RECONSTRUCTING MARRIAGE

European Family Law Series

RECONSTRUCTING MARRIAGE

The Legal Status of Relationships in a Changing Society

Caroline SÖRGJERD

intersentia
Cambridge – Antwerp – Portland

Intersentia Publishing Ltd.
Trinity House | Cambridge Business Park | Cowley Road
Cambridge | CB4 0WZ | United Kingdom
Tel.: +44 1223 393 753 | Email: mail@intersentia.co.uk

Distribution for the UK:
Hart Publishing Ltd
16C Worcester Place
Oxford, OX1 2JW
UK
Tel.: +44 1865 517 530
Email: mail@hartpub.co.uk

Distribution for the USA and Canada:
International Specialized Book Services
920 NE 58th Ave. Suite 300
Portland, OR 97213
USA
Tel.: +1 800 944 6190 (toll free)
Email: info@isbs.com

Distribution for Switzerland and Germany:
Stämpfli Verlag AG
Wölflistrasse 1
CH-3001 Bern
Switzerland
Tel.: +41 0 31 300 63 18
order@buchstaempfli.com

Distribution for other countries:
Intersentia Publishing nv
Groenstraat 31
2640 Mortsel
Belgium
Tel.: +32 3 680 15 50
Email: mail@intersentia.be

Reconstructing Marriage. The Legal Status of Relationships in a Changing Society
Caroline Sörgjerd

ISBN 978-1-78068-037-8
NUR 822

British Library Cataloguing in Publication Data. A catalogue record for this book is available from the British Library.

For my mother

ACKNOWLEDGEMENTS

"Feeling gratitude and not expressing it is like wrapping a present and not giving it."* Now that I am wrapping up this thesis, time has come to acknowledge those who have stood by me and assisted me in different ways on this journey.

First of all, I wish to express my sincere gratitude to my supervisor, Professor Maarit Jänterä-Jareborg. This thesis would not have been finished without her dedication, generosity, expertise and her meticulousness. Maarit has shown a devotion which extends far beyond what one can expect from a supervisor. For this I am deeply indebted to her. I have been fortunate enough to have an excellent assistant supervisor as well, Professor Anna Singer, who has participated actively in the formation of this thesis. Anna has contributed immensely with her sharp analysis and personal commitment. It has been an honor to work under these two women's guidance.

I also wish to thank Professor Håkan Andersson for providing me with a gateway into the world of science, available through his introductory course for new doctoral candidates. His lectures have inspired me in many ways and, not least, taught me to think "outside the box". Furthermore, I would like to thank Professor Rolf Nygren for valuable and thought-provoking discussions on legal history. My gratitude also goes to my fellow – past and present – doctoral candidate friends at the Department of Law, for encouragement, pleasant company and interesting discussions. I would especially like to thank Dr. Mosa Sayed for being my friend, and for sharing the experience of being a doctoral candidate with me. I also wish to express my gratitude to Maria Sörgjerd, Ylva Sörgjerd, Therèse Lejfalk, Helena Hillström, Victoria Enkvist and Jane Stoll for proofreading parts of my manuscript.

The comparative outlooks into the Dutch and Spanish legal systems have been significantly improved by input from legal experts in the Netherlands and Spain. I wish to thank Professor Katharina Boele-Woelki for her sharp input on my discussions concerning Dutch law, and Professor Cristina González Beilfuss for insightful and valuable comments on my account of Spanish law. Any remaining errors are mine. During my work with this thesis, I have been in contact with numerous authorities and experts, in Sweden and abroad. There is not enough room to thank each of them here, but a collective thank you is in order.

* William Arthur Ward.

Last but not least I would like to express my gratitude to my family. A special thank you goes to my parents-in-law Ylva and Peter, to my sister-in-law Karin, to my father Krister and to my brother Rasmus. Furthermore, I am deeply indebted to Jenny, my best friend and "diary" for her endless patience and support on a daily basis, and to my sister Therèse, who never feels far away although we live in different countries. This book has been dedicated to my mother Michèle, for all the sacrifices she made for me when I was growing up, and for always believing in me.

Finally, I wish to express my love and gratitude to my immediate family – Maria, Estelle and Lovisa – for their endless patience and support. You are amazing.

This book is a slightly modified version of my doctoral thesis, successfully defended on 11 February 2011 at Uppsala University, and takes into account questions and viewpoints presented at the public defense. For inspiration in this respect, I would like to thank my opponent Professor Eva Ryrstedt (Lund) and the board members – Professor Margareta Brattström (Uppsala), Professor Masha Antokolskaia (Amsterdam) and Professor Urpo Kangas (Helsinki). I would also like to thank Dr. Katharina Hilbig (Göttingen) for valuable input on German law and Dr. Helena Franzén for language revising this book. In this context, Professor Maarit Jänterä-Jareborg deserves an additional thank you for her continuing support and dedication.

My doctoral thesis was written within the multidisciplinary research programme Impact of Religion: Challenges for Society, Law and Democracy, established as a center of excellence at Uppsala University. The research programme provided financial means for the revision of my thesis after the public defense. For this I am deeply grateful. Financial means to write my doctoral thesis were provided by the Uppsala Faculty of Law and by a scholarship from Sigrid and Anna Åbergssons stipendiefond. Emil Heijnes Stiftelse för rättvetenskap contributed financially to the printing of this book. Like in the doctoral thesis, documents issued before 1 October 2010 have been taken into account in this book. Documents issued thereafter have only been considered selectively.

Caroline Sörgjerd
Uppsala, October 2011

CONTENTS

PART III – INTERNATIONAL AND EUROPEAN OUTLOOKS

ABBREVIATIONS

Art./Arts.	Article/Articles
BOE	Boletín Oficial del Estado
c	case
CEFL	Commission on European Family Law
Charter	Charter on Fundamental Rights of the European Union
CiU	Convergència i Unió
COM	European Commission Documents (European Union)
Council	Council of Europe
Ds	Departementsserien
ECHR/the Convention	European Convention of Human Rights
ECJ	European Court of Justice (European Union)
EEC	European Economic Community
e.g.	exempli gratia (for example)
etc.	et cetera (and the rest)
et al.	et alii (and others)
EU	European Union
f.	following (page)
FamPra.ch	Die Praxis des Familienrechts/La Pratique du Droit de la Famille
i.e.	id est (that is)
JT	Juridisk Tidskrift
LU	Lagutskottet
NJA	Nytt Juridiskt Arkiv (I) (case law from the Supreme Court, Sweden)
NJA II	Nytt Juridiskt Arkiv II
no.	number
p./pp.	page/pages
PACS	Pacte civil de solidarité
Para./Paras.	Paragraph/Paragraphs
PP	Partido Popular
Prop	proposition
PSOE	Partido Socialista Obrero Espagñol
RF	Regeringsformen

RH	Rättsfall från hovrätterna (case law from the Court of Appeals, Sweden)
SOU	Statens offentliga utredningar
Strasbourg Court	The European Court of Human Rights
SvJT	Svensk Juristtidning
TFEU	Treaty on the Functioning of the European Union
UN	United Nations
UU	Utrikesutskottet
v.	versus
Vol.	Volume

PART I

INTRODUCTION

1. INTRODUCTION

1.1. PURPOSE

What is marriage? The all-encompassing purpose of this thesis is to explore the essence of marriage. It will be suggested that marriage is not just a legal contract concluded by two persons for the purpose of settling their financial matters during marriage and in case of divorce. It will be suggested that there is also a symbolic dimension of marriage, which extends beyond the classical legal sphere, and is connected to the historical, religious and cultural functions of marriage in Swedish society.

The symbolic dimension of marriage was highlighted in Sweden in 2009, when the Marriage Code was extended to encompass couples of the same sex. The marriage reform of 2009 challenged the deeply rooted conception of marriage as an institution reserved for a man and a woman. The 2009 reform was not about same-sex couples acquiring the legal effects of marriage. The Registered Partnership Act of 1994 already provided same-sex couples with legal rules largely equivalent to those attached to marriage. The marriage enactment of 2009 was about accessing the *symbolic* dimension of marriage, and about the right to label the relationship "marriage". What characterizes the symbolic dimension of marriage; how does it influence the past, present and future understanding and function of marriage in Sweden, and why was the gender-neutral marriage reform of 2009 controversial in "secular"[1] and "liberal" Sweden in the twenty-first century?

In order to understand what marriage is and why extending the concept of marriage to encompass couples of the same sex faced a certain level of opposition in Sweden, it has been found adequate to reconstruct, identify and chart what marriage has symbolized in Sweden during the last three centuries. Who have been legally recognized as couples at different points in time, from society's point of view, with mutual rights and duties, and why have these unions been "chosen" above others? My ambition is to analyze the various forms and functions of different cohabitation models, and the content of different marriage enactments, for the purpose of understanding the concept of marriage in Sweden in the twenty-first century.

---

1 Although a majority of the Swedish population are members of the Church of Sweden (78 percent in 2008) only two percent of them state that they attend church services regularly. See Jänterä-Jareborg, Maarit, Religion and the Secular State, 2010, p. 672.

An established classification of marriage is to distinguish between two main functions, namely marriage as a *legal contract* and as a *civil status*.[2] Another way of expressing this is to speak in terms of two sometimes conflicting interests attached to marriage: on the one hand, promoting the community of the spouses as an entity and, on the other hand, protecting the individual freedom of the spouses. These two functions of marriage have shifted in importance over time in Sweden; a development which in the literature has been discussed in terms of marriage changing from a public to a private matter.[3] In chapter 4, the 1970s will be described as a turning point in Sweden in this respect.

Based on the 1969 government guidelines to the Family Law Commission (Familjelagssakkunniga), a new legal policy toward family law legislation was assumed in Sweden. The basic idea expressed through various enactments in the 1970s was to as far as possible trust the individual spouses to make rational decisions concerning their personal life. Against this background the spouses' individual – and mutual – autonomy in marriage was increased through legislation.[4] Cohabitation without marriage was also legally regulated in a special act at this point in time, namely in the 1973 Act on the Joint Dwelling of an Unmarried Couple. In chapter 4, it will be illustrated how the enactments of the 1970s contributed to changing marriage from being a public (state or church) concern toward resembling a private contractual matter between the parties. However, marriage is no ordinary contract and there was a limit to how far the Swedish legislator was willing to go in respect of abolishing moral values from the regulation governing marriage. Certain values remained protected in the marriage regulation, which limited the spouses' individual and joint autonomy in marriage.[5]

The practically oriented approach to family law legislation in the 1969 guidelines can be seen as the starting signal for legally regulating unmarried cohabiting couples of different sex in 1973, and more extensively in 1987.[6] This approach to family law legislation has also been of significance for the legal recognition of same-sex cohabiting couples. In 1987, a special cohabitees act was adopted for same-sex couples living together – the Homosexual Cohabitees Act.[7]

---

2 See, for instance, Agell, Anders, The Swedish Legislation on Marriage and Cohabitation, a Journey without a Destination, 1980, pp. 35 f. For a discussion of marriage as a status based contract, see also Agell, Anders, Äktenskapets giltighet – en civilrättslig och en förvaltningsrättslig fråga, 2002, pp. 21–39. See also Ryrstedt, Eva, Bodelning och bostad, 1998, pp. 19 f and 383 f.

3 See Ryrstedt, Eva, Bodelning och bostad, 1998, where the polarizing theme of marriage as a union based on community and individualism is analyzed.

4 See chapter 4.

5 See, for instance, sections 4.2.2.3 and 4.3.3.

6 The Cohabitees Joint Homes Act of 1987. In Swedish: Lag (1987:232) om sambors gemensamma hem. This Act replaced the 1973 Act on the Joint Dwelling of an Unmarried Couple. In Swedish: Lag (1973:651) om ogifta samboendes gemensamma bostad.

7 The Homosexual Cohabitees Act (Lag (1987:813) om homosexuella sambor).

In 1994 a formalized union modelled on marriage was introduced to same-sex couples, the Registered Partnership Act, and in 2009 a gender-neutral marriage act was enacted.[8] How did these enactments influence the essence of marriage in Sweden?

This thesis also aims to place the Swedish legal development toward recognition of same-sex couples in an international context. The Swedish gender-neutral marriage act will be compared with Dutch and Spanish enactments recognizing same-sex partners. Why was same-sex marriage introduced in these two countries? How have legal enactments to improve the position of same-sex couples been received by the Dutch and Spanish societies and the main religious communities in these two countries? Compared with the depth and length of the attention given to Swedish developments, the analyses of the developments in these two other countries remain on a surface level. The comparative part merely aims to provide illustrative outlooks into two jurisdictions which have produced similar enactments as the Swedish enactments, but against different historical and religious backgrounds. Moreover, certain aspects of the legal development concerning same-sex couples in the other Nordic countries will be touched upon.[9]

The same-sex marriage enactment of 2009 was about access to marital status, i.e. to the right to label a relationship "marriage". Marital status as such can also be of special significance at the European level. A final aim of this thesis is to round off the international perspective on marriage by taking into account relevant jurisprudence based on the European Convention of Human Rights (ECHR), as interpreted by the European Court of Human Rights (Strasbourg Court), dealing with the right to marry and to found a family, as well as the right to protection of one's private and family life. In addition, the significance of the marital status under European Union law will be accounted for, more precisely, in Council Directives and Regulations and in the jurisprudence of the European Court of Justice (ECJ). Furthermore, the European Union's own catalogue of human rights will be discussed – the Charter of Fundamental Rights of the European Union.[10]

---

8 These enactments will be thoroughly analyzed in chapter 6.

9 "Nordic countries" is here used for Sweden, Denmark, Norway, Finland and Iceland. These countries can also be called "Scandinavian countries". See section 7.4.

10 See chapter 8.

1.2. THE RESEARCH OBJECT

1.2.1. A STUDY AT TWO LEVELS

This thesis examines the concept of marriage at two different levels, namely (1) on the classical legal level, as expressed by the substantive marriage regulation, and (2) in respect of the symbolic dimension of marriage, expressed through the values attached to the marriage regulation and to the marital status in society.[11] Together, these two levels can be seen as characterizing the essence of marriage in Sweden. When studying the first level it is relevant to account for past law reforms in order to identify which interests have been considered to be worth protecting by law, and why these interests have had priority over others. For instance: what impediments to marriage have been established by law, what legal effects have been attached to marriage, and how have the rules on dissolution of marriage been designed?

When studying the second level – the symbolic dimension of marriage – the aim is to analyze what the institution of marriage has symbolized in the past and what it symbolizes today. This has been done by studying the function of marriage and by analyzing the values attached to the marital status from an ideological point of view. It will be claimed that the institution of marriage today to some extent is based on values which derive from the historical, cultural and religious functions of marriage as a "cornerstone of society" and which, as such, represents the most prominent cohabitation model. In this thesis it will be suggested that answers to what the essence of marriage is – and why introducing a gender-neutral marriage concept in Sweden was controversial – can be sought in sources outside of the traditional legal sphere. In other words, the essence of marriage is more than a legal contract and a civil status. It also contains a symbolic dimension based on values and connotations which cannot easily be controlled through legislation.

At the outset it should be mentioned that the intention is not to maintain a strict distinction between the account of the applicable regulation governing marriage and the symbolic values it expresses. The substantive marriage regulation is described for the purpose of providing a basis for observing and analyzing the symbolic values it contains and connotes. Also, the two levels – the regulatory and symbolic level – sometimes coincide. For example, impediments to marriage express considerations about what relationships are considered ethically undesirable from society's – or at a certain point in time the church's – point of view. Sweden's default marital property regime, in force since the 1920 Marriage Code, is constructed on the value-based principle of equality between husband and wife. Furthermore, a spouse's unilateral right to divorce, without stating any grounds for the divorce application, expresses values of individuality

[11] This will be illustrated in the following chapters and, finally, in section 9.2.2.

and freedom of choice and emphasizes the idea of marriage as a voluntary union based on the individual autonomy of the spouses.

1.2.2. THE TOPICALITY OF THE RESEARCH CHOICE

Questions concerning which couples should and which couples should not be safeguarded mutual rights and duties through legislation, and be recognized by society as a legally relevant family law unit, continue to preoccupy politicians, religious communities and the general public from their respective perspectives. In many Western countries a topical issue during the last decade has been whether or not to legally recognize same-sex couples in the statutory law. More than two thirds of the Member States of the EU have adopted or are preparing statutory registration schemes which include same-sex couples.[12] In October 2010, same-sex marriage was possible in Canada, Argentina, Belgium, Iceland, the Netherlands, Norway, Portugal, Spain, South Africa and Sweden.[13] Changing marriage into a gender-neutral concept challenges the deeply rooted idea of marriage as a union between one man and one woman, and has engaged politicians, church representatives and the general public in ethical, theological and legal discussions. The registration schemes and the marriage regulations available to same-sex couples differ in respect of the legal effects attached. In Portugal for instance, same-sex couples are able to conclude a marriage, but they are not able to adopt a child jointly.[14]

Legal recognition of same-sex couples is still a controversial issue in some European jurisdictions.[15] For instance, in Bulgaria, Estonia and Romania it has been specified in the law that marriage is reserved for different-sex couples.[16] On the global level, homosexual sexual acts between consenting adults are criminalized in several countries.[17]

---

12 Updated information about the legal status of same-sex couples in the world can be found at CBC News: www.cbc.ca/world/story/2009/05/26/f-same-sex-timeline.html. Accessed 26 October 2010. See also Boele-Woelki, Katharina, The Legal Recognition of Same-Sex Relationships Within the European Union, 2007–2008, pp. 1960 f. and Saez, Macarena, Same sex marriage, same sex cohabitation, and same sex families around the world, 2010.

13 CBC News: www.cbc.ca/world/story/2009/05/26/f-same-sex-timeline.html. Accessed 26 October 2010.

14 Saez, Macarena, Same sex marriage, same sex cohabitation, and same sex families around the world, 2010, p. 44.

15 Furthermore, Greece and Italy have no legal recognition of same-sex couples. Attempts to adopt family law rules for same-sex couples in Italy have failed. See Saez, Macarena, Same sex marriage, same sex cohabitation, and same sex families around the world, 2010, p. 25.

16 See www.fra.europa.eu/fraWebsite/attachments/FRA-LGBT-report-update2010.pdf. (p. 8) Accessed 5 December 2010. I have chosen to use the term "different-sex couple" to describe a relationship between a man and a woman, as a contrast to the term "same-sex couple".

17 For instance, in 2010 in the African state Malawi, a same-sex couple was sentenced to 14 years of prison for sodomy and indecency. The President issued a pardon after strong pressure from

A possible explanation for the controversy surrounding the legal recognition of same-sex couples is that family law is a field closely connected to changing values in society. As a result of its "value component", family law can be used to encourage certain behaviors in society, or to promote certain values found desirable at a political level. For instance, in respect of domestic equality, division of duties between the couple and non-discrimination on the basis of factors such as gender and sexual orientation, family law legislation not only *reflects* existing values, but can also be used to *create* new values through legislation. This can be seen as a form of "social engineering" in the field of family law, which was a central component of Swedish social democratic politics already during the establishment of the welfare state between 1930 and 1970.[18] Legal recognition of same-sex relationships in Sweden can be seen as an illustrative, contemporary example of such "social engineering", where legislation was used to promote a new, inclusive attitude toward homosexuals and same-sex couples in Swedish society.[19]

However, promoting specific values in the field of family law through legislation can be criticized as contradictory to the Swedish legislator's official policy to keep moral judgments in respect of cohabitation forms out of family law legislation. This policy – sometimes called the neutrality policy – was formulated in the early 1970s, based on the 1969 guidelines, at a time when the Swedish regulation governing marriage was reformed significantly and Sweden's first enactment on cohabitation without marriage was introduced.[20]

The legal status of unmarried cohabitees – of different as well as of the same sex – is another topical issue dealt with in this thesis. The "marriage-like" regulation of cohabitation without marriage in the Swedish Cohabitees Act of 2003 stands out in an international comparative context since it, like its predecessors – the 1973 Act and the 1987 Act – applies by default, i.e. without any registration procedure or other explicit act by the couple establishing their consent to being subjected to the rules of the Act. In chapter 5, the impact of different Swedish cohabitee enactments on the essence of marriage in Sweden will be analyzed.

1.2.3. THE CHOICE OF THE RESEARCH OBJECT – THREE ARGUMENTS

Why is it meaningful to analyze the Swedish concept of marriage, in light of the changing society and the legal recognition of unmarried couples? In other words:

---

the UN, but underlined that he condemned homosexual behavior. See Saez, Macarena, Same sex marriage, same sex cohabitation, and same sex families around the world, 2010, p. 1.

18 See section 4.1.2.3.

19 See section 6.5.1.

20 See sections 4.2.1, 4.2.4 and 5.2.3.

How can the research object be justified as more than an academic exercise, triggered by the recently enacted gender-neutral marriage regulation in Sweden?[21]

Firstly, it is of value to account for and analyze the impact of the Swedish gender-neutral marriage enactment on the essence of marriage. In order to understand how and why the same-sex marriage reform of 2009 challenged the essence of marriage, the institution of marriage must be thoroughly analyzed: more precisely, its past and present legal form and function in society. In this study it will be argued that marriage – contrary to what the Swedish legal development since the 1970s and the political aspiration toward neutrality might suggest – is not just any legal contract free from values. In fact, it is a more complex legal institution than we might have imagined.

The Swedish legislator was a pioneer in Europe with the implementation of the principle of equality between husband and wife in the Marriage Code of 1920, and with the practical and (alleged) value-free approach to marriage regulation, assumed in 1973. It will be argued in this study that irrespective of the practical approach to family law regulation, according to which the impediments to marriage were reduced to a minimum and divorce was turned into a unilateral right for each spouse, marriage has remained a value-based symbolic concept and the civil status of marriage is still of importance in society. Why is this so?

Secondly, it is of value to provide a foundation for future challenges relating to the essence of marriage. Such a foundation can be provided by a broader understanding of the institution of marriage from a historical, religious and cultural perspective. New challenges and conflicting values are likely to continue to emerge in the field of family law, for instance, as a result of immigration to Sweden from cultures with different outlooks on family law issues, views that may derive from religious values or hierarchical traditions. For instance, how should the Swedish legislator deal with demands for the statutory recognition of polygamous marriages and possible conflicts with the principle of equality between the individual spouses in Swedish family law? These issues are only briefly touched upon in this study, but I cherish a hope that the discussion as such can benefit from this study.[22]

Thirdly, comparing reasons for reform in Sweden in the field of legal recognition of same-sex couples with reasons for reform in two other jurisdictions, namely Spain and the Netherlands, can increase our understanding of the Swedish legal development and the essence of marriage in Sweden. The marriage regulation is a central component when reforming society by promoting certain political interests, for instance, the recognition of same-sex couples. This

---

21 These three arguments will be returned to and evaluated in section 9.3.

22 For a historical account for and a map of the occurrence of monogamy, polygamy (polygyni and polyandry) and group marriage in the world, see Westermarck, Edvard, The History of Human Marriage, vol III, 1925.

is visible in the Swedish, Dutch and Spanish legal developments toward a gender-neutral marriage concept, but the rhetoric at the political level varies in the jurisdictions studied, as a result of different political and religious backgrounds and traditions.

A gradual development toward recognizing the human rights of same-sex couples is visible also in the jurisprudence of the Strasbourg Court, when interpreting the European Convention of Human Rights. Furthermore, a development away from the previously predominating "spouse-only" approach, toward recognizing unmarried cohabiting couples as family members, can be observed in EU law. Moreover, human rights perspectives on same-sex couples have gained increased focus at the EU level, through the Charter of Fundamental Rights of the European Union.[23]

The comparisons with Spain and the Netherlands, as well as the outlooks on EU law and the jurisprudence of the Strasbourg Court, aim to illustrate that the connection between human rights and the legal recognition of same-sex couples in Europe have placed the institution of marriage and its symbolic dimension in the limelight. Access to marriage has become a symbol of full equality and a means for a country to advance itself as "progressive"[24] and "democratic" in a European context.

1.3. METHODOLOGY

1.3.1. SOURCES AND METHOD

This is a study for a Swedish LL.D-degree, i.e. a doctoral thesis in law in Sweden and written by a person only educated in law. It follows that the consulted sources are those customarily used in legal studies, namely statutory legal provisions and government initiated studies drafted in the form of committee reports, published in a special series.[25] Relevant case law from, in particular, the Swedish Supreme Court is also taken into account and, finally, contributions from legal literature.

Preparatory work to legislation are studied for the combined purpose of systemizing and clarifying the substantive content of the applicable law and identifying the underlying ideologies which have motivated legal enactments in Sweden at different points in time. Committee reports are particularly suitable

---

23 See section 8.2.4 and subsections.

24 The term "progressive" (liberal) is used here as a contrast to the term "conservative" or "regressive", against the backdrop of the prevailing human rights discourse in Europe, which emphasizes the value of improving the rights of the individual. This is also the terminology used by Antokolskaia, Masha, in: Harmonisation of Family Law in Europe, 2006, p. 25. However, Antokolskaia points out, using human rights as a universal standard can be problematic and is not entirely politically correct. The term "traditional" is also occasionally used as opposite to "liberal" or "progressive". See idem pp. 25 f.

25 "Statens offentliga utredningar" (SOU).

as points of departure when it comes to identifying shifting ideologies, because of their often extensive and ambitious commission and the represented expertise. As pointed out by Ole Lando, however, the preparatory work might contain a "hidden political agenda". For tactical or political reasons the explicitly stated motives may not always be the whole truth. This possibility should be kept in mind when studying the given motivations for reforms.[26]

Moreover, analyzing legal changes in respect of formalized and informal partnerships at the European level requires taking into account international treaties, EU regulations and EU directives, as well as relevant case law from the European Union's Court of Justice (ECJ). The jurisprudence of the European Court of Human Rights (Strasbourg Court), interpreting the 1950 European Convention on Human Rights, is also of relevance.

This study differs from a typical legal study in Sweden in the sense that sources from other disciplines have also been consulted and text analysis has been carried out when studying the form and function of marriage. An analysis of changing attitudes, varying political incentives and shifting moral and ethical values over time in society, benefits from consulting, inter alia, historical and sociological sources. In addition, theological sources have been taken into account: namely, official documents from the Church of Sweden, for instance, handbooks of the Church of Sweden dating as far back as 1693. This has been done for the purpose of determining the essence of marriage according to the church at different times. Analyzing these kinds of sources is in general difficult, since the conditions in society have shifted from one point in time to another. In this respect, however, the study is carried out selectively without intending to be exhaustive.

It can be questioned if it is desirable for a researcher to consult and use sources from other disciplines; keeping in mind the researcher's lack of knowledge of the other fields' methods, theories and sources. However, when studying a dynamic field such as family law with close links to societal developments it can also be considered a mistake not to consult adjoining academic disciplines.[27] From this perspective, studying for instance sociological features in connection with legal reforms can be necessary, irrespective of the methodological difficulties encountered, in order to gain a more comprehensive understanding of the legal development relating to marriage.[28] Moreover, when dealing with family law issues, it is difficult to clearly distinguish between the different disciplines.[29] In Swedish preparatory work to legislation, in committee

---

26 Lando, Ole, The Worries of a Comparatist, 2000, p. 26.

27 Of this opinion is, for instance, Malmström, Åke, Rättssociologiska forskningsuppgifter inom äktenskapsrätten, 1957, p. 233. The position taken by Malmström has been so frequently referred to in legal literature that it can be considered as established in Sweden, within family law research. The same line of reasoning applies to the necessity of consulting international sources of law. This will be elaborated on in section 1.3.2.

28 Malmström, Åke, Rättssociologiska forskningsuppgifter inom äktenskapsrätten, 1957, p. 233.

29 Malmström, Åke, Rättssociologiska forskningsuppgifter inom äktenskapsrätten, 1957, p. 233.

reports in particular, sociological and demographic research is often taken into account. This makes the delimitation regarding method and approach to other social sciences vague. Interdisciplinary outlooks are meant to add another dimension to our understanding of the concept of marriage. However, the legal perspective is central and all other sources are used selectively.

Another methodological difficulty is consulting foreign legal sources, here primarily from the Netherlands and Spain, dealing with the enactment of statutory rules on formalized same-sex unions. Apart from possible language barriers, analyzing foreign legal sources may not appear difficult at first glance. However, it is likely that legal traditions and methodology differ in the jurisdictions studied, making it important to proceed with caution.[30] The foreign sources I have consulted are primarily contributions to the legal literature, but also sociological reports and preparatory work to legislation have been taken into account.

In summary, the overall impression is that the use of sources from disciplines other than the legal, as well as foreign legal sources, is motivated as long as conclusions are drawn with caution and with an awareness of the possible differences in traditions and conceptions. The names of the institutions, for instance, "cohabitation without marriage" and "registered partnership," may vary from one country to another, as well as the legal effects attached.

1.3.2. THE FUNCTION OF LEGAL COMPARISONS IN THIS STUDY

In chapter 7 of this thesis the legal developments concerning same-sex couples in Spain and the Netherlands are analyzed. Including the legal position of unmarried cohabitees in general in the comparative chapter, irrespective of the sex of the couple, would have been fruitful. However, the focus is on same-sex unions in the Netherlands and Spain, for the reasons accounted for in sections 1.4.2, 1.4.3 and 1.4.4 below. In chapter 7, comparative outlooks into the Nordic enactments on registered partnership are also included, for the purpose of identifying general motivations to legislate in this field.

Why is a comparative perspective included in the account of the form and function of the institution of marriage in Sweden? At the outset it should be emphasized that the idea is not to provide an extensive legal comparison between Sweden, the Netherlands and Spain. The jurisdictions are not placed on "equal footing" in the sense that they are analyzed with equal thoroughness. Instead the

30 Strömholm, Stig, Användning av utländskt material i juridiska monografier, 1971, pp. 253 f., where he pointed out difficulties connected to analyzing foreign legal sources. It should be kept in mind, however, that the use of foreign law has become much more common since 1971 and is perhaps not as "unconventional" anymore. See also Bogdan, Michael, Komparativ rättskunskap, 2003, p. 40.

focus of the comparative chapter 7 is limited to investigating why the issue of legally recognizing same-sex unions has been on the legislative "agendas" in two other jurisdictions, namely in Spain and the Netherlands.

An often assumed point of departure when comparing legal systems, also seized upon here, is that *functionality* is vital.[31] It facilitates comparison if the object chosen for comparison – here the law enactments recognizing same-sex couples – fulfills the same basic *function* in the legal systems compared, in the sense that it contains a similar purpose and goal.[32] In all three jurisdictions compared a primary goal of the legal recognition of same-sex couples is anti-discrimination. It is noteworthy that in Spain, the Netherlands and Sweden, similar legislation has been adopted, irrespective of different societal, historical and religious backgrounds. The jurisdictions compared have followed a similar pattern when recognizing same-sex unions, first creating formalized institutions ("registered partnership" in the Netherlands and Sweden and "stable union" in Catalonia) open to same-sex couples, and then moving on to adopt a gender-neutral marriage regulation. The basic idea has been to, as far as possible, create legal parity between same-sex and different-sex cohabitation, based on the principle of equality. This similarity facilitates comparing the form and function of the different enactments.

A distinction can be made between (1) problem oriented comparative presentations of law and (2) descriptions of foreign law. In the latter case, foreign law is included for the purpose of enriching the analysis of the domestic legal system – not as an independent purpose.[33] In this thesis the comparative method used can be seen as a middle way between these two approaches. The jurisdictions compared here are not placed on equal footing as regards the attention given, the Swedish legal development being the center of attention.[34] However, the international comparisons are not only descriptions, but analyses aimed to illustrate why legally regulating same-sex relationships has been found to be

[31] See, for instance, Zweigert, K., Kötz, H., An Introduction to Comparative Law, 1998, p. 34 and Schwenzer, Ingeborg, Methodological Aspects of Harmonisation of Family Law, 2003, p. 146.

[32] Zweigert, K., Kötz, H., An Introduction to Comparative Law, 1998, p. 34. See also Bogdan, Michael, Komparativ rättskunskap, 2003, p. 74. Another approach to comparative law is to focus on differences rather than similarities. For instance Pierre Legrand emphasizes that deeply rooted cultural differences between the European countries, makes convergence of laws impossible. See Legrand, Pierre, European Legal Systems are not Converging, 1996, pp. 52–81.

[33] Strömholm, Stig, Användning av utländskt material i juridiska monografier, 1971, p. 252.

[34] "Equal footing comparison" can undoubtedly contribute considerably to the work of harmonizing laws (for instance in the European Union), by facilitating co-operation across borders, in particular from the perspectives of EU law, private international law and international family law. A connected problem, however, is that such research appears time-consuming and requires far-reaching linguistic skills or studies. For "equal footing" comparisons of European legal systems, see the work of the Commission on European Family Law: www.ceflonline.net/. Accessed 14 September 2010.

motivated in two other jurisdictions. The illustrative comparative outlooks also aim to create a more nuanced understanding of the legal development taking place in many European countries in respect of same-sex relationships.

Moreover, in chapters 3 and 4, certain international outlooks are provided into the French, German, Spanish and Dutch legal developments dealing with marriage in general, not just in respect of same-sex couples. The purpose of these comparative reflections is to place the seemingly rapid and progressive Swedish marriage regulation in a European setting. The sources primarily consulted in order to illustrate the national developments in broad outline are published by the Commission on European Family Law (CEFL), namely the general Principles concerning property relations between spouses, maintenance after divorce and the Principles concerning divorce.[35] Additional sources have been consulted when discussing the most recent developments.

1.4. DELIMITATION

1.4.1. THE TWOSOME RELATIONSHIP IN FOCUS

A general delimitation issue worth mentioning is the distinction between marriage and family. It is disputed whether being "family" requires children, or whether two adults living together as a couple constitute a family.[36] This controversy, however, is not the focus of this thesis. This thesis focuses on the relationship between two adults – unmarried cohabitees, spouses or registered partners – not on their relationship with children.[37] As mentioned above, the function of marriage has changed in Sweden from focusing on the marital status as a basis for family life, to focusing on the contractual side of marriage, i.e. the individual's autonomy and rights in marriage. Since the 1970s, to a great extent, this development is visible in Swedish enactments dealing with marriage.[38] Nevertheless, the marital status has remained significant in Sweden as a basis for the adult couple's community.

35 The Commission on European Family Law (CEFL) was founded 1 September 2001 and its main objective is to provide theoretical and practical research in relation to the harmonization of family law in Europe, inter alia by formulating a set of "Principles of European Family Law". See www.ceflonline.net/. Accessed 20 September 2010. See also sections 3.7 and 4.4.2, for comparative reflections.

36 The question of what the elements of the "family" are has, for instance, been raised by Dagmar Coester-Waltjen, Human Rights and the Harmonization of Family Law in Europe, 2008, p. 3.

37 Also in the International Encyclopedia of Comparative Family Law, the relationship between the adult couple is distinguished from their relationship with children and dealt with separately. See Glendon, Mary Ann, Rheinstein, Max, International Encyclopedia of Comparative Law, Vol. IV, Persons and Family, Interspousal Relations, 2007, p. 3.

38 See also Ryrstedt, Eva, Bodelning och bostad, 1998, pp. 383–402.

However, enactments on legal parenthood and a couple's relationship with children are analyzed as a part of the legal recognition of same-sex relationships. Opponents to reforms aimed to strengthen the position of same-sex couples tend to lean on the argument that a marriage between a man and a woman is the best environment – and a biological prerequisite – for having and raising children.[39] From this point of view, marriage can be seen as an institution aimed for procreation, and since a homosexual couple cannot reproduce jointly on their own they should not have access to marriage. This view, which can be linked to a "religious conception" of marriage, prevailed for centuries in Sweden and resulted in disapproval of homosexuality. Since all sexual acts should take place within marriage for the purpose of procreation, extramarital sexual behavior was criminalized and homosexuals, who could not marry, as a result, had no right to have sexual relations.[40]

It needs to be emphasized that marriage and procreation are two separate issues in Swedish legislation today.[41] A common notion is that procreation does not have to take place within marriage. Children have equal legal rights regardless of their parents' civil status. Single persons are allowed to adopt children, and the Swedish state provides financial support to single-parent households. On the other hand, the right to marry and to found a family is dealt with in the same article in the ECHR, namely Art. 12. This illustrates a general tendency to lump the concepts of marriage and family together. These two rights are also dealt with in the same Article (Art. 9) in the Charter of Fundamental Rights of the European Union.[42] The question of who should be recognized as a "family member" in the context of the free movement of EU citizens – is relevant when analyzing the legal development at the EU level (in chapter 8). In all other respects, the ambition here is to as far as possible focus on the adult couple living together in an intimate relationship, and not on their relationship with children.

---

39 This line of argument is frequently put forth by members of the Christian Democratic Party in Sweden. See, for instance, Motion to Parliament, (2007/08:C317), Könsneutralt äktenskap.

40 Coester-Waltjen, Dagmar, Coester Michael, International Encyclopedia of Comparative Law, Vol. IV, Persons and Family, Chapter 3, Formation of Marriage, 1997, p. 50. Also Vagn Greve, from a Danish perspective, notes that only married couples were allowed to have a sexual relationship and, as a consequence, it was self-evident to criminalize extramarital sexual relations. See Hvornår er bigami strafbart? 2009, p. 93.

41 Through the Gender Identity Act, Lag (1972:119) om fastställande av könstillhörighet, transsexuals who had undergone gender reassignment surgery were able to marry someone of their opposite assigned sex. This formally disconnected marriage from reproduction, since these couples were unable to procreate jointly.

42 Charter of Fundamental Rights of the European Union (2000/C 364/01). The wording of the Charter appears to clarify this distinction compared to the ECHR. The Charter will be accounted for in section 8.2.4.2.

1.4.2. WHY IS SWEDEN IN THE FOREFRONT? THREE ARGUMENTS

Why is the Swedish legal development in respect of informal and formalized unions the point of departure here? Several reasons lie behind the decision to focus on Sweden. *Firstly,* Sweden is internationally known for "pioneering" legislation in areas such as: gender equality within family law (emphasized already in the Marriage Code of 1920), the comparatively early introduction of no-fault divorce, the early legal recognition of cohabitation without marriage, as well as the successive development to legally recognize same-sex relationships.[43] Sweden was the first country in the world to officially regard cohabitation between two persons of the same sex as "a perfectly acceptable form of family life from society's point of view".[44] Sweden was also the first country in the world to legally regulate the situation of same-sex couples in a special family law enactment, namely through the "Homosexual Cohabitees Act" in 1987.[45] Moreover, Sweden was among the first to introduce a Registered Partnership Act in 1994, and a gender-neutral concept of marriage in 2009.[46]

The construction of the Swedish welfare state attracted large-scale international attention after World War II. In fact, the Swedish model has been described as: "the standard by which all other welfare states are to be measured".[47] The Swedish welfare state – established largely during the rule of the Social Democratic Party in Sweden between 1930 and 1970 – as well as the regulations of formalized and informal partnerships in Sweden – can be claimed to illustrate models for a "good order of things" based on solidarity and equal rights. From this perspective the Swedish legal developments are worthy of being placed in the forefront of this study.

Secondly, the central position of the Church of Sweden in Swedish society in the early twenty-first century – as well as its historically powerful position – motivates the special attention paid to this religious community in the present study. As mentioned above, alongside of the state, the religious communities have the authority to officiate at legally valid marriage ceremonies. It may appear inconsistent, especially from an international perspective, with Sweden's

43 See, for instance, Bradley, David, Family Law and Political Culture, 1996, where the Scandinavian states are pointed out as progressive in the field of family law.

44 Law Commission Report (LU 1973:20), p. 116. Author's translation.

45 Widergren, Bo, Ytterberg, Hans, Homosexuella sambor – innebörd och mottagande av en ny rättsfigur, 1990, p. 491.

46 This legal development will be analyzed in chapter 6.

47 Davidson, Alexander, Two Models of Welfare, 1989, p. 103. This reputation, based on the description by Marquis Childs in The Middle Way on Trial, 1980, has been questioned by Alexander Davidson, who nevertheless considers spreading a notion of the Swedish model among American readers to be valuable. See idem p. 103.

reputation as a secular country,[48] that religious communities are granted the privilege of exercising this authority.

Church marriages are popular in Sweden. In 2008, more than 40 percent of all marriages were officiated within the Church of Sweden and a majority of the Swedish population – around 70 percent in 2010 – are members of the Church of Sweden.[49] However, these high figures, it has been pointed out, do not accurately reflect the extent of the population's belief in God.[50] Only two percent of the members of the Church of Sweden attend worship services regularly and only 23 percent of the population state that they believe in God.[51] The contradiction between on the one hand, a weak belief in God, and on the other hand, high figures of participation in church services such as conclusion of marriage, adds another dimension when studying the essence of marriage in Sweden and why adopting a gender-neutral marriage concept was a controversial issue in Sweden. Moreover, the progressive decision of the Church of Sweden to officiate at same-sex marriages motivates special focus. The Church of Sweden is one of few religious communities in the world to officiate at same-sex marriages, and almost all other churches in Sweden are opposed to the idea of concluding marriages between two men or two women.[52]

Thirdly, practical reasons are of interest when focusing on Sweden. A profound analysis of symbolism, values and conditions in society presupposes extensive knowledge about the culture, traditions and language of the jurisdictions focused on. Such knowledge and detailed insight often requires that the jurisdiction focused on is also the author's home ground.

---

48 The Church of Sweden was also the state church of Sweden until the year 2000, see Government Bill (Prop 1997/98:116). But the church's authority to officiate legally valid marriages has been kept in spite of the reform of 2000. See Jänterä-Jareborg, Maarit, Religion and the Secular State, 2010, p. 672. As pointed out by Maarit Jänterä-Jareborg, the term "secularism" can mean different things. See pp. 673–677. This will be further analyzed in section 4.2.4.2.

49 See www.svenskakyrkan.se/default.aspx?id=645562. Accessed 24 May 2011.

50 Jänterä-Jareborg, Maarit, Religion and the Secular State, 2010, p. 672.

51 Jänterä-Jareborg, Maarit, Religion and the Secular State, 2010, p. 672, with reference to statistics by the Church of Sweden and the figures presented in the European Barometer Study of 2005.

52 However, the Swedish Mission Church (Missionskyrkan) has decided that it is up to each congregation to decide whether or not to celebrate same-sex marriages. By June 2010, however, no such marriages had been reported. See Jänterä-Jareborg, Maarit, The Same-Sex Marriage Reform with Special Regard to Concerns of Religion, 2010, p. 1507. See also section 6.3.2.4. Also Norrmalms Baptist församling, Judiska församlingen; Stockholm and Liberala Katolska Kyrkam i Sverige are Free Churches which have to some extent agreed to marry same-sex couples in Sweden. See http://www.sydsvenskan.se/sverige/article546491/Fa-samfund-ar-villiga-att-viga-samkonade-par.html. Accessed 18 January 2011.

1.4.3. WHY THE NETHERLANDS AND SPAIN?

Two additional jurisdictions – Spain and the Netherlands – where the legal developments regarding same-sex couples during the last decade resemble that of Sweden have been chosen as the basis for comparative observations. In both of these jurisdictions, the institution of marriage appears to have been the "target" of same-sex couples and their interest groups when seeking official approval of their relationships. My aspiration is that an analysis of the driving forces to legislate in the field of same-sex relationships in Spain and the Netherlands will increase the understanding of the Swedish legal developments in this field and their impact on the essence of marriage in Sweden.

An aspect which makes the legal recognition of same-sex couples in Spain interesting to study is the historically powerful position of the Roman Catholic Church in Spanish society. However, it has only been possible to briefly touch upon this aspect within the framework of this thesis. Moreover, the Spanish legislative history is special, as a result of the dictatorship of General Franco during 1935–1975. Keeping this relatively recent political past in mind, as well as the central position of the Roman Catholic Church in Spanish society, it might appear unexpected that Spain was the third country in the world to introduce gender-neutral marriage regulation in 2005, and that Catalonia was the first predominantly Roman Catholic region in the world to adopt a formalized relationship scheme open to couples of the same sex in 1998. Although in Spain a marriage can be celebrated either in a civil procedure or within a religious community, same-sex marriages can thus far only be concluded in the civil form, since no churches in Spain appear willing to marry same-sex couples.[53]

An interesting aspect regarding the Netherlands is that civil marriage is the only legally valid form of contracting a marriage according to Dutch law. Couples, whether of the same sex or of different sexes, who desire church participation in connection with their marriage, can ask for a church blessing of their marriage or registered partnership only after the civil ceremony. This blessing is irrelevant from a legal perspective, but can have an emotional or religious meaning for the couple. Unlike in Sweden and Spain, in the Netherlands there exists no "double track system" with a possibility to choose between a legally valid church marriage and a civil marriage. How did this system for conclusion of marriage influence the gender-neutral marriage enactment and the political rhetoric in the Netherlands?

Another interesting feature of Dutch law is that registered partnership is available to same-sex as well as different-sex couples. In the Netherlands, couples

---

53 However, it appears that the US-based Metropolitan Community Churches (MCC), which is planned to open in Madrid during the autumn of 2010, is planning to officiate at a same-sex marriage in Madrid, between two Spaniards living in Canada. See for instance www.rawstory.com/rs/2010/0704/spain-church-samesex-marriages/. Accessed 14 September 2010.

of different sex and couples of the same sex who wish to formalize their relationship can choose between registered partnership and marriage. The Dutch registered partnership, which is very similar to marriage, appears to function today as a "marriage lite," which is easier to dissolve than a marriage and generally perceived as less "symbolically charged" than a marriage.[54] In Sweden, avoiding creating a "second-class marriage" has been an explicit goal stated in the preparatory work to legislation concerning cohabitation without marriage.[55] The regional registration schemes in Spain – called stable unions – also apply to same-sex and different-sex couples, but unlike the Dutch and Swedish registered partnership acts, these unions are not "marriage-like" institutions.[56]

1.4.4. THE FOCUS ON SAME-SEX COUPLES

The same-sex marriage enactment in Sweden is of special interest because it highlights the symbolic dimension of marriage. Why was the institution of marriage chosen by politicians and same-sex couples as the goal of equality achievements, and why was registered partnership not a sufficient alternative to marriage in this respect? In a somewhat dramatic sense the introduction of a gender-neutral marriage concept and the connected tension between the religious communities and the state can be seen as the ultimate challenge of marriage – an illustration of man challenging God and the biblical story of the Creation.[57] The responses of the Catholic Church in Spain to the gender-neutral marriage enactment are especially illustrative and clearly expressed in this respect.

We witness an increasing demand for the legal recognition of same-sex unions in the Western world, creating debates because of different outlooks on what the purpose of marriage is and whether or not same-sex couples qualify for serving this purpose. The Swedish same-sex marriage enactment of 2009 is important because it highlighted the importance of access to marriage, and the symbolic value of being able to label the formalized union "marriage".

1.5. OUTLINE

This dissertation is divided into four parts. Part I consists of only one chapter (chapter one), Part II of chapters two to six, Part III of chapters seven to eight

---

54 See, for instance, Schrama, Wendy, Registered Partnership in the Netherlands, 1999, p. 323. See also Boele-Woelki, K, Curry-Sumner, I, Jansen M, Schrama W, Evaluatie van 'Wet openstelling huwelijk' en van het geregistreerd partnerschap, 2006, p. 252.

55 See chapter 5.

56 See chapter 7.

57 See chapter 6.3.3.1 and section 9.2.2.

and Part IV of the concluding chapter nine. Part I is an introductory background, providing a gateway to the research object. Part II is centered on the Swedish legal development in respect of marriage, including the enactments of alternative cohabitation models, namely cohabitation without marriage and registered partnership. Part III places the Swedish development in an international context and Part IV is the conclusion.

In Part II, the outline follows a historical timeline and each chapter is centered on a relevant enactment governing marriage. Each chapter deals with a specific theme, the core of which is captured in the heading of the chapter. The analysis strives to analyze ideological, religious, sociological and legal issues related to marriage and to illustrate what interests, needs and legal considerations have justified the chosen legal enactments at different points in time.

In Part III, the Swedish legal development toward the legal recognition of same-sex couples is placed in an international comparative setting, through comparisons with the Netherlands and Spain (chapter 7). Chapter 7 also contains a brief overview of the legal development concerning same-sex couples in the Nordic countries. Thereafter, issues concerning changing cohabitation models will be analyzed at the EU level and according to the ECHR (chapter 8). Finally, in Part IV, the main observations and findings of this study will be summarized and the future form and function of the institution of marriage in Sweden will be discussed (chapter 9).

PART II

MARRIAGE IN SWEDEN: FROM DIVINE TO GENDER-NEUTRAL

2. MARRIAGE AS A GIFT OF GOD

2.1. THE POINT OF DEPARTURE

What was the essence of marriage in 1734? What regulation applied and what interests formed the values relating to marriage, expressed through the law? The codification of Swedish law in 1734, with a special book on the law of marriage – the Marriage Code – forms the starting point for the analysis of marriage and other informal "marriage-like" unions, such as cohabitation without marriage, in Swedish society.

In 1734, the Church of Sweden, after more than a century of struggles to control the moral values attached to people's sexual behavior, finally obtained monopoly on concluding the marriage ceremony. As a result, the Code of 1734 introduced the requirement that a marriage, to be legally valid in Sweden, had to be celebrated in the Church of Sweden – the Swedish Evangelical Lutheran state church.[58] Until then a legally valid marriage could be entered into also according to old Germanic marriage customs.

2.2. TOWARD THE MARRIAGE CODE OF 1734 – CONFLICTING INTERESTS

2.2.1. GERMANIC MARRIAGE CUSTOMS VERSUS CANONICAL LAW

In Sweden marriage customs were written down for the first time in the country's provincial laws of the eleventh and twelfth centuries.[59] The provincial laws were a collection of customs that had been passed on through an oral tradition from generation to generation before they were finally written down. According to these "pre-Christian"[60] Germanic marriage customs, conclusion of marriage was

58 This coincided with the Council of Trent (1545–1563). See, for instance, Agell, Anders, Äktenskapets giltighet – en civilrättslig och en förvaltningsrättslig fråga, 2002, p. 21. See also Sundberg, Jacob, Familjerätt i omvandling, 1969, pp. 16–18.

59 Inger, Göran, Svensk rättshistoria, 1997, pp. 14–16.

60 Sweden was Christianized during the tenth century, but it was a time-consuming process and pre-Christian (Germanic) provincial customs lingered on for centuries. See Carlsson, Lizzie, Jag giver dig min dotter (Part I), 1965, p. 15. See also Carlsson, Lizzie, Jag giver dig min dotter, (Part II), 1972, p. 6.

an economic settlement between two families, which was negotiated internally and privately without involving the public. In general, marriage was not a personal matter for the future spouses to decide, but an economic matter for their families to negotiate.[61]

According to the provincial laws, marriage was to be concluded in three stages, namely (1) the marriage contract, (2) the marriage ceremony and (3) the bedding.[62] Only after all of these three stages had been completed, did the marriage gain legal force and the wife became a part of the husband's household, which as a rule constituted a hierarchical farming production unit and included not only immediate family members, but also several generations and servants.[63] Also dissolution of marriage was a private economic matter to be dealt with by the two families.[64]

During the tenth century, when Catholicism was introduced, new interests began to surface in Sweden, which challenged the pre-Christian marriage customs, namely Catholic values expressed in canonical law.[65] According to canonical law, marriage is a sacrament, insoluble in nature and preferably –initially not necessarily – concluded in the Catholic Church.[66] Sexual activity outside of marriage was a sin and elevating the institution of marriage to a sacrament – monogamous and indissoluble – can be seen as a means to counteract extramarital sexual behavior.[67] It can be mentioned that annulment was a possible way out of a marriage, without contradicting the Catholic idea of marriage as a sacrament. Annulment meant establishing that there had never been a valid marriage in the first place.[68] Moreover, an important aspect of marriage according to canonical law compared to the customary law was the idea that marriage is based on the consent of the spouses-to-be – not on their parents' consent or the consent of a guardian.[69]

---

61 For a thorough account of marriage in the old Swedish society, see Carlsson, Lizzie, Jag giver dig min dotter, I and II, 1965 and 1972. See also Korpiola, Mia, Between betrothal and bedding, 2009.

62 Westring, Hjalmar, Den nya giftermålsbalken jämte dithörande författningar med förklaringar, 1933, p. 15. See also Melby, Kari, Pylkkänen, Anu, Rosenbeck, Bente, Carlsson Wetterberg, Christina, Inte ett ord om kärlek, 2006, p. 28.

63 Melby, Kari, Pylkkänen, Anu, Rosenbeck, Bente, Carlsson Wetterberg, Christina, Inte ett ord om kärlek, 2006, pp. 28–30. See also Schmidt, Folke, The Prospective Law of Marriage, 1971, p. 195.

64 Carlsson, Lizzie, Jag giver dig min dotter, 1972, p. 3.

65 Carlsson, Lizzie, Jag giver dig min dotter, 1972, pp. 6 f.

66 Carlsson, Lizzie, Jag giver dig min dotter, 1972, p. 5. See also Katolska kyrkans katekes, 1996, Para. 1640.

67 Rheinstein, Max, König, René, International Encyclopedia of Comparative Law, Vol. IV, Persons and Family, Chapter 1, Introduction, 2006, p. 6.

68 Annulment of marriage will be further discussed in sections 2.7 and 3.4.2.2.

69 Melby, Kari, Pylkkänen, Anu, Rosenbeck, Bente, Carlsson Wetterberg, Christina, Inte ett ord om kärlek, 2006, pp. 28–30. See also Schmidt, Folke, The Prospective Law of Marriage, 1971, p. 32.

Breaking with old Swedish marriage customs, which had been passed on from generation to generation, was a time-consuming process filled with conflicting interests.[70] Attempts to turn marriage into a church matter, governed by canonical law, instead of an economic settlement between families, caused tension between defenders of old traditions and religious adherers.[71] Families, especially wealthy ones, have been considered reluctant to turn over the important decisions regarding marriage to their children, since marriage could involve considerable financial interests. In other words, they were concerned that "consent-based" marriage might jeopardize the family's control over its fortune and real estate property.[72] Masha Antokolskaia has underlined that the introduction of marriage without parental consent was contrary to the interests of the noble clans and quite a progressive idea, which contributed to paving the way to personal freedom, for instance, in respect of choosing a marriage partner.[73] Moreover, Antokolskaia has pointed out that many basic concepts of family law used today, in fact derive from canon law – the *ius commune*[74] applicable in many European countries from the medieval times until the Reformation – for instance, the notion of marriage as a monogamous, heterosexual and life-long union.[75]

It is unclear to what extent the canonical standpoint was generally adopted in Sweden prior to the Reformation, which was carried out toward the end of the sixteenth century, when Lutheranism replaced Catholicism in Sweden.[76] According to Lizzie Carlsson, who focused on the early regulation on betrothal and marriage in Sweden in her doctoral thesis and following research, the "pre-Christian" marriage customs were the primary basis for the provincial laws, although the increasing influence of the Catholic Church in Sweden in the tenth and eleventh centuries might have, to some extent, influenced the provincial laws.[77] At least in respect of divorce law, Lars Tottie has pointed out that the papal edicts regarding marriage as an indissoluble union were never completely enforced in Sweden.[78]

---

70 Jänterä-Jareborg, Maarit, Religion and the Secular State, 2010, p. 672. See also Carlsson, Lizzie, Jag giver dig min dotter, 1965, p. 48.

71 Carlsson, Lizzie, Jag giver dig min dotter, 1972. p. 6.

72 Korpiola, Mia, An Uneasy Harmony, 1999, p. 127. See also Carlsson, Lizzie, Jag giver dig min dotter, 1965, p. 51.

73 Antokolskaia, Masha, Harmonisation of Family Law in Europe, 2006, pp. 132 f.

74 According to Antokolskaia, medieval uniform canon law was on the one hand, a mixture of Roman-Jewish, Germanic traditions, and on the other hand, the church's own family ideology developed during the Middle Ages. See Harmonisation of Family Law in Europe, 2006, pp. 55 f.

75 Antokolskaia, Masha, Harmonisation of Family Law in Europe, 2006, p. 154.

76 Law Commission Report of 1913, p. 371.

77 Carlsson, Lizzie, Jag giver dig min dotter, 1972, p. 19. This book was the continuation of the research subject in her doctoral thesis, Jag giver dig min dotter, 1965.

78 Tottie, Lars, The Elimination of Fault in Swedish Divorce Law, 1980, p. 131. See also Antokolskaia, Masha, Harmonisation of Family Law in Europe, 2006, p. 136. This has also been noted by Bradley, David, Family Law and Political Culture, 1996, p. 7.

2.2.2. THE REFORMATION – FROM CATHOLICISM TO LUTHERANISM

A key event when investigating the concept of marriage in Sweden is the Reformation, a period of church transformation, finally accomplished in 1593.[79] The year 1593 marked the end of the struggle between the members of the Catholic Church and supporters of the Lutheran faith in Sweden and the beginning of a strict religious era, which aimed to foster the inhabitants in accordance with the Lutheran faith.[80] The reorganization from being a Roman Catholic country to being an Evangelical Lutheran state did not go smoothly, not only due to religious tensions, but also because of economic and political factors. In the literature it has been pointed out that an economic aspect of the Reformation was that the royalty realized that they could lay their hands on the wealth of the Roman Catholic Church, by challenging the political order of the pope as the head of the church and the state.[81]

This development – the transfer of power from the Catholic Church to the Swedish state (the king) in close cooperation with the introduction of the Lutheran faith – had an impact on the religious concept of marriage. According to canonical (Catholic) law, marriage was a sacrament and the Pope was the independent, sole leader of the church, whereas the Lutheran (protestant) position viewed marriage as a gift of God to humanity.[82] In the view of Masha Antokolskaia, the Lutheran conception strengthened the dignity of marriage. From Antokolskaia's point of view, although marriage is no sacrament in the Lutheran faith, it is by no means the "second best" choice of lifestyle, i.e. secondary to the supremacy of the celibate state with the celibacy of the Catholic priests as the desirable model.[83]

In the long run, as will be illustrated below, the theoretical distinction between church law and civil law would turn out to be significant for introducing legal grounds for divorce. In 1734, however, this distinction was of little practical importance, as church and state values coincided. The king was the head of the church, which was a part of the government of the country. As pointed out by Max Rheinstein, this intertwinement of the positions of the king and the church made a liberalization of divorce law imperceptible at that point in time.[84] Assigning the king undivided power as sole legislator did not change the central

[79] Law Commission Report of 1913, pp. 79–82. See also Inger, Göran, Svensk rättshistoria, 1997, p. 71.

[80] Inger, Göran, Svensk rättshistoria, 1997, p. 71. For a thorough analysis of the impact of the Reformation, see Andrén, Åke, Sveriges Kyrkohistoria, Reformationstid, 1999.

[81] Jänterä-Jareborg, Maarit, Religion and the Secular State, 2010, p. 672. See also Andrén, Åke, Sveriges Kyrkohistoria, Reformationstid, 1999, pp. 8 f.

[82] Law Commission Report of 1913, p. 79.

[83] Antokolskaia, Masha, Harmonisation of Family Law in Europe, 2006, p. 169.

[84] Rheinstein, Max, Marriage Stability, Divorce, and the Law, 1972, p. 153.

position of religion in Swedish society. On the contrary, the religious engagement appears to have increased and culminated when the church finally obtained a monopoly on performing marriages in 1734.[85]

After the Reformation, an interest common to the church and state was to strengthen the position of the Lutheran faith in Sweden by counteracting all dissenting religious faiths. In line with this ambition, the practice of religions other than the Lutheran was criminalized in the Church Act of 1686,[86] and could lead to the death sentence according to the Marriage Code of 1734.[87] In fact, already in the seventeenth century, unity in respect of religion was laid down as a basis for the 1634 Instrument of Government.[88] The idea of religion as the connecting factor in a state – *vinculum reipublicae* – remained significant during most of the eighteenth century.[89] Normative efforts of the church to foster its congregation are reflected in its endeavor to sharpen the civil punishments for unwanted sexual relations and behavior. For instance, adultery, incest, bestiality and homosexual acts were forbidden on pain of death.[90] God's law was absolute and the book of Genesis directly applicable.[91]

2.2.3. THE PERIOD OF ENLIGHTENMENT – THE IMPACT ON MARRIAGE

In the legal literature, the process toward liberalizing regulation governing marriage in the West, illustrated in the coming chapters of this thesis, has been linked to the period of Enlightenment. As Masha Antokolskaia puts it: "Enlightenment thought lays at the beginning of the process of the liberalization of the family".[92] Antokolskaia characterizes the Enlightenment ideology as a progressive "modernity project", based on universal values such as peace, prosperity, happiness, justice and freedom, which started in the eighteenth century and still continues.[93] In other words, the Enlightenment ideology can be

85 This has been pointed out by: Nygren, Rolf, Kyrkorätt, Äktenskap och sekularisering – I, 1989, pp. 27 f.

86 Sundberg, Jacob, Familjerätt i omvandling, 1969, p. 33. The Church Act of 1686 remained in force for 300 years, replaced by the Church Act of 1992. See Inger, Göran, Kyrkolagstiftningen under 1600-talet, 2002, p. 231.

87 Jägerskiöld, Stig, Kring tillkomsten av 1734 års lag, 1984, p. 12.

88 Sundberg, Jacob, Familjerätt i omvandling, 1969, p. 33.

89 Normann, Carl-E, Enhetskyrka och upplysningsidéer, 1963, p. 8.

90 Österberg, Eva, Historiska perspektiv, Kyrkan, äktenskapet och konstruktionen av det "normala", 2004, p. 44. Östberg claims that Sweden in the eighteenth century was fundamentalistic and strived to control people's sexuality in a way that had no European equivalent outside of the Nordic countries and Scotland.

91 Jägerskiöld, Stig, Kring tillkomsten av 1734 års lag, 1984, p. 19.

92 Antokolskaia, Masha, Harmonisation of Family Law in Europe, 2006, p. 195.

93 Antokolskaia, Masha, Harmonisation of Family Law in Europe, 2006, pp. 32 and 265 f.

seen as the starting point for regarding marriage as a means to achieve personal happiness – not merely as a religious and social duty.[94]

Also Max Rheinstein has observed the impact of the ideas of the Enlightenment on the institution of marriage. Rheinstein has held that the ideas of humanism and the Enlightenment reached Sweden, and was accepted by intellectuals, at a comparatively early stage in time. Furthermore, Rheinstein – who regarded the Swedish divorce laws of the eighteenth century as "liberal" because of the possibility to obtain a divorce by means of royal dispensation – links this to the impact of Enlightenment ideas on the intellectual climate in Sweden.[95]

The Enlightenment ideas and the "modernity project", according to Antokolskaia, were not realized in the whole of Europe until the 1960s, after 200 years of struggles against opposition in Europe.[96] The division into conservative and progressive factions in Europe can be claimed to have remained relevant during the entire time and to have contributed to creating tension in connection with enactments dealing with marriage, most recently in connection with gender-neutral marriage.[97]

2.3. SWEDEN IN THE EIGHTEENTH CENTURY – THE STATE, CHURCH AND SOCIETY

2.3.1. THE CHURCH OF SWEDEN'S SPECIAL INTEREST IN MARRIAGE

In 1734, the main element laying down the predominating values in Swedish society was religion, as interpreted by the Church of Sweden. The Church of Sweden showed special interest in the institution of marriage, requesting exclusive rights to perform the marriage ceremony.[98] In 1734, the Church of Sweden finally reached this goal.

Marriage was the platform for family formation, and the family was the fundamental unit on which society relied completely, in order to ensure procreation and agricultural production in the Swedish farming society.[99] There was no welfare state, taking care of individuals. Instead the family cared for its

94 Antokolskaia, Masha, Harmonisation of Family Law in Europe, 2006, p. 193.
95 Rheinstein, Max, Marriage Stability, Divorce, and the Law, 1972, p. 153.
96 Antokolskaia, Masha, Harmonisation of Family Law in Europe, 2006, pp. 265 f.
97 See chapters 6 and 7.
98 Österberg, Eva, Historiska perspektiv, Kyrkan, äktenskapet och konstruktionen av det "normala", 2004, p. 44.
99 Committee Report (SOU 1938:57), p. 38. See also Österberg, Eva, Historiska perspektiv, Kyrkan, äktenskapet och konstruktionen av det "normala, 2004, p. 44. See also Schmidt, Folke, Äktenskapsrätt, 1974, p. 22.

own members and provided services such as childcare and old-age-care.[100] In short the family based on marriage was an indispensable unit, without which the individual would not survive.[101] Seen from this perspective, it is understandable that the Church of Sweden and the state showed special interest in the institution of marriage and actively discouraged divorce.[102]

Furthermore, as noted by Vagn Greve, changes in family patterns can be perceived as an "attack" on society as such, and an offense against what is understood to be "good morality".[103] Through the monopoly on concluding marriages, the Church of Sweden could set the moral standard in society, the basic idea being to only allow sexual relationships within marriage.[104] In eighteenth century Sweden, the purpose of marriage was procreation, and referring all sexual relationships to marriage in order to serve this purpose, was a means to counteract and morally forbid unwanted extramarital sexual behavior.[105] Sexual relationships outside of marriage threatened the indispensable family unit and risked creating illegitimate children and single mothers, which there was no welfare state to provide for and protect.

Despite the church's efforts to limit sexual acts to marriage, extramarital sexual behavior could not be completely controlled by the church. The so-called incomplete marriages, deriving from provincial marriage customs, were legally recognized in the Code of 1734. In the Code of 1734, according to the rules on incomplete marriage, a man's promise to marry a woman, followed by sexual intercourse, could be legally recognized as a marriage. A basic condition for recognition was that a man by promising to marry a woman had persuaded her to have sexual intercourse with him and then failed to go through with the planned marriage.[106]

---

100 Committee Report (SOU 1972:41), p. 87. See also Österberg, Eva, Historiska perspektiv, Kyrkan, äktenskapet och konstruktionen av det "normala", 2004, p. 44. See also Carlsson, Lizzie, Jag giver dig min dotter, 1965, p. 29.

101 Also servants formed an important part of this productive unit. See Schmidt, Folke, The Prospective Law of Marriage, 1971, p. 195.

102 Committee Report (SOU 1972:41), p. 87.

103 Greve, Vagn, Hvornår er bigami strafbart? 2009, p. 93. Greve was speaking of Danish conditions but parallels can be drawn to Sweden. For an extensive analysis of the origin and development of the institution of marriage and of moral ideas, see Westermarck, Edvard, The History of Human Marriage, vol I-III, 1925. Westermarck was a Finnish social anthropologist, philosopher, and sociologist.

104 Report of the Church Board, Kyrkostyrelsens skrivelse 2009:6, Vigsel och äktenskap, pp. 47 f.

105 Sundby, Olof, Luthersk äktenskapsuppfattning, 1959, p. 22.

106 The Church Act of 1686, Chapter 15, Sections 13–14. See also Nygren, Rolf, Kyrkorätt, Äktenskap och sekularisering – II, 1989, p. 53. The incomplete marriages will be dealt with in sections 2.5.4.1 and 2.5.4.2.

2.3.2. SOCIETY IN GENERAL – BASIC FEATURES RELATED TO MARRIAGE

Not only religious aspects of marriage, as interpreted by the Church of Sweden, were of importance for the institution of marriage in eighteenth century Sweden. The conditions in society in general also had an impact on marriage, by establishing the prerequisites for the everyday lives of the population.

Society in eighteenth century Sweden was built upon a patriarchal structure. Women were under the legal guardianship of their fathers until marriage and then the husband took over as legal guardian[107] of his wife.[108] The Marriage Code of 1734 did not change the legal position of women in this respect. Women inherited half as much as men. This inferior position of women is connected to the historically essential value of the family land and the family's interest in keeping it in the family in the future.[109] However, it should be kept in mind that women were to some extent compensated for their weaker financial position in inheritance law through the institutions of morning gift and dowry, which will be further analyzed in section 2.6.2.

Moreover, the wife was only entitled to half the amount of the marital property compared the husband, and the wife's property was administered by her husband. Through marriage, the woman became entitled to take her husband's name and, more importantly, to achieve his family status.[110] The family was the foundation of society and the social status of the family was a significant component of the class society.[111]

It has been pointed out in the literature that the legal position of women as inferior to men and women's lack of legal capacity should *not* be interpreted as a general indication that women were disrespected by their husbands and by society. Many marriages were built on companionship, and the woman was a valuable part of the household. The husband and wife had different

107 The wide English term "guardian" encompasses both of the Swedish terms "förmyndare" and "målsman". Thus the "guardian" handled the woman's property and affairs, as well as spoke on her behalf in court (in most cases).

108 Hafström, Gerhard, Den svenska familjerättens historia, 1972, p. 54. The husband's guardianship had two exceptions: when the wife was charged with a crime and when husband and wife had conflicting interests. In the former case, the woman spoke for herself. In the latter case, an administrator would be appointed by the court. It can be mentioned that the woman remained under her husband's guardianship until the Marriage Code of 1920 was enacted. The Marriage Code of 1920 entered into force on 1 January 1921. See also the Law Commission Report of 1918, p. 135.

109 Before 1260, women's right to inheritance was limited. Daughters only inherited if there was no son in the family. In 1260, this was altered so that a daughter inherited half as much as a son. See Carlsson, Lizzie, Jag giver dig min dotter, 1965, p. 30.

110 The Marriage Code of 1734, Chapter 9, Section 1. See also Almquist, Jan Eric, Den svenska familjerättens historia, 1943, pp. 44 f., and Agell, Anders, Brattström, Margareta, Äktenskap, Samboende, Partnerskap, 2008, p. 51, with further references.

111 Jägerskiöld, Stig, Kring tillkomsten av 1734 års lag, 1984, p. 13.

responsibilities. During marriage, the woman had an important role within the household, as *husfru* (mistress of the house) in charge of the household and the servants, whereas the man was head of the house toward the outside community.[112] Also, upon the death of the husband the widow took over her husband's position and authority as head of the household and of the farming unit that it usually constituted.[113]

The Marriage Code of 1734 contained a prohibition against wife battering.[114] In fact, the prohibition, pursuant to its wording, went both ways, i.e. it also prohibited women from beating their husbands.[115] The practical impact of the provision appears to be uncertain. In the literature, some have interpreted this prohibition against wife abuse as nothing but an expression of an unwillingness to *encourage* a husband to beat his wife, whereas in practice, a husband was allegedly considered entitled to do so, pursuant to his *patria potestas*.[116] As Lizzie Carlsson points out, there is no evidence to be found in the preserved protocols from the courts which supports the idea that wife abuse was a common feature in eighteenth century Sweden.[117]

However, the legal authority of the man to administer corporal punishment to the servants – pursuant to his role as master of the house – appears to have been utilized occasionally.[118] This authority was kept in the law, as part of the master's domestic responsibilities until 1858.[119] The master of the house was not allowed to carry out excessive violence toward a servant, which resulted in making the servant "lame or disfigured".[120]

---

112 Andersson, Gudrun, Myndig eller omyndig? 1996, p. 17. The responsibility of caring for the household depended on the status and economy of the family. When analyzing the position of women, not only legal factors but also societal norms and habits must be taken into account, pp. 16 f. See also Hafström, Gerhard, 1972, pp. 55 f.

113 The woman's important position upon the death of her husband has been pointed out by Carlsson, Lizzie, Jag giver dig min dotter, 1965, p. 29.

114 The Criminal Code (Misgiernings Balk) Chapter 36, Section 1.

115 "Hvilken man af hat, eller i dryckenskap, eller för annor qvinnos skul, slår hustru sina blå eller blodig, lahm eller lytt; vare thet alt i tveböte. Slår hustru man sin; stånde samma rätt." In short, this quote stated that a man who beat his wife, because of hate or under the influence of alcohol, or for the sake of another woman, "blue and bloody" or "lame or disfigured", was to pay fines. It is also stated that in respect of a woman who beat her husband, the same rules applied.

116 Jägerskiöld, Stig, Kring tillkomsten av 1734 års lag, 1984, p. 13. See also Hafström, Gerhard, Den svenska familjerättens historia, 1972, p. 52. See also Carlsson, Lizzie, Jag giver dig min dotter, 1965, p. 28. The term *patria potestas* is a Roman concept meaning the power vested in the father in capacity of the head of the family with respect to his wife and children.

117 Carlsson, Lizzie, Jag giver dig min dotter, 1965, p. 28.

118 Carlsson, Lizzie, Jag giver dig min dotter, 1965, p. 29.

119 Schmidt, Folke, The Prospective Law of Marriage, 1971, p. 195.

120 This prohibition is laid down in the same provision as the prohibition against spousal battery, i.e. in the Criminal Code (Misgierningsbalk), Chapter 36, Section 1. If the husband had in fact a legal right to beat his wife and children, this right was abolished in the Criminal Code of 1864. See Hafström, Gerhard, Den svenska familjerättens historia, 1972, p. 52.

2.4. NOVELTIES REGARDING MARRIAGE – THE CODE OF 1734

2.4.1. CONCLUSION OF MARRIAGE

The Code of 1734, the first Codification of rules applicable to the whole Swedish state, contained several legislative novelties. The idea is to briefly present the innovations of the Marriage Code here and return to the subjects below for further analysis. A significant novelty in the 1734 Code was the above-mentioned introduction of church marriage as the only legally valid form of concluding a marriage. From the point of view of the Church of Sweden, obtaining the exclusive right to legally marry couples strengthened its position in society and challenged the provincial marriage customs, according to which marriage was an economic settlement between families.[121] Moreover, introducing one system for conclusion of marriage – the religious ceremony according to the Church Act – most likely offered administrative advantages and clarity.[122] Prior to the 1734 codification, a marriage could be contracted under informal conditions, which risked creating confusion in respect of the validity of the marriage.[123] This risk was diminished through the requirement that a valid marriage had to be celebrated within the church. But the so-called incomplete marriages, which will be dealt with in sections 2.5.4.1, 2.5.4.2 and 2.5.4.3 below, continued to give rise to legal effects until 1915.

Another novelty was the establishment of marriageable ages for men and women in the Marriage Code of 1734. Neither the Church Act of 1686, nor the provincial laws contained any lower age-limits for conclusion of marriage. In the Church Act, it was merely stated that neither men nor women should marry before reaching a lawful and mature age.[124] According to the Marriage Code of 1734, Chapter 1, Section 6, the age-limit for marriage was set at 15 for women and 21 for men. Marriage before these ages required dispensation by the king.[125] Establishing an age-limit for men at 21 years of age was, most likely, a considerable sharpening compared to the "maturity criterion" applied by the church, according to which the age of 15 usually sufficed for conclusion of marriage.[126] There does not appear to have been an exact age-limit for women in the Church Act. It is likely that the age of puberty was generally applied.[127]

121 See section 2.2.1.
122 Committee Report (SOU 2007:17), p. 108.
123 Committee Report (SOU 2007:17), p. 108.
124 Law Commission Report of 1913, p. 134.
125 Law Commission Report of 1913, p. 134. This will be further discussed in section 2.5.2.1.
126 Law Commission Report of 1913, p. 134.
127 Law Commission Report of 1913, p. 134.

2.4.2. DISSOLUTION OF MARRIAGE

Another noteworthy novelty in the Marriage Book of the Code of 1734 was the codification of rules on dissolution of marriage. As of 1734, applications for dissolution of marriage were decided by the court, not the church.[128] This change, however, did not mean that divorce became easier to obtain. In reality, due to the strong religious influence, it was nearly impossible to obtain a divorce, even if the law provided such a possibility in exceptional cases.[129] A court proceeding was preceded by an arduous church procedure, for the purpose of reconciling or deterring the spouses from going through with the divorce.[130]

The grounds for dissolution of marriage were twofold, namely (1) *hor*[131] (adultery) and (2) *egenvilligt övergivande* (arbitrary abandonment), laid down in the Marriage Code, Chapter 13. Substantively, these two grounds were no novelties. The same two grounds for divorce had been included in the provincial laws, but were challenged by the canonical perception of marriage as a sacrament which could not be dissolved.[132] After the Reformation, the Lutheran conception of marriage as a gift of God to humanity – not a sacrament – took over and the two grounds for divorce (adultery and arbitrary abandonment) could be reintroduced in the Church Acts of 1572 and 1686, and finally in the Marriage Code of 1734.[133]

2.5. THE FORMS AND CONDITIONS OF MARRIAGE – THE CODE OF 1734

2.5.1. BETROTHAL

The institution of *trolovning* (betrothal) is an illustrative example of the efforts made by the Church of Sweden to strengthen its position in Swedish society, in competition with the wide-spread provincial marriage customs. Thus, in the Marriage Code of 1734, betrothal was made obligatory prior to marriage, and marriage had to be celebrated in the Lutheran Church of Sweden. It can be mentioned that "betrothal" was the religious term, whereas "marriage contract"[134] (fästning) was the ancient legal term for the preliminary stage to

128 Law Commission Report of 1913, p. 372.
129 Jägerskiöld, Stig, Kring tillkomsten av 1734 års lag, 1984, p. 15.
130 Nygren, Rolf, Kyrkorätt, Äktenskap och sekularisering – I, 1989, p. 28. This will be further discussed in section 2.7.
131 The Swedish term *hor* should not be confused with prostitution. *Hor* or "adultery" here refers to sexual intercourse with somebody other than the spouse.
132 Law Commission Report of 1913, pp. 79 and 371.
133 Law Commission Report of 1913, p. 371.
134 The English translation "Marriage contract" is used by Anders Agell in: The Swedish Legislation on Marriage and Cohabitation, a Journey without a Destination, 1980, p. 19.

marriage.[135] However, as mentioned above, the Lutheran Church of Sweden failed to completely replace the "marriage contract" with the corresponding religious institution of betrothal. Irrespective of the rules on betrothal, marriages continued to take place without the participation of the church. As will be discussed in section 2.5.4.2 these marriages could on certain conditions be recognized as incomplete marriages and give rise to the legal effects of marriage.

Conclusion of betrothal required an overt declaration in the presence of the *giftoman*[136] and four witnesses, two from the husband's side of the family and two from the wife's.[137] A valid betrothal also required the participation of a minister of the Church of Sweden.[138] The idea was to avoid "secret marriage" arrangements – in the literature also called "clandestine marriages"[139] – concluded without the participation of the church. The existence of such "secret marriages" can be seen as an example of the church's difficulties to control sexual relations. Another formal prerequisite for a valid betrothal was the establishment of the woman's *hemgift* (dowry). The regulation of dowry, which will be further discussed below, was kept unchanged in the Marriage Code of 1734, as an absolute prerequisite for marriage.[140]

If the betrothed unanimously wished to call off their planned marriage – provided that they did not have children – the vicar could draw up a certificate of dissolution. If only one of them had a change of heart, a court was to decide whether or not the petitioning spouse had reasonable grounds for the application

135 Committee Report (SOU 1972:41), pp. 116 f.

136 Since the Swedish term *giftoman* is difficult to translate, the Swedish term is used here. The giftoman was authorized to decide matters concerning the daughter's as well as the minor son's marriage. Andersson, Gudrun, Myndig eller omyndig? 1996, p. 19. The consent of the giftoman was not required if the woman was a widow, wishing to remarry. See Westring, Hjalmar, Den nya giftermålsbalken jämte dithörande författningar med förklaringar, 1933, p. 29.

137 Westring, Hjalmar, Den nya giftermålsbalken jämte dithörande författningar med förklaringar, 1933, p. 15. These formalities were not compulsory. The absence of the consent of the giftoman could only result in invalidity of the marriage if the giftoman petitioned accordingly. Also a written promise to marry was considered a valid betrothal, with the approval of the giftoman, see p. 16. According to the Church Act of 1686, Chapter 15, Section 10, conclusion of a marriage contract required four witnesses, whereas conclusion of betrothal only required two male witnesses, one from each side, except parents and giftoman. See Sveriges kyrkolag af år 1686, 1844–1845, p. 148.

138 Committee Report (SOU 1972:41), p. 116.

139 Antokolskaia, Masha, Harmonisation of Family Law in Europe, 2006, p. 109. It can be noted that according to Göran Lind, the term *matrimonium clandestinum* (secret marriage) was used in several different contexts, meaning (1) marriages contracted in the presence of witnesses, but without the participation of the church, (2) marriages of which there was no evidence of validity other than the parties' own statements, (3) marriages contracted without parental consent and (4) marriages contracted without banns (after the introduction of banns as an obligatory element in 1216). In summary, it was a question of relationships which lacked one or several formal prerequisites. See Lind, Göran, Common Law Marriage, 2006, p. 107.

140 Inger, Göran, Svensk rättshistoria, 1997, p. 142.

and, if this was not the case, award the other spouse pecuniary damages.[141] If the petitioner was the one to blame for the dissolution, that person was not allowed to enter into a marriage with another person until the case had been settled. Settlement involved arranging economic dealings and possibly also paying damages.[142]

When the Marriage Code of 1734 was drafted, regulating betrothal appears to have been problematic. More precisely, this was because it was suspected that betrothal tended to be entered into light-heartedly and that making separation difficult by deterring from separation through attaching far-reaching legal effects to betrothal risked resulting in unhappiness which could lead to coldness between the couple.[143] The legal solution chosen to avoid hasty betrothals and prevent secret marriages was to require that betrothal was preceded by *lysning* (banns).[144] Banns meant publically announcing the coming betrothal in the church three Sundays in a row, for the purpose of investigating whether impediments to marriage existed.[145] Banns were mandatory, but according to the Marriage Code of 1734, exemption from banns could be granted, if there was no time because the husband-to-be was summoned for military service. It can be mentioned that also the Church Act of 1686 allowed exemption from banns, but only if either party was dying.[146]

Traditionally, excluding impediments through banns had been the responsibility of the giftoman.[147] Making banns the responsibility of the church was a means to strengthen the position of the Church of Sweden in society, by increasing its participation in the establishment of marriages.

---

141 Law Commission Report of 1913, 106 f. See also Committee Report, (SOU 1972:41), p. 116. Rules on dissolution of betrothal can be found in the Marriage Code of 1734, Chapter 4. As regards church law, see the Church Act, Chapter 16, as commented in: Sveriges kyrkolag af år 1686, 1844–1845, pp. 161–173.

142 Westring, Hjalmar, Den nya giftermålsbalken jämte dithörande författningar med förklaringar, 1933, p. 16. The person to blame for the break-up was not entitled to take back gifts.

143 Law Commission Report of 1913, p. 106.

144 In 1216, the regulation of banns was first introduced as a prerequisite for marriage in a letter from the Pope, as an attempt to avoid "secret marriages". See Carlsson, Lizzie, Jag giver dig min dotter, 1972.
Carlsson, Lizzie, Jag giver dig min dotter, 1972, p. 99.

145 Committee Report (SOU 1972:40), p. 141.

146 Inger, Göran, Svensk rättshistoria, 1997, p. 141.

147 Committee Report (SOU 1972:41), p. 141. See also Inger, Göran, Svensk rättshistoria, 1997, p. 89 and the Law Commission Report of 1913, p. 106.

2.5.2. WHO COULD MARRY WHOM?

2.5.2.1. Impediments to Marriage

Marriage in eighteenth century Sweden was a voluntary union, in the sense that no one should be forced to marry.[148] Yet, a woman could not marry without the consent of her giftoman. This person was usually her father. According to the Marriage Code of 1734, however, the mother filled in if the father was deceased.[149] An impediment to marriage could be either *dispensable* or *indispensable*, depending on what interests a specific impediment aimed to protect and how fundamental the connected values were.[150] Marriage without the consent of the giftoman was a dispensable impediment. A marriage concluded against the wishes of the woman's giftoman could, however, result in missed inheritance rights.[151] In practice, this can be seen as having reduced the impression of marriage in the eighteenth century as a voluntary union based on the consent of the parties. Other *dispensable* impediments of the Marriage Code of 1734 were: underage, certain diseases and disfigurement (impediment to betrothal), remarriage in certain situations, priest celibacy[152] and marriage to members of other Christian denominations than the Lutheran.

The *indispensable* impediments were: affinity or blood relationship,[153] already existing marriage or betrothal and adultery.[154] Existing marriage or betrothal made the second marriage invalid.[155] Adultery, committed by one or both parties was an impediment to marriage in the Code of 1734 and the marriage could be

---

148 See the Code of 1734, Chapter 1, Section 5.

149 It appears that granting the mother equal power as the father in this respect was criticized. See Andersson, Gudrun, Myndig eller omyndig? 1996, p. 34.

150 Hafström, Gerhard, Den svenska familjerättens historia, 1972, pp. 26–31 (dispensable impediments) and 31–36 (indispensable impediments).

151 Jägerskiöld, Stig, Kring tillkomsten av 1734 års lag, 1984, p. 15. See also Hafström, Gerhard, Den svenska familjerättens historia, 1972, p. 32.

152 The fact that priest celibacy remained an impediment tot marriage in protestant Sweden is noteworthy as a remnant of the impact of the Catholic faith and Canonical Law.

153 Cousins could marry each other upon dispensation. In 1845, this was changed so that cousins were allowed to marry one another without dispensation. Thus the impediment of affinity ended with the prohibition against marriage to a niece or nephew. In the Marriage Code of 1920, marriage between a sibling and the other sibling's offspring (i.e. niece or nephew) was made a dispensable impediment, since it was no longer considered medically justified to keep it as indispensable. See Westring, Hjalmar, Den nya giftermålsbalken jämte dithörande författningar med förklaringar, 1933, p. 37. See also Hafström, Gerhard, Den svenska familjerättens historia, 1972, p. 28.

154 Persons who had committed adultery together were forbidden to marry each other, unless the innocent spouse of one of them was deceased or remarried or consented to the adulterous parties marrying each other. See Hafström, Gerhard, Den svenska familjerättens historia, 1972, p. 31.

155 Westring, Hjalmar, Den nya giftermålsbalken jämte dithörande författningar med förklaringar, 1933, p. 38.

annulled upon the request of the innocent spouse (of the adulterous spouse), or upon request of the district attorney.[156]

The rules on invalid marriage and annulment of marriage in the Code of 1734 appear rather vague, leaving several questions regarding the effect of invalidity unanswered.[157] As a result, it was sometimes unclear if an annulment procedure was required to establish a marriage as invalid. A possible explanation for this obscurity is that the legislator and the church in 1734 were quite uninterested in the institution of annulment, perhaps because this was a canonical remainder from pre-Lutheran times.[158]

As briefly mentioned in section 2.4.1, in the Marriage Code of 1734 lower age-limits for men and women wishing to marry were established in the law for the first time: 21 years for men and 15 years for women.[159] However, marriage to an under-age person was a dispensable impediment and not a ground for dissolution. The king could grant dispensation from the age-limit in an individual case.[160] In practice, the higher age-limit for men compared to women resulted in many applications for dispensation which motivated lowering the age-limit for men from 21 to 17 years, through an ordinance in 1756.[161]

It is noteworthy that the age-limit for women was much lower than for men. A possible explanation for this difference could be that the husband had to take on the responsibility as the legal guardian of his wife, which included a duty to financially support her. It can be assumed that fulfilling this responsibility required that the husband had reached a certain level of maturity, and this can justify the age-difference between men and women. Another possible explanation why different age-limits applied to men and women could be that safeguarding population growth was a concern of the legislator and favoring procreation was necessary, in a time when bad crops and diseases were a threat in this respect.[162]

The Marriage Code of 1734 followed a general tendency to reduce the number of impediments for the purpose of easing the burden of administration in dispensation matters.[163] Nevertheless, the impediments to marriage in the Marriage Code of 1734 were extensive by modern standards. It has been pointed

---

156 Hafström, Gerhard, Den svenska familjerättens historia, 1972, pp. 30 f.

157 Committee Report (SOU 1972:41), p. 158.

158 Law Commission Report of 1913, p. 310. See also Westring, Hjalmar, Den nya giftermålsbalken jämte dithörande författningar med förklaringar, 1943, pp. 64 f.

159 The Marriage Code of 1734, Chapter 1, Section 6. In 1892, in a statute issued by the king, the age-limit for women was raised to 17 years. By 1920, it was 18 years for women and 21 years for men. According to Westring, the idea was that women were not mature enough to become wives and mothers before this age. See Westring, Hjalmar, Den nya giftermålsbalken jämte dithörande författningar med förklaringar, 1933, p. 28. The Church Act, Chapter 15, Section 5 prescribed that mature age was needed and referred to the Marriage Code.

160 Inger, Göran, Svensk rättshistoria, 1997, p. 141.

161 Ordinance of 8 December 1756. See Hafström, Gerhard, Den svenska familjerättens historia, 1972, p. 31.

162 Inger, Göran, Svensk rättshistoria, pp. 141 f.

163 Committee Report (SOU 1972:41), pp. 124 f.

out by Dagmar Coester-Waltjen and Michael Coester that there is a connection between the rules on dissolution of marriage and the impediments to marriage, in the sense that restrictive divorce rules are often combined with an extensive catalogue of impediments.[164] According to their view, impediments to marriage could be used as a device to avoid creating unhappy and unstable marriages.[165] In other words, if a marriage is difficult to dissolve, as was the case under the 1734 Code compared to later enactments, it was especially urgent to restrict and control access to it through impediments.

2.5.2.2. The Legal Authority to Celebrate Marriages

The central position of the Church of Sweden is also reflected in the rules governing authority to celebrate marriages. According to the Marriage Code of 1734, the authority to officiate at legally valid marriages was reserved for ministers of the Church of Sweden, who were of the Lutheran faith as interpreted by the church. This was the only acceptable religious faith in Sweden.[166] In fact, the practice of religions other than the Lutheran was criminalized in the Church Act of 1686[167] and could lead to the death sentence according to the Marriage Code of 1734.[168]

The Swedish Lutheran marriage service applied also to foreigners living in Sweden and wishing to marry in Sweden. It was possible, through dispensation from the king, for members of Christian religious communities other than the Lutheran to marry Lutherans.[169] In practice, however, the Church of Sweden actively discouraged its members from marrying members of religious communities other than the Lutheran.[170]

---

164 Coester-Waltjen, Dagmar, Coester Michael, International Encyclopedia of Comparative Law, Vol. IV, Persons and Family, Chapter 3, Formation of Marriage, p. 3.

165 Coester-Waltjen, Dagmar, Coester Michael, International Encyclopedia of Comparative Law, Vol. IV, Persons and Family, Chapter 3, Formation of Marriage, p. 3.

166 In the late 1800s, groups excluded from the right to church marriage, were granted admission to a civil marriage ceremony. According to the Dissenter Act of 1860 (Dissenterlag), religious communities other than the Church of Sweden could be legally recognized and the pastors of these communities could be authorized to conclude legally valid marriages. However, there was a problem. Betrothal had to be combined with banns and banns, in turn, required child baptism followed by confirmation. These religious customs were not practiced in all religious communities. To come to terms with this problem another Dissenter Act was introduced in 1873, providing denominations (in practice mainly Baptists) with access to civil marriage. In 1908 civil marriage was made available to everyone. See Committee Report (SOU 1972:41), p. 142, Hafström, Gerhard, Den svenska familjerättens historia, 1972, p. 43, Nygren, Rolf, Kyrkorätt, Äktenskap och sekularisering – II, 1989, p. 46 and Winroth, Alfred, Äktenskaps ingående, 1892, pp. 43–48.

167 Sundberg, Jacob, Familjerätt i omvandling, 1969, p. 33. The Church Act of 1686 remained in force for 300 years, replaced by the Church Act of 1992. See Inger, Göran, Kyrkolagstiftningen under 1600-talet, 2002, p. 231.

168 Jägerskiöld, Stig, Kring tillkomsten av 1734 års lag, 1984, p. 12.

169 Committee Report (SOU 2007:17), p. 109.

170 The Church Act of 1686, Chapter 15, Section 8, see Sveriges kyrkolag af år 1686, 1844–45, p.146.

2.5.3. THE APPLICABLE MARRIAGE SERVICE

2.5.3.1. The Marriage Service: Background and Wording

According to the Marriage Code of 1734, it was required that the religious marriage ceremony was celebrated by the Church of Sweden in the church.[171] As a result, unlike in Sweden today, there was no civil ceremony available as an option to the church ceremony. The Marriage Code of 1734 did not contain a specific "church section". Instead the Church Act of 1686 was applicable alongside of the Marriage Code, complementing state law by laying down the mandatory liturgy governing conclusion of marriage.[172] The Church Act only regulated a few details concerning conclusion of marriage, for instance, the requirement that marriage had to be preceded by banns.[173] The wording and components of the liturgical ceremony were laid down in the Church Handbook of 1693.[174] According to the handbook, the marriage ceremony started with an admonition by the minister to the congregation:

> "[...] God himself has founded marriage and placed the man as the head of the woman, so that he shall be her superior, rule her in fear of God to the best; and love her like Christ loved the congregation and gave his life to her. [...]"[175]

The presence of God is pervasive in the whole ceremony and the couple is initially reminded of their duty to live in a "God-fearing" manner. The liturgy cited above depicts marriage as a union based on a strict hierarchical structure, with the husband as his wife's master, in accordance with the husband's capacity as the legal guardian of his wife. However, the superior position of the husband did not give him the right to abuse his wife. On the contrary, he was to love her just as Christ had loved and died for his congregation. In fact, the woman, due to

171 In 1614, the church's position had become well-established and powerful enough to enable carrying out the requirement that the marriage ceremony was to take place in the church in order to be legally valid. See the Law Commission Report of 1913, p. 82.

172 Inger, Göran, Den svenska kyrkolagen 300 år, 1986. pp. 168–170.

173 The Church Act of 1686, Chapter 15, Section 18.

174 Handbok, ther vti är författat, huruledes gudstiensten med christelige ceremonier och kyrckioseder, vti wåra församlingar skall blifwa hållen och förhandlad, 1693. It can be mentioned that in the nineteenth century, the handbook was revised again in 1811 and 1894. The liturgy dealing with the marriage ceremony, however was laid down in 1882 and kept until 1917. In 1917, the wording of the marriage service was modernized slightly, but it was still quite traditional and the woman's role is described in terms of behaving so that she is of help to her husband. See Handbok för svenska kyrkan: steadfast av konungen år 1917, Svenska kyrkans diakonistyrelses bokförlag, 1918, p. 164.

175 "[...] Gud sielf hafwer stichtat ächtenskapet, och satt mannen till qwinones hufwud, at han skall wara hennes förman, regera henne i gudz fruchtan, til thet bästa, ther til älska henne, såsom Christus älskade församlingen, och gaf sig sielf i döden för henne." Handbok, ther vti är författat, huruledes gudstiensten med christelige ceremonier och kyrckioseder, vti wåra församlingar skall blifwa hållen och förhandlad, 1693, pp. 107 f. Author's translation.

perceived "gender weaknesses", was believed to be in need of the man's protection: "And like the man is gifted with greater reason and stronger nature than the woman; he shall use these God's gifts for her assistance, and not for oppression," the handbook specifies.[176]

The minister then moved on to discussing the role and obligations of the wife in relation to her husband. The woman was to love her husband and hold him as her superior, bearing in mind that she had been created for the purpose of assisting her husband. In other words: "She shall not rule over him. The woman was created for the sake of the man; not the man for the sake of the woman".[177] In the ceremony, the hierarchical nature of marriage was compared to the relationship between God and mankind. In other words, the husband's superior position to the wife was a reflection of God's superiority in relation to man.

Once these basic features of marriage had been laid down by the minister, following the liturgy, he continued with the actual questions. First he turned to the man, asking if he was willing to take the woman as his lawfully wedded wife to love in sickness and in health.[178] Thereafter, the woman was asked the same question. This procedure of consent was followed by a short prayer and a blessing of the bride's ring. The man then took the ring and offered it to the woman, as a symbol of commitment, and once again expressly declared his decision to marry the woman and to love and honor her. As the woman accepted the ring, she also expressly repeated her consent to marrying the man and to loving him in sickness and in health. Finally, it should be noted that the reproductive function and purpose of marriage are emphasized several times in the prayers, through the minister's request for God's blessing that the marriage be fruitful.[179]

An overall impression of the marriage ceremony, applicable in 1734, is that laying down the hierarchical order, with God as superior to man and the man as superior to the woman, was a central component of the religious marriage ceremony. However, the strict hierarchy of marriage did not contradict the element of love in the relationship. Husband and wife were to love each other as God loved his people. Moreover, it was confirmed that husband and wife needed one another. The woman needed the man for guidance and protection and the

176 "Och såsom mannen är begåfwat med större förnuft och starchare natur än qwinnan; så skal han och bruka sådana Gudz gåfwor henne till bistånd, och icke till förtrychelse. Handbok, ther vti är författat, huruledes gudstiensten med christelige ceremonier och kyrckioseder, vti wåra församlingar skall blifwa hållen och förhandlad, 1693, p. 108. Author's translation.

177 "Icke skal hon biuda til att råda öfwer honom. En qwinna är skapat för mannens skull; och icke mannen för qwinnones skull." Handbok, ther vti är författat, huruledes gudstiensten med christelige ceremonier och kyrckioseder, vti wåra församlingar skall blifwa hållen och förhandlad, 1693, p. 108. Author's translation.

178 "älska [varandra] i nöd och lust", Handbok, ther vti är författat, huruledes gudstiensten med christelige ceremonier och kyrckioseder, vti wåra församlingar skall blifwa hållen och förhandlad, 1693, p. 110.

179 Handbok, ther vti är författat, huruledes gudstiensten med christelige ceremonier och kyrckioseder, vti wåra församlingar skall blifwa hållen och förhandlad, 1693, pp. 110 and 119.

man needed the assistance and company of the woman, for the purpose of procreation as well as companionship. Marriage was a life-long union brought together by God, in the sense that: "God has brought together man and woman, so that no man can put them asunder".[180] However, unlike in the Catholic faith, marriage was no sacrament in the Lutheran faith.

2.5.3.2. An Alternative Wording of the Marriage Service

The 1693 Church Handbook contained an alternative phrase, which was to be applied if the spouses were not expected to have children. In the alternative wording, a prayer focusing on the value of companionship replaced the prayer for a fruitful marriage: "widowbrides and those with no hope of offspring".[181] It is noteworthy that there existed such an alternative prayer for couples who could not be expected to have children together. The idea of blessing also twosome unions without any prospect of procreation appears to have been based on the biblical idea that it is not good for the man to be alone.[182] The existence of such a service can be seen as a glimpse of another dimension of marriage in the eighteenth century, namely the notion of marriage as a basis for a close twosome companionship, without necessarily being linked to procreation. However, the main impression is that this dimension of marriage is overshadowed in the liturgical ceremony, by the values dealing with the hierarchical structure of marriage. Also from a biblical perspective, it was the man who was considered to be in need of company and the woman was given to him in this context.

2.5.4. THE "INCOMPLETE MARRIAGE"

2.5.4.1. Background – the Church Battling with Old Customs

Incomplete marriage is a remnant of Germanic marriage customs, laid down in the provincial laws of the eleventh and twelfth centuries. According to the provincial laws, which have been discussed in section 2.2.1, marriage was in short concluded through a promise to marry (a marriage contract), followed by a marriage ceremony and consummated through the bedding, without the

180 "dher Gud man och qwinna så hafwer sammanfogat, at ingen menniska them åtskilia kan." Handbok, ther vti är författat, huruledes gudstiensten med christelige ceremonier och kyrckioseder, vti wåra församlingar skall blifwa hållen och förhandlad, 1693, p. 109. Author's translation.

181 "Enkiebrudar/och them som äro utom förhoppning om lifsfrucht." Author's translation. Handbok, ther vti är författat, huruledes gudstiensten med christelige ceremonier och kyrckioseder, vti wåra församlingar skall blifwa hållen och förhandlad, 1693, p. 119.

182 Genesis 2:18.

participation of the church.[183] In 1734, the mutual ambition of the church and the king was to strengthen the position of the church, by making religious marriage the only legally valid form of concluding a marriage.

However, not all provincial customs could be done away with through the Code of 1734. Betrothal followed by sexual intercourse could be legally recognized as a marriage. Also a sexual relationship without betrothal could, under certain circumstances, be granted some legal effects of marriage. These "incomplete marriages"[184] – incomplete in the sense that no church ceremony had taken place – were included in the Code of 1734.[185] In fact, incomplete marriages, which were not uncommon, were recognized by the Church of Sweden in 1686 and included in the Church Act.[186] Also the Catholic Church, as a rule, appears to have recognized marriages concluded according to the old Swedish provincial customs,[187] without the participation of the church.[188]

Incomplete marriages continued to give rise to legal effects in the statutory law until 1915, when the Act on Conclusion and Dissolution of Marriage was enacted.[189] Various reasons were given for the abolishment of rules on incomplete marriage. It was held, for instance, that rules on incomplete marriage contradicted the idea of marriage as a voluntary, publicly declared union, since a court could establish such an incomplete marriage against the will of one

183 For a thorough account of these old Swedish traditions, see Carlsson, Lizzie, Jag giver dig min dotter, 1965. Skrifter utgivna av Institutet för rättshistorisk forskning grundat av Gustav och Carin Olin, p. 13 f. See also Carlsson, Lizzie, Jag giver dig min dotter, 1972.

184 The term *ofullständigt äktenskap* (incomplete marriage) is not used in the Marriage Code of 1734. However, it is used in later publications, travaux préparatoires included. See, for instance, Law Commission Report of 1913, pp. 96–105, for an account of the rules on incomplete marriages in Sweden.

185 See section 2.5.4.2.

186 The Church Act of 1686, Chapter 15, Sections 13–14. This regulation can be traced back to the Bible, more precisely to Exodus, Chapter 22, Verse 16. See Law Commission Report of 1913, p. 86.

187 This was the case as long as marriage had not been concluded in breach of the impediments dealing with incest. A marriage contracted in breach of an impediment based on close affinity could at least in theory be prosecuted as illegal extra-marital fornication. However, according to Lizzie Carlsson, such "fornication" was rarely prosecuted. Jag giver dig min dotter, 1972, pp. 97 f.

188 It is unclear why the Catholic Church recognized old provincial marriage customs contracted without church participation. Three possible scenarios have been described in the literature: (1) canonical law was adopted in the provincial laws, (2) there were two independent parallel developments or (3) canonical law was influenced by the provincial laws. See Carlsson, Lizzie, Jag giver dig min dotter, 1972, p. 93. These three options are, according to Carlsson, widely accepted in research. Göran Lind provides a pragmatic explanation why the Catholic Church recognized marriages contracted without the participation of the church, namely that the Catholic Church could reach more people in society by recognizing such marriages as legally valid and thus strengthen its position in a society where Germanic marriage customs were deeply rooted. Lind, Göran, Common Law Marriage, 2006, p. 108.

189 Lagen den 12 november 1915 om äktenskaps ingående och upplösning. See also Committee Report (SOU 1972:41), p. 117.

party.[190] It can be noted that the Swedish Cohabitees Act of 2003, as well as its predecessors, the acts of 1973 and 1987, apply "marriage-like" rules by default, i.e. without establishing that the couple consents to being subject to legislation. The similarity of approach is interesting.[191]

2.5.4.2. The Incomplete Marriage Regulation

The central provision in the Marriage Code of 1734, dealing with incomplete marriage, is found in *Chapter 3, Section 9*. According to the provision, a court could, when a woman had entered into betrothal with a man and then had sexual intercourse with him, establish the two as husband and wife.[192] Such a decree provided the woman with a right to community of property. Moreover, the relationship constituted an obstacle to marriage to another person. However, the husband did not become the legal guardian of the wife in an incomplete marriage, nor did he have the right to administer her property.[193]

According to *Chapter 3, Section 10*, it was laid down that a man and a woman, after a promise to marry which was followed by sexual intercourse, were obliged to marry each other in the church, if the promise to marry had been declared valid, or if the man had attended church together with the woman in his capacity as her "betrothed".[194] The scope of this provision appears somewhat unclear.[195] It has been considered likely that the legal effects pursuant to Chapter 3, Section 10, were limited to those attached to betrothal – not to marriage.[196] To summarize, a sexual encounter *without betrothal* appears, under certain conditions, to have given rise to the legal effects of betrothal (Section 10), whereas sexual intercourse *after betrothal* could give rise to the legal effects of marriage (Section 9).

In 1755, an ordinance was adopted prescribing that, in case the man and the woman in situations covered by Chapter 3, Section 10, refused to contract a formal church marriage, they should be summoned to *domkapitlet* (the chapter of the church) to receive warnings and admonition. If they continued to refuse

190 Agell, Anders, The Swedish Legislation on Marriage and Cohabitation, a Journey without Destination, 1980, p. 20.

191 See chapter 5.

192 See, for instance, Agell, Anders, The Swedish Legislation on Marriage and Cohabitation, a Journey without a Destination, 1980, pp. 19 f. See also Almquist, Jan Eric, Den svenska familjerättens historia, 1943, p. 39.

193 Almquist, Jan Eric, Den svenska familjerättens historia, 1943, pp. 39 f. Also in case of the death of a spouse the legal effects of an incomplete marriage differed compared to the legal effects of a "regular" marriage. See Agell, Anders, The Swedish Legislation on Marriage and Cohabitation, 1980, p. 20.

194 In Swedish the term used in this context is *kyrkotagning*, meaning that the man had brought the woman to church to receive a special blessing ceremony, normally after the birth of a child. See Inger, Göran, Svensk rättshistoria, 1997, p. 140.

195 Law Commission Report of 1913, p. 102.

196 Law Commission Report of 1913, p. 102.

marriage, a court could impose a short-term imprisonment.[197] If they still continued to refuse marriage, they were once again to be summoned to the chapter of the church for an admonition. If this did not convince them to marry each other, the matter could finally be turned over to the king, who could make an exception to the rule regarding marriage and instead allow dissolution of the relationship.[198]

A final provision is worth mentioning in the context of incomplete marriages in the eighteenth century, namely *Chapter 5, Section 1*. According to this provision, marriage made an "illegitimate child" legitimate, if conceived (1) during betrothal, (2) after a promise to marry or (3) *i lönskaläge* (without betrothal or a promise to marry). Under this provision, also the child's mother was entitled to be covered by the legal effects of marriage.[199] The content of this provision is unclear, but it appears to have been applied as a supplement to Chapter 3, Sections 9–10, in situations when a child was conceived outside of marriage. A possible theory is that the provision was applied as an alternative ground according to which the man could be forced to marry the woman.[200] Children conceived during betrothal were treated as children born to married parents, and were thus entitled to inheritance and a proper upbringing.[201] Otherwise, in 1734, children born to unmarried parents had no inheritance rights.[202] Children born "out of wedlock" were only entitled to a meager upbringing during the parents' lifetime.[203]

2.5.4.3. The Function of Incomplete Marriage in the Swedish Legal System

2.5.4.3.1. The "Feminist"[204] Alternative to Marriage?

It is possible to discuss incomplete marriage from what one today would call a feminist perspective. The Law Commission Report of 1913, which formed the basis, inter alia, for abolishing incomplete marriage from the law, pointed out

197 Law Commission Report of 1913, p. 101.

198 Law Commission Report of 1913, p. 101.

199 Law Commission Report of 1913, p. 103.

200 In 1915 this provision granted the unmarried woman who had a child the right to certain legal effects of marriage without being forced to marrying. Law Commission Report of 1913, pp. 104 f.

201 Inger, Göran, Svensk rättshistoria, 1997, p. 143.

202 Parents, however, had the right to inheritance from their children. This discrepancy was discussed in connection with the enactment of the Marriage Code of 1734, but found to be motivated as a compensation for the parents' duty to maintain the children. See Hafström, Gerhard, Den svenska familjerättens historia, 1972, p. 86.

203 Hafström, Gerhard, Den svenska familjerättens historia, 1972, p. 86.

204 The term "feminist" has been placed in quotation marks since it is rather premature to use the term in this context. In Sweden, the term "feminist" was first used in 1902, without a clear meaning. It was not until the 1970s that the term gained ground in Sweden. See www.ne.se/lang/feminism? i_whole_article=true. Accessed 14 September 2010.

that the incomplete marriage regulation offered an unmarried woman a possibility to obtain some legal rights attached to marriage without being bound by an actual marriage.[205]

Already in the 1880s, according to Jacob Sundberg, the rules for incomplete marriage were occasionally used deliberately by women who wished to have access to the legal effects of marriage, without being under a husband's legal guardianship and without being covered by restrictive divorce rules.[206] According to Sundberg, this advantage of incomplete marriage attracted attention also outside of Sweden, for instance in Germany.[207] Sundberg did not find it surprising that objections to abolishing incomplete marriages came primarily from women.[208]

The number of women deliberately using the incomplete marriage regulation for the purpose of enjoying legal rights of marriage without being bound by marriage (if there were in fact such women in the eighteenth and nineteenth centuries) must have been extremely low. Above, the central role of marriage in Swedish society has been accounted for. Marriage was the platform for family formation and the family provided essential "welfare services" – in default of a welfare state – and different commodities for members of the family. The legal position of children born outside of marriage was poor. Avoiding the legal guardianship of a husband did not mean that a woman attained majority. Obtaining the legal rights and the financial and social protection attached to the marital status was most likely, for the most part, considered to be something positive and desirable from the perspective of women – not something to avoid.

It appears therefore most unlikely that incomplete marriage was widely used by women as a means to avoid being covered by strict rules on divorce. The predominating outlook on the function of marriage appears to have been that marriage was a life-long union, although in theory possible to dissolve. More accessible divorce rules might not have been in the best interest of women in the eighteenth century. As Masha Antokolskaia, points out, the importance of taking into account the contextual dimension should not be forgotten here. For example, Antokolskaia observes that the medieval prohibition against divorce did not aim to prevent spouses who no longer loved each other from ending their marriage.

---

205 Law Commission Report of 1913, p. 105. Through a reform in 1884, an unmarried woman reached majority at the age of 21, but a married woman even after that age remained under hur husband's legal guardianship until 1921 when the 1920 Marriage Code entered into force.

206 Sundberg, Jacob, Familjerätt i omvandling, 1969, p. 54. See also Andersson, Gudrun, Myndig eller omyndig? 1996, p. 23.

207 Sundberg, Jacob, Familjerätt i omvandling, 1969, p. 54.

208 Sundberg, Jacob, Familjerätt i omvandling, 1969, p. 54. Furthermore, according to my opinion it appears that these women's alleged objections to the abolishment of incomplete marriage were, most likely, silenced by the preparations of something far better – the emancipation of women from the legal guardianship of their husbands through the Marriage Code of 1920.

The primary idea in the medieval context was to improve the position of women by protecting them from being repudiated by their husbands.[209]

Keeping in mind the societal, legal and religious context in which the incomplete marriage regulation applied, it appears unlikely that it functioned as an alternative to marriage, which was deliberately chosen and preferred by a certain group of women in Swedish society, who were opposed to the institution of marriage and the position of the wife under the Code of 1734. Moreover, sexual relationships outside of marriage were criminalized in the Code of 1734. Although the sanctions for consenting sexual relations outside of marriage were abolished from the Criminal Code in 1864, such behavior could still, theoretically, be fined according to the Marriage Code of 1734.[210]

2.5.4.3.2. A Predecessor to the Contemporary Model of Cohabitation without Marriage?

Certain similarities can be observed, as well as significant differences, between incomplete marriage (abolished in 1915) and cohabitation without marriage (legally regulated in a special family law enactment in Sweden since 1973). Also Anders Agell noticed this, and accounted for the incomplete marriage regulation in different contexts, for the purpose of providing a general background to the "modern" rules on unmarried cohabitation.[211]

It can be argued that protection of a weaker party, usually the woman, is the general idea and basis for both the incomplete marriage regulation and the rules underlying the contemporary institution of cohabitation without marriage. However, although some similarities between the two sets of rules might be discernable, significant contextual differences make comparisons difficult. For instance, establishment of an incomplete marriage did not require that the couple live together, which is a basic prerequisite for application of the Cohabitees Act.[212] Cohabitation without marriage was, as mentioned above, even criminalized until 1864.

Nevertheless, the incomplete marriage regulation can be seen as in line with Sweden's early acceptance of sexual relationships outside of marriage. This could, in part, explain why the legal recognition of unmarried cohabitees through special cohabitee acts, in force and substantively widened several times since the 1970s, has not been particularly controversial in Sweden. As David Bradley puts

209 Antokolskaia, Masha, Harmonisation of Family Law in Europe, 2006, pp. 132 f.

210 The Marriage Code of 1734, Chapter 12, Section 3. According to Jacob Sundberg, it appears that legal charges in such situations presupposed that the woman had become pregnant and that her family pressed charges of alimony in order for criminal procedures to be initiated. See Familjerätt i omvandling, 1969, p. 53.

211 Agell, Anders, The Swedish Legislation on Marriage and Cohabitation, a Journey without a Destination, 1980, pp. 19 f.

212 See section 5.3.1.

eral ethic in contemporary Scandinavian family laws ıvely strong secular tradition, itself reflected in earlier relationships. The prevalence in Sweden of cohabitation ırriage ceremony is a manifestation of this."[213] It is possible .sh recognition of extramarital sexual relationships has, at ıt, influenced the moral climate in Sweden in respect of legal .d of family law, carried out in the twentieth century.

ection of a Weaker Party and Recognition of Couples Unable to ırry in the Lutheran Church – the Central Functions of Incomplete ıarriage

ıcomplete marriage has been described as an example of the church's .ies to break with the provincial marriage customs. The incomplete ıge regulation can also be seen as an expression of the church's care for the ›rivileged" unmarried woman who had been exploited by a man, by viding her with access to the legal effects of marriage.

Furthermore, the incomplete marriage regulation appears to have been ıpplied in respect of couples who could not, or would not, marry in the Lutheran Church: for instance, couples who married according to the provincial customs, as described in section 2.2.1. The incomplete marriage regulation could also be used to recognize marriages between members of other religious communities. In the mid 1800s, Jewish and Lutheran persons were not able to marry each other in Sweden. Instead they either travelled abroad – mainly to Denmark[214] – or established relationships without the participation of the church. According to Jacob Sundberg, this appears to have created a special interest in the incomplete marriage regulation.[215]

In summary, it appears that the possibility to encompass more couples under the marriage regulation – also those who were not married in the eyes of the Lutheran faith and the state – offered a practical solution to the problems with illegitimate children and unmarried cohabitation. The idea of the law being used for the purpose of solving practical problems recurs as a characteristic feature of the regulation governing marriage in the 1970s, as will be illustrated in chapters 4 and 5.

213 Bradley, David, Family Law and Political Culture, 1996, p. 3.

214 Civil marriages were allowed in Denmark from 1851. See Hafström, Gerhard, Den svenska familjerättens historia, 1972, p. 44. See also Nordisk familjebok http://runeberg.org/nfbe/0213.html. Accessed 20 September 2010.

215 Sundberg, Jacob, Familjerätt i omvandling, 1969, pp. 50 f.

2.6. THE LEGAL EFFECTS OF MARRIAGE

2.6.1. THE POSITION OF THE WIFE

When studying the legal effects of marriage in the 1734 Marriage Code, conclusion close at hand is that the wife appears to have been almost a "possession" of the husband, because of his legal guardianship over her. There was no such thing as "gender equality," and the husband administered his wife's possessions. The hierarchical structure – the roles expected to be played by husband and wife – was also reinforced in the applicable marriage liturgy.[216] However, women were not mere possessions of men. The woman had an important position and function in Swedish society and within the family, namely as wife and mother. Moreover, the wife was the head of any servants in the house. These were significant responsibilities in the eighteenth century context.

Moreover, the woman, although legally subordinate to her husband, enjoyed certain legal protection, laid down in the Code of 1734. According to the Marriage Code of 1734, the spouses' joint estate consisted of their "marital property" and each spouse's separate property.[217] The marital property was owned jointly by the spouses, although administered by the husband.[218] Without the consent of her husband, the woman was unable to administer the estate.[219] A novelty in the Marriage Code of 1734 was that the wife became entitled to dispose of her marital property share and her separate property in form of a will. The husband's administration rights were limited in the sense that he could not sell or mortgage his wife's share of the estate.[220]

Separate property was (1) real estate[221] owned prior to the marriage or acquired through inheritance, (2) gifts or property acquired through a will, with

216 See section 2.5.3.

217 Hafström, Gerhard, Den svenska familjerättens historia, 1972, p. 67. It can be mentioned that rules on spouses' property relations, laid down in the provincial laws, remained in force alongside of the 1734 Code. The differences between these two parallel regulations were abolished in 1845 and 1898. See Schmidt, Folke, Äktenskapsrätt, 1974. pp. 61 f.

218 Westring, Hjalmar, Den nya giftermålsbalken jämte dithörande författningar med förklaringar, 1933, p. 112. See Olivecrona, Om makars giftorätt i bo, 1878, pp. 2 f.

219 According to an ordinance of 1874, the married woman's position was strengthened, as she was granted the right to administer some of her own property, and the husband's guardianship was exempted in this regard. See Hafström, Gerhard, Den svenska familjerättens historia, 1972, p. 54.

220 Hafström, Gerhard, Den svenska familjerättens historia, 1972, p. 67. For a thorough account of rules on limitations on the husband's administration rights, see pp. 69–73.

221 A traditional distinction between *stadsrätt* (city law) and *landsrätt* (country-side law) in respect of real estate was made in the Marriage Code of 1734, Chapter 10, Sections 2 and 5. According to city law, all property, including real estate, became jointly owned through marriage, whereas country-side law exempted real estate. Which law to apply depended on where the real estate was situated. See the Law Commission Report of 1918, p. 136.

the condition that the property be the spouse's separate property or (3) property made private in a contract concerning property relations.[222]

The marital property regime, as a main rule, granted a greater share of the estate to the husband than to the wife upon the death of a spouse. The husband's share was two thirds, whereas the wife's share was one third of the estate. In some cases however, the spouses took equal shares. These inheritance rules will not be accounted for in detail in this context.[223]

2.6.2. THE DOWRY AND MORNING GIFT

The financial position of the wife, should the marriage end, was regulated through the rules on the dowry and morning gift. The Marriage Code of 1734 did not contain any provisions on spousal support. Such regulation can be seen as superfluous, since the husband was the legal guardian of the wife and marriage in principle a life-long union.[224] The father of the bride – who was normally her giftoman – provided the bride with a gift (normally assets, but it could also be a pecuniary sum) called *hemgift* (dowry), which functioned as a form of inheritance advance.[225] In fact, the dowry existed already in the provincial laws, and was kept in the Marriage Code of 1734.

The *morgongåva* (morning gift) was also aimed at securing the bride's future financial situation, but was paid by the husband. The morning gift functioned as widow's pension, and was available to the wife upon the death of the husband.[226] The morning gift was considered the separate property of the wife, but the sum was administered by the husband during the marriage. As of the Marriage Code of 1734, the morning gift – despite its beneficial name "gift" – was no longer a voluntary transaction. Even if no explicit agreement on morning gift had been

---

222 In Swedish: äktenskapsförord. The regulation can be found in the Marriage Code of 1734, Chapter 8, Section 1. See also Law Commission Report of 1918, p. 166 and Hafström, Gerhard, Den svenska familjerättens historia, 1972, pp. 69 f. As a rule, debts deriving from before the marriage were to be paid with the property that the spouse in debt owned prior to the marriage, whereas debts of one or both spouses during marriage were to be paid with the spouses' joint property. See the Marriage Code of 1734, Chapter 11, Sections 2 and 3.

223 Hafström, Gerhard, Den svenska familjerättens historia, 1972, p. 65. It appears that the regulation of morning gift was supposed to compensate the wife's subordinated position as regards her share of the marital property, see pp. 64 f. In 1845, new principles were introduced in the law, granting the woman the right of inheritance upon the death of her husband, as well as the general right to half of the marital property. See pp. 65 f.

224 Ryrstedt, Eva, Bodelning och bostad, 1998, p. 41.

225 Hafström, Gerhard, Den svenska familjerättens historia, 1972, pp. 57–59, where the development and history of dowry is described. The dowry had different forms and functions over time and regionally in Sweden, and will not be further discussed here.

226 Hafström, Gerhard, Den svenska familjerättens historia, 1972, pp. 60 f.

reached prior to the marriage, the woman was entitled to a certain share of the estate (an estimated morning gift) in case of her husband's death.[227]

It appears that looking after the financial interests of the woman was found worth protecting in the Code of 1734. The morning gift (and the dowry) was aimed to protect the wife financially. These rules counterbalanced to some extent the married woman's lacking legal authority to administer her property and her less favorable position in the inheritance law. The morning gift was kept until 1920, when husband and wife obtained mutual inheritance rights.[228]

2.7. DISSOLUTION OF MARRIAGE: GROUNDS FOR DIVORCE

Before the tenth century, when canonical law was introduced in Sweden,[229] dissolution of marriage is believed to have been fairly easy to achieve. Divorce was, most likely, accessible through a simple oral declaration by the spouses that they wished to terminate their marriage contract, in the presence of witnesses or at the *Ting* (the session for main hearing in Sweden).[230] Along with the introduction of Catholicism in tenth century Sweden followed a morally strict view on dissolution of marriage, which has been described in section 2.2.1.

According to the Marriage Code of 1734, the grounds for divorce were twofold. Divorce could be granted in case of (1) *hor* (adultery) and (2) *egenvilligt övergivande* (malicious desertion).[231] These two grounds for divorce were retained more or less unchanged in the law for two centuries.[232] Also, if a spouse was absent for a long time (at least six years in practice) and no information about his or her whereabouts was available, the other spouse could be granted permission to remarry.[233] Divorce was not easily accessible according to the provisions in the 1734 Code. The final decision as regards dissolution of marriage was adjudicated by the Court, but the church still had the important task of attempting to reconcile the spouses before the Court decided in the matter.[234] The church's participation aimed to convince the spouses to continue with their marriage, either by deterring the spouses from divorcing or by reconciling

227 Hafström, Gerhard, Den svenska familjerättens historia, 1972, p. 61. The provisions regarding the morning gift were kept in the law until 1920, see p. 62. In 1845, the rules on the morning gift were revised so that they applied unconditionally, even when the spouses had children together. This had not been the case previously. See Law Commission Report of 1918, p. 142.

228 Inger, Göran, Svensk rättshistoria, 1997, p. 199.

229 See section 2.2.1.

230 See Law Commission Report of 1913, p. 370. See also Almquist, Jan Eric, Den svenska familjerättens historia, 1943, pp. 65 f.

231 The Marriage Code of 1734, Chapter 13.

232 Committee Report (SOU 1972:41), p. 179.

233 The Marriage Code of 1734, Chapter 13, Section 6.

234 Law Commission Report of 1913, p. 372.

them.[235] Refusal to continue with the marriage could result in pecuniary fines and a one year decree on *skillnad till säng och säte* (legal separation).[236] The point of departure in respect of divorce in the Marriage Code of 1734 was the same as in the Church Act of 1686: divorce should be difficult to obtain and be limited to cases when a spouse had severely offended the other.[237]

In the eighteenth century, the basic idea promoted by the church and the state was that spouses wishing to dissolve their marriage were sinners in violation of God's commandments, and it was the job of the church minister to inform them that they were carrying out a scheme of the devil.[238] In cases when only one of the spouses wished to dissolve the marriage, heavy fines could be imposed on that spouse.[239] Keeping these prerequisites in mind, it is understandable that judicial divorce was a rare, although not insignificant, feature in Sweden under the 1734 Code.[240]

The king was authorized to grant divorce on grounds other than the ones established in the code, for instance, dispensation due to hatred and loathing between the spouses. The chapters of the church then issued letters of divorce. For instance, incurable disease could give rise to dispensation from the restrictive divorce criteria in the Code of 1734.[241] The king's authority to grant divorce on grounds other than those included in the 1734 Code was established in court jurisprudence – not in statutory law. This has in the literature been interpreted as a sign of the controversial character of the topic of divorce.[242] Already in 1810, the case law that had developed in the field of dispensation matters was included in the statutory law, in a special ordinance, for the purpose of easing the heavy administrative burden of the numerous dispensation cases before the king.[243]

Max Rheinstein has suggested that although being divorced in Sweden was not "exactly praiseworthy" the fact that the powerful king was the one granting

235 See, for instance, Hafström, Gerhard, Den svenska familjerättens historia, 1972, p. 79.

236 The Marriage Code of 1734, Chapter 14.

237 Westring, Hjalmar, Den nya giftermålsbalken jämte dithörande författningar med förklaringar, 1933, pp. 179 f.

238 Inger, Göran, Svensk rättshistoria, 1997, p. 93.

239 Law Commission Report of 1913, p. 372.

240 Nygren, Rolf, Kyrkorätt, Äktenskap och sekularisering – I, 1989, p. 28. See also Rheinstein, Max, Marriage Stability, Divorce, and the Law, 1972, p. 153.

241 Hafström, Gerhard, Den svenska familjerättens historia, p. 81. In fact, according to Hafström, dispensation was granted already in the 1660s.

242 Almquist, Jan Eric, Den svenska familjerättens historia, 1943, p. 67.

243 Hafström, Gerhard, Den svenska familjerättens historia, 1972, pp. 80 f. Thus the following additional grounds for divorce were introduced: (1) exile, (2) imprisonment for life, (3) ambush or conspiracy to the other spouse's life, (4) true madness during four years and without hope of improvement and (5) on motion of the king's own discretion. These additional grounds were regulated in an ordinance which remained in force until it was replaced by the 1915 Act on Conclusion and Dissolution of Marriage. Committee Report (SOU 1972:41), p. 179.

dispensation might have added "a certain aura of respectability".[244] It is possible that the position of the king as head of the state and the church might have contributed to decreasing the social stigma most likely attached to divorce in eighteenth century Sweden. However, on the whole, and keeping in mind the limited grounds for divorce which applied, divorce must have been a rare and exceptional feature, by no means found "respectable" in society. As Masha Antokolskaia has pointed out, dissolution of marriage during the spouses' lifetime, according to the protestant view in general, was a legal sanction for matrimonial offences, not a remedy for the breakdown of the marriage.[245]

2.8. THE ESSENCE OF MARRIAGE UNDER THE 1734 CODE – SUMMARIZING ANALYSIS

The overall impression of the analysis of the institution of marriage under the 1734 Code is that marriage was a divine institution, based on a strict hierarchical structure with the husband as master over his wife. This is illustrated in the marriage liturgy analyzed in section 2.5.3 above. In 1734, the Church of Sweden was a powerful institution and religion, as interpreted by the Church of Sweden, a pervasive element which united the country. A central objective with the marriage regulation was to further strengthen the position of the Church of Sweden. For instance, the practice of religions other than the Lutheran was criminalized in the Church Act of 1686.[246] Also the king found unity in respect of religion desirable, and this was established as a basic rule in the Instrument of Government of 1634.[247]

The introduction of the religious marriage ceremony as a mandatory criterion for conclusion of a legally valid marriage also illustrates the powerful position of the Church of Sweden in 1734. However, the church did not manage to break completely with the Germanic marriage customs. Incomplete marriage was recognized in the Code of 1734. This early recognition of sexual relations outside of marriage can be seen as having laid the foundation for a permissive moral climate in Sweden toward cohabitation without marriage in the future.

The religious influences contributed to turning marriage into a voluntary union, based on the consent of the couple, as opposed to the previous predominating function of marriage, under the provincial laws, as a means of arranging financial affairs between families. It should be mentioned, however, that the woman could be disinherited by her parents, should she marry against

244 Rheinstein, Max, Marriage Stability, Divorce, and the Law, 1972, p. 153.
245 Antokolskaia, Masha, Harmonisation of Family Law in Europe, 2006, p. 174.
246 See, for instance, Sundberg, Jacob, Familjerätt i omvandling, 1969, p. 33.
247 See, for instance, Sundberg, Jacob, Familjerätt i omvandling, 1969, p. 33.

the wishes of her giftoman.[248] This weakened the conception of marriage as a voluntary union in 1734, based on the consent of the individual spouses-to-be.

The religious concept of marriage, depicted in the marriage liturgy, emphasized the husband's duty to treat his subordinated wife with the same kindness as God treats mankind. This can also be seen as a shift toward an emphasis on marriage as a union based on love. Already in the Church Handbook of 1686 there was a special alternative wording in the marriage ceremony, applicable to spouses who were not expected to have children. This alternative wording focused on the value of companionship instead of procreation.[249] It is noteworthy that marriage as a companionship between two persons was recognized by the church already in the Church Handbook of 1693.

---

[248] Jägerskiöld, Stig, Kring tillkomsten av 1734 års lag, 1984, p. 15. See also Hafström, Gerhard, Den svenska familjerättens historia, 1972, p. 32.

[249] Handbok, ther vti är författat, huruledes gudstiensten med christelige ceremonier och kyrckioseder, vti wåra församlingar skall blifwa hållen och förhandlad, 1693, p. 119.

3. MARRIAGE BETWEEN TWO EQUALS

"[...] [T]he spouses shall, as far as possible,
be placed side by side, as equally free and independent persons,
without any legally established right for one to decide
over the other or alone in joint family matters."[250]

3.1. THE POINT OF DEPARTURE

What was the essence of marriage under the Marriage Code of 1920? The Marriage Code of 1920 replaced the Code of 1734, which had been in force for almost two centuries. During this time span significant changes had taken place in Swedish society. The hierarchical structure of marriage, as well as the impact of connected religious values, as interpreted by the Church of Sweden, had loosened up in favor of a focus on equal participation of the spouses in their family matters and in respect of administration of their property. Love was the basic component of marriage, experienced as something more than deep affection.[251]

The most significant novelty in the Marriage Code of 1920, reflecting the changing values in society, was that women were granted full legal capacity. The idea of spouses as two individuals with equal rights and duties toward each other, illustrated in the quote above from a government bill, had gained ground in Sweden and created pressure to replace the previously prevailing hierarchical view on marriage, described in chapter 2. These new ideas and values were transferred into legislation through comprehensive enactments dealing with marriage during 1915–1920. How did these enactments and the principle of equality between men and women influence the essence of marriage in Sweden?

---

250 "[...][M]akarna böra, så långt möjligt är, ställas bredvid varandra såsom lika fria och självständiga personer utan någon i lag stadgad rätt för den ena att bestämma vare sig över den andre eller över familjens gemensamma angelägenheter." NJA II 1921, p. 6. Author's translation.

251 Law Commission Report of 1913, p. 108.

3.2. TOWARD THE MARRIAGE CODE OF 1920 – RELEVANT ENACTMENTS AND NORDIC LEGAL COOPERATION

3.2.1. THE ENACTMENTS OF 1908 AND 1915

3.2.1.1. Civil Marriage as an Option to Religious Marriage

The introduction of civil marriage as an option available to all couples in 1908 once and for all put an end to the exclusive authority of the Church of Sweden to conclude legally valid marriages, which had been laid down in the Code of 1734. The first step toward introducing a general possibility for couples to choose between a civil and a religious marriage ceremony was taken in the late eighteenth century, when religious communities other than the Lutheran Church of Sweden were authorized to solemnize marriages.[252] However, at that time, the religious communities only concluded marriages between their own members. During the second half of the nineteenth century, a civil marriage ceremony was designed for couples who were unable to marry in church because they belonged to non-Christian religious communities, for instance a Jewish church.[253] However, marriage concluded in the religious form remained the main rule, and civil marriage the exception.

In 1908, the two forms for concluding a marriage – the religious and the civil – were placed on par in the law, establishing the partners' freedom of choice in this regard.[254] In the Marriage Code of 1920, as established already in the 1915 enactment, the term *vigsel* (marriage ceremony) was applied to both the civil and the religious marriage ceremonies.[255] As a result, Chapter 4 Section 1 of the Marriage Code of 1920 read: "Marriage is concluded through a church or a civil ceremony".[256] The enactment of 1908 can be seen as an early example of the legislator increasing couples' freedom of choice, which would develop into the predominating characteristic and goal of the regulation governing marriage in the 1970s.[257]

---

252 In 1781, Christian religious communities other than the Lutheran were authorized to marry couples, and in 1782 the Jewish community was also granted such authority. See the Law Commission Report of 1913, p. 279.

253 In 1863, a Government Decree was adopted allowing marriage between a Christian and a Jew. See the Law Commission Report of 1913, p. 279.

254 Act of 6 November 1908.

255 The Swedish term *vigsel* does not easily translate into English, but it refers to the legally binding marriage ceremony.

256 Author's translation. The same terminology was used in the 1915 Act on Conclusion and Dissolution of Marriage. See also Westring, Hjalmar, Den nya giftermålsbalken jämte dithörande författningar med förklaringar, p. 68. This wording was kept in the Marriage Code of 1987, which still applies today.

257 See chapter 4.

3.2.1.2. The Enactment of 1915: Conclusion and Dissolution of Marriage

Through an enactment in 1915, new rules governing conclusion and dissolution of marriage were introduced. The enactment of 1915 contributed to making marriage more personal and individualistic, as opposed to the hierarchical and "top-down" structure of the Code of 1734. The church's involvement in marriage was reduced through the Act of 1915. For instance, betrothal was turned into an informal agreement between the couple and the impediments to marriage were reduced. Moreover, divorce was made more accessible and the Church of Sweden was disconnected from the function as mediator between spouses. These reforms will be accounted for in detail below.

In 1913 the Law Commission questioned if the church should at all be involved in the establishment of legally valid marriages, or if civil marriage should be introduced as the only legally valid form of concluding a marriage in Sweden.[258] However, the "double track" system which still applies today was kept, providing couples with the right to choose between a civil and a religious marriage ceremony. The Law Commission's main motivation for retaining the freedom of choice between a religious and a civil marriage ceremony was that the freedom to choose the most appealing ceremonial marriage form would favor the marriage frequency. The problem of couples cohabiting outside of marriage was also mentioned as a reason for keeping the religious marriage ceremony as a legal option. More precisely, preserving couples' freedom of choice in respect of the marriage ceremonies was believed to counteract the risk that couples avoided marriage altogether, and chose to live together as unmarried cohabitees, because civil marriage did not match their personal values or religious beliefs.[259] In addition, the popularity of church marriage in society was a strong (and in my opinion more convincing) argument in favor of retaining the freedom of choice in 1913.[260]

3.2.2. NORDIC LEGAL COOPERATION

3.2.2.1. Harmonization of Marriage Law

In the 1920s, a "Nordic model" of marriage was created through the introduction of largely harmonized laws in the Nordic countries.[261] The Swedish enactments dealing with marriage around 1920 were influenced by the goal of achieving

---

258 Law Commission Report of 1913, p. 280.

259 Law Commission Report of 1913, p. 280.

260 Law Commission Report of 1913, pp. 280 and 605. Also when the gender-neutral marriage concept was adopted in Sweden in 2009, the popularity of church marriage motivated retaining the double track marriage system. This will be discussed in section 6.3.5.

261 Agell, Anders, Äktenskap, samboende, partnerskap, 2004, pp. 85 f.

harmonized marriage laws in the Nordic countries. In 1910, Sweden initiated a Nordic harmonization project, which resulted in uniform laws regarding legal separation and divorce. Within the next few years this project was extended to cover also matrimonial property rules.[262]

The basis for the legal cooperation was established in 1872, when the first of the so-called "Nordic Lawyers' Meetings" was held. During these meetings, issues concerning legal harmonization were discussed, family law included.[263] Nordic legal cooperation was considered urgent to achieve, since marriages between citizens of the different Nordic countries were common.[264] Similarities in respect of customs and conditions of life of the Nordic people have been pointed out as factors which facilitated the harmonization of laws in the region.[265] It was considered especially urgent to harmonize rules dealing with conclusion of marriage, particularly those dealing with the impediments to marriage.[266] Also in respect of dissolution of marriage, the regulation took into account the interest of achieving Nordic harmonization.[267] Certain basic features dealing with the legal effects of marriage were also harmonized, for instance, the basic idea that the net value of the spouses' property should be divided equally upon dissolution of the marriage.[268] Rules relating to the relationship between children and parents, and the social and public aspects of family law, have on the contrary, never been subject to significant legal cooperation between the Nordic countries.[269]

It should be clarified that different interpretations of the term "harmonization" can be found in the legal literature. The term can be used in a broad sense, covering "every process that results in an increase in the degree of legal uniformity".[270] From this point of view, harmonization includes efforts to produce general guidelines which can be adopted by different countries.[271] The term can also be used to describe concerns to encourage countries to find

262 Lødrup, Peter, The Reharmonisation of Nordic Family Law, 2003, p. 19. See also Law Commission Report of 1918, p. 4 and NJA II, 1910 no. 2, pp. 1–13.

263 Lødrup, Peter, The Reharmonisation of Nordic Family Law, 2003, p. 19. In fact, Nordic legal cooperation was on the carpet already in the early nineteenth century, when law books were being revised and new criminal laws drafted. Inger, Göran, Svensk rättshistoria, 1997, pp. 180 f. In the early 1900s, the Nordic countries with legal cooperation in the field of marriage were Sweden, Denmark and Norway. These countries are also commonly referred to as the Scandinavian countries. Later on also Finland and Iceland were included in the harmonization of marriage laws. See section 7.4.2. It can be mentioned that Finland was a part of Russia until 1917 and Iceland was a part of Denmark until 1942. See also Schmidt, Folke, The Prospective Law of Marriage, 1971, pp. 191–218.

264 Law Commission Report of 1913, pp. 4 f.

265 Law Commission Report of 1913, p. 4.

266 Law Commission Report of 1913, p. 4.

267 Agell, Anders, Äktenskap, samboende, partnerskap, 2004, pp. 14 and 85 f.

268 Government Bill (Prop 1986/87:1), p. 42.

269 Lødrup, Peter, The Reharmonisation of Nordic Family Law, 2003, p. 18.

270 Antokolskaia, Masha, Harmonisation of Family Law in Europe, 2006, p. 16.

271 Lødrup, Peter, The Reharmonisation of Nordic Family Law, 2003, p. 18.

common legal solutions, without imposing a unified set of rules on them.[272] According to both of these views, a distinction is made between *harmonization of laws*, on the one hand, and *unification of laws*, on the other hand. According to Peter Lødrup, the Nordic "harmonization" model appears to be more like a "unification of laws", keeping in mind the close resemblance in the substance and structure of the laws adopted as a result of the legal cooperation projects during the first half of the twentieth century.[273]

Also Maarit Jänterä-Jareborg underlines that the term "harmonization" should not be confused with the term "unification", the latter meaning strivings to achieve identical (uniform) rules. The term "harmonization", Jänterä-Jareborg points out, is wider and encompasses the process to bring legal rules closer together, and the level of ambition varies in this respect.[274] The term harmonization is here used in this wide sense, to describe the Nordic legal cooperation, even though the result and the political ambition could be claimed to qualify, to some extent, as a "unification" of laws. The Swedish divorce regulation of 1915[275] and the marital property regime of 1920, like the corresponding enactments in Denmark and Norway, have attracted attention abroad for the liberal grounds for divorce and the aim to create equality between spouses, expressed decades before similar developments took place in Europe in general.[276]

In this chapter, as well as in the following, focus is on the Swedish legal development - not on the legal development in the other Nordic countries. However, as pointed out by Lødrup in 2010, because of a common cultural heritage, geographical vicinity and historical intertwinement of the Nordic countries, there is and was "a Nordic model based on the same ideas on the institution of marriage, divorce, maintenance and matrimonial property".[277] The existing differences today, according to Lødrup, are not of "fundamental character" for the basic legal framework created through the early Nordic legal cooperation.[278] However, as pointed out by Urpo Kangas, it should be noted that the similarities between the legal systems in the Nordic countries concern a few special civil laws only, and the Nordic legal systems do not generally function

---

272 Meulders-Klein, Marie-Thérèse, Towards a European Civil Code on Family Law? 2003, p. 106. See also Lødrup, Peter, The Reharmonisation of Nordic Family Law, 2003, p. 18.

273 Lødrup, Peter, The Reharmonisation of Nordic Family Law, 2003, p. 18.

274 Jänterä-Jareborg, Maarit, En harmoniserad familjerätt för Europa? Internationellt privaträttsliga och rättsjämförande perspektiv, 2009, pp. 328 f.

275 The 1915 Act on Conclusion and Dissolution of Marriage was incorporated into the Marriage Code of 1920, in principle unaltered. The small alterations made can be found in Law Commission Report of 1918.

276 Agell, Anders, the Swedish Legislation on Marriage and Cohabitation, a Journey without a Destination, 1980, p. 12. See also Bradley, David, Family Law and Political Culture, 1996, p. 9. See sections 3.2.2.2 and 3.7.2.2.

277 Lødrup, Peter, The Reharmonisation of Nordic Family Law, 2003, p. 22.

278 Lødrup, Peter, The Reharmonisation of Nordic Family Law, 2003, p. 22.

according to the same principles.[279] However, a feature common to the legal developments in the Nordic region is that the principle of equality between husband and wife was introduced in the marriage regulation at a comparatively early point in time.[280]

3.2.2.2. Why were the Nordic Countries Pioneers with Equality between Spouses?

The question why the Nordic countries were the first to implement the principle of equality between spouses in the regulation governing marriage has puzzled legal scholars. Different explanations as to why the Nordic countries were pioneers in this field have been given in the literature. Masha Antokolskaia has noted that the Swedish marriage enactments, like the other Nordic counterparts, were not the result of a political revolution, but of what she calls a "gradual process of modernization".[281] Antokolskaia has pointed out that in 1920 the Nordic region neither had a developed economy, nor a particularly strong influence of liberal ideology, which could have explained the radical legal solutions in the field of marriage.[282]

According to David Bradley, the liberal Nordic family laws are to some extent the result of a relatively strong secular tradition.[283] In chapter 2 above, the battle between old and new customs in Sweden has been described and the church's "failure" to eradicate all provincial marriage customs from the law has been accounted for. The recognition of incomplete marriages in the Code of 1734 can be seen as an early example of a liberal view on extramarital sexual relations, which might have lingered on in the Swedish mentality and laid the foundation for the liberal Marriage Code of 1920. However, this factor alone does not suffice as an explanation for why Sweden – and the Nordic region – was the first in Europe[284] to modernize its family law legislation based on the principle of equality between husband and wife.

Cohabitation without marriage was considered to be a cause of the decreasing marriage frequency in Sweden when the Marriage Code of 1920 was enacted.[285] An explanation for the decreasing interest in marriage and the increasing number of couples cohabiting without marriage, given in the Law Commission Report of 1913, was that the regulation governing marriage was based on "traditional" values, which were no longer generally represented in society, in

279 Kangas, Urpo, Divorce System and Maintenance of Former Spouses in Scandinavian Countries, 2007, p. 38. The topic of Nordic harmonization will be further analyzed in section 7.4.
280 See section 3.7.2.2.
281 Antokolskaia, Masha, Harmonisation of Family Law in Europe, 2006, p. 234.
282 Antokolskaia, Masha, Harmonisation of Family Law in Europe, 2006, p. 234.
283 Bradley, David, Family Law and Political Culture, 1996, p. 3.
284 Antokolskaia, Masha, Harmonisation of Family Law in Europe, 2006, p. 234.
285 NJA II 1921, p. 6.

particular the husband's legal guardianship over the wife.[286] Time was ripe to "modernize" the marriage regulation and make the institution of marriage a more attractive choice.[287] Against this background, couples' tendencies to cohabit without marriage and the social problems linked to this can be seen as having formed the basis for the Marriage Code of 1920 and its equality focus.

It is also possible that the goal of achieving Nordic legal cooperation in the field of marriage to some extent "speeded up" the modernization of marriage laws in the Nordic region. From this point of view, the necessity of harmonizing Nordic marriage laws provided an incentive to thoroughly evaluate the applicable law for the purpose of solving problems of cross-border marriages.

In addition, as Peter Lødrup has pointed out, the need for Nordic legal harmonization was assessed by legal experts, Supreme Court judges and law professors who were given the mandate to draft the law proposals – not politicians. According to Lødrup, this might be an explanation why the Nordic harmonization project was successful.[288]

3.3. NOVELTIES REGARDING MARRIAGE – EQUALITY BETWEEN SPOUSES AS THE BASIS FOR THE MARRIAGE CODE OF 1920

The emancipation of women in 1920 necessitated various changes in the marriage regulation. A new marital property regime was introduced in the Marriage Code of 1920, which granted husband and wife equal rights and duties in respect of their property – the deferred community of property regime.[289] As regards the spouses' relationship with their children, equality between the spouses was expressed by placing husband and wife on par as legal guardians of their joint children.[290] The Marriage Code of 1920 facilitated access to divorce compared to the Code of 1734, which only permitted divorce on the grounds of adultery and desertion.[291] Previously, the conception of divorce was that a couple wishing to divorce should be reproached and more or less "forced" to stay married.[292] In the

---

[286] "[...] [D]et intrång i kvinnans självständighet och självbestämningsrätt, som äktenskapet på grund av målsmanskapet innebär, torde särskilt inom vissa samhällslager vara ett av skälen till äktenskapsfrekvensens sjunkande och det ökade antalet konkubinat." NJA II 1921, p. 6. Author's translation.

[287] NJA II 1921, p. 6.

[288] Lødrup, Peter, The Reharmonisation of Nordic Family Law, 2003, p. 20.

[289] This system will be accounted for in section 3.5.2 below.

[290] NJA II 1921, p. 9.

[291] In 1810 the king's authority to grant dispensation was legally established and a few additional narrowly defined grounds for divorce after dispensation were established. It can be mentioned that the 1915 Act on Conclusion and Dissolution of Marriage first applied the "liberal" grounds for divorce.

[292] According to the Code of 1734, Chapter 14, Section 1, spouses unable to reconcile could be fined. See Westring, Hjalmar, Den nya giftermålsbalken jämte dithörande författningar med

Marriage Code of 1920, this attitude was replaced by efforts to help the spouses reconcile, the idea being that this protected and defended the family as a desirable unit in society.[293]

The idea of marriage as a mutual project, based on equality, to which each spouse contributed according to his or her capacity, was central in the Marriage Code of 1920. In Chapter 5, Section 1, this is illustrated through the basic principle that: "Husband and wife owe each other faithfulness and respect; in consultation they are to devote themselves to safe-guarding the best interest of the family."[294]

However, the principle of equality did not mean challenging the traditional roles of husband and wife. The spouses' duty to contribute to the maintenance of the family could be fulfilled in different ways. In Chapter 5, Section 2, it was established that: "Spouses are obliged to, according to their ability, through pecuniary allowance, work in the home, or in other ways provide the support for the family, which considering the spouses' conditions can be seen as suitable. [...]"[295] In accordance with the provision, the wife's work in the home was to be valued equally as the husband's work outside the home. In other words, focus was on improving the situation of the housewife – not on enabling married women to work outside the home.

In fact, a traditional division of duties was much desired from the point of view of the legislator. It was thought to favor the best interest of the family that the wife cared for the home, whereas the husband provided financially for his family.[296] The principle of equality between the spouses was discussed on these premises in the preparatory work to the Marriage Code of 1920: "With regard to the interest of the family, it is probably often best if the wife primarily devotes herself to caring for the home. How her work in the home should be arranged must, nevertheless, be for her to decide."[297] In other words, strengthening the woman's situation as a housewife was the desirable goal in 1920.[298] Equality in

förklaringar, 1933, p. 202. The fines in this context were abolished in 1860. See Law Commission Report of 1918, p. 396.

293 Inger, Göran, Svensk rättshistoria, 1997, p. 261. See also Law Commission Report of 1913, p. 202. See the Marriage Code, Chapter 14.

294 "Man och hustru äro skyldiga varandra trohet och hänsyn; de hava att i samråd verka för familjens bästa." Author's translation of the Marriage Code of 1920, Chapter 5, Section 1. In 2009, this provision was made gender-neutral. This will be further discussed in chapter 6.

295 Makarna äro pliktade att, var efter sin förmåga, genom tillskott av penningar, verksamhet i hemmet eller annorledes bidraga till att bereda familjen det underhåll, som med avseende å makarnas villkor må anses tillbörligt. [...]" Author's translation.

296 NJA II 1921, pp. 8 and 23.

297 "Av hänsyn till familjens intresse är det nog ofta lyckligast, om hustrun i främsta rummet ägnar sig åt vården av hemmet. Huru hennes arbete i hemmet skall ordnas måste dock ankomma på henne själv." NJA II 1921, p. 8. Author's translation.

298 NJA II 1921, pp. 7 f.

"modern" terms of questioning gender roles, the division of duties in particular, was not to speak of at that point in time.[299]

It was considered important that married women were able to decide independently in matters concerning their work in the home.[300] In order to ensure that the wife, although not earning an income of her own, could decide in household matters on a day to day basis, a possibility to enjoin the husband to provide funds for this purpose was introduced in the Marriage Code, Chapter 3, Section 3.[301] This provision also applied in situations when the wife failed to support the family financially, but this was still an unusual scenario in 1920, when only four percent of all married women in Sweden carried out paid work.[302] However, it was not out of the question for women to have paid work outside the home. In special cases, it was in fact considered necessary, namely if the family needed two incomes to survive.[303]

3.4. THE FORMS AND CONDITIONS OF MARRIAGE – THE MARRIAGE CODE OF 1920

3.4.1. BETROTHAL

In the Law Commission Report of 1913, marriage was described as a union based on love and mutual sympathy.[304] In line with this more "personalized" and "privatized" conception of marriage betrothal was turned into an informal personal matter between the couple, instead of a formal requirement handled by the church. Existing betrothal was no longer an impediment to marriage to another person.[305] In fact, betrothal could be concluded through a simple oral agreement between the couple. Betrothal could be dissolved unilaterally and without any specific form regulated by law. There remained, however, certain rules as regards duty to pay damages if betrothal did not lead to marriage, provided that children had been conceived in the meantime.[306]

---

299 Equality in the sense of granting men and women equal opportunities and rights has marked the Swedish welfare state since the 1970s. Gunnarsson, Åsa, Familjen – en genusforskningens utmaning, Familjeföreställningar, om familjens betydelse inom juridik, ekonomi och forskning, 2001, p. 12. See also section 4.1.2.

300 NJA II 1921, p. 8.

301 NJA II 1921, pp. 7 f.

302 NJA II 1921, p. 26. See also Agell, Anders, Individ, familj, stat, 1984, p. 721.

303 NJA II 1921, p. 8.

304 Law Commission Report of 1913, p. 108.

305 Westring, Hjalmar, Den nya giftermålsbalken jämte dithörande författningar med förklaringar, 1933, pp. 16 f. For provisions on betrothal, see the Marriage Code of 1920, Chapter 1, Sections 1–6.

306 The Marriage Code of 1920, Chapter 1, Section 3.

It was no longer found desirable to "force" persons to go through with a planned marriage because of the binding nature of betrothal.[307] The purpose of betrothal was described in the 1913 Law Commission Report as offering two persons the opportunity to get to know each other before marriage. Strict rules on betrothal, established in the Code of 1734, were seen as contradictory to the view that betrothal should be a "test period" to see if the couple was compatible for marriage.[308] Turning betrothal into a private matter instead of a church matter can be seen as an example of a "legislative trend" in Sweden toward decreasing the church's influence in marriage during the twentieth century, in favor of a more secular (and private) order.[309]

The conception of marriage primarily as a union based on love and sympathy and, from this point of view, incompatible with formal betrothal appears strikingly "modern", in the sense that betrothal was regarded as a "test period", offering the parties a chance to get to know one another. Since the 1960s, cohabitation without marriage can be claimed to have functioned as such a "test period" in Sweden. In the 1920s, however, it was not a question of the legislator suggesting that the couple live together before marriage, for the purpose of determining if they were suited for marriage in the future. On the contrary, in 1920, extramarital relationships were regarded rather as a threat to marriage.[310] Nevertheless, legally binding formal rules on betrothal were considered outdated and to possibly deter couples from marriage. From this point of view, making betrothal an informal matter between the parties was actually a means to promote marriage.[311] At the same time, the "de-formalizing" of betrothal indicates a new dimension of marriage, which enunciated the voluntary feature of marriage as a union based on mutual love and commitment. In section 3.4.4 it will be claimed that this dimension also showed in the wording of the religious and civil marriage ceremonies.

3.4.2. IMPEDIMENTS TO MARRIAGE

3.4.2.1. Underlying Functions

Not all intimate relationships are permitted in society. Establishing impediments to marriage is a means for the state (or previously the church) to decide and signal which relationships are considered morally unacceptable. Only relationships which qualify according to certain ethical or moral standards are granted access to the institution of marriage. A development toward decreasing

307 Law Commission Report of 1913, p. 108.
308 Law Commission Report of 1913, p. 107.
309 This will become more visible in connection with the enactments of the 1970s, discussed in chapter 4.
310 See section 3.2.1.
311 Law Commission Report of 1913, p. 107.

the number of impediments in the regulation governing marriage is noticeable in Sweden during the twentieth century. This development is in line with the idea of marriage gradually evolving into becoming an institution serving primarily the interests of two individuals, instead of an institution primarily serving the interests of the state (or the church). However, in the 1920s, the list of impediments to marriage was still rather extensive. In fact, the impediments which aimed to avoid hereditary or contagious diseases were extended compared to the Code of 1734, including also mental illness[312] and venereal disease.[313]

In the Act of 1915, which was implemented into the Marriage Code of 1920, the procedure to examine impediments to marriage was simplified so that the couple's assurance on their honor that there were no impediments to marriage, of affinity or disease, was sufficient, as well as their assurance that they were not already married to another person.[314] This is an explicit example of marriage gradually changing from a public to a private matter. However, as mentioned above, the regulation of banns functioned as a complementary guarantee that there were no impediments to marriage.

3.4.2.2. Annulment and Invalidity

The distinction between, on the one hand, *invalidity of marriage* and, on the other hand, *annulment of marriage* was retained in the Marriage Code of 1920. As described in section 2.2.1, annulment derived from the Catholic faith, and established a way to end a marriage without interfering with the notion of marriage as an insoluble sacrament. This religiously based institution was kept in the Marriage Code of 1920, although the situations when it could be applied were limited compared to previously.

An *invalid marriage* did not have to be annulled through a court procedure, but was treated like there had not been a marriage in the first place. Invalidity arose in situations when the formal prerequisites of marriage had been severely

312 According to Hjalmar Westring, mentally ill persons had in practice been excluded from marriage prior to the Code of 1920 as well. His main impression is that the impediments regarding illnesses became more lenient in the Marriage Code of 1920, because of the introduced possibility to be granted dispensation. See Westring, Hjalmar, Den nya giftermålsbalken jämte dithörande författningar med förklaringar, 1933, p. 27.

313 The Marriage Code of 1920, Chapter 2, Sections 5 and 6. These impediments were dispensable. Furthermore, a marriage contracted in violation of these impediments could be annulled, provided that proceedings were initiated within the prescribed time-period of six months. The spouse with the illness had to initiate proceedings of annulment within six months of recovery, and the other spouse within six months from the time of discovery. In respect of the impediment of venereal disease, the proceedings needed to be initiated by the spouse without the disease within three years from the conclusion of the marriage. See the Marriage Code of 1920, Chapter 10, Section 2, and Chapter 10, Section 3, Paragraph 3.

314 Committee Report (SOU 1972:41), p. 142. Impediments to marriage were regulated in the Marriage Code of 1920, Chapter 2, Sections 1–12.

neglected at the time when the marriage was concluded, for instance, if the officiating person was not authorized to marry the couple.[315]

A marriage could also be *annulled* through a court procedure, in case of an indispensable impediment. Annulment court procedures could be initiated by a spouse or by the public prosecutor, in respect of impediments relating to affinity in the direct descending line and between siblings. In fact, the public prosecutor was obligated to initiate annulment procedures in case of close affinity between the spouses, irrespective of whether or not the spouses had been aware of the impediment.[316] The prohibition against being married to more than one person at a time was also an indispensable impediment and annulment procedures by the attorney general were required.[317]

Some impediments were not severe enough from an ethical point of view to lead to invalidity or annulment of marriage. Marriage to a former spouse's relative in the direct descending line is an example of such a "dispensable" impediment.[318] This impediment had no genetic relevance, but was still considered motivated to uphold for ethical reasons in 1920.

3.4.2.3. Adoption – Indispensable Impediment yet Possible to Bypass

In the Marriage Code of 1920, affinity through adoption was included as an indispensable impediment to marriage. More precisely, marriage between an adoptive parent and his or her adopted child was prohibited, but only for as long as the adoption ties remained from a legal point of view.[319] The basic idea was not to prevent marriages between an adopted child and his or her adoptive parent, but to avoid a system where adoptive ties are transformed into marital ties. The adoption could be annulled, for instance, through an agreement between the adoptive parent and the adopted child, and marriage could then be concluded between them.[320]

Marriage between adopted siblings was not an impediment to marriage in 1920.[321] It appears contradictory that marriage to a former spouse's relative was an impediment to marriage due to ethical reasons, whereas marriage to an adoptive sibling was not an impediment. It also appears inconsistent that

---

315 The Marriage Code of 1920, Chapter 4, Section 9.

316 The Marriage Code of 1920, Chapter 2, Section 7 and Chapter 10, Section 1. See also Westring, Hjalmar, Den nya giftermålsbalken jämte dithörande författningar med förklaringar, 1933, pp. 181 f. and p. 185.

317 The Marriage Code of 1920, Chapter 2, Section 10, as well as Chapter 10, Section 1.

318 The Marriage Code, Chapter 2, Section 9. Committee Report (SOU 1972:41), p. 139.

319 This provision was first enacted on 14 June 1917. See the Marriage Code of 1920, Chapter 12, Section 12.

320 The Act on Adoption of 14 June 1917, Sections 19–24, where the prerequisites for annulling the adoption were laid down.

321 It appears that the impediment of affinity in this context only applied to relatives by blood. See Committee Report (SOU 1972:41), p. 139.

marriage between an adoptive parent and an adopted child, although easy to bypass, was an impediment to marriage, whereas adoptive ties between siblings was not. It appears that ethical considerations and valuations on desirable family formations, from society's point of view, differed considerably in 1920 compared to today, the view on affinity created through adoption in particular.

3.4.2.4. Age-Limits for Conclusion of Marriage

The Marriage Code of 1920 raised the marital age for women to 18 from 17 years and the marital age for men was set at 21 years. Dispensation from the lower age-limits was possible and marriage in violation of the age-limits was not a ground for an annulment procedure.[322] It can be noted that marriage before the ages of 18 and 21 for women and men respectively, if they had not been married before, required parental consent according to the Marriage Code of 1920, Chapter 2, Section 2. The consent of both parents was required, in line with the spouses' equal position as legal guardians of their children.

The higher age-requirement for men – 21 years of age – was no novelty in the Marriage Code of 1920. It was established already in the Marriage Code of 1734 and found suitable to retain in 1920, with reference to "the comparatively late development of the individual", irrespective of the significant number of applications for dispensation from the age-limit.[323] It was also taken into account in the Law Commission Report of 1913 that the higher age-limit for men corresponded with recent legal developments in other countries in Europe.[324]

Retaining a higher age-requirement for men appears inconsistent with the principle of equality between the spouses in the Marriage Code of 1920. In 1734 this difference could be defended with reference to the husband's duty to provide financially for his wife and children and his authority to administrate her property. However, in the Marriage Code of 1920 the idea was to place husband and wife on an equal footing in this respect. On the other hand, it can be argued that the higher age-requirement for men in 1920 was in line with the generally prevailing view on the spouses' division of duties. As mentioned above, only four percent of all women were gainfully employed at this point in time in Sweden.

322 The Marriage Code, Chapter 2, Section 1 and Chapter 10 (about annulment) and Chapter 2, Sections 3 and 4 about the impediment of incapacity and the right to a court decision in case of the guardian's lacking consent for incapacitated persons to marry.

323 Law Commission Report of 1913, p. 134. The number of dispensations are compiled on p. 138 of the 1913 Committee Report.

324 In Sweden, it was taken into account by the Law Commission, that raising the man's marital age was a trend in Europe, for instance in Germany and Switzerland. Under the German Code, the age-limit had been set at 20 years, but in practice marriage required that the man had reached majority, which was set at 21 years. In Switzerland, the age-limit had been sharpened from 18 to 20 years. In Denmark the age was set at 20 years. In France, Holland, Belgium, Hungary, Italy and Portugal, however, the age of 18 sufficed for men and dispensation could be granted before that age. See Law Commission Report of 1913, p. 135.

Thus in practice the husband's duty to provide financially for his wife remained a reality in most families. From this point of view, upholding a higher age-limit for men than for women can be seen as being justifiable in 1920, i.e. for the purpose of ensuring that the husband was mature enough to provide for the family and to handle the family finances.

The age-requirement for women – 18 years of age – was a sharpening of the previous minimum age requirement for women set at 17 years through a statute in 1892, which in turn had been a sharpening of the woman's minimum marital age of 15 in the 1734 Code.[325] This new sharpening was justified for the purpose of protecting the young woman. In the Law Commission Report of 1913, it was taken into account that women's education normally was not finished before the age of 18. As a result, before the age of 18 women could not be expected to have sufficient experience of life or adequate self-knowledge to understand the importance of choosing her husband and the responsibilities of motherhood.[326] It is noteworthy that protecting the young woman from concluding a marriage in haste and with poor judgment was taken into account by the Law Commission in 1913. Furthermore, the age-limits for men and women were aimed to safeguard that marriage was built on a solid and lasting foundation. In other words, raising the age-limit for women, and retaining a difference between men and women in this respect, appears to have been considered a means to prevent and counteract unhappy marriages which risked ending in divorce.[327]

3.4.3. THE MARRIAGE CEREMONY: TERMINOLOGY AND FORMALITIES

3.4.3.1. Formal Requirements

Unlike betrothal, which was made an informal matter, the marriage ceremony remained guarded by formalities in the Marriage Code of 1920. As under the Code of 1734, the marriage ceremony still had to take place in the presence of witnesses.[328] Moreover, the simultaneous presence of both parties when consenting to the marriage was kept as a mandatory requirement, for the purpose of safeguarding the voluntary feature of marriage.[329]

325 Westring, Hjalmar, Den nya giftermålsbalken jämte dithörande författningar med förklaringar, 1933, p. 28.

326 Law Commission Report of 1913, p. 136. See also Westring, Hjalmar, Den nya giftermålsbalken jämte dithörande författningar med förklaringar, 1933, p. 28.

327 Law Commission Report of 1913, p. 136.

328 The Marriage Code of 1920, Chapter 4, Section 8.

329 The Marriage Code of 1920, Chapter 4, Section 8. See Westring, Hjalmar, Den nya giftermålsbalken jämte dithörande författningar med förklaringar, 1933, p. 76.

Couples retained the right to choose between two forms for conclusion of marriage: the civil and the religious, a right which had been established in 1908. As mentioned in section 3.2.1 above, offering a "double track" system for conclusion of marriage can be seen as being aimed to strengthen the attraction of marriage and, at the same time, counteract cohabitation without marriage. Ministers of the Church of Sweden continued to have the capacity to officiate legally valid marriages, confirmed in an explicit provision in the Marriage Code. In respect of ministers of other religious communities, legal capacity to officiate at marriages had to be granted by the king.[330] It can be noted that whereas the civil marriage ceremony was generally available to all couples qualifying to marry, access to the religious form presupposed that at least one party was a member of the church.[331]

3.4.3.2. Terminology and Symbolism: Vigsel and Giftermål

A novelty in the Marriage Code of 1920 was that the Swedish term *vigsel* (marriage ceremony) was applied to the civil as well as the religious marriage ceremonies. In the 1908 Act, different terms had been used in Swedish which do not easily translate into English. The term *vigsel* had been applied to the religious ceremony, whereas the civil ceremony had been called *giftermål*. In society in general, the terms were used interchangeably and it was found desirable to create correspondence between the terminology used in society and the terminology applied in the law.[332] Interestingly enough, the same controversy regarding whether both ceremonies could qualify as vigsel arose in connection with the same-sex marriage reform in 2007.[333]

The terminological equalization aimed at strengthening the symbolic value of civil marriage, which, it was held, was sometimes conceived of as being of lower dignity than a marriage concluded in the religious form.[334] The Law Commission appears to have been preoccupied with issues dealing with the symbolic dimension of marriage already in 1913.[335]

330 The Marriage Code of 1920, Chapter 4, Section 2, Paragraph 2.

331 This was a leniency compared to the Act of 1908, according to which both spouses-to-be had to be members of the church of Sweden in order to marry in the church. In the Marriage Code of 1920, the same requirement, that at least one was a member of the congregation, was applied in respect of other religious communities authorized by the king to officiate at marriages. In respect of non-Christian religious communities, however, both parties had to be members. See Chapter 4, Section 2, Paragraph 2.

332 Law Commission Report of 1913, p. 282.

333 This will be discussed in section 6.5.2.1.

334 Law Commission Report of 1913, p. 282.

335 This will be further analyzed in section 9.1.2.

3.4.3.3. *Capacity to Celebrate Marriages*

In the Marriage Code of 1920, the Church of Sweden retained a privileged position, in capacity of the state church. All ministers of the Church of Sweden had the capacity to officiate at marriages according to a provision in the Marriage Code.[336] A couple was free to choose a specific minister of their congregation to perform the marriage ceremony and the officials were obligated to meet the request of a couple for a specific minister to perform the marriage.[337] In theory it was possible to force a minister of the church to solemnize a marriage of, for instance, a previously divorced person, even against that minister's conscience.[338] The Church of Sweden was also the state church at that time, and officiating marriages was *myndighetsutövning* (an exercise of authority). It followed that a minister was a civil servant, who could be ordered to pay damages for professional misconduct, should he[339] refuse to marry, for instance, a divorced member of the congregation.[340]

In 1970, the issue of whether or not a minister of the church could refuse to officiate at marriages was clarified by the Supreme Court. In the case, a minister of the Church of Sweden had refused to remarry a previously divorced member of the congregation.[341] The Court established that ministers of the Church of Sweden were obligated to officiate at marriages, and that clearly refusing to do so constituted professional misconduct. In the present case, however, the minister's response to the couple wishing to marry had not been final and conclusive in this respect. For the purpose of avoiding similar situations in the future, an ordinance regarding marriage officials was adopted.[342] According to this ordinance, each chapter of the church was responsible for informing the couple of which ministers were available on an individual basis for solemnizing marriages. The question of whether or not an authorization to marry should also entail an obligation to marry would arise once again in connection with the introduction of a gender-neutral marriage concept in 2009. At this point in time, however, the Church of Sweden was no longer the state church. The same-sex marriage enactment will be discussed in chapter 6.

As regards the civil marriage ceremony, the authority to marry differed depending on where the couple lived. In certain cities the members of the

---

336 The Marriage Code of 1920, Chapter 4, Section 5, Paragraph 1. Unlike in respect of the above-mentioned authority to officiate at civil marriages, the authority of the ministers of the Church of Sweden was not limited to a specific region, but applied in the entire country.

337 Westring, Hjalmar, Den nya giftermålsbalken jämte dithörande författningar med förklaringar, 1933, pp. 71 f.

338 Westring, Hjalmar, Den nya giftermålsbalken jämte dithörande författningar med förklaringar, 1933, pp. 71 f.

339 The first female ordination took place in 1960.

340 Schmidt, Folke, Äktenskapsrätt, 1974, p. 40.

341 See decision by the Supreme Court, NJA 1972 p. 612.

342 See Statute (1975:1047) om vigselförrättare i vissa fall.

magistrate[343], or lacking such members, the chairman of *stadsstyrelsen* (the local authority), were authorized marriage officials. The term "magistrate" is no longer applicable, as the state has been divided into municipalities, according to new principles. Unlike ministers of the church, civil officials with capacity to marry couples were not authorized to marry couples outside their jurisdiction. In other cities, situated "on the country-side", *landsfiskalen* (the superintendent) was authorized to perform civil marriages. Moreover, the king could grant authorization to other persons in respect of a specific region.[344] A novelty in the Marriage Code of 1920 was that an authorization to officiate at civil marriages constituted an *obligation* of the concerned official to officiate at marriages within the district of authorization.[345]

3.4.4. THE MARRIAGE CEREMONIES IN 1920[346] – THE RELIGIOUS AND THE CIVIL COMPARED

According to the basic rule, which still applies today, liturgical details as regards the religious marriage ceremony were laid down in church law, whereas the wording of the civil marriage ceremony was issued by the king in a statute.[347] In 1920, the applicable church service was found in the Church Handbook from 1882.[348] The civil ceremony was established in a statute from 1915.[349]

3.4.4.1. The Civil Marriage Ceremony

In the civil marriage ceremony, according to the 1915 Statute, the marriage official addressed the couple with the following words:[350]

> "The purpose of marriage is the well-being of the individual and the upholding of society. You have declared your wish to enter into matrimony with one another."

---

343 Lagfaren ledamot av magistraten. See Westring, Hjalmar, Den nya giftermålsbalken jämte dithörande författningar med förklaringar, 1933, pp. 72 f. From medieval times until the mid 1800s, the magistrate was the highest governing body for the cities, with jurisdiction of its own. The mayor was the chairman of the magistrate.

344 The Marriage Code of 1920, Chapter 4, Section 5.

345 The Marriage Code of 1920, Chapter 4, Section 5, Paragraph 2.

346 These ceremonies applied before the Marriage Code of 1920 was adopted, and continued to apply thereafter.

347 In the Marriage Code of 1920, Chapter 4, Section 8, Paragraph 3, it was laid down that the Church Handbook applies to the content of the religious marriage service.

348 Svenska kyrkohandboken, 1882. Chapter 7 regulates marriages.

349 Statute, KF d. 3 december 1915 om vad vid borgerlig vigsel skall iakttagas.

350 The marriage ceremony is quoted by: Westring, Hjalmar, Den nya giftermålsbalken jämte dithörande författningar med förklaringar, 1933, p. 77. Author's translation.

"Do you N.N. take this N.N to be your lawful wedded wife to love for better or for worse?"

Answer: Yes.

"Do you N.N. take this N.N. to be your lawful wedded husband to love for better or for worse?"

Answer: Yes

"Give each other your hand in confirmation of this." (Before the handshake, the man may place a ring on the woman's left ring finger.)

"Empowered by my office, I pronounce you husband and wife. Never forget the promise of life-long faithfulness that you have given [each other]. Live with one another in mutual respect, love and confidence, and bear in mind your responsibility toward future generations. May unity and happiness remain in your marriage and guard your home."[351]

The civil ceremony expressed certain values, through the emphasis on life-long faithfulness, and describing marriage as the basis for having children. In the Marriage Code of 1920, fault still influenced the outcome of divorce proceedings. Keeping this is mind prescribing life-long faithfulness in the civil marriage ceremony appears natural. It is noteworthy, however, that also after the 1970s – when fault was made irrelevant for the outcome of divorce proceedings and ancillary matters such as maintenance claims – the wording of the civil marriage ceremony was kept more or less unaltered. The wording of the ceremony turned out to be more long-lived than the law.[352]

3.4.4.2. The Religious Marriage Ceremony

As regards the religious marriage ceremony applicable in 1920, the liturgical ceremony, laid down in the 1882 Handbook of the Church of Sweden, followed the same basic pattern as the civil ceremony. The minister first asked the man and then the woman if they wished to enter into matrimony with each other, reminding them of the presence of God. The marriage ceremony contained, in

351 In Swedish, the last paragraph reads: "I kraft av mitt ämbete förklarar jag Eder för äkta makar. Glömmen aldrig det löfte om trohet för livet, I nu haven avlagt. Leven med varandra i inbördes aktning, kärlek och förtoende, och besinnen Edert ansvar mot kommande släkten. Endräkt och lycka förblive i Edert äktenskap och hägne Edert hem." Author's translation.

352 See Statute (Förordning) (2006:214) med närmare föreskrifter om vigsel och registrering av partnerskap som förrättas av domare eller särskilt förordnad förrättare, Section 4. This Statute was replaced by Statute (Förordning) (2009:263) om vigsel som förrättas av särskilt förordnad vigselförrättare, when the gender-neutral marriage regulation was adopted in Sweden in 2009 and the wording was revised and modernized. See section 6.6.1.

addition, prayers and quotations from the Bible. The handbook contained a divine definition of marriage and a traditional description of the duties of the spouses, and prescribed that the minister address the couple accordingly:

> "In God's, the Father's and the Son's and the Holy Spirit's, name. Dear Christian! Marriage is founded by God himself, for the upholding of society and for united spouses' mutual help, to ease the troubles of life, relieve oncoming worries, and through a careful upbringing prepare the bliss of descendents. [...] The husband's duty is to love and honor his wife and by sense and kindness more and more seek to win her trust. So shall also the wife with love and affection meet her husband, tenderly participate with him in the care of their house, and so behave, that she pleases the husband, to the assistance of whom she has been given. [...]"[353]

In fact, the liturgy cited above was included already in the 1811 Church Handbook. The emphasis on the spouses' mutual relationship built on love and solidarity was at that time a radical break from its predecessor the 1693 liturgy, described in section 2.5.3. The liturgy of 1811 was criticized at the 1873 Synod of the Church of Sweden. More precisely, it was discussed if the word *tillgivenhet* (affection) should be replaced by the word *undergivenhet* (submission).[354] In the handbook of 1894, however, the word "affection" was kept. This can be seen as an early example of the Church of Sweden contributing to creating equality between men and women in society.[355]

3.4.4.3. Comparisons between the Two Ceremonies

In the religious and the civil marriage ceremonies applicable in 1920, the basic message of mutual *kindness and participation* as significant components of marriage is a characteristic common feature, although the religious service is longer and more detailed than the civil ceremony. Also the purpose of safeguarding *"the upholding of society"* is the same in the civil and the religious ceremonies, linking procreation to marriage.

However, the quotation above from the 1882 Handbook expresses several values which appear contradictory to the intentions expressed by the legislator when the Marriage Code of 1920 was adopted. The emancipation of women from

---

353 "I Guds, Faders och Sons och den Heliga Andes, namn. Dyre kristne! Äktenskapet är af Gud sjelf stiftadt, till samhällets bestånd och till förenade makars inbördes hjelp, att lätta lifvets mödor, mildra mötande bekymmer, och igenom en sorgfällig uppfostran bereda efterkommandes sällhet. [...] Mannens plikt är, att älska och ära sin hustru, och genom förstånd och välvilja mer och mer söka att vinna hennes förtroende. Så bör och hustrun med kärlek och tillgifvenhet möta sin man, ömt deltaga med honom i omsorgen om deras hus, och så skicka sig, att hon må täckas den make, hvilken hon gifven är till hjelp. [...]" Svenska kyrkohandboken, 1882, p. 164. Author's translation.

354 Report of the Church Board, Kyrkostyrelsens skrivelse 2009:6, p. 50.

355 Report of the Church Board, Kyrkostyrelsens skrivelse 2009:6, p. 50.

the husband's legal guardianship was combined with an ambition to improve the legal situation of the married woman. Improving the legal situation of women was a means of breaking with the "old-fashioned" hierarchy of the Marriage Code of 1734. It was feared that couples refrained from marrying because they did not approve of the "traditional" (outdated) connotations to marriage.[356] The church service expressed that the wife was given "to the assistance" of her husband, her duty being to behave so that she pleased her husband. Keeping in mind the political attention paid to the principle of equality in Sweden around the year 1920, the maintained religious ceremony's reference to the woman as a "gift" to the man, obligated to assist him, appears outdated and even offensive.

It should be kept in mind, however, that in the 1920s equality was essentially a matter of improving the situation of housewives, by attempting to increase the value of their work in the home – and not aimed to challenge traditional gender roles.[357] The woman was considered best suited for working in the home, and in that sense she can be seen as "assisting her husband". The value of women's participation in the spouses' home was confirmed already in the quote from the 1882 Church Handbook. Keeping this in mind, perhaps the values connected to the civil and the religious marriage ceremonies were not so different in 1920 after all.

Nevertheless, speaking expressly in terms of the woman being given to the assistance of her husband was contrary to the political ambition relating to the emancipation of married women from their husbands' legal guardianship in 1920. The church ceremony signaled that the religious concept of marriage was different and more "traditional" than the "secularly inspired" civil ceremony. This can be seen as an early example of how the values in society tend to change faster than religious values, such as those of the Church of Sweden; a phenomenon which would become more obvious during the twentieth century.[358] It can be claimed that the religious values of the ceremony of 1882 – deriving from the Bible and applied by the Church of Sweden until replaced by a slightly altered wording in 1917[359] – lived on in Swedish society and created controversy in connection with the introduction of a gender-neutral marriage concept in 2009. This will be further analyzed in chapter 6.

---

356 See section 3.2.1.

357 See section 3.3.

358 According to Jacob Sundberg, the Church of Sweden's role as the "Folk Church" caused future problems, when the state adopted reforms which contradicted old church values, for instance in respect of remarrying divorced persons, marrying persons belonging to other religious communities and female ordination. See Familjerätt i omvandling, 1969, pp. 48 f. Also former Archbishop Hammar, K.G. Hammar has pointed out that attitudes in society have changed faster than within the Church of Sweden. See Svenska kyrkans utredningar 2005:1, p. 32.

359 The language was slightly modernized in the 1917 ceremony, the phrase stating that the woman was given to the man's assistance has been replaced by a phrase stating that she shall "behave so that she is of help to him". ("så skicka sig, att hon må bliva honom till hjälp"). Author's translation. The message of the woman's subordination to the man remains in the 1917 service. Although she is not literally said to be given to the assistance of her husband, her duty is, nevertheless expressed in terms of helping him. See Handbok för svenska kyrkan, 1918.

3.5. LEGAL EFFECTS OF MARRIAGE

3.5.1. ADJUSTING THE LAW TO THE VALUES IN SOCIETY

It can be questioned how novel the ideas of equality of the Marriage Code of 1920 really were. In the travaux préparatoires to the Marriage Code of 1920, it was pointed out that an ambition with the law revision was to adjust the values expressed by law to the predominating values in society, by abolishing the husband's guardianship of his wife and authorizing the wife to participate equally in decisions concerning the family.[360] Such an order was widely accepted and already practiced in society. It was considered an advantage that the "new" legal system with the woman actively in charge of the household had already successfully been "tested out" in practice, thereby ensuring that the reform would be well-received and match the values and habits in society.[361]

However, the idea that the woman was in charge of the household was no novelty in Sweden. Already in 1734, the married woman was in charge of the household in capacity of the "matron of the house", and was in this capacity authorized to make decisions in matters concerning the household, although she was obligated to follow any rules that the husband may have prescribed in this respect.[362]

3.5.2. THE REVISED MARITAL PROPERTY REGIME

New rules governing the spouses' economy were required when the system with husbands as legal guardians of their wives was abolished in 1920. The political aim to create equality between the spouses was incorporated into the marital property regime of the Marriage Code of 1920 – the deferred community of property system.[363] This system was based on the principle that each spouse retained the ownership of property owned by him or her *prior* to the marriage, as well as property which had been acquired *during* the marriage. The marital property regime included inherited property and property acquired as a gift, unless explicitly stated otherwise by the donor or in a will. Each spouse was given individual responsibilities and rights in respect of his or her property and independency toward creditors.[364] Glendon and Rheinstein have summarized

---

360 NJA II 1921, p. 6 and Law Commission Report of 1918, Lagberedningens förslag till revision av giftermålsbalken och vissa delar av ärvdabalken. IV. Förslag till giftermålsbalk m.m. 1918:15, p. 163.

361 NJA II 1921, p. 8.

362 Law Commission Report of 1918, p. 160.

363 It can be mentioned that since 1900, there had been several motions to Parliament, proposing reforms of the marital property regime. The basic idea suggested was to challenge the husband's right to administer the wife's property. As a result, in 1912, the wife's consent to certain dispositions of the husband involving her separate property was introduced in the law. See Law Commission Report of 1918, p. 154.

364 Hafström, Gerhard, Den svenska familjerättens historia, 1972, p. 75.

the aim of the deferred community accordingly: "during marriage, [the idea is] to leave each spouse free to deal with and manage his property, but upon death or other termination to treat the spouses as if they had lived under a system of universal community."[365]

The deferred community of property system differed considerably from the earlier system, according to which the spouses' property in principle was owned jointly, with sole administration rights for the husband. In the Marriage Code of 1920, each spouse obtained a latent claim for half of the total value of the marital property, but the claim could only be realized upon dissolution of the marriage, through death or divorce. This latent claim was guarded by a requirement for the other spouse's consent for certain important legal acts. If the owner neglected to act accordingly, the other spouse could turn to court and apply for a *boskillnad* (separation of estate).[366] A duty to take proper care of the marital property during marriage was also included.[367] A spouse's shortcoming in this respect could lead to a liability to financially compensate the other spouse.[368] Moreover, it can be mentioned that new rules on succession law were introduced, through which the spouses received mutual inheritance rights.[369]

As mentioned in section 3.3, the basic idea behind the deferred community of property system was to increase the status of the housewife and of her unpaid work in the home. In other words, the housewife's shouldering of the necessary work in the joint household made the husband's career possible.[370] In order to give the woman more independent authority in capacity of housewife, as mentioned above, a possibility to enjoin the husband to provide funds for this purpose - a household allowance - was introduced in the Marriage Code of 1920.[371] This provision was "gender-neutral", i.e. not exclusively reserved for women, but in effect designed for the purpose of strengthening the position of women.[372]

The marital property regime reflects the values attached to marriage in 1920. There was a limit to the principle of equality between men and women, in the sense that the law protected and encouraged a traditional division of duties. In the applicable civil and religious marriage ceremonies, accounted for in section

365 Glendon, Mary Ann, Rheinstein, Max, International Encyclopedia of Comparative Law, Vol. IV, Persons and Family, Interspousal Relations, 2007, p. 101.

366 Westring, Hjalmar, Den nya giftermålsbalken jämte dithörande författningar med förklaringar, 1933, pp. 113 f. In the Marriage Code of 1987, separation of estate was replaced by the possibility for spouses to jointly apply for *bodelning under äktenskap* (division of property during marriage).

367 The Marriage Code of 1920, Chapter 6, Section 3.

368 The Marriage Code of 1920, Chapter 13, Sections 5–7. A spouse could also receive compensation if the other spouse had used his or her marital property to increase the value of his or her private property, Chapter 13, Section 8.

369 See Brattström, Margareta, Singer, Anna, Rätt arv, 2007, pp. 22 f. Succession law will not be dealt with here.

370 Law Commission Report of 1918, p. 166.

371 The Marriage Code, Chapter 5, Sections 2 and 3. See also NJA II 1921, pp. 7 f.

372 NJA II 1921, pp. 7 f. and p. 26.

3.4.4, the reproductive function of marriage was central. The division of duties between men and women in 1920, supported in the Marriage Code, also appears to have connected marriage to procreation. In practice, married men and women appear to have continued with their lives in more or less the same fashion as before women were emancipated from the legal guardianship of their husbands. Nevertheless, introducing a legal possibility for a married woman to have gainful employment without the permission of her husband was a significant reform. Giving women's right to participate equally in family matters statutory support – inter alia through the deferred community of property regime – laid the foundation for the future course of events and was a prerequisite for the changes to come in respect of marriage and divorce rules in the 1970s.[373]

3.5.3. SPOUSAL MAINTENANCE

3.5.3.1. The Regulation

The emancipation of women made explicit rules on spousal maintenance necessary in the Marriage Code of 1920. The duty to maintain was twofold according to the Marriage Code of 1920. There was (1) a mutual obligation for each spouse *during the marriage* to contribute to family needs, through money, work in the home or by other means.[374] As a last resort, if one spouse obviously neglected the duty to maintain the other, a court could order the payment of maintenance during marriage.[375] If the spouses lived apart due to breakdown of the marriage, the right to maintenance remained, unless the spouse in need was responsible for the separation.[376] The maintenance obligation also remained during legal separation.[377]

Moreover, maintenance claims could (2) be initiated by a spouse *upon dissolution of the marriage*.[378] Maintenance could either be paid periodically or as a lump sum, the former being the main rule.[379] The right to maintenance upon

373 See section 4.2.

374 The Marriage Code of 1920, Chapter 5, Sections 2 and 5.

375 According to Hjalmar Westring, court proceedings on maintenance during marriage were considered detrimental to the marriage and offensive in general. Therefore, obvious neglect was demanded, which excluded court proceedings as a result of every little disagreement between the spouses. Westring, Hjalmar, Den nya giftermålsbalken jämte dithörande författningar med förklaringar, 1933, pp. 90 f. If a spouse, after a year, had paid more than his (or her) share according to Section 2, the other spouse could be obligated by the court to compensate the injustice, Chapter 5, Section 6.

376 The Marriage Code of 1920, Chapter 5, Section 7.

377 The Marriage Code of 1920, Chapter 11, Section 25.

378 The Marriage Code of 1920, Chapter 11, Section 26.

379 The right to maintenance ceases if the receiver remarries. Westring, Hjalmar, Den nya giftermålsbalken jämte dithörande författningar med förklaringar, 1933, pp. 229 f. The right also ceases if spouses break off their legal separation and continue living together in matrimony. See the Marriage Code, Chapter 11, Section 30.

dissolution of the marriage was related to the question of guilt, in the sense that the spouse responsible for the breakdown was excluded from the right to claim maintenance. It can be mentioned that maintenance in respect of children was regulated in a separate act, which will not be dealt with here.[380]

3.5.3.2. Maintenance and Equality – A Contradiction?

When the Marriage Code of 1920 was enacted, the Law Commission considered it to be urgent to establish rules on spousal maintenance. More precisely, it was held that the weaker party – usually the woman – risked being left without financial support in case of divorce.[381] In fact, according to the Law Commission, possibly well-founded divorce applications had occasionally been denied, for the purpose of avoiding that one spouse was left without any financial means upon divorce.[382]

The introduction of a duty for a spouse – usually the husband – to maintain the other spouse – usually the wife – after divorce was in line with the much desired traditional division of duties in 1920. Since married women were not expected to work outside the home, it was difficult for them to find a job after divorce. The rules on maintenance can be seen as reinforcing the traditional gender roles. The man was supposed to keep providing for his wife financially, even after divorce. From this point of view, there was no contradiction between maintenance and equality in the 1920s. Furthermore, it should be kept in mind that marriage was in most cases still a life-long commitment in the 1920s, since divorce was uncommon.

Table 1. The Marriage Frequency in Sweden between 1900 and 1935[383]

Year	Population	Marriages	Divorces
1900	5 136 441	31 478	405
1905	5 294 885	30 888	448
1910	5 522 403	33 162	609
1915	5 712 740	33 182	847
1920	5 904 489	42 918	1 325
1925	6 053 562	37 419	1 748
1930	6 142 191	43 858	2 218
1935	6 250 506	51 306	2 718

380 Act 11 June 1920 concerning children born in wedlock (lagen om barn i äktenskap, nr 407).
381 Law Commission Report of 1913, p. 448.
382 Law Commission Report of 1913, p. 448.
383 Committee Report, (SOU 2007:17), p. 203, with reference to the National Central Bureau of Statistics.

The table shows that in 1915, the number of divorces amounted to 2.5 percent of the total number of marriages concluded that year. Although this number would increase the coming years, divorce remained uncommon in Sweden during the 1920s. From this point of view, the urgency of rules governing maintenance after divorce appears exaggerated.

In respect of the limited number of women who did go through a divorce in the 1920s, however, the possibility to obtain maintenance might have been significant. The divorced woman's chances of being gainfully employed were limited after a long marriage, during which she had worked in the home and taken care of the spouses' children.[384] Moreover, in the Law Commission Report of 1913 it was held that it could be humiliating for the woman to be "forced" to be gainfully employed after a divorce.[385] This clearly signals that women could not be expected to work outside the home. This line of argument demonstrates how deeply rooted the traditional division of duties between the spouses was in 1920, and on what terms the principle of equality was discussed.

3.6. THE DISSOLUTION OF MARRIAGE

3.6.1. "COPENHAGEN DIVORCES" AND THE NEED FOR LAW REFORM

A considerable ideological change had taken place in Swedish law and society at the time of the enactment of the Marriage Code of 1920, compared to the values reflected in the Marriage Code of 1734. It was no longer considered to be in society's best interest to protect and encourage marriages which had broken down completely, by deterring the spouses from divorcing. Nevertheless, as will be illustrated below, obtaining a divorce was time-consuming.[386]

Between 1860 and 1915, a loophole in the law offered a shortcut to the otherwise difficult and time-consuming divorce procedure.[387] A couple agreeing to divorce could enter into an agreement on how their property was to be divided in case of divorce, and then stage the "abandonment" of one spouse. The other spouse then travelled abroad – often to Copenhagen, Denmark – for some time, and thereby enabled the spouse who was seemingly "left behind" to claim divorce on the ground "arbitrary abandonment".[388]

---

384 Law Commission Report of 1913, pp. 448 f.

385 Law Commission Report of 1913, p. 448.

386 See section 3.6.2.1.

387 Law Commission Report of 1913, p. 384.

388 Law Commission Report of 1913, pp. 384. This has also been discussed by, Nygren, Rolf, Kyrkorätt, Äktenskap och sekularisering – I, 1989, p. 29. Arranging economical affairs beforehand was necessary. Otherwise the "abandoning" spouse would lose his or her right to marital property. See also Inger, Göran, Svensk rättshistoria, 1997, p. 201. See also Law Commission Report of 1913, pp. 384.

This shortcut to divorce, often referred to as "Copenhagen divorce", was much disliked by the Law Commission when preparing the 1915 Act on Conclusion and Dissolution of Marriage. The general idea was that "Copenhagen divorces" bypassed the law and, as a result, risked undermining people's general respect for the law. Furthermore, this shortcut to divorce was only available to wealthy couples who could afford a stay abroad, during which the "abandonment" was established.[389] It was pointed out as "unfair" by the Law Commission that wealthy spouses could stage abandonment through a trip abroad, whereas the poor who could not afford such a trip had to go through the "mediation" procedure by the church. This, the Law Commission pointed out, was often perceived as "offensive" from the perspective of the couple who could not afford a trip to Copenhagen.[390]

3.6.2. PRELIMINARY STAGES TO DIVORCE: LEGAL SEPARATION AND MEDIATION

3.6.2.1. Legal Separation

Legal separation was introduced in the Marriage Code of 1920, as a new feature regarding marriage breakdown.[391] The point of departure was that divorce was granted on the ground of "deep and constant discord" – after a legal separation of one year – if the spouses still found their marriage to be intolerable.[392] If the spouses were in agreement to dissolve the marriage, their word that the marriage had broken down was sufficient for granting legal separation by court order. No further investigation of underlying reasons was required. Accepting the spouses' word that the marriage had broken down, without any further investigations, was a considerable "modernization" of the law, in line with the general development of the concept of marriage from being a public concern and interest, toward becoming more of a private concern of the couple. However, the issue of divorce was not left completely to the "whim" of the spouses. The Law Commission emphasized that the provisions on legal separation aimed at preventing hasty divorces, and thus protected the institution of marriage, which was considered important.[393]

389 Law Commission Report of 1913, p. 384.

390 Law Commission Report of 1913, p. 384.

391 Previously, as a last resort in divorce matters, practice had been to order the spouses to live apart for one year, after fines and warnings by the Church Council, in accordance with the king's Statute of 1860. See Committee Report (SOU 1972:41), p. 170. The underlying purpose and procedure differed from the regulation of legal separation.

392 The Marriage Code of 1920, Chapter 11, Sections 1 and 3.

393 Law Commission Report of 1913, p. 385.

During the legal separation, the spouses were required to live apart and without sexual contact, the idea being for them to consider if marital life had truly come to an end and to avoid that applications for divorce were made in haste.[394] After at least a year of incessant legal separation, the court granted the divorce, upon the request of either spouse.[395] The fact that the spouses had not resumed married life during the legal separation was seen as an indication that the breakdown of the marriage remained. However, the requirement that the couple did not live together during the legal separation does not appear to have been absolute. In case law divorce appears to have been granted irrespective of the fact that the spouses were living together after the legal separation.[396]

3.6.2.2. Mediation

The rules on mediation, introduced in 1915, indicate a shift toward a "softer" view on the institution of marriage, and a development toward assigning more credit to the spouses' ability to decide if their marriage should end, without unnecessary public interference. The participation of the church in issues concerning marriage was decreased, for instance through the abolishment of the system of church warnings, laid down in the Code of 1734. The participation of the Church of Sweden prior to divorce had been aimed to deter spouses from divorcing. In the Marriage Code of 1920, however, the idea was still to reconcile the spouses, but the method used to achieve this goal was different. The job of the mediator – a minister of the church or another specially appointed unbiased third party[397] – was to help the spouses to understand each other.

Under the Marriage Code of 1920, mediation was used, prior to a judgment on legal separation, in case of (1) deep and constant discord,[398] (2) disputes about maintenance,[399] (3) disputes about payment to a spouse for participation in the other spouse's business,[400] or (4) disputes concerning administration of the other spouse's marital property.[401] As a rule, mediation appears to have been required before a decision on legal separation could be granted.[402] However, as pointed out by the 1918 Law Commission, legal separation could be granted without

394 Law Commission Report of 1913, pp. 391 f.

395 The Marriage Code of 1920, Chapter 11, Section 3.

396 Law Commission Report of 1913, p. 403.

397 It was up to the administrative agencies to decide whether a civil mediator should be appointed. The Marriage Code, Chapter 14, Section 2.

398 See also Chapter 15, Section 8.

399 The Marriage Code of 1920, Chapter 5, Sections 2, 3, 5, 6, 7, 8, 9 and 10.

400 The Marriage Code of 1920, Chapter 8, Section 6.

401 The Marriage Code of 1920, Chapter 8, Section 7.

402 The Act on Conclusion and Dissolution of Marriage, Chapter 6, Section 1 and 2. See also The Marriage Code, Chapter 15, Section 8. For more details on mediation, see Westring, Hjalmar, Den nya giftermålsbalken jämte dithörande författningar med förklaringar, 1933, pp. 283 ff.

mediation, in order to avoid that one spouse through obstructing mediation, delayed the judgment on legal separation.[403]

Introducing rules on mediation was considered a necessary consequence of the emancipation of women, and of the legal principle that husband and wife decide jointly in economic matters of the family. Against this background, the Law Commission noted, it was inevitable that the participation of women would create conflicts between the spouses. Mediation was a means to help the spouses reconcile when conflicts arose between them.[404]

3.6.3. GROUNDS FOR DIVORCE

Divorce could be granted without legal separation, upon the request of one spouse, according to the 1920 Marriage Code, in a number of cases, enumerated in a "divorce catalogue".[405] These grounds were the same as those included in the 1915 Act on Conclusion and Dissolution of Marriage. Divorce was available if a spouse:

(1) had remarried in breach of the law (bigamy),
(2) had sexual intercourse or fornication with somebody other than the spouse,
(3) had infected the other spouse with a venereal disease,
(4) had attempted to take the other spouse's life, or had committed aggravated assault on the other spouse or the children,
(5) had been convicted for certain felonies,
(6) abused alcohol, or
(7) was mentally ill.

The grounds for immediate divorce were mainly clarifications laid down in statutory law of previously applicable principles. Novelties in the 1915 Act were the grounds of bigamy, venereal disease and criminal fornication other than adultery.[406] The extensive "divorce ground catalogue," the immediacy of divorce in these situations and the access to legal separation were quite radical from an international perspective, and contrary to the previous function of divorce as a last resort in exceptional cases.[407]

---

403 Law Commission Report of 1918, p. 396.

404 Law Commission Report of 1918, p. 398.

405 The Marriage Code of 1920, Chapter 11, Sections 7 through 13 See Westring, Hjalmar, Den nya giftermålsbalken jämte dithörande författningar med förklaringar, 1933, pp. 199–236. The great majority of all divorces in the 1920s were preceded by legal separation. See Schmidt, Folke, Äktenskapsrätt, 1974, p. 122. In most cases under the divorce catalogue access to divorce presupposed that the application was filed within six months from gained knowledge of the conditions.

406 Westring, Hjalmar, Den nya giftermålsbalken jämte dithörande författningar med förklaringar, 1933, p. 204.

407 See section 3.7.2.

3.7. THE ESSENCE OF MARRIAGE IN 1920 – SUMMARIZING ANALYSIS AND COMPARISONS

3.7.1. SUMMARIZING ANALYSIS

The institution of marriage in the Marriage Code of 1920 appears ambiguous, standing with one foot in the "traditional" old-fashioned outlook on marriage and with the other foot in the "modern". The institution of marriage had two sides, which the law tried to battle and balance. A shift toward a "personalized" outlook on marriage is visible, which centered on confidence in the individual spouses' ability to act as two equals. In this spirit, betrothal was turned into an informal matter. Moreover, divorce was made easier to obtain. It was no longer considered motivated to force spouses to continue with a marriage which had broken down, through deterrent church mediation. Instead mediation was introduced for the purpose of helping the couple reconcile. The participation of the Church of Sweden in such services was no longer indispensable, as civil mediators existed.

These novelties regarding marriage appear "modern" in the sense that they enunciated the idea of marriage as primarily a personal and private matter instead of primarily a state or church concern. Abolishing church warnings by an official of the Church of Sweden as a mandatory feature in divorce proceedings, and making divorce more accessible through the introduction of the wide "divorce ground catalogue", can be seen as indicating a shift toward marriage becoming a union based on the individual spouse's autonomy; a feature of marriage which would grow stronger in Sweden during the decades to come, especially in the 1970s.[408]

However, under the 1920 Marriage Code, these modern values, centering on the principle of equality between husband and wife, appear to have remained primarily relevant on a theoretical level. Married women were legally emancipated, but in practice, nevertheless, the traditional roles played by husband and wife remained intact. Women continued to work in the home and secure the population growth by having and raising children, whereas men were responsible for providing for the family financially. The Marriage Code of 1920 protected this "traditional" side of marriage, for instance, through the spousal maintenance rules. Husbands (although the provisions in the Marriage Code were gender-neutral) were in practice the ones expected to provide financially for their wives during marriage, as well as after marriage in the rare case of divorce.[409] In fact, as mentioned above, it was considered degrading for a divorced woman to have to be gainfully employed in the 1920s.

Nevertheless, the ideological significance of the Marriage Code of 1920 should not be underestimated. Through the Marriage Code of 1920, the legal

---

408 See section 4.2.

409 Only 1325 divorces were registered in 1920.

concept of marriage was emphasized as a mutual project based on equality, to which each spouse contributed according to his or her capacity, in contrast to the previous notion of marriage as a patriarchal institution. During the decades to come, the principle of equality between husband and wife in the 1920 Marriage Code would gradually become established in society as well.[410]

In other words, the Marriage Code of 1920 laid the ideological foundation for the coming legislative and societal changes relating to marriage. In fact, establishing the theoretical and ideological basis in the law in this respect was the aim expressed by the legislator in 1920 – not to challenge gender roles and the established division of duties in the family: "[...] [T]he spouses shall, *as far as possible*, be placed side by side, as equally free and independent persons, without any *legally established* right for one to decide over the other or alone in joint family matters."[411]

3.7.2. INTERNATIONAL COMPARISONS: PERSPECTIVES ON THE SWEDISH LEGAL DEVELOPMENT

3.7.2.1. How Progressive was the Swedish Marriage Code of 1920?

The Swedish Marriage Code of 1920 has a reputation for being ahead of its time in a European perspective,[412] containing the liberal divorce rules of the 1915 Act and the deferred community of property regime, based on the principle of equality between husband and wife. How does the ideology behind and the applicable rules of the Swedish Marriage Code of 1920 – the rules on spouses' property relations, divorce and maintenance – compare to the corresponding marriage regulations applicable in Spain, the Netherlands, France and Germany? How progressive was the Swedish Marriage Code of 1920?

It should be underlined once again that the idea here is not to provide any extensive account of the substantive regulation of four additional European countries. The idea is limited to making some general observations, by sketching in a broad outline the course of events in four other European jurisdictions. This is done primarily on the basis of the national reports published by the Commission of European Family Law (CEFL) concerning property relations between spouses and divorce and maintenance of former spouses,[413] in order to identify characteristic "liberal" features in the Swedish Marriage Code of 1920.

410 This will be illustrated in chapter 4.
411 As quoted initially in this chapter. NJA II 1921, p. 6. Author's translation. Emphasis added.
412 Agell, Anders, Brattström, Margareta, Äktenskap, Samboende, Partnerskap, 2008, pp. 39 f.
413 European Family Law in Action, Volume IV: Property Relations between Spouses, Edited by, Boele-Woelki, Katharina, Braat, Bente and Curry-Sumner, Ian, Intersentia 2003, European Family Law in Action, Volume I: Grounds for Divorce, Edited by, Boele-Woelki, Katharina, Braat, Bente and Curry-Sumner, Ian, Intersentia 2003 and European Family Law in Action, Volume II: Maintenance between Former Spouses, Edited by, Boele-Woelki, Katharina, Braat, Bente and Sumner, Ian, Intersentia 2003.

3.7.2.2. *Equality and the Legal Position of Married Women*

A novelty of the Swedish Marriage Code of 1920 was that women were emancipated from the legal guardianship of their husbands and became entitled to administer their own property. As described above, through the Marriage Code of 1920, the legal concept of marriage developed toward becoming more of a mutual project based on equality, to which each spouse contributed according to his or her capacity, women often through household work and men through gainful employment. Household work was explicitly included in the 1920 Marriage Code, as a means of contributing to the marriage. The new marital property regime of the Swedish Marriage Code of 1920 – the deferred community of property regime – can be seen as being based on the principle of creating equality between husband and wife, by safeguarding the married woman's right to a share of the husband's eventual wealth in case the marriage ended.

In France, an enactment in 1907 aimed at protecting the rights of the married woman, by granting her the right to administrate earnings gained through a profession of her own. However, this right could not be fully realized until the married woman officially obtained legal capacity to conclude agreements without her husband's consent. This was achieved through two subsequent enactments, in 1938 and 1942.[414] The married woman's authority to conclude agreements concerning the spouses' mutual life was, to some extent, already recognized in French case law prior to the 1938 reform, namely through an assumption that a wife was acting in compliance with her husband's wishes when concluding agreements concerning their mutual life.[415] It can be noted that also pursuant to the Swedish Code of 1734, the predecessor to the 1920 Marriage Code, married women were authorized to enter into certain agreements concerning matters relating to running the household on a daily basis.[416]

In 1965, a comprehensive reform concerning the spouses' property relations was carried out in France, but it did not aim particularly at creating equality between the spouses. According to the marital property regime of 1965, all property owned prior to the marriage, as well as gifts and assets acquired through succession, was the personal property of each spouse. The marital property regime only included property which had been acquired *during* the marriage. Although each spouse was authorized to administrate and dispose of his or her personal assets, the husband remained "head of the community" with sole authority to administer the marital property. Equality between husband and wife through equal rights of participation in matters concerning their joint

---

414 European Family Law in Action, Volume IV: Property Relations between Spouses, 2003, question 2, p. 60. French Report written by Ferrand, Frédérique and Braat, Bente, and available at www.ceflonline.net/. Accessed 26 October 2010.

415 European Family Law in Action, Volume IV: Property Relations between Spouses, 2003, question 2, p. 60. French Report written by Ferrand, Frédérique and Braat, Bente.

416 See section 2.6.1.

property, introduced in Sweden through the Marriage Code of 1920, was not introduced in French marriage regulation until 1985.[417]

In Germany, the constitutional requirement of equality between husband and wife was implemented in the regulation governing marriage in 1953, through rules guaranteeing the woman administration rights in respect of her property.[418] Prior to this, pursuant to the Civil Code of 1900, the marital property regime – based on the principle of separation of property – provided the husband with the right to administer, not only his own property, but also property which the wife had brought into the marriage. This was, however, found contrary to the constitutional requirement of equality. In 1958 a new marital property regime was introduced in Germany[419], i.e. the community of accrued gains, which contained provisions stating that the wife's household work was equally valuable as the husband's gainful employment, by establishing household work as a means of contribution. According to the wording of the German Civil Code, household work was exclusively assigned to the wife until 1976.[420]

In the Netherlands, the incapacity of married women was abolished through legislation in 1957, and women became authorized to administer their property as well as the spouses' community property. However, a provision stating that the husband was the "head" of the marriage was kept in the Dutch Civil Code until 1970.[421]

In Spain, equality between men and women was not established until 1981, delayed by the dictatorship of General Franco, between 1939 and 1975. During this political regime, traditional gender roles were promoted through the law, in a strictly Catholic religious climate.[422] It can be mentioned, however, that for a short time prior to this regime, namely during the Second Spanish Republic (1931–1936), the principle of equality between husband and wife was expressed in the Constitution: "marriage is based upon equality of rights for both sexes [...]".[423] The Spanish Republic marked a temporary break from an otherwise long predominance of the Catholic faith and traditional Catholic values concerning married life. However, the Republic only lasted for three years and it would be

417 European Family Law in Action, Volume IV: Property Relations between Spouses, 2003, question 2, p. 60. French Report written by Ferrand, Frédérique and Braat, Bente.

418 See The German Constitution of 1949, Art. 117 on upholding anti-constitutional family law, (violating article 3(2) of the Constitution) until 1953.

419 Gleichberechtingungsgesetz of 18 June 1957, Bundesgesetzblatt Part I, p. 718.

420 See section 1356 (1) BGB until 1976. European Family Law in Action, Volume IV: Property Relations between Spouses, 2003, question 2, p. 62. German Report written by Martiny, Dieter and Dethloff, Nina, and available at www.ceflonline.net/. Accessed 26 October 2010.

421 European Family Law in Action, Volume IV: Property Relations between Spouses, 2003, question 2, p. 67. Dutch Report written by Boele-Woelki, Katharina, Schonewille, Fred and Schrama, Wendy, and available at. www.ceflonline.net/. Accessed 26 October 2010.

422 See section 7.3.4.1.

423 European Family Law in Action, Volume I: Grounds for Divorce, 2003, question 2, p. 51. Spanish Report written by Martín-Casals, Miquel, Ribot, Jordi, Solé, Josep, p. 5, and available at www.ceflonline.net/. Accessed 26 October 2010.

another 50 years before an enactment striving to create equality between men and women was adopted at the federal level in Spain.[424]

Against the background sketched above, identifying the main developments concerning spouses' property relations and the position of women in Spain, Germany, France and the Netherlands, the Swedish Marriage Code of 1920 stands out as liberal. The ideology of marriage as a mutual project, in which both spouses participate as two equals, was not recognized by the laws of the other countries, for political or other reasons, until several decades later, at a time when Sweden was ready to take the principle of equality and individual autonomy of the spouses one step further.[425] Explanations to why Sweden (and the other Nordic countries) was a pioneer in the field of equality between spouses have been discussed in section 3.2.2.2.

3.7.2.3. Access to Divorce

The Swedish divorce rules in the 1915 Act on Conclusion and Dissolution of Marriage, transferred to the Marriage Code of 1920, facilitated access to divorce significantly. As mentioned above, an ideological change had taken place in Sweden. As a result, it was no longer considered to be in society's best interest to protect and encourage marriage stability in all situations, by deterring the spouses from divorcing. As a result, deep and permanent breakdown of the marriage was recognized as a ground for divorce, after a legal separation decree, and various fault-based divorce grounds proving for an expedient divorce were included in an extensive "divorce catalogue".[426] If the spouses were in agreement to dissolve the marriage, their word that the marriage had irreparably broken down was enough for the court to grant a legal separation decree. No further investigation of underlying reasons was required. The divorce catalogue of fault grounds gave a spouse the unilateral right to immediate divorce, without legal separation.[427]

Divorce based on mutual consent was introduced in France through the Reform Act of 1975. Its predecessor only recognized divorce based on fault.[428] In respect of unilateral applications for divorce, the 1975 enactment contained various fault grounds, and, for instance, six years of de facto separation as a

---

424 See sections 4.4.2.1–4.4.2.3 for more comparative reflections.

425 See chapter 4.

426 The grounds for divorce in the Marriage Code of 1920 have been accounted for in section 3.6.3.

427 See section 3.6.3 and European Family Law in Action, Volume IV: Property Relations between Spouses, 2003, question 2, p. 52. Swedish Report written by Jänterä-Jareborg, Maarit, Brattström Margareta and Walleng Kajsa, and available at www.ceflonline.net/. Accessed 26 October 2010.

428 European Family Law in Action, Volume I: Grounds for Divorce, 2003, question 2, p. 30. French Report written by Ferrand, Frédérique, and available at www.ceflonline.net/. Accessed 26 October 2010.

ground for divorce, which made the French model of 1975 quite inaccessible from the point of view of a spouse wishing to dissolve the marriage contrary to the other spouse's wishes.[429]

In Germany, the divorce law in force between 1900 and 1938 was based on fault as the only ground for divorce. A court decided which spouse was to blame for the breakdown of the marriage, with consequences primarily in the area of spousal maintenance. The only situation when fault was irrelevant under the German law was when divorce was granted on the ground of mental illness.[430] In 1938, during the Third Reich, a new marriage act was introduced, which allowed divorce, either based on fault grounds, or on the ground of irretrievable breakdown of the marriage for three years without prospects of continuation. In the latter situation, if the spouse to blame for the breakdown of the marriage asked for divorce, the other spouse could contest it. Until the 1970s, divorce was difficult to obtain unilaterally in Germany, as an "innocent" spouse could prevent divorce by contesting it, even after 20 years' separation.[431] In 1976, the divorce law was modernized. The law in force since then is based on the principle of broken marriage as the sole ground for divorce.[432]

In the Netherlands, divorce based on the irretrievable breakdown of a marriage was introduced as the sole ground for divorce in 1971, replacing all grounds previously enumerated in the law. Divorce by consent still does not exist as an autonomous ground for divorce in the Netherlands.[433]

During the second Spanish republic (1931–1939), when the state adopted laws to demonstrate distance toward Catholic values, divorce based on the mutual consent of the spouses was introduced in the Spanish Constitution of 1932. Divorce upon the request of one of the spouses was possible on certain grounds, and legal separation was an alternative way out of a marriage, pursuant to the 1932 Constitution.[434] When Franco took over, however, in line with the Catholic faith, which regards marriage as a sacrament, the divorce regulation of the Republic was abolished. The only "way out" of a marriage which had broken

---

429 See section 4.2.2.2.

430 European Family Law in Action, Volume I: Grounds for Divorce, 2003, question 2, p. 31. German Report written by Martiny, Dieter, and available at www.ceflonline.net/. Accessed 26 October 2010.

431 Erstes Eherechtsreformgesetz of 14 June 1976 (Bundesgesetzblatt Part I, p. 1421), See European Family Law in Action, Volume I: Grounds for Divorce, 2003, question 2, p. 32. German Report written by Martiny, Dieter.

432 European Family Law in Action, Volume I: Grounds for Divorce, 2003, question 2, p. 33. German Report written by Martiny, Dieter. See also The German Civil Code, Sections 1565–1566.

433 European Family Law in Action, Volume I: Grounds for Divorce, 2003, questions 2 and 4, pp. 44 and 89. Dutch Report written by Boele-Woelki, Katharina, Cherednychenko, Olga and Coenraad, Lieke, and available at www.ceflonline.net/. Accessed 26 October 2010.

434 European Family Law in Action, Volume I: Grounds for Divorce, 2003, question 2, pp. 50 f. Spanish Report written by Martín-Casals, Miquel, Ribot, Jordi and Solé, Josep, and available at www.ceflonline.net/. Accessed 26 October 2010.

down was through initiating annulment proceedings, or through a decree on legal separation. All grounds for separation functioned as sanctions for the reprehensible conduct of a spouse, and were only available upon the request of the innocent spouse.[435] Only after the end of the Franco Regime could a secular marriage regulation be adopted in Spain and the development toward achieving equality between men and women and toward making divorce more accessible could begin.[436]

The extensive Swedish "divorce catalogue" in the Marriage Code of 1920, which enumerated the grounds upon which one spouse could be granted divorce without a legal separation, had no equivalence in the other jurisdictions discussed above. Also access to a one year legal separation prior to divorce, based on mutual consent of the spouses, stands out as quite radical in a contemporary European context. However, the divorce regulation in force in Spain during the Second Republic (1931–1939) appears to have been more "progressive" than the Swedish Marriage Code of 1920, by allowing divorce based on mutual consent.

In Spain, a recurring reason for legislating in the field of family law appears to have been a willingness to demonstrate either dissociation from or support for religious values concerning marriage. This was visible during the Second Spanish Republic, when Catholic values were abolished from the law in favor of a secular law. It was also visible when Franco took over, through a renewed focus on the Catholic faith in family values expressed by law. After the Franco regime, once again, the law developed in a secular direction, and legislation has been adopted based on values which are contrary to the values of the Catholic Church, e.g. the same-sex marriage enactment and the enactment enabling (unilateral) "divorce on demand".[437]

In section 7.3.1 it will be suggested that against the background of a totalitarian political regime, adopting laws generally perceived as "progressive" can be a means of reinforcing democracy. Spain was not the only jurisdiction experiencing an authoritarian political regime after World War II. Also recent German legal history is marked by the Third Reich, and the following division of the country into two parts. According to Masha Antokolskaia's interpretation, in legal cooperation with the other Nordic countries, "progressive" marriage regulation has been adopted in Sweden without the incentive of a political revolution for the purpose of breaking with the past, but rather as a result of a gradual development.[438]

---

435 European Family Law in Action, Volume I: Grounds for Divorce, 2003, question 2, p. 51. Spanish Report written by Martín-Casals, Miquel, Ribot, Jordi, Solé, Josep.

436 Comparative reflections on the developments after the 1970s will be provided in section 4.4.2.

437 The Spanish same-sex marriage regulation will be discussed in section 7.3.3. The 2005 divorce reform will be discussed in section 4.4.2.3.

438 Antokolskaia, Masha, Harmonisation of Family Law in Europe, 2006, p. 234. See also section 3.2.2.2.

Another general observation, common to all the jurisdictions discussed here, is that fault was an element in divorce proceedings in all jurisdictions studied until the 1970s, and continues to be of direct or indirect relevance even today in some of them, as well as in many other countries.[439] Although the Swedish divorce reform of 1915 aimed to facilitate access to divorce, fault remained relevant as a ground for divorce with an impact on decisions regarding ancillary matters. For instance, only the "innocent" spouse was entitled to maintenance payments during legal separation and after divorce. Since women were not expected to have gainful employment in Sweden at that time, divorced women depended on spousal maintenance, and the question of who was to blame for the breakdown of the marriage could be decisive for their financial well-being.[440] However, in the Netherlands, according to principles developed in jurisprudence, the judge could decide whether or not to grant maintenance payments, regardless of fault, as long as the person petitioning for divorce was also the applicant in the maintenance claim.[441] The Swedish 1978 enactment dealing with spousal maintenance after divorce, which codified principles established in case law, will be further analyzed from a comparative perspective in section 4.4.2.

---

439 See sections 4.2.2.2 and 4.2.2.3.

440 See section 3.5.3.1 and 3.5.3.2.

441 European Family Law in Action, Volume II: Maintenance between Former Spouses, 2003, question 56, pp. 24 f. Dutch Report written by Boele-Woelki, Katharina, Cherednychenko, Olga and Coenraad, Lieke.

4. TOWARD INCREASED AUTONOMY IN MARRIAGE – THE ENACTMENTS OF THE 1970s AND THE MARRIAGE CODE OF 1987

4.1. LAYING THE FOUNDATION FOR AN ALTERED CONCEPT OF MARRIAGE

4.1.1. THE 1970S – "MODERN" VALUES RELATING TO MARRIAGE GAINING GROUND

In the 1970s, the political idea of achieving equality between men and women became more than just a legally established principle. The principle of equality gained ground also in the everyday customs of the Swedes. Ideas and values relating to marriage, only vaguely discernible in the 1920s, were explicitly expressed through the law, namely in enactments dealing with conclusion and dissolution of marriage and spousal maintenance after divorce. Through the law reforms of the 1970s, the spouses' autonomy in marriage increased, the basic idea being that the spouses were the best judges to decide matters concerning their own personal life, for instance in respect of deciding if their marriage should continue or be dissolved. Through law reform in the 1970s, marriage was enhanced as primarily a matter between the spouses – not primarily as a state or church concern.

Masha Antokolskaia refers to the family law enactments in Europe of the 1960s and 1970s as a "family law revolution" and holds that the "modernization project" initiated during the Enlightenment was completed through this revolution.[442] The result, according to Antokolskaia, was that traditional values gave way to a more pluralistic society, where different family values can co-exist.[443] This "modernization" was allegedly the most far-reaching in Sweden, where comparatively radical enactments dealing with marriage were adopted already in the 1970s, and were reinforced through the Marriage Code of 1987.[444]

---

442 Antokolskaia, Masha, Harmonisation of Family Law in Europe, 2006, pp. 261 and 265.

443 Antokolskaia, Masha, Harmonisation of Family Law in Europe, 2006, p. 261.

444 Antokolskaia, Masha, Harmonisation of Family Law in Europe, 2006, p. 269. Also Mary Ann Glendon has pointed out that Sweden from a comparative perspective has gone quite far when implementing the idea of a "clean break" between the spouses upon divorce. See Glendon, Mary Ann, The Transformation of Family Law, 1989, pp. 224–227.

How "progressive" was the Swedish regulation governing marriage, adopted in the 1970s, in a European context? How and why did the enactments of the 1970s and the Marriage Code of 1987 change the essence of marriage in Sweden?

4.1.2. THE ESTABLISHMENT OF THE SWEDISH WELFARE STATE: 1930–1970

4.1.2.1. The Swedish Social Democratic Party

The Social Democratic Party has played a central role in the above mentioned "modernization project" in Sweden – i.e. in transplanting the family law principles and values coined in the Marriage Code of 1920, into Swedish society. In 1932, the Social Democratic Party won the general election. Deep recession prevailed in Sweden in the 1920s and the unemployment was high. Unemployment figures between 30 and 50 percent have been discussed in the literature in respect of the Swedish labor force, which consisted primarily of farmers,[445] and industrialization has been seen as the main cause.[446]

The Social Democratic Party based its winning election campaign on constructive reform programs to come to terms with the high unemployment figures. The basic political approach to the problem was to provide meaningful jobs and pay market wages. This would be financed by raised taxes and was expected to result in an expansion of the business sector. In other words, more job opportunities would be created which, in turn, would strengthen the Swedish economy in general.[447]

Another focus of the Social Democrats was the importance of reformative social policy efforts in the home, the goal being to create the so-called Folk Home.[448] The term "Folk Home" was used by the leader of the Social Democratic Party, Per Albin Hansson, in 1928, in attempt to describe the prerequisites of a desirable society according to social democratic politics.[449] The connected values

445 Childs, Marquis, Sweden: The Middle Way on Trial, 1980, p. 15.

446 Davidson, Alexander, Two Models of Welfare: the Origins and Development of the Welfare State in Sweden and New Zealand, 1989, p. 92.

447 In 1936, the working hours for rural laborers were regulated in the law, and in 1938 the situation of laborers was further improved by guaranteeing all workers an annual two-week paid vacation. These reforms were financed with higher progressive taxes on income, inheritance and wealth, whereas taxation of corporations was maintained on a low level. See Hadenius, Stig, Swedish Politics during the 20th Century, 1988, p. 39–41.

448 In Swedish: Folkhemmet, as translated by Bäckström, Anders, et al., Religious Change in Northern Europe, 2004. The term "People's Home" is another possible translation. See Hadenius, Stig, Swedish Politics During the 20th Century, 1988, p. 41.

449 Protocol of the Second Chamber, 1928, p. 11. The term originated from nineteenth century bourgeoisie and was reinterpreted and launched again by the Social Democrats. See also Davidson, Alexander, Two Models of Welfare: the Origins and Development of the Welfare State in Sweden and New Zealand, 1989, p. 102.

laid the foundation for the establishment of the welfare society, which, in turn, changed the values and practices relating to marriage.

4.1.2.2. The Folk Home

> "The foundation of the home is community and solidarity. The good home does not know of any privileged or neglected, pets or stepchildren. Here no one looks down upon the other, here no one seeks to gain advantages at the expense of others, and the strong do not oppress and rob the weak. In the good home equality, care, cooperation and helpfulness prevail. Applied to the large Folk and Citizen's Home, this would imply the deconstruction of all social and economical barriers, which now separate the citizens into rich and poor, propertied and poverty-stricken, robbers and robbed."[450]

This quote is a famous section of a political speech delivered in 1928 by the leader of the Swedish Social Democratic Party – Per Albin Hansson. In this speech, the concept of the Folk Home was introduced as a part of the political program of the Social Democrats. The Folk Home was used by the Social Democrats as an umbrella term to describe the Social Democratic Party's political program to create a welfare state, which aimed to improve the living conditions of broad categories of citizens.[451]

The "home" was used as a metaphor for society, the idea being that the family functions as a democratic society in miniature, reflecting the same basic small-scale needs as society as a whole. The family concept intended in this context was the "nuclear" family,[452] with the generally established division of duties between the spouses. In the 1930s, marriage was the preferable cohabitation form and the basis for childrearing. The declining marriage frequency and the increasing number of children born to unmarried parents were seen as caused by the high unemployment.[453]

The Swedish Social Democrats managed to establish the concept of the Folk Home in Swedish society by linking it to nativity, which was a problem in the

---

450 "Hemmets grundval är gemensamheten och samkänslan. Det goda hemmet känner icke till några privilegierade eller tillbakasatta, inga kelgrisar och inga styvbarn. Där ser icke den ene ner på den andre, där försöker ingen skaffa sig fördel på andras bekostnad, den starke trycker icke ned och plundrar den svage. I det goda hemmet råder likhet, omtanke, samarbete, hjälpsamhet. Tillämpat på det stora folk- och medborgarhemmet skulle detta betyda nedbrytandet av alla sociala och ekonomiska skrankor, som nu skilja medborgarna i privilegierade och tillbakasatta, i härskande och beroende, i rika och fattiga, besuttna och utarmade, plundrare och utplundrade." Expressed by Per Albin Hansson, Protocol of the Second Chamber, 1928, p. 11. Author's translation.

451 Hadenius, Stig, Swedish Politics during the 20th Century, 1988, p. 41.

452 The term nuclear family is here used to describe the immediate monogamous family, consisting of husband, wife and their children, as opposed to the previously dominating large farm households consisting of many relatives.

453 Committee Report (SOU 1936:59), pp. 17 f. (figures on children born to unmarried and married parents, respectively) and p. 65.

1930s. In fact, as pointed out by David Bradley, Swedish birth rates in the 1930s were the lowest in all of the developed states.[454] The low nativity in the 1930s accentuated the need of a new social policy in order to come to terms with the problem. The Social Democrats connected the low nativity and the trend toward smaller families to financial insecurity. This problem, the Social Democratic Party claimed, could be solved through their political program, which was based on the idea of the Folk Home.[455] The financial insecurity for families was especially manifest in these times of depression, which contributed to making the Folk Home metaphor appealing to the general public.[456]

4.1.2.3. The Reform Program of the 1930s: Alva and Gunnar Myrdal as Two Key Ideologists

The Social Democrats governed Sweden without interruption between 1930 and 1976, during the establishment of the welfare state. Comprehensive reforms in the field of family law were introduced during this time-period. From this point of view, the ideology of the Social Democrats was a central component of the establishment of the welfare state in Sweden, which, in turn, would provide a basis for the change in respect of values relating to marriage during the decades to come.

Alva and Gunnar Myrdal were two key Social Democratic politicians who have been given much credit for the reformation of society and living conditions in Sweden.[457] In their extremely influential book "Kris i befolkningsfrågan" (Crisis in the Population Issue),[458] they discussed problems relating to the

---

454 Bradley, David, Family Law and Political Culture, 1996, p. 39.

455 According to David Bradley, Different political approaches were considered when explaining this problem. The Conservatives explained the low figures with reference to affluence. The Liberals blamed a long decline accentuated by depression, whereas the small National Group of the Conservative Party produced racist arguments. The Communists viewed the "pronatalist policy" as a means of keeping the armed forces and surplus wages at a cheap price. See Family Law and Political Culture, 1996, p. 39.

456 It has been pointed out that the depression further accentuated a long decline in nativity in Sweden. See Bradley, David, Family Law and Political Culture, 1996, p. 39. Moreover, industrialization and urbanization have been pointed out as key factors to the dropping nativity figures, establishing a new way of life compared to in the rural society. Also, the use of birth-control measures played a role in the context of dropping nativity figures. See Popenoe, David, Disturbing the Nest, 1988, p. 106.

457 Alva Myrdal was one of the most prominent women in Swedish public life at this time and for decades to come. In 1982 she won the Nobel Peace Prize. Her husband, Gunnar Myrdal, was a minister of the social democratic government and a member of the commission on housing, established in 1935.

458 Author's translation. Before this book, the concerns for the shrinking population had been expressed mainly in conservative political circles. In 1910, for instance, the spreading of information on contraceptives was forbidden by the conservatives, in an effort to secure labor in the military sector as well as in agriculture, under the threat of the declining population figures. See Popenoe, David, Disturbing the Nest, 1988, p. 107.

shrinking population, for the purpose of promoting the idea of the Folk Home as a basis for societal reform. In 1934, when the book was published, birth rates in Sweden reached the lowest point ever.[459] The Myrdals proposed a series of reforms, which aimed at encouraging couples to marry and have children by granting them support in various forms.[460] The book of the Myrdals attracted much political attention and influenced the political agenda in the 1930s.[461]

In the 1930s, issues dealing with sexuality and procreation, in relation to married as well as unmarried couples, were of general political interest. A committee report on sexuality was presented in 1936, which analyzed the sexual norms and habits in Sweden, inter alia, for the purpose of coming to terms with the declining nativity figures.[462] Gunnar Myrdal was the chairman of the Population Commission, which was appointed by the government to write the report. The commission was productive. In fact, 18 reports were produced by the commission and its sub-committees between 1935 and 1938.[463]

A dilemma in the context of the problem of dropping nativity figures was that the state, on the one hand, wanted more children, but on the other hand, preferred children born to married parents.[464] In the Committee Report of 1936, it was pointed out that intimate extramarital relationships, based on love and mutual respect, were often a pre-stage to marriage and condemning such relationships was thus not considered fruitful.[465]

During the following decades, although somewhat delayed by World War II, several of the ideas of the Myrdals were adopted by Parliament.[466] The basic political aim was to through legislation promote and favor marriage - not cohabitation without marriage - but at the same time emphasize the spouses' autonomy toward one another.[467] To encourage conclusion of marriage, marriage loans were introduced to young couples who were otherwise financially unable to

---

459 At that time, each Swedish woman bore in average 1.7 children, which were 60 percent fewer children than 50 years earlier. In order to secure the population, it was considered necessary to reach an average birthrate of 2.3 children per woman. See Popenoe, David, Disturbing the Nest, 1988, p. 106.

460 Popenoe, David, Disturbing the Nest, 1988, p. 107.

461 Committee Report (SOU 1938:57), p. 30.

462 Committee Report (SOU 1936:59).

463 Popenoe, David, Disturbing the Nest, 1988, p. 110.

464 Committee Report (SOU 1936:59), p. 65.

465 Committee Report (SOU 1936:59), p. 76.

466 In 1934, rent rebates were provided by the Commission on Housing, for families with children and house loans, as a means of assisting large families. In 1935, the Population Commission was appointed by the Minister of Social Affairs, a commission which, together with its sub-committees, proposed comprehensive reforms, most of which were based on proposals first introduced by the Myrdals in their book "Kris i befolkningsfrågan". See Popenoe, David, Disturbing the Nest, 1988, pp. 107 and 110.

467 Cohabitee relationships were often called: *Stockholm äktenskap* (Stockholm-marriages), named after the capital, since the habit of unmarried cohabitation was widely accepted there. See, for instance, Hirdman, Yvonne, Social Engineering and the Woman Question, 1994, p. 74.

set up a household. The idea was that such loans would raise the marriage rates as well as lower the age of persons marrying for the first time. This would in turn favor the nativity figures. Between 1938 and 1948, 17 percent of the married couples made use of the possibility to receive marriage loans.[468] Moreover, modest maternity bonuses were provided for women with a low family income, and maternity and childbirth services were provided for free.[469] Other enactments concerned the abolition of the act prohibiting advertising of contraceptives,[470] income tax deductions for each child, a guaranteed minimum time of absence in connection with pregnancy and childbirth for female civil servants and a prohibition against firing a female servant because she was pregnant.[471]

4.1.2.4. The Impact of the Welfare Reforms on Values Relating to Marriage

The social welfare reforms in Sweden produced new values concerning marriage and the family. During the twentieth century, Sweden changed from being an agrarian economy, where the whole family performed important work together, to an industrialized economy, where women's work in the home was not looked upon as productive.[472] Women's participation in the labor market was not, however, unproblematic, and *kvinnofrågan* (question of women's rights) became prioritized in Swedish welfare politics.[473] There was a conflict in interests between the need to increase the participation of women in the industrialized society and, at the same time, maintain the home as an important base for the family. The introduction of publically subsidized childcare facilities offered a solution to this problem and made it easier for married women to combine gainful employment with having children.[474]

When women entered the labor market, their financial independence increased, which made it possible for them to focus on their own individual needs. As will be illustrated below, the marriage reforms of the 1970s were characterized by increased autonomy for the individual. For instance, divorce became a realistic option from a financial point of view for women who wished to leave the marriage. In a divorce law reform of 1973, divorce was turned into a personal right for each

---

468 Popenoe, David, Disturbing the Nest, 1988, p. 111, with reference to: Kälvemark, Ann-Sofie, More Children of Better Quality? 1980 p. 69.

469 Committee Report (SOU 1936:15).

470 For more information, see Committee Report (SOU 1936:51). See also Government Bill (Prop 1938:146).

471 Popenoe, David, Disturbing the Nest, 1988, p. 111. See also Committee Report (SOU 1938:13).

472 Committee Report (SOU 1938:57), pp. 38 f.

473 Committee Report (SOU 1947:46). See Myrdal, Alva, Folk och familj, 1944, Chapter 22. See also Hirdman, Yvonne, Att lägga livet till rätta, 1989, p. 14.

474 Hirdman, Yvonne, Social Engineering and the Woman Question, 1994, p. 72. See also Myrdal, Alva, Folk och familj, 1944, pp. 150–152 and Popenoe, David, Disturbing the Nest, 1988, p. 110. Mary Ann Glendon holds that families still perform important services for the state by caring for their members, although this role has changed in the welfare state. See The Transformation of Family Law, 1989, p. 306.

spouse, available, more or less, on demand. This chain of events influenced the division of duties in the family, as women started to work outside the home.

Furthermore, the link between sexuality and procreation weakened in Swedish society, when issues concerning sexuality became generally regarded as a personal matter and an expression of intimacy.[475] Sexual relations were no longer limited to marriage. In fact, already in the Committee Report of 1936, the official policy in respect of sexual relationships without marriage was that such relationships were tolerated, if the couple was in a long-term loving relationship – not if it was a question of casual sexual encounters.[476] This standpoint, most likely, contributed to laying the foundation for the legal recognition of cohabitation without marriage in 1973.[477] Moreover, the social acceptance of sexual relationships outside of marriage, and the view on the sexual act as serving a purpose other than procreation, can be seen as having opened up for social acceptance and the legal recognition of homosexual relationships.[478]

4.2. THE FAMILY LAW ENACTMENTS OF THE 1970S

4.2.1. A "NEUTRAL" APPROACH TO FAMILY LAW MATTERS: THE 1969 GUIDELINES

> "New legislation should [...] be neutral as far as possible with regard to various forms of cohabitation and divergent moral concepts. Marriage has had and should have a central place within family law, but we ought to endeavour to ensure that family law legislation does not include any regulations, which create unnecessary difficulty or inconvenience for those who have children and establish a family without getting married."[479]

The point of departure for the comprehensive law reforms of the 1970s was formulated in the 1969 guidelines to the government, quoted above. In the

---

475 This has been pointed out in: Report of the Church Board, Kyrkostyrelsens skrivelse 2009:6, p. 54. Also access to contraceptives for women contributed to this development.

476 Committee Report (SOU 1936:59), p. 76.

477 The Act on the Joint Dwelling of an Unmarried Couple (Lag om ogifta samboendes gemensamma bostad), which entered into force on 1 January, 1974. This act will be analyzed in section 5.2 and subsections.

478 See chapter 6.

479 "En ny lagstiftning bör [...] så långt som möjligt vara neutral i förhållande till olika samlevnadsformer och olika moraluppfattningar. Äktenskapet har och bör ha en central plats inom familjerätten, men man bör försöka se till att den familjerättsliga lagstiftningen inte innehåller några bestämmelser som skapar onödiga svårigheter eller olägenheter för dem som skaffar sig barn och bildar familj utan att gifta sig." Guidelines by the head of the Ministry of Justice to the Commission on Family Law, 15 August, 1969, Riksdagsberättelsen 1970, Ju 52, p. 81. See Committee Report (SOU 1972:41), p. 58. As translated by Graversen, Jørgen, Family Law as a Reflection of Family Ideology, 1990, p. 79.

commentaries and the legal literature, this quote has formed the basis for the idea of a so-called "neutrality policy" in Swedish family law legislation.[480] The 1969 guidelines were the basis for the comprehensive enactments of the 1970s, aimed to decrease provisions in the marriage regulation which contained moral judgments concerning cohabitation forms. In this spirit, for instance, impediments to marriage were reduced to an absolute minimum and no fault divorce was introduced. The guidelines were also the basis for adopting a special act on unmarried cohabitation. The 1973 Act on the Joint Dwelling of an Unmarried Couple and the impact of neutrality in respect of cohabitation without marriage will be discussed in chapter 5.

In the Government Bill of 1973, the moral impact of legislation was discussed. The point of departure for the enactments dealing with marriage was, in accordance with the guidelines, that legislation should solve practical problems and respect the individuals' right to decide which ethical norms to live by.[481] This was a significant change compared to the earlier political method to favor marriage in the law through different financial subsidies. At the same time taxation law was changed so that spouses were treated as two individuals with their own taxable incomes. According to the old taxation rules, spouses' taxable incomes had been treated as one entity, which could disfavor spouses with a high income and even compel them to divorce and then live together outside of marriage for tax related reasons.[482] This was contrary to the idea of neutrality in cohabitation models.

Furthermore, in the spirit of decreasing the normative features in the marriage legislation, the impediments to marriage were reduced and divorce was made an unconditional legal right.[483] Restrictive divorce rules were believed to have but a marginal effect on the number of dissolutions. Marriage was a voluntary union and the basic idea, expressed in the Government Bill of 1973, was that restrictive divorce rules were incompatible with the notion of marriage as a voluntary union.[484] In the Committee Report, it was pointed out that no one should be forced to stay in a marriage, from which he or she wished to be freed.[485] It can also be mentioned that a clear distinction between marriage and procreation was made through a statute in 1972, permitting transsexuals to marry someone of their opposite assigned sex.[486]

480 Discussions in the legal litterature on the neturality policy and its impact on Swedish family law legislation will be analyzed in sections 4.2.4 and 5.2.3.2.

481 Government Bill (Prop 1973:32), p. 84.

482 Government Bill (Prop 1973:32), pp. 83 f. See also Sundberg, Jacob, Marriage or No Marriage in Swedish Law, 1971, pp. 230 f.

483 These enactments will be discussed in section 5.2.

484 Government Bill (Prop 1973:32), pp. 91 f.

485 Committee Report (SOU 1972:41), p. 187.

486 The Gender Identity Act, Lag (1972:119) om fastställande av könstillhörighet.

The proposals put forth by the Law Commission resulted in enactments, adopted at three stages,[487] namely (1) rules on conclusion and dissolution of marriage in 1973, (2) rules on spousal maintenance in 1978 and, finally, (3) adoption of the Marriage Code of 1987.

4.2.2. THE 1973 ENACTMENTS – CONCLUSION AND DISSOLUTION OF MARRIAGE

4.2.2.1. Minimizing Impediments to Marriage

4.2.2.1.1. Marriage between "Half-Siblings"

An ambition to diminish moral values from the regulation governing marriage is visible in the enactments dealing with impediments to marriage. The basic idea in the 1973 enactment was that the number of impediments should be reduced to a minimum, since impediments could no longer obstruct de facto cohabitation.[488] Only couples who were fundamentally unwanted from society's point of view should be prohibited from marrying each other, because of heavy social (ethical) or medical (genetic) considerations.[489] The impediment for mentally disabled persons to marry – the so-called medical impediment – was abolished in 1973, as well as the impediment for a person to marry his or her niece or nephew. The genetic risk for future offspring in these situations was not considered grave enough to suffice as a reason to prohibit these relatives (or persons with a mental disability diagnosis) from marrying each other.[490]

However, the impediment preventing relatives in the direct descending or ascending line, or brother and sister, from marrying each other was kept in 1973. In respect of "half-siblings" – i.e. siblings with only one biological parent in common – this impediment was made dispensable. Dispensation from the

---

487 It can be mentioned that some rules relating to marriage had already been enacted. In 1956, a commission was appointed for the purpose of revising the Marriage Code, and in 1964 its results were presented in Committee Report (SOU 1964:34–35). The Government Bill was presented in 1968, (Prop 1968:136). For instance, through this reform, the age-limit for conclusion of marriage without parental consent was established at 18 years of age for both men and women. Dispensation from this impediment was possible upon application at the County Administrative Board. Moreover, the regulation of banns was discarded from the law in 1969. As a result, consideration of impediments to marriage alone determined if two persons could or could not marry each other. In the Government Bill of 1973, revising the marriage regulation step by step was considered a good idea, keeping in mind the failure to revise the entire regulation at once in the Committee Report of 1964 and the Government Bill of 1968. See Government Bill (Prop 1973:32), p. 87.

488 Government Bill (Prop 1973:32), p. 68.

489 Government Bill (Prop 1973:32), p. 94.

490 Government Bill (Prop 1973:32), pp. 97 f.

impediment could be granted by the County Administrative Board.[491] The motivation for making marriage between half-siblings a dispensable impediment was based primarily on biology, more precisely on the low genetic risk for the siblings' joint future offspring.[492]

Ethical aspects of allowing half-brothers and sisters to marry each other were discussed in the Government Bill. The basic idea supporting the abolishment of this impediment was that half-siblings usually did not grow up together. As a result, it was held, marriage upon dispensation could be morally justified in some cases.[493] In the Committee Report, the possibility was mentioned that half-siblings who grew up without knowledge of their affinity met as adults, became attracted to each other and began cohabiting and even had children jointly. In such a scenario it was considered justifiable to enable them to marry each other.[494] Consequently, the provision in the Criminal Code which prohibited sexual intercourse between half-siblings had to be abolished.[495]

The Swedish law reform, which made marriages between half-brothers and sisters possible upon dispensation, attracted international attention as an example of the quite radical Swedish political policy of the 1970s aimed to abolish moral judgments from the marriage regulation.[496] Also in Swedish society the reform was much publicized and aroused wide public support, because of a decision by the Court of Appeals in 1967.[497] In the case, two half-siblings, born by the same mother, grew up in different homes, met as adults, fell in love, and were then prosecuted for incest. During the criminal proceedings, a child was born into their relationship. The couple was found guilty of incest, but in the end they were granted a pardon by the government and no sanction was imposed on them. They were thus able to continue living together and raising their child.[498]

In 1971, Jacob Sundberg regarded this case as another example of the general moral decay in Swedish society. Adultery had been decriminalized in 1937, and

491 The Marriage Code, Chapter 2, Section 3. Also marriage between a sibling and the other sibling's offspring was made possible after such dispensation and the impediment prohibiting marriage to a previous sister-, brother- or parent-in-law was abolished. The basic idea was that concern for children of the previous marriage could not be decisive in this context. See Government Bill (Prop 1973:32), p. 99.

492 Government Bill (Prop 1973:32), p. 99.

493 Government Bill (Prop 1973:32), p. 99.

494 Committee Report (SOU 1972:41), p. 138.

495 Chapter 6, Section 5, Paragraph 2 of the Criminal Code.

496 See, for instance, Glendon, Mary Ann, The Transformation of Family Law, State, Law and Family in the United States and Western Europe, The University Chicago Press, 1989, p. 57, Bradley, David, Family Law and Political Culture, 1996, p. 1 and Antokolskaia, Masha, Harmonisation of Family Law in Europe, 2006, pp. 288–290.

497 Decision by the Court of Appeals, 10 October, 1967. See Sundberg, Jacob, Familjerätt i omvandling, 1969, pp. 68 and 81. See also Sundberg, Jacob, Marriage or No Marriage, 1971 p. 231 and Glendon, Mary Ann, The Transformation of Family Law, 1989, p. 57.

498 Sundberg, Jacob, Marriage or No Marriage, 1971 p. 231.

since 1962 bigamy could only result in a fine.[499] The outcome of the 1967 case showed, according to Sundberg, that even incest was losing its social stigma in Sweden.[500] Sundberg believed that the law should be used for the purpose of conducting moral supervision in society, and he was critical toward the legislator's policy based on the 1969 guidelines.[501] According to Sundberg's view, allowing marriages between half-siblings upon dispensation damaged the concept of marriage in the sense that it lost some of its "substance".[502]

It can be noted that changing the prohibition against marriage between half-siblings from an indispensable to a dispensable impediment did not mean that marriage between half-siblings was considered legally acceptable in Sweden. In the Committee Report of 1972, it was pointed out that the fact that the impediment as such was kept in the law was meant to be an official signal to society that sexual relationships between half-siblings, just like between other siblings, were *not* considered morally defendable.[503] Furthermore, an application for dispensation could be rejected by the County Administrative Board, for instance, if the half-siblings had grown up together.

Nevertheless, Sundberg has a point in that reducing the impediments to marriage in 1973, and changing the impediment concerning half-siblings from indispensable to dispensable, had an impact on the essence ("substance") of marriage. Through the reforms of the 1970s, several enactments were passed which contributed to changing the outlook on marriage from focusing on the marital status toward emphasizing the contractual side of marriage, i.e. the individual autonomy of the spouses. It could be claimed that practical reasons for reform were given priority to symbolic and moral reasons. From this point of view, the enactments of the 1970s can be seen as having strengthened the connotations to marriage as a contract, which could be entered into and exited out of more or less freely.

However, the fact that certain impediments to marriage were retained, the prohibition against marriage between half-siblings, for instance, indicates that there was a limit to how far the idea of enhancing marriage as a contract, resembling any contract within the law of obligations, could be extended even in the "progressive" 1970s in Sweden. Marriage retained its characteristic symbolic function to signal official approval of those couples granted access and disapproval of those denied access.[504]

---

499 Sundberg, Jacob, Marriage or No Marriage, 1971, p. 231.
500 Sundberg, Jacob, Marriage or No Marriage, 1971, p. 231.
501 Sundberg, Jacob, Marriage or No Marriage, 1971, p. 231. The 1969 guidelines and critical voices in the legal literature will be further discussed in section 5.2.3.2.
502 Sundberg, Jacob, Familjerätt i omvandling, 1969, p. 81.
503 Committee Report (SOU 1972:41), p. 138.
504 See section 9.2.2.

4.2.2.1.2. Affinity through Adoption

Genetic considerations were also visible in the retained possibility for an adoptive parent to marry his or her adopted child. According to the Marriage Code of 1920, adoption was an indispensable impediment, but it was easy to bypass. Marriage between an adopted child and his or her adoptive parent automatically broke the adoption ties.[505] Marriage between adopted siblings was also possible under the Marriage Code of 1920 and kept in connection with the 1973 reform. In 1973, affinity through adoption was no longer an impediment to marriage, and marriage between an adoptive parent and his or her adopted child broke all adoptive ties. As mentioned above, however, adoption between half-siblings required dispensation from the general impediment of affinity.

In the Committee Report of 1972, a parallel was drawn between, on the one hand, *half-siblings* and, on the other hand, *adopted siblings*. It was pointed out that the same ethical considerations might apply to marriage between siblings through adoption as to marriage between half-siblings. Still, adopted siblings were able to marry each other without a dispensation procedure, whereas half-siblings were restricted by the requirement of a dispensation procedure. For dispensation to be granted, it was normally required that the half-siblings had not lived together while growing up for the dispensation to be granted.[506] Siblings through adoption, who most likely had grown up in the same home, however, were allowed to marry each other without dispensation. This difference appears contradictory and ethically objectionable. In the Committee Report, this inconsistency was found justifiable with reference to biology, more precisely, to the complete absence of a genetic risk for the possible joint future offspring of the two persons affiliated through adoption.[507] The genetic risk for a future offspring was small in respect of half-siblings, which motivated introducing a possibility for them to marry each other, but only upon dispensation. As Mary Ann Glendon puts it: "The area is one where the law seems to be characterized more by vague and somewhat inconsistent notions about legitimacy than by systematic consideration of the purposes of regulation."[508]

The overall impression is that minimizing the impediments to marriage was in compliance with the general development toward regarding marriage as a personal matter, which the state should as far as possible avoid interfering with through provisions containing ethical values. In this spirit, genetic concerns replaced ethical ones, and resulted in what today appears to be an absurd legal situation. An additional factor which contributed to this absurd outcome and motivated reducing the impediments to marriage to an absolute minimum level

---

505 See section 3.4.2.2.

506 Committee Report (SOU 1972:41), p. 138.

507 Committee Report (SOU 1972:41), pp. 138 f. This inconsistency is not discussed in the Government Bill of 1973.

508 Glendon, Mary Ann, The Transformation of Family Law, 1989, p. 57.

was that impediments to marriage could in practice no longer stop couples from living together. As a result, extensive impediments to marriage were ineffective. Furthermore, few impediments and liberal dispensation grounds favored the autonomous feature of marriage. Moreover, as described in chapter 2, extensive impediments to marriage had been a way for the church – the Catholic Church in particular – to take control over sexual morality issues. From this point of view, reducing the impediments to a minimum could be seen as an effort to "free" the marriage regulation from religious values, in favor of a more "secular" concept of marriage.[509]

4.2.2.2. Divorce as a Unilateral Right

Even before the 1973 divorce enactment, Swedish divorce law, with liberal grounds for divorce, was one of the most permissive in Europe.[510] However, the basic idea prior to 1973 still appears to have been that marriage from a legal point of view was concluded for life.[511] In 1973, this perception changed, as divorce was facilitated and emphasized as an individual and unconditional right for each spouse:

> "[...][N]ew rules on dissolution of marriage are founded on the basic idea that conclusion as well as continuation of marriage should be based on the parties' free will to live together, subject to marriage regulation. This means that a spouse's wish to dissolve the marriage should always be respected."[512]

The 1973 enactment dealing with divorce reduced the public intervention in divorce issues to a minimum. An immediate right to divorce was introduced (1) if the spouses were in agreement to divorce and there were no children in the family, (2) if the marriage was entered into by coercion and (3) if either spouse was under the age of 18 when the marriage was concluded and no permission from the authorities had been obtained, or if marriage had been concluded contrary to certain impediments.[513] Divorce was also available to each spouse

---

509 According to David Bradley, secularizing the law was a deliberate political strategy. This will be further discussed in section 4.2.4.2 and 9.2.2.

510 Agell Anders, The Swedish Legislation on Marriage and Cohabitation, a Journey without a Destination, 1980, p. 12. See also Bradley, David, Family Law and Political Culture, 1996, p. 13 and Antokolskaia, Masha, Harmonisation of Family Law in Europe, 2006, p. 315. See also section 3.7.2.1.

511 Committee Report (SOU 1972:41), p. 57. The idea that marriage had served as a life-long union until the reform was expressed in the 1969 guidelines.

512 [...] [N]ya regler för upplösning av äktenskapet bygger på den grundläggande tanken att såväl äktenskapets uppkomst som dess bestånd skall bygga på parternas fria vilja att leva tillsammans under äktenskapets regelsystem. Detta innebär att makes vilja att upplösa äktenskapet alltid skall respekteras." Government Bill (Prop 1973:32), p. 74. Author's translation.

513 The Marriage Code of 1987, Chapter 5, Section 5.

immediately (4) if the spouses had lived apart for at least two years.[514] Access to immediate divorce in situations 2 and 3 replaced previously applicable annulment procedures. The public prosecutor was given the authority to initiate divorce proceedings when it was likely that a marriage had been concluded despite impediments referring to the affinity of the spouses or in case of bigamy.[515] If the spouses had lived apart for two years or more, no reconsideration period was required, even if they had children.[516]

The eradication of fault in Swedish divorce law meant that a party's possible "misconduct" in any respect was made irrelevant for the divorce proceedings. Since then, a spouse's wrongdoing does not influence the property adjustment or custody proceedings. In many jurisdictions, divorce cannot be obtained before the couple has agreed on all legal consequences.[517] In Sweden, however, the couple need not be in agreement about ancillary matters – maintenance or child custody for instance. Divorce can be granted irrespective of disputes about consequences, which can be dealt with in separate proceedings. Furthermore, family counseling replaced mediation as a new optional feature of divorce procedures.[518] Compulsory mediation conflicted with the view of the individuals concerned as capable of dealing with their own situation. Also, forcing couples (in some cases) to participate in mediation was found counterproductive, the obligation per se risking creating a negative attitude, which could result in conflicts between the spouses.[519]

The changes in Swedish society, which laid the foundation for the focus on the individual's needs and rights, have been described in section 4.1.2.4. Turning divorce into a personal right was in compliance with the aim in the preparatory work to eliminate ethical norms and moral values from marriage legislation and to trust the individual spouses as capable to make rational decisions about their marriage.[520] Furthermore, trusting the individual had an economic dimension. By making divorce a right for each spouse, the couple was encouraged to settle practical and economical issues on their own, without involving the courts in time-consuming and costly proceedings. Staying out of court was also thought to reduce conflicts between the spouses, the idea being to avoid a system where

---

514 The Marriage Code of 1987, Chapter 5, Section 4.

515 The Marriage Code of 1987, Chapter 5, Section 5, Paragraph 3. Since 1994, registered partnership is covered by this provision.

516 The Marriage Code of 1987, Chapter 5, Section 4.

517 Boele-Woelki, Katharina, Ferrand, Frédérique, Gonzáles Beilfuss, Cristina, Jänterä-Jareborg, Maarit, Lowe, Nigel, Martiny, Dieter, Pintens, Walter (Editors), Principles of European Family Law, Regarding Divorce and Maintenance Between Former Spouses, 2004. See also section 4.4.2.2.

518 Government Bill (Prop 1973:32), p. 74. In respect of rules on mediation in other European jurisdictions, see European Family Law in Action, Volume I: Grounds for Divorce, 2003, question 17, pp. 225–237.

519 Government Bill (Prop 1973:32), p. 73. See section 3.6.2.2.

520 See section 4.2.1.

lawyers are hired to determine who is to blame for the breakdown of the marriage and how much the guilty party should pay.[521] However, there were and still are limitations to how far the individual could be trusted in this respect. The state still intervened in the individual's private sphere by the requirement in law that a reconsideration period should run out prior to divorce in certain situations, namely if the couple had children, or if only one of them wished to dissolve the marriage.[522]

The official policy not to obstruct dissolution of marriage through restrictive legislation did not mean that the legislator was indifferent as to whether or not couples stayed married. The legislator was still concerned with the increasing divorce figures, which motivated combining the right to divorce with a reconsideration period.[523]

Year	Population	Marriages	Divorces
1960	7 497 967	50 149	8 958
1965	7 772 506	59 963	9 563
1970	8 081 229	43 278	12 943
1975	8 208 442	44 103	25 383
1980	8 317 937	37 569	19 887
1985	8 358 139	38 297	19 763

The declining marriage frequency was also considered problematic. In the Government Bill of 1973, a connection was made between the decreasing number of marriages concluded annually in Sweden and the increasing number of couples cohabiting and having children without being married. It was pointed out that for some unmarried couples the mere risk of having to expose their private life in a future divorce proceeding could be a disincentive to marry in the first place.[524] From this point of view, the 1973 enactment, which turned divorce into a right for each spouse, can be seen as an attempt to come to terms with this problem and encourage unmarried couples to marry. This indicates that although the legislator aimed to avoid expressing moral values concerning desirable cohabitation models, it was still found desirable that couples married. In other words, marriage retained its unique position as the optimal cohabitation model, despite the introduction of divorce as a unilateral right for each spouse.

---

521 Government Bill (Prop 1973:32), p. 89.

522 A period of reconsideration could also be decreed upon the joint application of the spouses. See section 4.2.2.3.

523 See section 4.2.2.3. The figures in the table are from the National Central Bureau of Statistics (SCB), www.scb.se. Accessed 20 September 2010.

524 Government Bill (Prop 1973:32), p. 89.

4.2.2.3. *The Period of Reconsideration – An Ethical Remainder in the Law*

Irrespective of the ambition of the Swedish legislator in the 1970s, to as far as possible abolish moral values from the regulation governing marriage, some clearly value-based provisions were retained in the law. The individual right to divorce has since 1973 one restriction, which still applies today: the requirement of a six-month period of reconsideration in certain situations.[525] A conflict of interests can be identified between, on the one hand, an adult individual's unilateral right to divorce and, on the other hand, the desire to protect children of the family from abrupt decisions to dissolve the marriage. When these interests were balanced the result was to prescribe an obligatory (minimum) six-month reconsideration period, if either spouse lived with a child under the age of 16 and had legal custody of the child. Also "step-children" were included in the provision, the idea being that the emotional ties between these children and their "social parent" could be strong, and that a hasty divorce therefore would risk being detrimental to the children's wellbeing.[526]

A certain level of flexibility applies in respect of the period of reconsideration. There is no prerequisite demanding that the couple live apart during this period. This is a difference compared to the previously applicable rules regarding legal separation, according to which the couple, as a rule, was required live apart during one year prior to the divorce.[527] It can be noted that if the couple has lived apart for two years prior to the divorce application, each spouse has the right to divorce without a reconsideration period.[528] Furthermore, the reconsideration period always applies upon the mutual request of the spouses. In this situation granting the spouses a period of reconsideration is in line with the policy to respect their autonomy as a couple.

---

525 The reconsideration period begins when the application for divorce is handed in to the court, or – when the application is not mutual – in connection with the service of the application for divorce. When the six-month reconsideration period has expired, divorce shall be issued, provided that either spouse makes such a plea. If no plea is made within a year from the first application for divorce, the case is written off. The Marriage Code of 1987, Chapter 5, Section 3 and Chapter 14, Section 14.

526 Government Bill (Prop 1973:32), pp. 111 f.

527 A certain level of flexibility is also visible in case law. See the Court of Appeal, RH 1994:29 and RH 1998:5. According to the first case, it was established that a spouse who at first conceded to divorce had a right to a reconsideration period after a change of heart before the judgment gained legal force. According to the second case, it was established that spouses who, when the reconsideration period had expired, made a plea for divorce but then changed their minds, had the right to continue with the reconsideration period until one year had expired. It can be mentioned that in most cases, the divorce procedure is written, not oral, Chapter 14, Section 12. See also Agell, Anders, Brattström, Margareta, Äktenskap, Samboende, Partnerskap, 2008, p. 45.

528 The Marriage Code of 1987, Chapter 5, Section 4. The Court normally finds information on personal registration showing that the spouses have been listed on different addresses for two years sufficient.

Anders Agell noted an inconsistency in the rules dealing with the reconsideration period and criticized the legislator in this respect. More precisely, according to Agell, it was inconsistent to, on the one hand, promote the abolishment of moral values from the marriage regulation, and, on the other hand, retain a reconsideration period which expresses moral values concerning family stability.[529] Anders Agell has a point. It appears contradictory that the legislator in 1973 found it motivated to prohibit a spouse without children from divorcing for six months, when the general point of departure was that ethical values should be abolished and divorce was, in this spirit, regarded as a unilateral right for each spouse. In the Government Bill of 1973, the obligatory reconsideration period was considered a justifiable restriction of the individual spouse's right to divorce, motivated for the purpose of avoiding hasty divorces, in situations when the consequences of the hasty decision affected somebody else, namely the objecting spouse or the children of the family.[530]

However, based on recent Swedish medical research, it is possible to question if the period of reconsideration does in fact protect the interests of children. This research has indicated that experiencing divorce as a child does not automatically lead to poor mental health as a young adult.[531] The decisive factor in this respect appears to be if the child experienced severe conflicts between the parents.[532] From this point of view, it could be claimed that the reconsideration period, which postpones divorce for at least six months, does not necessarily decrease the conflicts between parents, but on the contrary risks creating more harmful conflicts during the time when the spouses are forced to remain financially and legally connected to each other through marriage.

On the other hand it is possible that the reconsideration period in fact prevents hasty decisions to divorce in some cases, and thus protects the interests of the spouses and the children of the family. In 2010, approximately 12 percent of all divorce applications – requested (1) jointly, (2) by one of the spouses or (3) as a result of children in the family – were written off after a reconsideration period.[533] In 1973, introducing a minimum six-month period of reconsideration, replacing the one year legal separation, was a legislative compromise between the

529 Agell, Anders, the Swedish Legislation on Marriage and Cohabitation, a Journey without a Destination, 1980, p. 43.

530 Government Bill (Prop 1973:32), p. 75.

531 Ängarne-Lindberg, Teresia, Grown-Up Children of Divorce – Experiences and Health, Linköping University Medical Dissertations No. 1173, 2010.

532 Lecture given by docent Michael Gähler, Swedish Institute for Social Research, Stockholm University, at the Uppsala Faculty of Law, 24 April 2008, 6 pm – 8 pm. See also Gähler, Michael, Self-Reported Psychological Well-being among Adult Children of Divorce in Sweden, 1998, pp. 209–225.

533 Unpublished data collected and provided by the National Courts Administration (Domstolsverket).

interests in counteracting divorce and trusting individuals to make rational and carefully considered decisions concerning their marriage.[534]

The reconsideration period can be seen as an ethical remainder in the law, which illustrates that there was a limit to how far the Swedish legislator was ready to go in 1973, in respect of turning marriage law into a private matter with minimal public intervention. The fact that a reconsideration period has been at all retained in Swedish law indicates that the Swedish legislator is not indifferent to whether or not couples stay married and that moral values are still relevant in respect of the marriage regulation. Marriage has a special value and it has not been found desirable to completely turn it into a private matter between the spouses.

It can be questioned if this line of reasoning is still relevant in Sweden in the twenty-first century or if time is ripe to abolish the reconsideration period from Swedish divorce regulation. As pointed out above, abolishing the period of reconsideration can be motivated as being in line with the general legal development toward trusting the individual to make rational decisions. A repeal of the period of reconsideration can also be found to be motivated with reference to the medical research which has indicated that conflicts between parents are harmful to children – not divorce as such. From this point of view, the reconsideration period might perhaps, in some situations, create or increase rather than reduce the conflicts between the spouses.

On the other hand, the period of reconsideration does not prevent divorce; it only postpones it for six months, unless the couple does in fact decide to continue with their marriage during this time-period. As will be illustrated below, Swedish divorce rules are quite "liberal" from a European perspective.[535] Under Swedish law the spouses need not even be in agreement on ancillary matters in order to obtain the divorce decree. Furthermore, the Swedish reconsideration period does not appear to be subject to much debate in the media as "outdated" or contrary to the values in society. Against this background the overall impression is that a six-month period of reconsideration, after which divorce is always granted upon the request of a spouse, is not an unreasonable limitation of the individual's autonomy.

---

534 It can be mentioned that in the Government Bill of 1973, it was pointed out that 25 percent of all cases of legal separation were not followed through. In some cases this was, most likely, because divorce had been obtained on a different ground during the legal separation. Still, it was found likely that for the most part the divorce was not followed through after the legal separation because the spouses had resumed their marriage. See Government Bill (Prop 1973:32), p. 109. (It can be noted that the institution of legal separation was abolished in 1973. See section 3.6.2.1.).

535 See section 4.4.2.

4.2.2.4. *The Marriage Ceremony – Radical Proposals Rejected*

The legislator's limit to how far the "privatization" of marriage could be pushed in the 1970s is also visible in two radical committee proposals concerning the marriage ceremony, which were not endorsed in the 1973 Government Bill. The Committee Report of 1972 contained a proposal to abolish all ceremonial elements of marriage from the Marriage Code – the civil and the religious forms. The idea proposed was to base marriage solely on the couple's mutual, written agreement to marry.[536] All that would be required for the marriage to be legally valid would be notification of a public official with legal capacity to administer and register such agreements.[537] According to the proposal, marriage would be established without any ceremony, whether civil or religious. The registration of the agreement alone would be the constitutive factor for the establishment of a legally valid marriage. However, couples who wanted a ceremony, religious or civil, were free to organize one together with the officiating person in connection with the registration of the agreement.[538] But all such additional religious ceremonial aspects would be totally irrelevant from a *legal* viewpoint.

The government abstained from putting forth a bill in accordance with the proposal, mainly due to contradictions with the UN Convention of 1962 on Consent to Marriage, Minimum Age for Marriage and Registration of Marriages.[539] In particular, the abolishment of the requirement that witnesses be present at the conclusion of marriage would have been contrary to the 1962 Convention, the idea being that witnesses function as guarantors that the marriage is concluded voluntarily.[540]

Another proposal, discussed in the 1972 Report, was to replace the marriage ceremony with a simple oral announcement by the couple at *Folkbokföringen* (the Civil Register), expressing their decision to marry each other. The idea was to simplify conclusion of marriage. Couples who wanted a ceremonial framing of their marriage would be free to combine the registration procedure with a voluntary additional ceremony (without legal effects).[541]

However, the committee itself dismissed this idea as being too complicated, since it was assumed that most couples would still want a church ceremony. It was held that couples should not be required to go through two marriage procedures, a mandatory registration and an optional additional (legally

---

536 Committee Report (SOU 1972:41), p. 10.

537 Committee Report (SOU 1972:41), p. 145.

538 Committee Report (SOU 1972:41), p. 150.

539 United Nations Convention No. 7525, Consent to Marriage, Minimum Age for Marriage and Registration of Marriages. (Konvention angående samtycke till, minimiålder för samt registrering av äktenskap, New York den 10 december 1962 (Sö 1964:29). See Government Bill (Prop 1973:32), p. 103.

540 Government Bill (Prop 1973:32), p. 103.

541 Committee Report (SOU 1972:41), p. 148.

irrelevant) ceremony.[542] Also, it was pointed out that uncertainty as to when the marriage would gain legal force might arise, since couples would not know exactly when the registration of their marriage "contract" took place.[543]

In the end, the existing order with the possibility to choose between a religious and a civil ceremony, both producing a legally valid marriage was retained.[544] This can be seen as further enhancing the autonomous feature of marriage, in the sense that the spouses' freedom to choose between two different ceremonies was preserved.

As a means of encouraging couples who objected to a "ceremonial marriage" to nevertheless find it appealing to conclude a marriage, a shorter version of the civil marriage ceremony was introduced in 1973. According to this simplified civil ceremony, the marriage official simply asked the couple, in the presence of two witnesses, if they wished to marry one another. The words spoken during the marriage ceremonies – the religious and the civil – will be analyzed and compared in section 6.6.1. The rejection of the proposals to abolish the marriage ceremony indicates that there was a limit as to what extent marriage could be "informalized". In other words, the retention of the institution of marriage, to be concluded in a special ceremonial form, was still found to be motivated in Sweden in 1973.

4.2.3. THE 1978 ENACTMENT – SPOUSAL MAINTENANCE

4.2.3.1. Maintenance after Divorce[545]

The maintenance enactment of 1978, applicable after divorce, clearly illustrates the new outlook on the spouses as two capable and independent individuals. A guiding principle in the 1978 reform was that the legal effects of marriage should end when the marriage ended.[546] This principle was laid down in 1978, in a specific provision in the Marriage Code: "Following a divorce, each spouse shall

542 Committee Report (SOU 1972:41), pp. 148 f.

543 Committee Report (SOU 1972:41), p. 149.

544 In the Marriage Code of 1987, Chapter 4, Section 1, the prerequisites for the conclusion of a valid marriage ceremony are laid down: "Marriage is concluded through a marriage ceremony in the presence of relatives or other witnesses." Author's translation.

545 Provisions on maintenance deal with, on the one hand, maintenance toward children and, on the other hand, maintenance toward a spouse or a former spouse. Provisions dealing with children are placed in *Föräldrabalken* (the Code on Parents and Children) and will not be dealt with here.

546 Government Bill (Prop 1978/79:12), p. 139. From a comparative European perspective, this is not the predominating view. See European Family Law in Action, Volume II, Maintenance Between Former Spouses, 2003. In Germany a widely accepted principle in case law is that of lasting post-divorce solidarity of the spouses, p. 46. German Report written by Martiny, Dieter.

be responsible for his or her own support."[547] Husband and wife were to be treated as two equals, each responsible for his or her own material well-being.

Granting maintenance for any period following a divorce is a rare exception to this rule. Exceptions were, however, found to be motivated for the purpose of protecting women in situations when there was a need of maintenance, created as a result of the marriage, and the other spouse had the financial ability to pay.[548] As pointed out in the Government Bill of 1973, only 25 percent of all married women were financially independent. This was, inter alia, explained with reference to a combination of insufficient availability of childcare and a general lack of job opportunities.[549] It was also pointed out in the bill that it was common that one spouse, usually the wife, had a much weaker financial situation than the other spouse. Often the wife had contributed to making the husband's career possible, by working in the home and caring for the children instead of making a career of her own. In these situations maintenance payments could be motivated, primarily during a transitional period following the divorce. Payments during a longer period could also be awarded in exceptional situations when only one of the spouses had worked outside the home, and it was found unlikely that the other spouse would be able to provide financially for himself or herself after divorce.[550]

It can be noted that already before the 1978 enactment, the courts were restrictive when it came to awarding maintenance after divorce.[551] In other words, the 1978 enactment merely laid down principles in the statutory law, which had previously been established in case law. Giving these principles statutory support was, nevertheless, significant and further underlined the idea of marriage as a voluntary union which each spouse could freely leave. The maintenance regulation after divorce also illustrated a limit to the trust placed in the two adult individuals to freely decide matters concerning their finances, due to the fact that husband and wife were not in practice two equals from an economic point of view. As a result, financial independence after divorce was made the guiding principle, which signaled to society that this was the desirable goal for spouses to strive for, but that spousal maintenance could still be awarded in certain situations to protect a spouse who had worked in the home. In other words, the community of the spouses during marriage could still continue to have repercussions if their community ended.[552]

---

547 "Efter äktenskapsskillnad svarar varje make för sin försörjning." As translated by the Swedish Ministry of Justice, 1995. The Marriage Code of 1987, Chapter 6, Section 7.

548 Government Bill (Prop 1978/79:12), p. 138.

549 Government Bill (Prop 1973:32), pp. 66 f.

550 Government Bill (Prop 1978/79:12), pp. 138 f.

551 Government Bill (Prop 1978/79:12), pp. 138, 189, 140.

552 See Ryrstedt, Eva, Bodelning och bostad, 1998, p. 49.

4.2.3.2. Maintenance during Marriage

The restrictive view on maintenance after divorce does not apply to the spouses' financial obligations toward one another *during* marriage. On the contrary, during marriage, the community of the spouses is central and they are expected to share expenses. The guiding principle is that spouses should be entitled to the same standard of living. In the Marriage Code of 1987, Chapter 6, Section 1 it is laid down that: "Spouses shall, each according to his or her ability, contribute to the maintenance needed to meet their joint and personal needs."[553] The obligation to contribute financially during marriage can be fulfilled with money or domestic work.[554] This principle was introduced in the Marriage Code of 1920, where the possibility to contribute through household work was explicitly mentioned, and of considerable practical and symbolic relevance, in contrast to the old patriarchal rules with the husband as the legal guardian of his wife.[555]

In 1978, however, although the principle remained the same, household work was no longer mentioned in the provision. In the Government Bill of 1978, it was found inappropriate to comment on division of duties in the law, the point of departure being that: "[...] the regulation in the Marriage Code shall clearly be based on the idea of equality between men and women, which shall prevail in the home as well as in professional life."[556] This outlook was in line with the policy that women should not be encouraged to work in the home. On the contrary they should be gainfully employed and financially independent.[557]

In the Committee Report of 1977, it was discussed whether it was motivated to keep the provision dealing with maintenance *during* marriage.[558] The maintenance regulation applicable during marriage – as well as in case of divorce – it was argued, could be contrary to the basic idea of the spouses as two financially independent persons. Moreover, maintenance regulation during marriage could be seen as contrary to the basic principle that each spouse is economically independent during marriage, entitled to administer his or her own property and responsible for his or her own debts.[559] Furthermore, the practical need of a provision enabling the court to oblige a spouse to support the

---

553 "Makarna skall, var och en efter sin förmåga, bidra till det underhåll som behövs för att deras gemensamma och personliga behov skall tillgodoses." As translated by the Swedish Ministry of Justice, 1995. This principle applies also during a reconsideration period.

554 Committee Report (SOU 1977:37), p. 102.

555 The Marriage Code of 1920, Chapter 5, Section 2. See also Ryrstedt, Eva, Bodelning och bostad, 1998, p. 42.

556 [...] regleringen i GB [bör] klart bygga på den jämställdhet mellan män och kvinnor som bör råda både i hemmet och i förvärvslivet. Government Bill (Prop 1978/79:12), p. 136. Author's translation.

557 See sections 4.1.2.3–4.1.2.4, for a discussion, inter alia, on the changing values concerning women's gainful employment.

558 Committee Report (SOU 1977:37), p. 106. See also Government Bill (Prop 1978/79:12), p. 135.

559 The Marriage Code, Chapter 1, Section 3. Author's translation.

other spouse during marriage was questioned, considering that court proceedings in this situation were uncommon.[560]

In the end, however, the regulation was retained. The provision stating that husband and wife were entitled to the same standard of living was not considered contrary to the political aim to work for increased equality through promoting economic independency of the spouses also during marriage.[561] Another reason given in the Government Bill for keeping the provision was that lawyers and family counselors considered them to be useful guidelines and tools to avoid court proceedings. The very mention of a spouse's possibility to initiate court proceedings and demand maintenance payments during marriage, it was held, could be a deterrent from initiating and going through with court proceedings in matters dealing with the spouse's economy in general.[562]

The maintenance regulation applicable during marriage and upon divorce can be seen as containing conflicting aims.[563] During marriage, the community and solidarity of the spouses are emphasized through the maintenance regulation. The spouses are entitled to the same standard of living, and different forms of contributions are considered equally important to the family's well-being, i.e. contributions through gainful employment and through unpaid work in the home. The community of the spouses is also reflected in the symbolic provision on faithfulness, which after some deliberations in the Government Bill of 1973 was kept for symbolic reasons. According to this provision "Spouses shall show faithfulness to and consideration of one another. They shall jointly take care of their home and children and in consultation promote the best interest of the family."[564]

Whereas the idea of marriage as a community between the spouses predominates in the rules on maintenance during marriage, the individual spouse is the main focus of the maintenance regulation when the marital union has broken down and there is no family community left to preserve, i.e. after divorce. Against this background, the maintenance regulation applicable during marriage appears to be a deviation from the general aim to avoid moral input by the legislator in spouses' personal matters. It expresses a concern for the family unit based on marriage, which suggests that the legislator, irrespective of its practical argumentation in general in respect of marriage law, was still interested in preserving marriage as a relevant cohabitation model in Swedish society.

560 Government Bill (Prop 1978/79:12), p. 135.
561 Government Bill (Prop 1978/79:12), p. 135.
562 Government Bill (Prop 1978/79:12), p. 135.
563 See Ryrstedt, Eva, Bodelning och bostad, 1998, pp. 41–48.
564 "Makar skall visa varandra trohet och hänsyn. De skall gemensamt vårda hem och barn och i samråd verka för familjens bästa." The Marriage Code of 1987, Chapter 1, Section 2. As translated by the Swedish Ministry of Justice, 1995. See section 4.3.3.

4.2.3.3. *The Maintenance Regulation – Summarizing Reflections*

The maintenance regulation applicable *after divorce* illustrates the changes in respect of gender roles that had taken place in Sweden between the 1920s and the 1970s. In the 1970s, the housewife was no longer the preferable "societal norm" to be protected through the marriage regulation. Nevertheless, in practice, a traditional division of duties still existed in many families, which justified maintaining certain protective provisions – maintenance provisions for instance. The spousal maintenance regulation after divorce is the result of balancing two contradictory interests, on the one hand, the basic idea that all legal effects of marriage should end through divorce when a community of interests no longer exists between the (former) spouses and, on the other hand, the practical need of protecting and reimbursing a financially weaker party, often the woman. The contractual function of marriage, based on the individual's autonomy, has been prioritized as the guiding principle in the rules on spousal maintenance after divorce, and maintenance is only exceptionally available in this situation.

As pointed out by Eva Ryrstedt, the basic idea concerning maintenance *during marriage* has remained in principle the same since the Marriage Code of 1920 was enacted, irrespective of the major changes that have taken place in Swedish society, particularly in respect of women's gainful employment.[565] During marriage, the idea of marriage as a mutual project – a joint enterprise – is reflected and protected in the maintenance regulation. The principle of marriage as a joint enterprise, ventured into jointly by two autonomous individuals, has even motivated retaining in the legislation a possibility for a spouse to turn to court and demand maintenance payments during marriage, if the other spouse failed to provide it, the idea being that spouses are entitled to live on the same financial standard during marriage. Upon divorce, on the contrary, the contractual function of marriage is prioritized in the law and the economic independency of the spouses is placed in the forefront.

The opposing outlooks on the spouses' financial obligations toward each other *during marriage* and *after divorce* have been considered problematic in the literature. Eva Ryrstedt has argued that the right to maintenance *during marriage* has to a certain extent made the basic idea that each individual spouse owns his or her property (albeit restrained by a latent claim upon dissolution according to the default system) ineffective.[566] In other words, the contradiction lies in the fact that protecting the community of the spouses has remained the guiding principle during marriage, but the contractual and individualized view on marriage has been added and applies upon divorce. Against this background, Ryrstedt has suggested that it would be adequate to slightly increase a spouse's right to receive maintenance payments *after divorce*, during a transitional

565 Ryrstedt, Eva, Bodelning och bostad, 1998, p. 48.
566 Ryrstedt, Eva, Bodelning och bostad, 1998, pp. 48 and 401 f.

period.[567] Through such a system, according to Ryrstedt, the community which has existed between the spouses during marriage would be dissolved more gradually, and more accurately take into account the spouses' community and conditions of life during marriage. This line of reasoning is based on the assumption that if a spouse needs maintenance payments after divorce, this is most likely the result of the spouses division of duties – and their community in interests – during the marriage.[568] Slightly increasing a spouse's possibility to receive maintenance payments after divorce could be seen as a means of "honoring" the community of the spouses during marriage (for a transitional period) and thus, in a sense, protect the symbolic value of marriage as something more than a revocable contract.[569]

In chapter 9, it will be claimed that the institution of marriage has a special symbolic dimension which has contributed to retaining its position as a relevant cohabitation model in Sweden. It will also be claimed that marriage, partly because of this symbolic dimension, remains useful as a legal institution in Sweden.[570] However, protecting the symbolic dimension of marriage does not necessarily mean that legal rules which extend the community of the couple to life after divorce are desirable. Furthermore, increasing the possibility for a spouse to receive maintenance payments after divorce might not be in line with the predominating values in society and the principle of equality between men and women. In respect of maintenance after divorce, the interest of achieving equality between men and women through promoting financial independence of the spouses, in my opinion outweighs the interest of honoring the community that the spouses had during marriage. Furthermore, the idea of divorce as a unilateral right, which appears to be well-established in Swedish society, is in line with the basic idea that all legal effects of marriage should end upon divorce. The complex question whether or not the Swedish rules on spousal maintenance after divorce are too restrictive will be further analyzed from a comparative perspective in section 4.4.2.4.

567 Ryrstedt also mentions the possibility of combing this with rules resembling the Norwegian rules on *återgångsdelning*. According to these rules, spouses would be able to keep property which each of them had brought into the marriage, or acquired during marriage through a gift or a will from a third party, out of the property division upon divorce. In this way the property subject to division would be the property more directly acquired during the marriage and (perhaps) because of the marriage. See Ryrstedt, Eva, Bodelning och bostad, 1998, p. 402. This will not be further discussed here.

568 Ryrstedt, Eva, Bodelning och bostad, 1998, p. 402.

569 See section 9.2.

570 See sections 9.2, 9.3 and 9.4.

4.2.4. THE REFORMS OF THE 1970S – DISCUSSIONS OF LEGAL POLICY

4.2.4.1. *The Impact of Neutrality on the Swedish Legal Development*

The enactments accounted for above laid the foundation for the "modern" concept of marriage, based on the 1969 guidelines to the 1972 committee. The possible impact of "neutrality", as expressed in the 1969 guidelines, on the Swedish legal development concerning marriage has been subject to discussion in the legal literature. Anders Agell emphasized the damage that he believed the neutrality policy caused family stability in Sweden.[571] Agell was of the opinion that marriage had lost most of its ideological and religious meaning in Swedish society in 1973 and could even be claimed to constitute a revocable contract. Against this background, Agell argued, openly promoting marriage should not have been controversial in Sweden.[572] Instead, however, the neutrality policy based on the 1969 guidelines contributed to the decline of marriage rates and to the decrease of the significance of the institution of marriage in Sweden.[573] Also Jacob Sundberg criticized the 1969 guidelines for contributing to "the disappearance of a positive interest in marriage as an institution."[574] He noted that marriage had been turned into a civil contract, which could be entered into and dissolved by contract, and criticized the permissive attitude toward divorce in connection with the 1973 enactment.[575]

The idea of a neutrality policy as a decisive component of Swedish family law developments during the last three decades has gained an international hearing, inter alia, because of the contributions from the legal literature referred to above.[576] In Masha Antokolskaia's interpretation, the Swedish marriage enactments in the 1970s, as well as the rejected proposals for reform discussed above, by breaking with the traditional values connected to marriage, reflect an

---

571 Agell, Anders, Should and Can Family Law Influence Social Behaviour? 1998, pp. 126 f. The neutrality policy is thoroughly analyzed by Anders Agell in: Agell, Anders, Samboende utan äktenskap, 1985, pp. 84–113.

572 See Agell, Anders, the Swedish Legislation on Marriage and Cohabitation, a Journey without a Destination, Scandinavian Studies in Law, 1980, pp. 13 and 35–37.

573 Agell, Anders, The Swedish Legislation on Marriage and Cohabitation, a Journey without a Destination, 1980, pp. 35 f. For a discussion of marriage as a status based contract, see also Agell, Anders, Äktenskapets giltighet – en civilrättslig och en förvaltningsrättslig fråga, 2002, pp. 21–39.

574 Jacob Sundberg, as quoted by Glendon, Mary Ann, Comparative Law as Shock Treatment: A Tribute to Jacob W.F. Sundberg, 1993, p. 69.

575 Sundberg, Jacob, Marriage or No Marriage in Swedish Law, 1971, pp. 234. See also Glendon, Mary Ann, Comparative Law as Shock Treatment: A Tribute to Jacob W.F. Sundberg, 1993, p. 69.

576 See, for instance, Antokolskaia, Masha, Harmonisation of Family Law in Europe, 2006, p. 289.

"ideological pluralism".[577] Antokolskaia has a point. It appears reasonable to assume that the enactments of the 1970s, based on the policy to as far as possible avoid expressing moral values in respect of cohabitation models in family law legislation, laid the basis for legally recognizing other cohabitation models in the future, i.e. cohabitation without marriage and registered partnership. In other words, by moving away from the traditional notion of regarding the institution of marriage as the superior cohabitation model, favored in the law through special public state benefits, it was possible to reflect diversity in moral values through the law. However, in 1973, the level of diversity reflected in the marriage regulation was still limited. Marriage was still the only legally recognized cohabitation model, although a certain minimum level of legal protection was provided for unmarried different-sex couples.

According to David Bradley, it is primarily one ideology that shines through in the 1969 guidelines and the enactments they gave rise to, namely the political ideology of the Swedish Social Democratic Party.[578] Also Jacob Sundberg made a connection between the social and legal acceptance of unmarried cohabitees in Sweden and what he regarded as the prevailing "socialist ideology".[579] According to Bradley, the Swedish law reforms dealing with marriage in the 1970s were part of an "ideologically motivated program."[580] This program, Bradley argued, centered on an "egalitarian agenda" formulated by the Swedish Social Democrats in the late 1960s.[581] In this ideological program, improving equality between men and women was a central feature and "social engineering" – in the sense of actively attempting to change attitudes and behavior through legislation – was the means used to achieve this goal.[582] In other words, the policy was to use an interventionist approach in family matters to change traditional gender roles and connected attitudes in society.[583]

Social engineering in Sweden, according to Bradley, had been used already during the establishment of the Swedish welfare state, and would continue to be employed, for instance, to achieve a legal and following societal recognition of same-sex couples in the 1990s.[584] In fact, in the 1930s the Social Democratic politicians who were dedicated to reforming Swedish society in the field of the family, with Alva and Gunnar Myrdal at the cutting edge, called themselves *sociala ingenjörer* (social engineers).[585] It can be noted that the term "social engineers" was by no means a Swedish invention. It was an internationally

577 Antokolskaia, Masha, Harmonisation of Family Law in Europe, 2006, p. 288.
578 Bradley, David, Family Law and Political Culture, 1996, p. 264.
579 Sundberg, Jacob, Marriage or No Marriage in Swedish Law, 1971, pp. 230 f.
580 Bradley, David, Family Law and Political Culture, 1996, p. 264.
581 Bradley, David, Family Law and Political Culture, 1996, pp. 264 f.
582 Bradley, David, Family Law and Political Culture, 1996, pp. 264 f.
583 Bradley, David, Family Law and Political Culture, 1996, p. 2.
584 Bradley, David, Family Law and Political Culture, 1996, p. 2. Registered partnership will be discussed in chapter 6.
585 Myrdal, Alva and Gunnar, Kris i befolkningsfrågan,, 1935, p. 335.

established term used to describe societal reform, elaborated by the American legal scholar Roscoe Pound in the 1930s.[586]

It could be argued that David Bradley is reading too much into the 1969 guidelines and their impact on the legal development in Sweden. Even if the guidelines did in fact express the political "egalitarian agenda" of the Social Democratic Party, most of the ideas, such as the enforcement of a far-reaching neutrality policy, were rejected already in the Committee Report of 1972.[587] The political interest in equality – between men and women and between same-sex and different-sex couples – was not necessarily linked to the guidelines, but could have arisen anyhow, and have done so in many countries, as expressions of human rights based inter alia on the idea of non-discrimination, or simply as a response to practical needs in society. After all, many jurisdictions legally recognize the rights of unmarried couples and same-sex couples without speaking in terms of "neutrality".

It could be that the head of the Swedish government's justice department, by speaking in terms of neutrality in the 1969 guidelines to the Commission, merely sought to justify a progressive law reform, which had become necessary in Sweden, as a result of changing values in society concerning extramarital sexual relations. Furthermore, the welfare state had already laid the foundation for focusing on the principle of equality. From this point of view, a "neutral" approach to cohabitation models might have been a political justification for giving societal values and habits statutory support.[588] Bradley has a point that the focus on equal rights is especially manifest in the Swedish legal development, as a motivation for reform. Swedish politics have shown an ideological sensitivity toward different forms of unequal treatment, between men and women as well as between different-sex and same-sex couples. However, these questions are not limited to the political agenda of the Social Democratic Party, but prioritized issues by most political parties in Parliament.

Furthermore, the political interest in creating gender equality is not necessarily a purely ideological political vision to create a more fair and just society. There is also an economic side to gender equality, which might have created a political incentive to facilitate women's access to the labor market. If the spouses are both gainfully employed during marriage, the risk of one of them becoming a financial burden on society after divorce diminishes. Through the 1978 enactment, as well as according to guiding principles developed in case law before then, spousal maintenance after divorce is a rare exception to the rule that each spouse shall provide for his or her own support after divorce.[589] Without a political focus on gender equality, however, this would have risked becoming an

586 Friedmann, Wolfgang, Legal Theory, 1967, p. 336–344.
587 Committee Report (SOU 1972:41), p. 93.
588 See section 4.1.2.4.
589 See section 4.2.3.1.

expensive policy for the welfare state; a policy which divorced persons without means of providing for themselves financially would have turned to for economic support. Thus there is a connection between gender-equality and economics. Encouraging women to have gainful employment was motivated not only from an ideological perspective in the construction of a "just" society, but also for practical and economic reasons.

4.2.4.2. Abolishing Religious Values and Creating a Secular System: A Deliberate Political Agenda?

Was diminishing the impact of religion and religious values in the marriage regulation a deliberate political aim in Sweden in the 1970s? According to David Bradley, a central goal of the Social Democrats' ideological agenda has been to abolish moral values deriving from religion from Swedish marriage regulation and to strengthen marriage as a secular concept. Through the 1973 reform, Bradley has argued, a step in this direction was accomplished by abolishing certain restrictions on marital capacity and the rules on annulment of marriage.[590] Also Folke Schmidt has pointed out that the institution of "legal separation" appears to be a remnant of religious (Lutheran) values reflected in the law.[591] It can be questioned if the Swedish policy, based on the 1969 guidelines to the 1972 committee, to avoid moral values in marriage legislation in respect of couples' private life, focused especially on abolishing *religious* values for the purpose of turning marriage into a secular institution.

If the motivations for reform in the preparatory work are studied, secularizing Swedish marriage regulation does not appear to have been a deliberate strategy in the 1970s. Marriage annulment was abolished because it was rarely used, and the impediments to marriage were all reduced to a minimum, inter alia because the impediments no longer prevented de facto cohabitation.[592] Furthermore, the religious marriage ceremony was retained in the law as an option to the civil ceremony in 1973. If there was a political "agenda" to secularize marriage in the 1970s, as alleged by Bradley, it still remains rather "hidden".

As pointed out by Maarit Jänterä-Jareborg, the term "secularism" can mean different things. It can mean (1) that functions previously handled by the church are taken over by secular bodies in society. It can also mean (2) that participation of the public in church activities is low and it can mean (3) that religion is kept out of the public arena, more precisely, that religion is turned into a private and personal matter for the individual.[593] Sweden is largely secular in the first two

---

590 Bradley, David, A Family Law for Europe? Perspectives for the Unification and Harmonisation of Family Law in Europe, 2003, p. 65. See chapter 2.

591 Schmidt, Folke, The Prospective Law of Marriage, 1971, p. 198. However, it is not clear if this was the case.

592 Committee Report (SOU 1972:41), pp. 127, 163.

593 Jänterä-Jareborg, Maarit, Religion and the Secular State, 2010, p. 673.

senses, and the 1973 reforms contributed to secularizing Swedish marriage law in these respects, but the third sense of secularism is more complicated.[594]

It can be argued that the reforms of the 1970s "secularized" Sweden in the third sense referred to above. In other words, religion and religious values, underlying any legal situations, were treated in the same manner as moral values in general, namely as private matters. Thus it was not a question of politicians setting out to eradicate religion from marriage law, but of launching a new outlook on the relationship between the public (including the Church of Sweden, which was then the state church) and the individual, based on trust in the individual's ability to make the (right) decisions. In chapter 9 it will be argued that marriage cannot be completely free from moral values. As long as marriage is retained as an institution which socially sanctions certain relationships by granting them access to the marriage regulation, and signals disapproval of others by preventing marriage in accordance with the impediments to marriage, moral judgments are made about who qualifies for serving the purpose of marriage in society. In chapter 9, it will be suggested that such moral judgments are not based solely on legal considerations. It is possible that the historically dominating position of religion in respect of determining moral issues relating to marriage have continued to influence our understanding of marriage in Sweden in the twenty-first century.

4.3. THE MARRIAGE CODE OF 1987

4.3.1. THE DEFINITION OF MARRIAGE

The Marriage Code of 1987 entered into force on 1 January 1988, largely as a compilation of earlier enactments. The most significant and "radical" novelties regarding marriage had been introduced in the 1973 enactment. Nevertheless, the Marriage Code of 1987 contained a few novelties. A structural innovation in the Marriage Code of 1987 was that five fundamental principles dealing with marriage were collected and laid down in the first introductory chapter, in different sections (§). Thus marriage was characterized as a union between a man and a woman (1§), built on faithfulness and joint responsibilities (2§), where each spouse administrates his or her property and is individually responsible for any debts (3§). Moreover, marriage presupposes that the spouses divide duties among themselves and keep each other informed about financial matters (4§). Finally, marriage is dissolved through death or divorce (5§). In the Government Bill it was stated that these provisions were placed in the first introductory chapter for the purpose of defining and clarifying the concept of marriage.[595] One could say

594 Jänterä-Jareborg, Maarit, Religion and the Secular State, 2010, p. 673.
595 Government Bill (Prop 1986/87:1), p. 112.

that these principles as a whole demonstrated what values were considered to be decisive for the essence of marriage in 1987, in the sense that the principles illustrated what characterized the institution of marriage.

4.3.2. THE DEFERRED COMMUNITY OF PROPERTY REGIME: NOVELTIES

The deferred community of property regime, adopted in 1920, was kept in the Marriage Code of 1987.[596] However, certain adjustments and clarifications were made for the purpose of achieving a more equal and just division of property upon divorce.[597] The possibility to modify an unjust economic outcome of a division of property was extended, for the purpose of favoring the interests of the spouse owning most of the marital property, especially in case of marriages of short duration.[598] Furthermore, the rules compensating a spouse financially for the other spouse's dispositions to decrease the value of the marital property were simplified from a technical point of view, and a one-year time-limit was introduced in this respect.[599] Moreover, the possibility for the spouse with the greatest need to take over the joint dwelling was modified to encompass not only such a dwelling which constituted marital property, but also a dwelling which was private property pursuant to a contract on property relations.[600] The requirement that a spouse taking over a dwelling should financially compensate the other spouse was kept.[601]

Through the 1987 Code, the institution of *boskillnad* (separation of estate) – according to which the spouses could turn to court and demand that all their property was to be their private property – was replaced by a possibility for them to jointly apply for division of property during marriage.[602] Increasing the autonomy of the couple in this respect was in line with the general aim of the 1973 law reform, i.e. to enhance marriage as a private matter between the two individuals concerned and to minimize public interference. The spouses should as far as possible be trusted to make their own financial decisions.[603] Also,

---

596 See section 3.5.2.

597 Government Bill (Prop 1986/87:1), p. 1.

598 This possibility replaced the previous possibility to hold a spouse financially liable for neglecting to take proper care of the matrimonial property. Government Bill (Prop 1986/87:1), p. 49. Furthermore, it can be mentioned that the formal requirement of a written agreement in form of a marital property contract for the validity of gifts between spouses was abolished, although the registration requirement in respect of a gift was maintained, in order to achieve protection against the spouse's creditors.

599 Government Bill (Prop 1986/87:1), pp. 48–51.

600 The Marriage Code of 1987, Chapter 11, Section 8.

601 Government Bill (Prop 1986/87:1), p. 2. See also the 1987 Code, Chapter 11, Section 8.

602 Government Bill (Prop 1986/87:1), pp. 52 f. See also section 3.5.2.

603 See sections 4.2.1 and 4.2.2.

enhancing the spouses' autonomy to make decisions concerning their property by laying down in the statutory law their right to deviate from the deferred community of property regime in the 1987 Marriage Code was in line with the changes that had taken place in Swedish society since the 1920 Marriage Code was adopted.[604] In 1920, when the deferred community of property regime was first introduced, women worked in the home and men were gainfully active. In 1987, however, as a rule, women had a financial income of their own and the law could thus to a greater extent open up for allowing husband and wife to make their own financial decisions as two equals.

4.3.3. FAITHFULNESS AND THE SPOUSES' JOINT RESPONSIBILITIES: "UPGRADED" TO CHAPTER 1

Keeping in mind that the basic idea was to abolish ethical values from the marriage regulation, it is noteworthy that the provision of faithfulness was kept in the Marriage Code of 1987:

> "Spouses shall show faithfulness and consideration for one another. They shall jointly take care of their home and children and in consultation promote the best interest of the family."[605]

Prior to the introduction of no-fault divorce, disloyal behavior, adultery for instance, could have an impact on ancillary matters such as child custody disputes.[606] Since 1973, however, the provision of faithfulness is a normative guideline without any legal implications or sanctions attached. It expresses, on the one hand, the obligation of faithfulness and, on the other hand, the emphasis on equality between men and women, through the request that they jointly care for the home and the children.[607]

The provision on faithfulness was subject to much debate in the 1970s. In the Committee Report of 1972, abolishing the provision was advocated. Upholding the obligation of faithfulness in the law was considered outdated and risked deterring couples – especially young couples – from marrying.[608] In the Government Bill of 1973, however, the provision was kept, since it was thought to be valuable for protecting the solidarity in marriage.[609] The fact that this

604 The Marriage Code of 1987, Chapter 10, Section 4.

605 "Makar skall visa varandra trohet och hänsyn. De skall gemensamt vårda hem och barn och i samråd verka för familjens bästa." The Marriage Code of 1987, Chapter 1, Section 2. As translated by the Swedish Ministry of Justice, 1995.

606 Government Bill (Prop 1973:32), p. 86.

607 Government Bill (Prop 1973:32), pp. 66 f.

608 Committee Report (SOU 1972:41), p. 100.

609 Government Bill (Prop 1973:32), p. 89.

provision was kept in the law, and that it was placed in the first chapter, which set out to define the concept of marriage, can be claimed to further underline the idea of marriage as a joint enterprise of the spouses.

In 1977, changing the wording of the provision was suggested. The proposal, discussed in a committee report, was to replace the expression in the provision that "husband and wife shall show faithfulness and consideration to one another" with the more modern wording that "husband and wife shall show one another loyalty and consideration". The old version was thought to accredit sexual fidelity too much significance.[610] However, in the Government Bill of 1978 the original wording was kept unaltered as a remainder that solidarity between spouses remains a relevant feature of marriage, which still "defends its place as an introduction to the provisions on the legal effects of marriage."[611] In the Marriage Code of 1987, the "faithfulness provision" not only qualified as an introduction to the provisions laying down the legal effects of marriage, but as an introduction to the entire Marriage Code. In the Government Bill it was underlined that the concept "faithfulness" is to be interpreted in a wider sense than sexual fidelity. It is based on the ideas of loyalty and solidarity of the spouses.[612]

The spouses' loyalty toward one another is also included in their obligation to jointly care for the home and the children, laid down in the same provision.[613] In the Government Bill of 1973, it was pointed out that even though considerable efforts had been made to achieve equality between spouses, more work remained to be done. For instance, women were still paid less than men for the same work on the labor market. Thus the provision was still motivated to retain.[614] In the Government Bill, it was also pointed out that establishing in the law that domestic work and taking care of children are duties for both spouses can have a positive impact on general attitudes, and thus contribute to a higher level of equality between women and men in society.[615]

---

610 Committee Report (SOU 1977:37), pp. 16 and 37 f.

611 [...] försvarar sin plats som en inledning till lagens bestämmelser om äktenskapets rättsverkningar." Government Bill (Prop 1978/79:12), p. 181. Author's translation.

612 Government Bill (Prop 1986/87:1), p. 113. Government Bill (Prop 1978/79:12), p. 180.

613 The Marriage Code of 1920, Chapter 5, Section 1, replaced by the Marriage Code of 1987, Chapter 1, Section 2. This was a significant political novelty in the Marriage Code of 1920.

614 Government Bill (Prop 1973:32), pp. 66 f.

615 Government Bill (Prop 1978/79:12), pp. 180 f.

4.4. THE ESSENCE OF MARRIAGE UNDER THE 1970–1987 ENACTMENTS: SUMMARIZING ANALYSIS AND COMPARISONS

4.4.1. MARRIAGE AS A UNION WITH "REVOLVING DOORS"

Through the family law enactments of the 1970s, the core values relating to marriage changed significantly. One could say that the reforms of the 1970s turned marriage, from a life-long union into an institution with "revolving doors", in the sense that marriage, pursuant to the enactments of the 1970s, not only could be entered into freely, but also exited out of freely by each spouse. The limitations to this slightly exaggerated metaphor have been accounted for above, namely that impediments to marriage were retained and a period of reconsideration was introduced. Not all "couples" qualified for marriage. Nevertheless, access into and exit out of marriage were significantly facilitated in 1973.

The basic idea was that the spouses were two independent individuals with autonomous rights and needs, equally competent to make decisions concerning their marriage. Their competence in this respect should be respected in connection with all law reforms dealing with marriage. As a result, the enactments adopted between 1973 and 1987 reduced the public interference in marriage, in respect of conclusion and dissolution of marriage, as well as in respect of the legal effects of marriage. The restrictions on marital capacity were reduced in 1973, which opened up for marriage between persons previously unable to marry each other due to affinity.

An important factor in Swedish society contributed to the changing values relating to marriage: the increasing custom to cohabit outside of marriage. Against this background it became relevant to ask if it is motivated to restrict access to marriage through extensive impediments, when the restrictions did not obstruct de facto cohabitation. People who cannot marry each other because of an impediment to marriage, can still live together in an informal relationship. Moreover, the reduction of the impediments to marriage in 1973 had given previously excluded couples access to marriage. This can be seen as illustrating a shift toward a wider outlook on the institution of marriage. As will be claimed in chapter 6, this approach would continue to expand and be re-evaluated, and eventually encompass also couples of the same sex. Moreover, a significant change was that marriage was no longer considered a life-long union from a legal perspective. This view was reflected in the enactments of 1973 and 1978, through the unilateral right to divorce, combined with a restrictive view on spousal support after divorce.

The concept of marriage has been discussed above in terms of two different functions, namely as a contract and a civil status. The marriage enactments of the 1970s and the 1987 Act can be seen as primarily focusing on the contractual side of marriage and toning down the civil status side.[616] Still, marriage was no ordinary or value-neutral "contract". The regulation governing marriage still included normative and ethical remainders, for instance, the six-month period of reconsideration, which applies in certain situations and signals that it is desirable from the point of view of the legislator to avoid hasty divorces.[617] Also, the "faithfulness criterion", which was kept in the introduction to the Marriage Code of 1987, although no legal consequences were attached, signals that marriage is governed by special values which make it different from a "regular" contract within the law of obligations.

According to my opinion, the government's lack of interest in replacing the marriage ceremony with a registration procedure, as proposed in the 1972 Committee Report, indicates that society had an interest, not only in maintaining marriage as a special institution, but also in safeguarding the formalities around it. In other words, there was a limit to how far the legislator was willing to go when it came to turning marriage into a private "contract" based on the autonomy of the individuals concerned.

4.4.2. INTERNATIONAL COMPARISONS: PERSPECTIVES ON THE SWEDISH LEGAL DEVELOPMENT

4.4.2.1. How Progressive were the Swedish Marriage Enactments of the 1970s?

The Swedish Marriage Code of 1920 has been described as quite "liberal" from a European perspective in section 3.7.2.1. The Swedish enactments of the 1970s, dealing with divorce and spousal maintenance after divorce, also have a reputation as "progressive". It has been considered remarkable that Sweden, together with the other Nordic countries, managed to introduce far-reaching reforms in sensitive areas such as marriage and divorce when a conservative atmosphere still prevailed in most other western European countries.[618] Masha Antokolskaia has called the Swedish family law enactments of the 1970s "the most sweeping marriage and divorce reform in Western Europe".[619] How "radical", were the Swedish divorce enactments of 1973 and the maintenance enactment of 1978, compared to, for example, the Dutch, Spanish, German and French enactments?

616 Also Eva Ryrstedt has held that the 1973 divorce enactment reflects marriage as a contract. See Bodelning och bostad, 1998, p. 398.

617 It could be argued that applying a "period of notice" (the reconsideration period) when ending the marriage "contract" can be seen as expected and in line with the law of obligations. However, in my opinion the fact that such a period was retained, despite the general aim to avoid moral values, signals that there was a special interest in preventing divorce and preserving marriage.

618 Antokolskaia, Masha, Harmonisation of Family Law in Europe, 2006, p. 269.

619 Antokolskaia, Masha, Harmonisation of Family Law in Europe, 2006, p. 272.

4.4.2.2. Divorce as a Unilateral Right for each Spouse

4.4.2.2.1. The Divorce Regulations: A Brief Summary

The Swedish divorce regulation, which still applies in 2010, dates back to 1973. Through this enactment divorce was turned into a unilateral right for each spouse. All grounds for divorce were abolished from the law, and fault was made totally irrelevant in divorce proceedings and in ancillary matters, such as child custody and maintenance cases.

The Swedish unilateral right to divorce is still, a decade into the twenty-first century, quite liberal compared to the French, German and Dutch enactments. In Spain, through a reform in 2005, divorce regulation resembling the Swedish was enacted.[620] According to rules enacted in 1981, legal separation for one or three years was obligatory prior to divorce under Spanish divorce law.[621] The only exception to this rule was if one spouse had tried to kill the other spouse or his or her children.[622] Under the new Spanish divorce legislation, no period of separation is required prior to the divorce application, and no grounds for divorce are stipulated in the law. Like under Swedish law, the petition for divorce as such, by one or both spouses, is sufficient for obtaining a court decision granting the divorce. A basic limitation established in the Spanish divorce law is that the marriage must have lasted three months prior to the divorce application.[623] There is no equivalence to the Swedish "reconsideration period" in Spanish divorce law, which at first glance could make the Spanish law appear more "divorce-friendly" and liberal than the Swedish.[624] However, under Spanish divorce law the spouses must present an agreement concerning all ancillary matters along with the joint application for divorce.[625] Most likely reaching such an agreement can be a lengthy process for couples who disagree in some respect, for instance, child custody or maintenance. In Sweden divorce is always granted after the six months have passed, upon the application of either spouse. From

620 European Judicial Network: http://ec.europa.eu/civiljustice/divorce/divorce_spa_en.htm. Accessed 18 September 2010.

621 European Family Law in Action, Volume I: Grounds for Divorce, 2003, question 11, p. 185. Spanish Report written by: Martín-Casals, Miquel.

622 European Family Law in Action, Volume I: Grounds for Divorce, 2003, question 4, p. 95. Spanish Report written by: Martín-Casals, Miquel.

623 European Judicial Network: http://ec.europa.eu/civiljustice/divorce/divorce_spa_en.htm. Accessed 18 September 2010. If one spouse abuses the other or a child of the family, no time-period is required.

624 See Ferrer Riba, Josep, Same-Sex Marriage, Express Divorce and Related Developments in Spanish Marriage Law, 2006, p. 142.

625 Such matters concern child custody and maintenance, division property and pension. See European Judicial Network: http://ec.europa.eu/civiljustice/divorce/divorce_spa_en.htm. Accessed 18 September 2010. See also Ferrer Riba, Josep, Same-Sex Marriage, Express Divorce and Related Developments in Spanish Marriage Law, 2006, p. 142.

this point of view, divorce on the whole appears more accessible in Sweden than in Spain, irrespective of the Swedish six-month reconsideration period.

Under French divorce law, according to a principle adopted in 1975 and kept in the Divorce Act of 2004, divorce is easy to obtain if the spouses are in agreement to dissolve the marriage, namely through a joint application based on their mutual consent. The spouses must also present a contract with arrangements concerning ancillary matters.[626] In respect of such a "contractual divorce",[627] no period of separation is required prior to the application and no ground for dissolution needs to be invoked.[628]

If only one spouse wishes to dissolve the marriage under French divorce law, a two-year separation of the spouses is required before divorce can be granted. After two years from the petition for divorce, irrespective of on what ground the petition was initially made, divorce may always be granted.[629] This was a liberalization compared to the previous act, according to which six years of separation was required upon unilateral divorce applications. Fault has been retained as an independent ground for divorce under the 2004 Divorce Act.[630] According to the French Civil Code, Art. 242, fault is: "a fact or a series of facts ascribable to the other which constitute a serious or continual violation of the duties and obligations of marriage and render intolerable the continuation of communal life."[631] The notion of fault is to be understood restrictively since the 2004 reform, and the basic idea is that financial consequences of divorce should not be dependent on the question of who is to blame for the breakdown of the marriage. Nevertheless, the judge has certain discretion in this respect.[632]

German divorce law does not recognize mutual consent as an independent direct ground for divorce. The only ground for divorce, recognized in the German Civil Code, is the "irretrievable breakdown" of the marriage.[633] Both spouses can invoke this ground, irrespective of who is to blame for the

626 European Family Law in Action, Volume I: Grounds for Divorce, 2003, question 29, p. 313. French Report written by: Ferrand, Frédérique.

627 Ferrer Riba, Josep, Same-Sex Marriage, Express Divorce and Related Developments in Spanish Marriage Law, 2006, p. 144.

628 European Family Law in Action, Volume I: Grounds for Divorce, 2003, question 22, p. 272. French Report written by: Ferrand, Frédérique.

629 Ferrer Riba, Josep, Same-Sex Marriage, Express Divorce and Related Developments in Spanish Marriage Law, 2006, p. 145.

630 Ferrer Riba, Josep, Same-Sex Marriage, Express Divorce and Related Developments in Spanish Marriage Law, 2006, p. 145.

631 See Ferrer Riba, Josep, Same-Sex Marriage, Express Divorce and Related Developments in Spanish Marriage Law, 2006, p. 145.

632 Ferrer Riba, Josep, Same-Sex Marriage, Express Divorce and Related Developments in Spanish Marriage Law, 2006, p. 145.

633 The expression "irretrievable breakdown" is not used in the Civil Code, but the word "breakdown" (scheitern). According to the Civil Code, a marriage fails if the marital community of the spouses no longer exists and there can be no expectation that the spouses will restore it. See European Family Law in Action, Volume I: Grounds for Divorce, 2003, question 4, pp. 80 f. German Report written by: Dieter, Martiny.

breakdown of the marriage.[634] A period of separation is required prior to divorce. If the spouses apply jointly for divorce, the marriage is irrebuttably presumed to have broken down permanently, if they had been separated for *one year* prior to the application. This time-period also applies if one spouse applies for divorce and the other consents. In respect of a unilaterally contested request for divorce, the presumption of marriage breakdown requires a three-year period of separation. Under German law, the breakdown of the marriage can also be proven through "hardship clauses", without using the presumption.[635] Fault or possible marital offences only play a marginal role in German divorce proceedings, namely by preventing the guilty party from access to a speedy divorce. The element of fault could even, in exceptional situations, prevent divorce from being granted at all at that specific time, if divorce because of special circumstances would result in such exceptional hardship that ordering the spouses to continue with the marriage is found necessary.[636]

The Dutch divorce regulation, which was enacted in 1971, resembles the German, in the sense that irretrievable breakdown of the marriage is the sole ground for divorce, but in situations when the spouses are in agreement to dissolve the marriage, it appears to be speedier to obtain a divorce under Dutch law than under German law. Divorce based on mutual consent is only possible when based on irretrievable breakdown, but the spouses' statements that the marriage has permanently broken down are sufficient as evidence in this respect. No further investigation is made by the judge.[637]

In respect of a unilateral divorce application under Dutch law – which the other spouse contests – the judge can ex officio investigate whether or not the marriage has broken down irreversibly. The applicant can also submit evidence by proving personal facts and circumstances which have lead to the permanent deterioration of the marriage, for instance, adulterous behavior of a spouse. Thus fault can to some extent be indirectly relevant in divorce proceedings under Dutch law. However, divorce can no longer be rejected because the petitioning spouse is to blame for the deterioration of the marriage.[638] Furthermore, it

---

634 European Family Law in Action, Volume I: Grounds for Divorce, 2003, questions 1, 4 and 11, pp. 3, 80 and 172. German Report written by: Dieter, Martiny.

635 European Family Law in Action, Volume I: Grounds for Divorce, 2003, question 4, pp. 80 f. German Report written by: Dieter, Martiny.

636 European Family Law in Action, Volume I: Grounds for Divorce, 2003, question 12, pp. 188–190. German Report written by: Dieter, Martiny.

637 European Family Law in Action, Volume I: Grounds for Divorce, 2003, question 4, p. 89. The Dutch Report is written by: Boele-Woelki, Katharina, Cherednychenko, Olga and Coenraad, Lieke.

638 European Family Law in Action, Volume I: Grounds for Divorce, 2003, question 12, p. 193. The Dutch Report is written by: Boele-Woelki, Katharina, Cherednychenko, Olga and Coenraad, Lieke.

appears that the element of fault can be taken into account in connection with maintenance claims and alimony payments.[639]

4.4.2.2.2. Comparative Reflections

According to the Swedish Marriage Code of 1987, divorce based on mutual consent can in principle be obtained within 24 hours, based on a joint written application by the spouses. However, it takes three weeks from the date of the court's decision for a divorce decree to gain legal force and become final. Until the three weeks have expired, the court decision can be appealed by either spouse. The spouses in general do not have to appear in court and they do not have to agree on ancillary matters for the divorce to be granted. Ancillary matters, for instance, child custody and division of property, if disputed, can be dealt with in separate proceedings. If the spouses have children under the age of 16, or if one spouse objects to the petition, a six-month period of reconsideration is decreed. The spouses can also jointly demand such a reconsideration period. If the spouses have lived apart for two years prior to the application, no period of reconsideration is required, even if they have children.[640]

In comparison with the jurisdictions surveyed above, the Swedish model appears accessible and fast. Divorce cannot be delayed longer than by six months by a spouse opposed to divorce. However, since the 2005 reform, Spain also stands out as a comparatively "divorce friendly" jurisdiction. Nonetheless, the above mentioned requirement that all ancillary matters must be settled in an agreement before divorce based on mutual consent can be granted in Spain, can delay Spanish divorce proceedings considerably.

A development toward excluding – or at least diminishing – the element of fault in divorce proceedings can be observed during the twentieth century in the jurisdictions discussed here. From a Swedish perspective, excluding fault from divorce proceedings can be seen as protecting the integrity of the individuals and indirectly increasing the accessibility of divorce, by avoiding deterring a "guilty" spouse from going through with a divorce out of fear for airing his or her personal life in court. It is a common belief in many European jurisdictions that fault grounds risk creating bitterness between the spouses, which can be detrimental to children's wellbeing.[641] As shown above, in France, Germany and the Netherlands fault can still be of some relevance in connection with divorce.

---

639 European Family Law in Action, Volume I: Grounds for Divorce, 2003, question 11, pp. 177 f. The Dutch Report is written by: Boele-Woelki, Katharina, Cherednychenko, Olga and Coenraad, Lieke.

640 See section 4.2.2.3.

641 Because of the risk of fault creating conflicts between parents, the French assumed a restrictive policy toward divorce based on fault. Fault was nevertheless retained as an independent ground. See Butruille-Cardew, Charlotte, The 2004 French Divorce Law and International Prospects, 2006, p. 144.

France is the only one of the jurisdictions compared that has maintained fault as a direct ground for divorce, although applied restrictively.

It may seem unexpected that Spain, which was the last of the jurisdictions studied here to "modernize" its divorce regulation in 1981, was among the first to implement the idea of divorce as a unilateral right (in 2005). Adopting sweeping reforms at different points in times, for the purpose of appearing progressive and breaking with the family values promoted by the Catholic Church, appears to be a recurring theme in the Spanish legal development in the field of family law.[642]

4.4.2.3. The "Clean Break" of Divorce – Termination of Legal Effects

Through the 1978 enactment, spousal maintenance after divorce was laid down as a rare exception in Sweden, the guiding principle being that all legal effects of marriage shall end when the marriage ends.[643] This enactment was no novelty in practice. It established principles in statutory law that had already been developed in case law.[644] Spousal maintenance pursuant to the Swedish Marriage Code of 1987 can be awarded where necessary for a transitional period after divorce or, exceptionally, for a longer period.

Also in Spain, the idea of divorce terminating all economic ties between the spouses is the main rule since the 2005 reform. The Spanish spousal maintenance regulation appears to be based on the idea of avoiding unfairness, which does not necessarily mean that the petitioning spouse must need maintenance payments to make a living, whereas the Swedish regulation on maintenance only applies if absolutely necessary from the economic perspective of the petitioner.

Also under German and French laws the point of departure is that the spouses are supposed to provide financially for themselves after divorce. In practice, however, if a spouse is unable to do so, maintenance can be awarded.[645] In Dutch divorce proceedings the judge has a wide discretion to grant maintenance upon the request of a spouse who does not have a sufficient income to provide for himself or herself after divorce. Although limited by the principle of the lack of means and the ability to pay, the judge's own conception of what is "fair" can be determining for the outcome.[646]

---

642 See sections 7.3.1 and 7.3.3.1.

643 Government Bill (Prop 1978/79:12), p. 139. From a comparative European perspective, this is not the predominating view. See also European Family Law in Action, Volume II, 2003, question 58, p. 53. The Swedish Report is written by: Jänterä-Jareborg, Maarit.

644 European Family Law in Action, Volume II, Maintenance Between Former Spouses, 2003, question 56, p. 31. The Swedish Report is written by: Jänterä-Jareborg, Maarit.

645 European Family Law in Action, Volume II, Maintenance Between Former Spouses, 2003, question 58, p. 46. The German Report is written by Martiny, Dieter and the French Report is written by Ferrand, Frédérique.

646 European Family Law in Action, Volume II, Maintenance Between Former Spouses, 2003, question 58, p. 49. The Dutch Report is written by Boele-Woelki, Katharina, Cherednychenko, Olga and Coenraad, Lieke.

4.4.2.4. Was the Swedish Maintenance Enactment of 1978 too Far-Reaching?

The Swedish maintenance enactment of 1978 was in line with the general outlook, (reflected in the enactments of the 1970s) on the spouses as two equal, capable and independent individuals. The guiding principle, which at the time was already well-established in case law, was that divorce terminates all inter-spousal financial consequences of the marriage – including their obligation to maintain each other.

Another aspect of the reform, mentioned in the Government Bill, was that limiting access to spousal maintenance upon divorce was thought to encourage married women to be financially independent during and after divorce.[647] The Swedish approach to spousal maintenance after divorce differed from the basic view expressed in the law of the other jurisdictions studied here. Even today, spousal maintenance after divorce appears to be more accessible in the other jurisdictions than in Sweden. The right to spousal maintenance after divorce can be argued to be a justified "safety valve", in situations when there is an imbalance in respect of the financial ability and the work capacity of the spouses.

It can be argued that the Swedish spousal maintenance reform of the 1978 – which gave principles developed in case law statutory support – was too extensive even from a Swedish perspective and incompatible with the actual living conditions in society. The rules are based on the idea of promoting equality through ending the marital obligations upon divorce. However, in the 1970s, only 25 percent of all married women had gainful employment. This was, inter alia, a result of insufficient availability of childcare and a lack of job opportunities.[648] In the Government Bill of 1973, it was held that the low number of financially independent married women in the 1970s was also the result of a traditional division of duties between husband and wife, according to which the wife was the primary caretaker of the spouses' children and the husband earned most of the family living. Because of this division of duties, spousal maintenance after divorce was retained as an exception to the rule of financial independence of the spouses during marriage and after divorce.[649]

An explanation for why spousal maintenance after divorce could be made the exception in Sweden – when it was still the main rule in most other European countries – was the impact of the Swedish welfare state. The welfare state can be seen as based on the idea of a "collective" financial responsibility of the citizens.[650] Along with the welfare state came a social security system with a minimum level of financial aid for the individual to fall back on as a last resort in situations when the individual could not provide for himself or herself. It should

647 Government Bill (Prop 1978/79:12), p. 139.

648 Government Bill (Prop 1973:32), pp. 66 f. The figure is based on the year 1973, when the divorce rules were adopted.

649 Government Bill (Prop 1978/79:12), pp. 138 f.

650 The Swedish welfare society has been analyzed in section 4.1.2 and subsections.

be emphasized, however, that the social security system was no alternative to spousal maintenance, in the sense that an individual could choose to turn to the state instead of an ex-spouse for support. If an individual's need of financial aid was the result of a marriage and the other ex-spouse had the financial ability to pay, spousal maintenance is the way to go – not welfare benefits.

The Swedish system is especially supportive toward single parent households, through various financial subsidies, for instance, child and housing benefits to facilitate parents' gainful employment. These benefits were not only available to single parent household, but can be seen as particularly important in single parent households and might to some extent help individuals get by financially despite the restrictive view on spousal maintenance after divorce.

A state-subsidized preschool system is generally available in Sweden. This significant part of the Swedish welfare state has, most likely, been a decisive factor for realizing the idea of marriage as a "clean slate" right for each spouse. Access to financially affordable childcare enables women, who are still the primary caretakers of children after divorce, to be gainfully employed and to work full time. Without this system, divorced women in general would be much more dependent on spousal maintenance after divorce, or upon society for receiving support or subsidies.

4.4.2.5. Progressive Swedish Marriage Regulation and European Harmonization

It appears that the Swedish enactments on spouses' property relations, divorce and spousal support after divorce were introduced decades before the other jurisdictions studied here adopted laws based on similar values. The values in the Swedish enactments of 1915 and 1920, dealing with access to divorce, did not, as a rule, gain a hearing in France, Germany and the Netherlands until the 1970s. In Spain, rules providing married women with the right to administer their property were adopted only in 1981.[651]

The Swedish enactments of the 1970s, once again, created a "gap" between Swedish divorce and maintenance rules and the rules applicable in the other countries. Spain also adopted liberal divorce rules in 2005, but Spanish spouses must agree on all ancillary matters before divorce based on mutual consent can be granted. The overall impression is that this gap between Sweden and the countries surveyed here still exists, to some extent. In France, fault is still an independent ground for divorce, although a restrictive approach is recommended. The Netherlands and Germany still apply irretrievable breakdown as the sole ground for divorce, the introduction of which made Sweden "liberal" from a European perspective in 1915. Against this background, the Swedish – and now also the Spanish – policy that a spouse's unilateral wish to dissolve a marriage

[651] European Judicial Network: http://ec.europa.eu/civiljustice/divorce/divorce_spa_en.htm. Accessed 18 September 2010.

should be respected (although in Sweden combined with a six-month period of reconsideration) is liberal from a European perspective.

The Swedish unilateral right to divorce appears liberal even compared to the Principles drafted by the Commission on European Family law, on the basis of the applicable divorce law in 22 European jurisdictions. These Principles set out to inspire national legislators in Europe to harmonize laws, for the purpose of facilitating the free movement of persons within the EU. However, the harmonization efforts of the CEFL are not limited to the European Union, but are meant to include and benefit also citizens of European states which are not members of the EU.[652]

According to the CEFL Principles, it is initially established that divorce by mutual consent and upon the request of one spouse should be permitted.[653] However, this main principle, in line with the most "divorce friendly" European regulations, such as the Swedish, is followed by a number of exceptions. In respect of divorce against the wishes of one of the spouses, factual separation for one year is required, unless this would mean exceptional hardship for the petitioner, for instance because of domestic violence.[654] Access to immediate divorce, according to the CEFL Principles, is only possible, without a reflection period of three to six months, if the spouses have no children and have agreed on all consequences.[655] However, as discussed above in relation to the Spanish divorce law of 2005, agreeing on all consequences can be time-consuming. From this point of view, Swedish divorce law appears more liberal than the CEFL Principles, as a divorce decree under the Swedish Marriage Code of 1987 can be granted before the couple has reached an agreement concerning ancillary matters.

The comparisons between the selected jurisdictions here, as well as the limitations of a spouse's unilateral right to divorce included in the CEFL Principles, indicates that Swedish divorce regulation is still liberal on the European legal arena. It is possible that others may follow the Swedish enactments on divorce and spousal maintenance after divorce. An interest in focusing on the individual's rights and autonomy has become more and more visible in Europe, under the influence of the human rights discourse, and the individual's unilateral right to divorce without judicial proceedings and before solving all ancillary matters may very well become politically prioritized.[656] The CEFL Principles

652 Jänterä-Jareborg, Maarit, En harmoniserad familjerätt för Europa? Internationellt privaträttsliga och rättsjämförande perspektiv, 2009, p. 337.

653 Principle 1:3, Principles of European Family Law Regarding Divorce and Maintenance Between Former Spouses, Commission on European Family Law, 2004, p. 24.

654 Principles 1:8 and 1:9, Principles of European Family Law Regarding Divorce and Maintenance Between Former Spouses, Commission on European Family Law, 2004, pp. 51 and 57.

655 Principle 1:5, Principles of European Family Law Regarding Divorce and Maintenance Between Former Spouses, Commission on European Family Law, 2004, p. 33.

656 Human rights aspects on the legal developments concerning cohabitation models will be analyzed in chapter 8.

may also have an impact on the legal development in this respect, as a source of inspiration for national legislators.

However, certain general problematic viewpoints concerning the CEFL Principles have been noted in the legal literature. Esin Örücü, although basically positive to the work of the CEFL and its Principles, has pointed out that it could be perceived as a "futile exercise" to promote harmonized rules through vaguely regulated principles, which leave a number of issues up to the national legislators to clarify. Moreover, Örücü points out that political, cultural and economic factors can justify defending the diversity in the national regulations dealing with divorce.[657] The Principles are drafted based on what the CEFL calls the "common core" in the 22 jurisdictions surveyed or, in the absence thereof, the "better law".

The CEFL Principles already have been a source of inspiration to national legislators. In 2008, the Dutch Attorney General referred to the CEFL Principles Regarding Parental Responsibilities, and the Portuguese divorce reform of 2007 appears to have been directly influenced by the CEFL Principles Regarding Divorce.[658] Against this background, it appears likely that the Principles will have an impact in any future efforts to harmonize family law in Europe, inter alia in order to facilitate EU Citizens' free movement across borders within the Union. Also, as Maarit Jänterä-Jareborg points out, harmonized rules in Europe are relevant, not only from the perspective of the free movement of EU citizens, but also from a symbolic point of view. Jänterä-Jareborg underlines that harmonized family law rules in the EU contribute to creating a common foundation of values in the EU – a European "identity".[659] Such a common foundation of values was the basis for the Nordic legal cooperation during the first half of the twentieth century.[660] Through this legal cooperation, the Nordic countries agreed on several legal solutions in respect of the regulation governing marriage, which are still considered "progressive" in many European countries in the twenty-first century.[661]

From a Swedish perspective, according to which the marriage regulation often appears to be more "liberal" than the CEFL Principles, certain legal compromises would have to be made in order to comply with the Principles. The adjustments required from a Swedish perspective to comply with the CEFL Principles would be much less comprehensive than the reforms necessary for many other European countries to meet the standards laid down in the Principles.

---

657 Örücü, Esin, The Principles of European Family Law put to the Test: Diversity in Harmony or Harmony in Diversity? 2007, p. 233.

658 www.ceflonline.net/. Accessed 21 September 2010.

659 Jänterä-Jareborg, Maarit, En harmoniserad familjerätt för Europa? Internationellt privaträttsliga och rättsjämförande perspektiv, 2009, p. 336.

660 See section 7.4.2. See also Jänterä-Jareborg, Maarit, En harmoniserad familjerätt för Europa? Internationellt privaträttsliga och rättsjämförande perspektiv, 2009, p. 337.

661 Jänterä-Jareborg, Maarit, Unification of International Family Law in Europe – A Critical Perspective, 2003, p. 216.

5. A "SECOND-CLASS" MARRIAGE? THE COHABITEE ACTS OF 1973, 1987 AND 2003

5.1. POINT OF DEPARTURE

In the 1970s, as pointed out in chapter 4, marriage in Sweden developed toward becoming more of a private and personal matter between two individuals, and less of a state or church concern. The idea of marriage as a union based on the autonomy of the individual was strengthened through law reform. The guiding political ideology was that the legislator should as far as possible trust the individual spouses to make rational decisions concerning their family life and avoid expressing moral values through the family law legislation. In this context, a special family law enactment regulating the situation of unmarried cohabiting couples was adopted – the 1973 Act on the Joint Dwelling of an Unmarried Couple.[662]

The Act of 1973 provided unmarried cohabitees with a right to take over a tenancy contract or a condominium (against compensation), upon dissolution of the cohabitation. The same right applied to married couples, but in respect of spouses, also real estate was included. In 1987, the second Cohabitees Act was adopted – the Cohabitees Joint Homes Act[663] – in which cohabitation under "marriage-like conditions" was made subject to rules regarding division of the net value of the joint home and household goods, acquired for the purpose of the couple's joint use. The Act of 1987 replaced the 1973 Act. In 2003 a "gender-neutral" Cohabitees Act was adopted for the main purpose of including same-sex and different-sex cohabitees in the same enactment, but the legislator seized the opportunity to clarify a few issues at the same time.

The Act of 1973 – although limited in scope – can be seen as a first symbolic step toward legally recognizing cohabitation without marriage as a "marriage-like" cohabitation model in Sweden, with certain status features attached.[664] The legal development in respect of cohabitation without marriage in Sweden provides an opportunity to analyze the differences between informal cohabitation

662 Lag (1973:651) om ogifta samboendes gemensamma bostad. The Act was included in the Real Property Law (*Jordabalken*).

663 Lag (1987:232) om sambors gemensamma hem.

664 See section 5.3.1 below.

and marriage. What are the differences between marriage and cohabitation without marriage in Sweden, substantively and symbolically? How has applying a special set of rules to unmarried cohabitees, modelled on the property division rules applicable to spouses, influenced the outlook on marriage in Sweden?

5.2. THE 1973 ACT ON THE JOINT DWELLING OF AN UNMARRIED COUPLE

5.2.1. PRACTICAL REASONS FOR ADOPTING THE ACT

In 1973, the marriage regulation underwent considerable substantive and symbolical changes in Sweden. At the same time the Cohabitees Joint Homes Act of 1973 was adopted. The motive for the enactment, given in the Government Bill, was that the 1973 Act was needed for the purpose of solving practical problems connected to the widespread habit of couples cohabiting outside of marriage. As mentioned in chapter 4, the government does not appear to have deliberately set out to bring forth changes of behavior through the Act: "The function of legislation regulating marriage as a cohabitation form [...] [is] to solve practical problems, not to favor one form of cohabitation over others.[665] In other words, the Cohabitees Act of 1973 primarily intended to adjust the law to the practical needs in society – not to encourage people to cohabit outside of marriage instead of marrying. As pointed out in the 1969 guidelines to the committee, the intention was not to diminish the importance of marriage.[666]

At the same time, the 1972 Commission on Family Law ("Familje-lagssakkunniga") was well aware of the impact that legislation can have on people's behavior. The 1969 guidelines to the Commission underlined that: "[T]here is no reason to relinquish the use of legislation on marriage and the family as one of several instruments in the reformative efforts toward a society where every adult individual can take responsibility for himself [herself] without being economically dependent on relatives and where equality between men and women is a reality."[667] However, reforming society can hardly be interpreted as

665 "Lagstiftningens funktion när det gäller äktenskapet som form för samlevnad anges vara att lösa praktiska problem, inte att privilegiera en samlevnadsform framför andra." Committee Report (SOU 1972:41), p. 91. Author's translation.

666 Guidelines by the head of the Ministry of Justice to the Commission on Family Law, 15 August, 1969, Riksdagsberättelsen 1970, Ju 52, p. 81. See Committee Report (SOU 1972:41), p. 58.

667 "[D]et finns ingen anledning att avstå från att använda lagstiftningen om äktenskapet och familjen som ett av flera instrument i reformsträvandena mot ett samhälle där varje vuxen individ kan ta ansvar för sig själv utan att vara ekonomiskt beroende av anhöriga och där jämlikhet mellan män och kvinnor är en realitet." Guidelines by the head of the Ministry of Justice to the Commission on Family Law, 15 August, 1969, Riksdagsberättelsen 1970, Ju 52, p. 81. The directives can also be found in: Committee Report (SOU 1972:41), p. 58. Author's translation.

the purpose of the substantially limited 1973 Cohabitees Act. The Act was introduced as a practical solution to the problems created by the increasing tendency of couples to live together outside of marriage, and to separate.

The 1973 Act was a product of the 1969 guidelines, which also formed the basis for the comprehensive marriage law reforms of the 1970s, discussed in chapter 4. The 1973 Act was marked by the same aspiration to reduce the ethical values from family law legislation as the other enactments.[668] Although the 1973 Cohabitees Act and the marriage and divorce enactments of the 1970s were adopted in the same general spirit, regulation on unmarried cohabitation appears less ideologically charged and more focused on solving practical problems than the other enactments. The practical impact of the 1973 Cohabitees Act appears marginal, when considering the limited legal effects attached to it, compared to other contemporary issues, for instance the launching of divorce as a unilateral right for each spouse.

Irrespective of the practical and pragmatic basis of the Act, the Cohabitees Act of 1973 was not free from values. The Act protected certain values at the expense of others, by balancing the relevant interests at stake. In the Government Bill, the values protected through the 1973 Cohabitees Act were identified as creating equality between men and women and protecting a weaker party. Protecting these values in the law, it was held, was in line with the prevailing interests and values in society.[669]

5.2.2. SOCIAL PROTECTION OF A WEAKER PARTY

The basic idea to protect the individual from injustice can be seen as a central component of the social welfare state and of the connected Social Democratic political program.[670] The 1973 Act on the Joint Dwelling of an Unmarried Couple introduced a possibility for a District Court, upon the request of a cohabitee, to evaluate and weigh the needs of each cohabitee, and to grant the cohabitee with the greatest need the right to take over the joint home when the cohabitation ended.[671] Avoiding socially offensive situations, for instance, that children and their caretaker had to move from their home upon separation,

[668] See sections 4.2.1 and 4.2.2.

[669] Government Bill (Prop 1973:32), p. 66.

[670] See section 4.2.

[671] Prior to the Act of 1973, an unmarried cohabitee could be entitled to take over a tenancy right in case of death or separation. In the latter situation, two prerequisites were necessary, namely that the cohabitee holding the tenancy contract was *unable to use the dwelling for the remaining tenure* and that he or she *consented to transferring the contract* to the other cohabitee. However, there was no legal possibility to balance the interests of the parties and to grant the cohabitee with the greatest need the right to take over the couple's joint dwelling upon separation. The absence of such a possibility, it was argued in the Government Bill of 1973, could give rise to unsuitable and even offensive results, especially when the cohabitee

because the tenancy right happened to belong to the other cohabitee, was explicitly mentioned in the bill as a motive for adopting the 1973 Act.[672]

The possibility to award the home to the cohabitee with the greatest need can be seen as a form of social welfare legislation, primarily protecting the interests of children and the interests of their primary caretaker – in reality often women. A traditional division of duties during the relationship, according to which the woman raised the couple's children and the man worked outside the home, was assumed to be common also in a cohabitee relationship, and could give rise to unfair results upon dissolution. When the cohabitation ended there was no family law regulation protecting the interests of the weaker party in the form of property division, maintenance rights and succession rights.[673]

The level of protection introduced through the 1973 Cohabitees Act remained limited. Not all types of homes were covered by the Act. Tenancy contracts were included, but real estate was excluded, and the right to take over a condominium required that financial compensation corresponding to its value was paid. However, the social protection provided by the right to take over a tenancy contract in Sweden should not be underestimated. Tenancy contracts are common in Sweden and also attractive, as the tenant enjoys extensive protection in the law, which makes it difficult for a landlord to cancel a legally binding contract. Moreover, as a result of the rent freeze in 1941, apartments in the cities were inexpensive to rent and a popular alternative to buying an expensive house in the crowded suburbs.[674] In other words, apart from the social value of being able to continue living in one's home, there was an indirect financial value in taking over the tenancy contract, namely, to avoid having to buy a new home because no new tenancy contract was available.

Also the right to take over a condominium against compensation had a social protection function when the 1973 Act was adopted. In the 1970's, condominiums were generally inexpensive in Sweden and the cohabitee taking over a condominium could in general afford to "buy out" the other cohabitee. Real estate, on the contrary, had a significant value and was thus entirely excluded from the Act of 1973. This indicates that there was a limit to the level of social protection deemed justified. Furthermore, as pointed out in the Government Bill, including real estate in the Cohabitees Act would have provided unmarried cohabitees with more extensive legal rights and duties than the corresponding marriage regulation applicable to spouses at that time, and this was not found desirable.[675] According to the rules applicable to spouses, if real estate had been made the separate property of a spouse – for instance through a marital property

obligated to leave the joint home had custody of, and was living with, the couple's children. See Government Bill (Prop 1973:32), pp. 132 and 213.

672 Government Bill (Prop 1973:32), p. 132.

673 Government Bill (Prop 1973:32), p. 132.

674 Sundberg, Jacob, Marriage or No Marriage in Swedish Law, pp. 225.

675 Government Bill (Prop 1973:32), p. 134.

contract or through a condition by a third party in a will – it could not be taken over by the other spouse upon divorce.[676] The reason for excluding real estate, which was the separate property of one spouse, was most likely linked to the historical significance of real estate in Sweden. In the Swedish farming population, real estate was passed on from generation to generation. In fact, special rules to ensure that real estate stayed in the family existed already in the provincial laws and were included in the Marriage Code of 1734.[677]

To summarize, it appears that the 1973 Act was, most likely, not intended as an ideological statement of the legislator. It was primarily adopted for the purpose of solving practical problems and avoiding unfair results upon the separation of unmarried cohabitees. Despite the limited scope of the Act (no rules to equalize the couple's financial situation were included) the right to take over a rented apartment or a condominium could be significant from a social and financial perspective.

5.2.3. "THE NEUTRALITY POLICY"

5.2.3.1. Conflicting Interests in the 1969 Guidelines

The guidelines of 1969 to the Commission on Family Law were the basis for the comprehensive changes in the marriage regulation in the 1970s, which can be seen as having strengthened the autonomous dimension of marriage.[678] But the guidelines also had an impact on the outlook on unmarried cohabitees and constituted the foundation for the 1973 Cohabitees Act.

According to the 1969 guidelines, legislation should be neutral to different cohabitation models.[679] The basic idea was to retain marriage as a central cohabitation model in family law legislation, but avoid rules which made it inconvenient for unmarried couples. Based on the 1969 guidelines, the idea of a "neutrality policy" has been developed, as a decisive element in marriage law reform in Sweden.[680] The idea of striving toward a "neutral" marriage regulation can be seen as a way of expressing the general aim to avoid ethical values in marriage regulation.

---

676 Government Bill (Prop 1973:32), p. 134.

677 As a result real estate – unlike other property – could qualify as separate property, which in practice meant that it fell outside of the administration right of the husband and prevented him from selling or otherwise disposing of the property. See section 2.6.

678 See sections 4.2.1, 4.2.4.1 and 4.2.4.2.

679 Guidelines by the head of the Ministry of Justice to the Commission on Family Law, 15 August, 1969, Riksdagsberättelsen 1970, Ju 52, p. 81. See Committee Report (SOU 1972:41), p. 58. As translated by Graversen, Jørgen, Family Law as a Reflection of Family Ideology", p. 79.

680 The neutrality policy is sometimes called the neutrality theory.

However, already in the Committee Report of 1972 it was observed that applying the idea of neutrality to cohabitation models was problematic, since the concept of neutrality contained contradictory aims.[681] It was pointed out that the aim of the neutrality policy was twofold. First, it aimed to *avoid that unmarried cohabitees and spouses were treated differently by the law when facing the same practical situation*. The basic idea was that differential treatment could be apprehended as "unjust" by spouses or cohabitees and should therefore be avoided as far as possible.[682] Second, the objective of the neutrality policy was also to grant couples the *freedom to choose* whether or not to marry, and to avoid forcing upon them legal effects which they had not requested.[683]

Although marriage and cohabitation without marriage are both voluntary unions, in the sense that no one may be forced into either union, there is one significant difference: a valid marriage requires that the prospective spouses, in the presence of a competent official, *explicitly consent* to marry each other and become spouses, which includes undertaking the connected rights and duties.[684] Couples choosing to cohabit without marriage in Sweden, on the other hand, become subjected to protective legislation *without any official procedure of consent* (by default).

In the 1972 report, the committee concluded that the two goals of the neutrality policy could not be attained at the same time. Balancing the two contradictory interests was necessary and the committee proposed a two-sided approach to the concept of neutrality.[685] Thus, neutrality in the sense of *equal treatment of cohabitees and spouses* was to be provided in the fields of social welfare law and taxation law, and neutrality in the sense of *protecting couples' freedom of choice whether or not to marry* was to be provided in the field of traditional family law, maintaining a clear distinction between marriage and cohabitation without marriage. The committee believed that applying the neutrality policy in the extensive sense of always treating cohabitees and spouses equally, would deprive the institution of marriage of its substantive content.[686] This was not desirable, since the idea was to retain marriage as a central institution in Swedish family law.[687] In other words, creating a legally recognized "alternative" to marriage was not to think of at this time. Nevertheless, limiting the individual's

681 Committee Report (SOU 1972:41), pp. 91 f.

682 Committee Report (SOU 1972:41), p. 91.

683 Committee Report (SOU 1972:41), p. 91.

684 A valid marriage contract presupposes a wedding ceremony. See Agell, Anders, Legal Issues of the Late 1990's, 1999, p. 199, with reference to a judgment by the Supreme Court in 1985 (Nytt Juridiskt Arkiv 1985 s 185).

685 Committee Report (SOU 1972:41), p. 91.

686 Committee Report (SOU 1972:41), p. 93.

687 Committee Report (SOU 1972:41), p. 93. The basic idea to keep marriage as the central cohabitation model was also expressed in the Government Bill (Prop 1973:32), p. 65 and in the guidelines by the head of the Ministry of Justice to the Committee on Family Law, 15 August, 1969, Riksdagsberättelsen 1970, Ju 52, p. 81.

freedom of choice was deemed necessary for the purpose of providing a basic level of social protection also in respect of unmarried cohabitees.

5.2.3.2. The Neutrality Policy and Cohabitation without Marriage: Criticism in the Legal Literature

The idea that legislation should be completely neutral as to whether or not couples chose marriage or informal cohabitation was dismissed already in the Committee Report of 1972 and the Bill of 1973. The idea of neutrality could not be fully realized, since adopting the Cohabitees Act of 1973 required prioritizing social protection over the individual's freedom to choose not to be covered by family law legislation. As a result, speaking in terms of "neutrality" in the context of cohabitation without marriage can be misleading.

Nevertheless, it has been claimed that the neutrality policy, laid down in the 1969 guidelines, had a negative effect on the marriage frequency in Sweden. According to Anders Agell, the alleged neutral position of the legislator toward cohabitation forms is to blame for the weakened position of marriage in society and for the high number of cohabitation without marriage. Agell has argued that the enactment of a special Cohabitees Act in 1973 undermined the institution of marriage, which he regretted, since in his opinion marriage provided the best regulation for couples living together – especially couples with children. Protecting family stability[688] should be in the interest of the legislator, Agell held, since statistics indicated that unmarried couples were more likely to separate than spouses.[689] According to Agell, the 1973 Cohabitees Act was a direct product of the alleged neutrality policy of the legislator.[690] Agell further argued that the idea of neutrality had been used strategically and arbitrarily. Neutrality was explicitly mentioned in preparatory work when it supported a particular reform, but disregarded when it did not serve that particular political interest.[691]

Another perspective on neutrality is to argue that it should have been carefully and systematically followed through, by extending all legal effects of marriage to unmarried cohabitees. In the first comments in Swedish legal literature, Folke Schmidt argued along these lines, pointing out that many cohabitee relationships involved the same emotional aspects and the same long-term commitment as a marriage. From this point of view, according to Schmidt, it would have been appropriate to treat cohabitees and spouses equally, by attributing to both cohabitation models the same legal effects, provided that a cohabitee could prove in the individual case that the relationship was in fact

688 In this context, the term "family stability" is used in the sense low break-up frequency of couples.

689 Agell, Anders, Should and Can Family Law Influence Social Behaviour? 1998, pp. 126 ff.

690 Agell, Anders, The Swedish Legislation on Marriage and Cohabitation, a Journey without a Destination, 1980, p. 21.

691 Agell, Anders, Samboende utan äktenskap, Rättsläge och rättspolitik, 1985, p. 85.

equal to a marriage.[692] In this way, according to Schmidt, the legislator would have been truly "neutral" to cohabitation models. The legislator was not ready to abandon the idea of marriage as a central cohabitation model in Sweden. Marriage remained relevant and unmarried cohabitees were only subject to limited regulation in 1973. In the Cohabitees Act of 1987, however, when rules on division of certain property were introduced, the legislator took one step in the direction advocated by Schmidt. Still, the regulation applicable to cohabitees remained far from identical to the regulation governing marriage.

Several arguments, other than a general ambition to retain marriage as a central institution, can be raised against applying the entire set of marriage regulation to unmarried cohabitees. Most importantly, such a solution would be incompatible with the idea of marriage as a voluntary union requiring the consent of the couple being subject to its legal rules. This "consent criterion" is missing in respect of the Cohabitees Act, which applies by default. Another argument against applying all legal effects of marriage to unmarried cohabitees is that not all unmarried cohabitees can be assumed to want to be covered by such extensive rules. Unmarried cohabitees belong to a diverse group and need different legal rules. Margareta Brattström identifies this diversity aspect, and exemplifies it with that there are (1) cohabitees who are in the beginning of their relationship, testing to live together. Moreover, there are (2) cohabitees who use cohabitation without marriage as an alternative to marriage because they do not wish to marry, and (3) cohabitees who do not have the time or the money to marry. Finally, Brattström points out that there are (4) cohabitees who falsely believe that they are covered by the same rules as spouses.[693] Only in respect of the last category of cohabitees (4) would applying the entire set of marriage rules to unmarried cohabiting couples be motivated and assumingly in compliance with the couple's wishes.

Moreover, the cohabitees may have different views on what rules should apply to their relationship, one party possibly being more committed than the other. In the absence of a ceremony or registration resembling the formal requirements applicable to spouses, it cannot be assumed that all cohabitees wish to be covered by the same rules as spouses. Eva Ryrstedt has criticized the Cohabitees Act for giving rise to unpredictable and sometimes random outcomes, arguing that if the idea of neutrality to cohabitation models is to be retained, all property assignable to either party's earnings and accrued during the cohabitation, should be subject to division upon dissolution.[694] Through such a wider scope of the cohabitee regulation, according to Ryrstedt, the regulation would as a whole

692 Schmidt, Folke, Äktenskapsrätt, 1974, p. 25.

693 Brattström, Margareta, The Protection of a Vulnerable Party when a Cohabitee Relationship Ends, 2006, p. 354.

694 Ryrstedt, Eva, Legal Status of Cohabitants in Sweden, 2004, p. 437. The randomness of the Cohabitees Act is also discussed by Ryrstedt in: Delning mellan sambor i Sverige, 2000, pp. 398–401.

more accurately reflect the economic co-operation and the community inferred by the cohabitation.[695]

It can be mentioned that through a law reform in 2001, New Zealand adopted far-reaching rules governing unmarried cohabitees.[696] More precisely, the deferred community property regime, which applies to spouses, was made applicable by default under certain conditions to so-called de facto (unmarried) couples as well.[697] According to the main rule, a "de facto" relationship must have lasted three years before the rules apply, but there are exceptions and it is not absolutely necessary that the unmarried couple cohabit for the rules to apply.[698] One could say that New Zealand has implemented the Swedish idea of "neutrality" in the far-reaching sense discussed above, by largely applying the same rules to spouses and unmarried couples, under certain circumstances.

The 1969 guidelines attracted considerable attention, not only in Sweden, but also internationally – too much attention, same say. Peter Lødrup toned down the practical relevance of the Swedish guidelines of 1969. According to Lødrup, the importance of the Swedish guidelines has been exaggerated in the legal literature in the context of unmarried cohabitation.[699] This observation appears to be well-founded. As has been pointed out earlier, the Act of 1973 was adopted for the main purpose of solving certain practical problems caused by increased cohabitation of couples outside of marriage, and not for the purpose of establishing the basis for a new political ideology – a "neutrality ideology".[700] The concept of neutrality has occasionally been used in what this author considers a misleading and imprecise manner, as an explanation for the Swedish legislator's assumed absence of a positive interest in the institution of marriage.[701] However, the Swedish legislator was not uninterested in marriage in 1973, and is not uninterested in marriage in 2010. The legislator adopted a different approach to cohabitation models in 1973, and decided not to actively promote marriage relative to other cohabitation models through legislation, but nevertheless said that marriage was still an important institution. Parliament's Law Commission explicitly underlined that the idea was to keep marriage as the primary form of family formation for the majority of the population.[702]

---

695 Ryrstedt, Eva, Legal Status of Cohabitants in Sweden, 2004, p. 437. See also Ryrstedt, Eva, Bodelning och bostad, 1998, pp. 416 and 429.

696 Briggs, Margaret, The Formalization of Property Sharing Rights for De Facto Couples in New Zealand, 2009, p. 341.

697 For a discussion of the 2001 marriage reform in New Zealand, see Atkin, Bill, Reflections on New Zealand's Property Reforms 'Five Years On', 2007, pp. 217–244. See also Briggs, Margaret, The Formalization of Property Sharing Rights for De Facto Couples in New Zealand, 2009, pp. 334–337.

698 Atkin, Bill, Reflections on New Zealand's Property Reforms 'Five Years On', 2007, p. 222.

699 Lødrup, Peter, The Reharmonisation of Nordic Family Law, 2003, p. 21.

700 See section 5.2.1.

701 See, for instance, Agell, Anders, Should and Can Family Law Influence Social Behaviour? 1998, pp. 126 ff.

702 Law Commission Report (LU 1973:20), pp. 74 f.

Had there been no interest in preserving marriage, it appears likely that the institution of marriage would have been abolished in the 1970s. The fact that marriage has been retained in the law and that the institution of registered partnership was modelled on marriage in the 1990's indicate that marriage still is a prominent cohabitation model in Sweden.[703]

5.2.4. STRUCTURE AND CONTENT

The Cohabitees Joint Homes Act of 1973 consisted of seven articles. A cohabitee relationship was defined as: "a marriage-like relationship between an unmarried man and an unmarried woman".[704] Upon the dissolution of such a "marriage-like" relationship, the cohabitee with the greatest need could be given the right to take over the couple's joint dwelling. Children were not a prerequisite for exercising this right, but children served as an assumption that the relationship was in fact marriage-like in the sense of the Act, as opposed to, for instance, friends or siblings living together.[705] In respect of couples without children, it could be motivated to grant one of the cohabitees the right to take over the dwelling, for instance upon the death of a cohabitee after a long relationship, or in situations when the woman was pregnant when the cohabitation ended. Also non-biological parental ties could be taken into account, e.g. if a cohabitee had custody of a child which was not the cohabitees' mutual child.[706] However, exceptional reasons were required in the absence of mutual children.

5.3. THE COHABITEES JOINT HOMES ACT OF 1987

5.3.1. LEGALLY RECOGNIZING A NEW STATUS?

In short, the 1987 Cohabitees Act consisted of four different types of legal rules.[707] *Firstly,* there were rules establishing a property system comparable to the deferred community of property regime applicable to spouses, although much more limited in scope. *Secondly,* there were provisions based on the Cohabitees Act of 1973, establishing a right to take over a dwelling. *Thirdly,* there were rules laying down a requirement of joint consent of the parties, or judicial

703 The future form and function of marriage will be analyzed in section 9.4.

704 The Act of 1973, Section 1.

705 The Act of 1973, Section 1.

706 Government Bill (Prop 1973:32), pp. 132–134. In the Committee Report (SOU 1972:41), the proposal was limited to only covering couples with children. In the Government Bill of 1973, however, such a solution was considered too limited.

707 A division into three categories has also been made by David Bradley. See Family Law and Political Culture, 1996, pp. 98 f.

authorization, for certain dispositions of the cohabitee property. There were also rules protecting the rights of third parties. *Fourthly*, upon the death of a cohabitee, the surviving cohabitee was entitled to economic compensation equal to a fixed amount of money from the cohabitee property of the deceased cohabitee.[708] However, the right to such compensation presupposed that the deceased cohabitee left behind property which qualified as "cohabitee property" according to the Act.

In the Committee Report of 1981, it was stated that: "There is no reason why cohabitation between unmarried persons should not be considered a fully respectable cohabitation form, serving a purpose of its own".[709] This statement in the Report can be claimed to illustrate a willingness to signal public approval of cohabitation without marriage. In other words, it can be claimed that attributing "marriage-like" legal effects to unmarried cohabiting couples was motivated, not only for practical reasons, but also for the symbolic purpose of recognizing cohabitation without marriage as a civil status in Sweden. According to Eva Ryrstedt, a certain touch of "status" is discernible in the 1987 Act, as well as in the 2003 Act. However, as Ryrstedt rightly points out, the legal significance of the "status" of unmarried cohabitation in Sweden is less comprehensive than the legal status attached to marriage, because of the differences in respect of legal effects.[710]

In my opinion, Ryrstedt has a point that the Cohabitees Act of 1987 can be seen as introducing an institution with certain status based features. Through the 1987 Act, one could say that part of the contractual dimension of marriage was made applicable to unmarried couples living together, more precisely, a limited version of the property division rules. In addition, through the 1987 Act, a new legal terminology was established; the term "cohabitees" was introduced, to describe an unmarried couple living together in accordance with the prerequisites laid down in the Act. It can be claimed that this terminology contributed to creating connotations to status, i.e. that a cohabitee relationship, covered by the Cohabitees Act, is generally perceived as more committed than a relationship where the parties involved refer to each other in terms of "boyfriend" or "girlfriend". In other words, cohabitation without marriage is not an independent civil status alongside of marriage in Sweden, but it can be claimed to have certain status-based features. However, because the Cohabitees Act applies by default, i.e. without a registration procedure establishing the consent

---

708 See the Cohabitees Act of 2003, Section 18. The compensation amounts to two *prisbasbelopp* (basic amounts). The value of one "basic amount" is established through a special act and is raised annually. See section 5.4.4.2. A similar provision applies to spouses, although the minimum sum which a spouse is entitled to is four basic amounts.

709 "Det finns heller inte något skäl, varför samboende mellan ogifta inte skulle kunna betraktas som en fullt respektabel samlevnadsform, som fyller en egen uppgift." Committee Report (SOU 1981:85), p. 116. Author's translation.

710 Ryrstedt, Eva, Bodelning och bostad, 1998, p. 423.

of the couple to being subjected to the rules of the Cohabitees Act, the civil status feature remains limited. In the Government Bill of 1987, the practical need of introducing more legal rules was the central motive for reform – not the ideological value of legal recognition.[711]

It can be noted that in the Committee Report of 1981, the so-called neutrality policy seems to reappear.[712] Statutory recognition of cohabitation without marriage through the enactment of more extensive rules was now considered to be the very intention of the neutrality concept formulated in the 1969 guidelines. However, the neutrality argument was not used in the following Government Bill as an argument in favor of legally recognizing the rights of unmarried couples, which suggests that this argument was in no way decisive for the enactment.[713] A likely explanation is that the neutrality policy reappeared in 1981 as one argument, among others, for legally regulating the economic effects of separation of unmarried couples, in the general spirit of decreasing the ethical values in the marriage regulation. As illustrated above, the term "neutrality" has become a value-charged concept in the policy debate, in respect of the question whether or not regulation on cohabitation without marriage has "threatened" the institution of marriage.[714]

Finally, it can be mentioned that when the Cohabitees Joint Homes Act of 1987 was adopted, a corresponding Act – "the Homosexual Cohabitees Act" – was enacted for same-sex couples.[715]

5.3.2. THE COHABITEES ACT AND THE MARRIAGE FREQUENCY: A BRIEF OBSERVATION

In 1973, when cohabitation without marriage was first regulated in statutory law, a main reason for adopting a special cohabitees act was that cohabitation without marriage often appeared to function as a preliminary stage to marriage, and it was found desirable to facilitate a "smooth transition" between unmarried cohabitation and marriage, for the purpose of assuring that couples would not be deterred from marrying by losing tax related benefits or other advantages.[716] It was pointed out that applying similar rules to any division of property upon the termination of the relationship was expected to "defuse" the step to formalizing the relationship by concluding a marriage.[717] The opposite outlook on cohabitation without marriage and its impact on the institution of marriage has

711 Government Bill (Prop 1986/87:1), p. 105. See also Committee Report (SOU 1981:85), p. 116.
712 Committee Report (SOU 1981:85), p. 116.
713 Government Bill (Prop 1986/87:1).
714 See section 5.2.3.2.
715 Lag (1987:813) om homosexuella sambor. See section 6.3.1.
716 Government Bill (Prop 1986/87:1), pp. 41 and 102.
717 Government Bill (Prop 1986/87:1), p. 102.

been provided in the literature, namely that regulating cohabitation without marriage in a special act has decreased the marriage frequency in Sweden.[718] In practice, however, the marriage frequency seems to have been more or less unaffected by the 1987 Cohabitees Act. Also the number of divorces have remained on the same level.[719]

Year	Population	Marriages	Divorces
1970	8 081 229	43 278	12 943
1975	8 208 442	44 103	25 383
1980	8 317 937	37 569	19 887
1985	8 358 139	38 297	19 763
1990	8 590 630	40 477[720]	19 357
1995	8 837 496	33 642	22 528
2000	8 882 792	39 895	21 502
2005	9 047 752	44 381	20 000

5.4. THE COHABITEES ACT OF 2003

5.4.1. WHY WAS THE ACT ADOPTED?

5.4.1.1. The Symbolic Value of Including Same-Sex and Different-Sex Cohabitees in the Same Enactment

In 2003, the cohabitee regulation was revised once again in Sweden.[721] In substance, the Act of 2003 is similar to its predecessor, the Cohabitees Joint Homes Act of 1987, only encompassing the cohabitees' joint dwelling and joint household goods, and providing for a division of that property upon termination of the relationship. Many provisions in the Cohabitees Act of 1987 were

718 See section 5.2.3.2.

719 The figures below have been retrieved from Statistics Sweden, www.scb.se. Accessed 2 December 2010.

720 It should be mentioned that the increased number of marriages in 1989 was connected to a law revision introducing new rules on widow's pension, which entered into force on 1 January 1990. The old rules on widow's pension were repealed, and a possibility for a surviving man or a surviving woman to receive a financial benefit during a limited time was introduced. The new rules were less advantageous and many couples married in 1989, in order to be covered by the old rules. However, it can be noted that generous transition rules were introduced, as well as a general exception in respect of women born prior to 1944, which made it possible to sometimes continue applying the old rules. See Brattström, Margareta, Makars pensionsrättigheter, 2004, p. 79.

721 The Cohabitees Act entered into force on 1 July 2003, replacing the Cohabitees Joint Homes Act (1987:232) and the Act on Homosexual Cohabitees (1987:813), encompassing both Acts in the same enactment. See Government Bill (Prop 2002/03:80), pp. 27 f.

transferred unaltered into the Act of 2003, but some terminological clarifications were made. The substantive rules in the Act will be accounted for in sections 5.4.2, 5.4.3 and 5.4.4.

In the Government Bill of 2003, the practical advantages of dealing with all unmarried cohabitees in the same enactment were underlined. It was held that the legislative technique used previously – to deal with same-sex cohabitees separately – was confusing and the legal effects appeared unclear.[722] However, although not mentioned explicitly in the bill, as a primary reason for adopting the Cohabitees Act of 2003, the symbolic significance of equal treatment of same-sex couples and different-sex couples can also be seen as a driving force behind the 2003 Act. Through the Act of 2003, the two enactments of 1987 dealing with unmarried cohabitees – the Cohabitees Joint Homes Act and the Homosexual Cohabitees Act – were merged into one Cohabitees Act, and this signalled to society that achieving equal treatment of couples, regardless of sex, was desirable.

As will be illustrated in the remaining chapters below, the idea of protecting the rights of homosexual individuals and treating same-sex and different-sex couples equally in the law had become a primary aim in Sweden, as well as in many other European countries in the early twenty-first century, in light of the predominating human rights discourse in Europe. In Sweden, this aim has resulted in several legal enactments, including a registered partnership act and a gender-neutral marriage enactment. As a result of the aim to not distinguish between couples in the law because of the sex of the individuals concerned, retaining two separate but equal cohabitee acts for same-sex and different-sex couples was neither desirable nor necessary.

5.4.1.2. Protection of a Weaker Party – Still a Central Goal

In the Government Bill of 2003, ideological reasons based on equality between same-sex and different-sex couples were not emphasized. Like its predecessors, the 2003 Act expressly set out to protect the financially weaker party upon termination of the relationship.[723] In fact, the aim to protect a weaker party appears to be even more clearly expressed in the Government Bill of 2003 than in the previous Bill of 1987. In 1987, protection of a weaker party was considered necessary primarily because of cohabitees' general reluctance to enter into agreements to safeguard a just outcome in case of dissolution.[724] In 2003, however, protecting a weaker party was announced as a general, all-encompassing purpose.[725]

---

722 Government Bill (Prop 2002/03:80), p. 26. See also Ryrstedt, Eva, Legal Status of Cohabitants in Sweden, 2004, p. 416.
723 Government Bill (Prop 2002/03:80), p. 25.
724 Government Bill (Prop 1986/87:1), p. 107.
725 Government Bill (Prop 2002/03:80), p. 25.

Regarding the earlier 1973 Act, it appears accurate to describe its main purpose in terms of providing a minimum level of social protection to a weaker party. The 1973 Act contained only a possibility to take over the home. In comparison, adding rules on the division of certain property does not increase the level of social protection, but it can still create a principle for the level of equality and fairness upon dissolution. Nevertheless, an outcome of a property division according to these rules can also appear random and unjust, as will be illustrated in section 5.4.1.3. Moreover, the cohabitees can jointly "opt-out" of the division of property by agreement. In the Act of 2003, the couple's autonomy was increased, which strengthened their freedom of choice,[726] but exercising this autonomy requires that both parties are in fact in agreement. If no agreement can be reached, which sets the property division rules aside, the rules of the 2003 Act apply as a default regime.

It appears that the Cohabitees Act still has a social protection function in respect of a weaker party, considering that not all provisions of the Cohabitees Act can be contracted out of, and because "it takes two to tango", i.e. to conclude an agreement setting the division of property rules in the Cohabitees Act aside. If no agreement is made, the property division rules apply and can equalize economic inequalities to the benefit of a financially weaker party.[727] Nevertheless, as a result of changes in Swedish society in the twenty-first century, the "protection function" of the Cohabitees Act of 2003 has decreased in importance. A truly financially weaker party who was in need of social protection in 1973 (in reality often the woman who raised the children) is rarer in twenty-first century Sweden. In chapter 4, the same development toward focusing on the autonomy of the individuals has been noted in respect of spouses, at the expense of the protective function of the regulation.

5.4.1.3. A Minimum Level of Protection? Unfair Results of the Act

An official goal of the Cohabitees Act of 2003 is to contribute, like its predecessors, to providing a *minimum level* of protection when the cohabitation ends.[728] The intention was not – it was underlined in the Government Bill of 2003 – to create a "second-class marriage" with a property regime of a lower dignity compared to the marital property regime, applicable to cohabiting couples.[729] It was underlined that the institution of marriage was still superior to other cohabitation models in respect of personal security and legal stability.[730] Nonetheless, it is likely that a cohabitee, who according to the default rules is

---

726 See section 5.4.3.1.

727 If there are third party stipulations in a will or connected to a gift, these cannot be set aside by the cohabitees through an agreement.

728 Government Bill (Prop 2002/03:80), p. 25.

729 Government Bill (Prop 2002/03:80), p. 25.

730 Government Bill (Prop 2002/03:80), p. 25.

obligated to transfer property owned by him or her, or the value of such property, to the other cohabitee when the relationship has ended, may regard this as far-reaching and far beyond a minimum level obligation. Furthermore, sociological research has indicated that many cohabitees have insufficient knowledge of the scope of the Cohabitees Act, and that an application for division of property may come as a surprise to the wealthier cohabitee.[731]

The overall impression is that the effects of the Act of 2003 can be quite far-reaching in situations when the unmarried cohabiteees have not "opted-out" of the rules on division of property and one cohabitee demands a division, especially in situations when the cohabitee obliged to pay a certain sum to the other was unaware of the scope of the Act. The division of property according to the Cohabitees Act of 2003 risks being perceived as "unfair" by the general public and at least one of the cohabitees. An outcome of a division of property according to the Act could be that the cohabitee who owned less property during the cohabitation comes out as the wealthier party after the property division. In Swedish legal literature, various examples are given of these kinds of situations.[732] For instance, a result which generally appears unfair is when one party purchases a home for the couple, through investing money earned from selling a previous apartment. Although owned alone by that cohabitee, the home acquired for the purpose of joint use becomes cohabitee property, and its value is to be divided equally upon dissolution of the cohabitation. The other cohabitee, whose property mainly consisted of, e.g. shares in companies, may keep this out of the division. An outcome which makes the cohabitee who owned less during the cohabitation wealthier than the other cohabitee after the division of property cannot be seen as in line with the alleged aim to protect a financially weaker cohabitee.[733]

Another situation which can be perceived as unfair is when a condominium, owned by one of the cohabitees, but defined as cohabitee property according to the Act, is sold during the cohabitation. The profit from the sale is then deposited in a bank account, and the couple moves into a rented apartment. Since the Cohabitees Act does not encompass money in bank accounts, the value of the joint home is no longer subject to division upon the dissolution of the

731 Committee Report (SOU 1999:104), pp. 245–249. See also Government Bill (Prop 2002/03:80), p. 25.

732 See Jänterä-Jareborg, Maarit in: Rechtregeln für nichteheliches Zusammenleben in Schweden, 2009, pp. 218–220, Ryrstedt, Eva, Legal Status of Cohabitants in Sweden, 2004, pp. 435–437, Ryrstedt, Eva, Delning mellan sambor i Sverige, 2000, pp. 398–401, and Brattström, Margareta, The Protection of a Vulnerable Party when a Cohabitee Relationship Ends, 2006, pp. 351 f.

733 Jänterä-Jareborg, Maarit, Rechtregeln für nichteheliches Zusammenleben in Schweden, 2009, p. 219. Jänterä-Jareborg points out that the rule on adjustment in § 15 of the Cohabitees Act of 2003 is most likely not applicable in this situation if the cohabitation has lasted for over five years, which was the case in her example.

relationship.[734] Furthermore, when a person moves into another person's home and they begin cohabiting, the home is not acquired "for the purpose of joint use" and thus not subject to division upon termination of the relationship. In this situation it does not matter if the cohabitee moving in has contributed by paying mortgages, or raised the value of the home through improvements; the home is still excluded from the scope of the Act because it was not acquired for the purpose of joint use.[735]

Various solutions to come to terms with random and unfair results of the Cohabitees Act have been discussed in the Swedish legal literature. Margareta Brattström underlines the necessity of securing a surviving cohabitee's financial situation, and advocates the introduction of a possibility for cohabitees to establish in a will that they wish to inherit each other as though they were married.[736] Eva Ryrstedt has held that the cohabitee regulation as a whole should reflect the economic co-operation of the couple and the economic community created as a result of the cohabitation. One way of achieving this is by making more property subject to division under the Cohabitees Act, i.e. not just the couple's joint home and chattels, acquired for the purpose of joint use.[737]

Unfair outcomes pursuant to the Cohabitees Act can under certain conditions, on an individual basis, be avoided in court by application of the adjustment provision in the Cohabitees Act (Section 15). This provision is modelled on a corresponding provision in the Marriage Code, and opens up for, if reasonable, deviation from the main rule of an equal division of the value of the property, so that the wealthier party keeps more than half.[738] Maarit Jänterä-Jareborg has advocated a more independent approach to cohabitation without marriage than the approach applied today, in order to avoid unfair and random outcomes of the Cohabitees Act. According to Jänterä-Jareborg, one way of achieving fairness and avoiding unreasonable results is to increase the adjustment possibilities of the courts in an individual case.[739]

Another possible means to avoid unfair outcomes upon the dissolution of a cohabitee relationship is to apply the principles developed in case law concerning unjust enrichment. According to these rules, a party can under certain conditions

---

734 Brattström, Margareta, The Protection of a Vulnerable Party when a Cohabitee Relationship Ends, 2006, pp. 351 f.

735 Brattström, Margareta, The Protection of a Vulnerable Party when a Cohabitee Relationship Ends, 2006, p. 351.

736 Brattström, Margareta, The Protection of a Vulnerable Party when a Cohabitee Relationship Ends, 2006, p. 353.

737 Ryrstedt, Eva, Legal Status of Cohabitants in Sweden, 2004, p. 437. See also Ryrstedt, Eva, Bodelning och bostad, 1998, pp. 416 and 429. See also section 5.2.3.2 above.

738 Requisites for application and jurisprudence relating to this provision are discussed by Agell, Anders, Brattström, Margareta, Äktenskap, Samboende, Partnerskap, 2008, pp. 274 f. See also Ryrstedt, Eva, Legal Status of Cohabitants in Sweden, 2004, p. 437. See also Ryrstedt, Eva, Bodelning och bostad, 1998, pp. 424–426.

739 Jänterä-Jareborg, Maarit, Rechtregeln für nichteheliches Zusammenleben in Schweden, 2009, p. 225.

be entitled to financial compensation, inter alia, for unpaid work or improvement of another party's property. In Sweden, however, this principle has only been subject to scrutiny by the courts in connection with matters belonging to the law of obligations – not in the family law context of unmarried cohabitees.[740] In Denmark and Finland, however, unjust enrichment claims have been used as a means to avoid unfairness upon the dissolution of a cohabitee relationship.[741] Moreover, in the Finnish Government Bill, which was approved by Parliament on 24 November 2010, such rules have been included.[742]

To summarize: the Swedish Cohabitees Act can give rise to results most likely perceived as random and "unfair" by the cohabitees and the general public, since it does not take into account each cohabitee's financial situation as a whole. Several possible solutions to come to terms with this problem and decrease the risk of unfair results upon dissolution of a cohabitee relationship have been accounted for above. The question of whether Sweden should adopt rules based on the Danish "cohabitation will", the Finnish Act (which e.g. takes into account the principle of unjust enrichment), or should find a different legal solution more suitable for Sweden, will not be solved here. According to my opinion, the Swedish Cohabitees Act should be subject to thorough legal scrutiny in a committee report, and the problems discussed above should be addressed.

5.4.1.4. *What is "Fair" in the Context of Cohabitation without Marriage?*

A basic difference between marriage and cohabitation without marriage is that marriage is contracted through an official procedure of consent, whereas cohabitation without marriage is not. The marriage ceremony aims to certify that both individuals concerned voluntarily consent to being subject to the marriage regulation. Since the Cohabitees Act applies by default – i.e. without a formal element through which the couple officially consent to being covered by special rules – all rules included in the Act can be seen as a limitation of the individual's freedom of choice.

In the Swedish preparatory work on proposed legislation, social similarities in the everyday lives of unmarried cohabitees and spouses have been emphasized.[743] The similarity is also visible in the term "marriage-like conditions", which was a requisite for the rules' application, expressed in the Cohabitees Act of 1987. This terminology is not used in the 2003 Cohabitees Act, because same-sex cohabitees are covered by the Act and they did not have access

740 Agell, Anders, Brattström, Margareta, Äktenskap, Samboende, Partnerskap, 2008, pp. 253 f.

741 Agell, Anders, Brattström, Margareta, Äktenskap, Samboende, Partnerskap, 2008, pp. 254. See also Government Bill, (RP 37/2010 rd), p. 14 (Finland).

742 Government Bill, (RP 37/2010 rd), p. 14. See also http://web.eduskunta.fi/Resource.phx/riksdagen/index.htx.

743 Government Bill (Prop 1973:32), p. 84, where it is assumed that married and unmarried couples in most cases live under the same social conditions.

to marriage at the time when the Act was adopted. However, this was merely a linguistic modification. No substantive change was intended in respect of the intimate characteristic of the relationships covered by the Act.[744]

A different outlook on cohabitees' social relationship is held by Marsha Garrison. More precisely, Garrison focuses on the *differences* between spouses and cohabitees, also on the Swedish arena. According to Garrison, the perception of what is "fair" when it comes to dealing with unmarried cohabitees in the law depends on how one views the relationship between the cohabiting couple. In Garrison's opinion, the situation of unmarried cohabitees is different from that of spouses, since the former are less likely to share monetary resources. The legislator should, consequently, refrain from interfering in unmarried couples' financial relations through statutory provisions.[745] Garrison even argues that applying "marriage-like" rules by default to unmarried cohabitees would "undermine the consistency, fairness, and integrity of the law".[746]

Tone Sverdrup, on the other hand, has argued along the lines of the Swedish legislator, underlining the similarities between unmarried cohabitees and spouses. Sverdrup's view is that cohabitees, although they do not necessarily earn the same amount of money, constitute a unit, in respect of consumption, work and investments. Sverdrup rightly points out that: "[cohabitees] eat the same food, go on the same holidays and share common financial responsibilities toward their children."[747] In other words, a cohabitee relationship is generally characterized by the same interdependency as a marriage. Sverdrup has observed that the cohabitee with the lowest income – often because she (or he) has worked part time in order to be the primary caretaker of the couple's children – will not have much money left for investments.[748] In this situation, statutory intervention, through cohabitee rules applicable by default, is a means to avoid unfairness.

These opposite approaches to cohabitation without marriage illustrate different interpretations of the concept of justice. The American philosopher Michael J. Sandel has pointed out that an established understanding of justice focuses on freedom as the central component.[749] Sandel has distinguished between two "camps" with opposite outlooks on how to achieve justice through freedom. There is the "laissez-faire camp," which believes that "justice consists of

744 Government Bill (Prop 2002/03:80), p. 27.

745 Garrison, Marsha, Marriage Matters: What's Wrong with the ALI's Domestic Partnership Proposal, 2008.

746 Garrison, Marsha, Marriage Matters: What's Wrong with the ALI's Domestic Partnership Proposal, 2008, p. 2.

747 Sverdrup, Tone, An Ill-Fitting Garment: Why the Logic of Private Law Falls Short between Cohabitants, 2009, p. 356. See also p. 368.

748 Sverdrup, Tone, An Ill-Fitting Garment: Why the Logic of Private Law Falls Short between Cohabitants, 2009, p. 356. See also p. 356.

749 Sandel also mentions other approaches to justice, for instance justice through virtue and good life, often identified with cultural conservatives on the political right. See Sandel, Michael J., Justice, What's the Right Thing to Do? 2009, p. 20.

respecting and upholding the voluntary choices made by consenting adults."[750] The public should, according to this interpretation of justice, refrain from interfering with personal choices through legislation. The opposite "camp", which Sandel describes as "egalitarian," believes that justice is achieved through fairness. From this point of view "[...] [J]ustice requires policies that remedy social and economic disadvantages and give everyone a fair chance at success".[751]

The Swedish Cohabitees Act of 2003 and its predecessors appear to represent the "egalitarian camp". The Swedish Cohabitees Act interferes with the individual's freedom to not be covered by legislation, through application by default. It limits the financially stronger cohabitee's autonomy in respect of his or her property, for the purpose of creating a fair financial and social outcome upon dissolution. In other words, the Cohabitees Act aims to create justice through fairness by remedying social and economic disadvantages of the financially weaker cohabitee. This approach is supported by Tone Sverdrup. Marsha Garrison, on the other hand, who emphasizes the importance of unmarried couples' right to be spared from the interference of special rules in their property relations, can be seen as defending what Sandel calls the "laissez-faire" attitude.

Interpreting the concept of justice as requiring an element of fairness appears consistent with the basic values promoted by the Social Democrats in Sweden already in the 1930s. An egalitarian idea based on fairness can be seen as a central component of the Swedish welfare state, established during the following decades, more precisely the idea of granting everybody a fair chance to succeed in society.[752] In fact, the Swedish welfare state appears to have created an ideal base for cultivating the principle of fairness – sometimes at the expense of the autonomy of an individual – for instance in respect of the relationship between rich and poor, men and women, married and unmarried, children of married parents and children of unmarried parents, and most recently, between heterosexual and homosexual couples. In these situations justice appears to have been linked to the egalitarian policy of creating fairness in society.[753]

---

750 Sandel, Michael J., Justice, What's the Right Thing to Do? 2009, p. 20.

751 Sandel, Michael J., Justice, What's the Right Thing to Do? 2009, p. 20.

752 See section 4.1.2.

753 On the topic of egalitarian political policies in Sweden, see also Bradley, David, Family Law and Political Culture, 1996, pp. 72–74.

5.4.2. THE FORMS AND CONDITIONS OF COHABITATION WITHOUT MARRIAGE: THE ACT OF 2003

5.4.2.1. Establishment of Cohabitation without Marriage

5.4.2.1.1. Substantive Content of the Act

In the Cohabitees Act of 2003, a cohabitee relationship is defined as: *"two persons living together in a relationship, on a permanent basis, sharing a household"*.[754] This general definition applies also outside of the scope of the Cohabitees Act, unless otherwise specified, which creates consistency in different fields of law. This is a clarification compared to earlier, when the determination of who were regarded as "unmarried cohabitees" varied depending on the legal context.[755]

The definition of a *relationship* in the Cohabitees Act of 2003 (Section 1) presupposes a sexual relationship, or that the relationship is of such intimacy that sexual activity usually occurs.[756] The term "relationship" replaced the earlier terminology "marriage-like conditions". The old terminology was criticized for being vague and outdated.[757] The reason why the term "marriage-like" was abolished also has to do with the inclusion of same-sex couples in the Act.[758] Including same-sex cohabitees in the same enactment as different-sex cohabitees can be seen as a primary reason for adopting the 2003 Act.[759] Since same-sex couples did not have access to marriage in Sweden in 2003, the term "marriage-like" appeared unsuitable.

Permanence as a requisite for application indicates that the relationship should be durable, or at least intended to be of some duration.[760] As regards *"sharing a household"* the definition presupposes that the couple has shared economy, or that there is a certain degree of cooperation concerning household expenses.[761]

---

754 In Swedish: "två personer som stadigvarande bor tillsammans i ett parförhållande och har gemensamt hushåll" (author's translation). In the Cohabitees Joint Homes Act of 1987, the corresponding applicable wording was: "one man and one woman".

755 Government Bill (Prop 2002/03:80), pp. 27 f.

756 Government Bill (Prop 2002/03:80), p. 27.

757 Government Bill (Prop 2002/03:80), p. 27. The term "marriage-like conditions" necessitated consultation of preparatory work, whereas the term "relationship" was said to be more precise and easily interpreted, see p. 27.

758 Government Bill (Prop 2002/03:80), p. 28.

759 Government Bill (Prop 2002/03:80), p. 1. See also section 6.4.2.

760 Government Bill (Prop 2002/03:80), pp. 27 f.

761 Government Bill (Prop 2002/03:80), p. 28.

5.4.2.1.2. "Non-Intimate" Relationships Excluded: Relatives and Friends

When the Cohabitees Act of 2003 was under preparation, it was discussed whether the scope of the Act should be extended to include also other types of relationships, such as adult siblings or parents and children living together. These kinds of households were, in the end, not included, since the persons involved were not considered to be in need of the legal protection laid down in family law legislation.[762] Excluding couples who would not be eligible to marry from the scope of the Cohabitees Act indicates that the symbolic value of cohabitation without marriage is in compliance with the values attached to marriage. Both the Cohabitees Act and the regulation governing marriage are applicable to relationships between two persons who are living together as a couple and are not closely related.

The Swedish decision not to extend the scope of the Cohabitees Act to encompass, for instance siblings, appears to be in line with European standards as asserted by the Strasbourg Court in two cases. In short, the basic message of the Strasbourg Court is that relationships resembling marriage – and perhaps the values connected to such relationships – are worth protecting through law. In the first case – Burden v. the United Kingdom (2008)[763] – two British sisters had been living together for 31 years in a home which they owned jointly. The question for the Strasbourg Court to decide was whether or not adult siblings living together should be treated like married couples (or civil partners according to British law), and thus be exempted from the liability to pay inheritance tax upon the death of one of them. The Strasbourg Court found that the situations of married and unmarried heterosexual cohabiting couples were not analogous for the purposes of survivors' benefits, since "marriage remains an institution which is widely accepted as conferring a particular status on those who enter it".[764]

The second case – Korelc v. Slovenia (2009)[765] – concerned the right to take over a dwelling upon the death of one of two friends living together to save money, in a non-sexual relationship. The Strasbourg Court found that since the men were not in a situation comparable to homosexual cohabitees, spouses or close family members, denying the surviving friend the right to take over the

---

762 Committee Report (SOU 1999:104), pp. 271 ff. Being classified as "cohabitees" in the sense of the Cohabitees Act is relevant, inter alia, for the right to receive accommodation allowance. It should be mentioned, however, that non-intimate couples living together, for instance relatives can be entitled to take over a tenancy right under certain conditions, which will not be discussed here. These rules should not be confused with the Cohabitees Act.

763 Burden v. The United Kingdom, (application no. 13378/05), 29 April 2008.

764 Burden v. The United Kingdom, Para. 63. In summary, the ECHR found that there had been no violation of Art. 14 of the ECHR (non-discrimination) in conjunction with Art. 1, protocol 1 (the right to the peaceful enjoyment of possessions). Relevant jurisprudence from the Strasbourg court dealing with same-sex and different-sex cohabitation will de discussed in section 8.3.

765 Korelc v. Slovenia, (application no. 28456/03), 12 May 2009.

home did not constitute discrimination. The Court held that "distinguishing between different forms of cohabitation does not necessarily give rise to discrimination prohibited by Article 14".[766]

In Sweden, the decision not to include "non-intimate" relationships in the Cohabitees Act has been motivated with practical arguments – not ideological arguments. Friends or relatives living together are not assumed to need special family law rules since their economy as a rule is not intertwined. Nonetheless, only including "marriage-like" relationships in the Cohabitees Act can be seen as a symbolic defense of the twosome, intimate relationship as worthy of special legal protection and public recognition. In other words, the legislator is not willing to extend the view on what types of couples should enjoy legal recognition and be protected through special legislation, be it spouses or unmarried cohabitees. Thus, cohabitation without marriage remains a "marriage-like" institution. The Swedish approach is well in line with the recent decisions of the Strasbourg Court.

5.4.2.2. A Registration Procedure Instead of Application by Default?

Introducing a registration procedure for unmarried cohabiting couples who wish to be covered by special legislation was considered when the Act of 2003 was enacted. A registration procedure would help clarify exactly when a cohabitee relationship is established. Such a procedure was, however, dismissed in the Government Bill of 2003, as being contradictory to the official aim of the Act, namely to offer a certain level of social protection.[767] There was a great risk, it was held, that the cohabitees most in need of protection would not be the ones registering their relationship.[768]

Another factor, which was taken into account when rejecting the idea of adopting a registration procedure for unmarried cohabitees, was that contracts are rare in cohabitee relationships.[769] It was pointed out that the couple often becomes aware of the need to regulate their mutual affairs only when the relationship has ended and they disagree on how to divide their assets. Moreover, when the relationship ends because of the death of a cohabitee, it is too late, for instance, to draw up a will.[770] It was considered likely that unmarried cohabitees would be just as disinclined to apply for any registration as they are to enter into

[766] Korelc v. Slovenia, Para. 90.

[767] Government Bill (Prop 2002/03:80), p. 27.

[768] Government Bill (Prop 2002/03:80), p. 27.

[769] Government Bill (Prop 2002/03:80), p. 25. The general problem of cohabitees' unwillingness to enter into agreements regulating their cohabitation was also noted in the English Report: the Law Commission, Consultation Paper No. 179, Cohabitation: The Financial Consequences of Relationship Breakdown, A Consultation Paper, published 31 May 2006, Sections 5.23 and 5.24.

[770] Government Bill (Prop 2002/03:80), p. 25.

family law agreements in general, and the aim to protect a weaker party would therefore risk being lost.[771]

The idea of introducing a registration requirement for cohabitation without marriage has been discussed in the preparatory work and in the legal literature on several occasions during the last few decades.[772] In his doctoral thesis, Göran Lind proposed that the Cohabitees Act should be replaced by a registration procedure, which should also apply to marriage.[773] Ingeborg Schwenzer proposed in the "Model Family Code", that the same legal effects that apply to marriage should be attributed to unmarried cohabiting couples without a registration procedure in three situations: (1) if the relationship has lasted for more than three years, (2) if the partners have a common child or (3) if one or both partners have contributed substantially financially or otherwise to the relationship.[774] The guiding principle advocated by Schwenzer is that assets acquired during the "partnership" should be divided equally between the partners.[775] Schwenzer applies the term "partnerships" to marital as well as non-marital relationships (marriage, registered partnerships and informal cohabitee relationships) in the three situations enumerated above. Furthermore, it can be mentioned that Schwenzer has posed the question if marriage should be at all legally regulated. However, because people appear to wish to give their relationship significance through a marriage ceremony, she has not advocated that marriage should be abolished as a legal institution.[776]

In Sweden, an informal "default model" for unmarried cohabitees has been preferred to a registration model, as a means of protecting a financially weaker cohabitee. Basing legal effects of unmarried cohabitation on a registration procedure has the advantage that the consent of the couple to being subjected to legal rules would be secured, and, as a result, the legislation would not necessarily have to be kept at a minimum level.

In this author's opinion, which is in line with the legal solution chosen in the Swedish Cohabitees Act, the disadvantages with a registration procedure for unmarried cohabitees outweigh the advantages. A "registration model" has a different target group than the Swedish "default model". A registration model would not solve the problems created through informal cohabitation, which has attracted the attention of the Swedish legislator since the early 1970s. The wide-spread societal habit to cohabit without marriage risks creating practical

---

771 Government Bill (Prop 2002/03:80), pp. 25 and 27.

772 The proposal of the 1972 Commission has been discussed in section 4.2.2.4.

773 Lind, Göran, Common Law Marriage, 2006, pp. 1030–1044.

774 Schwenzer, Ingeborg, in Collaboration with Dimsey, Mariel, Model Family Code From a Global Perspective, 2006, pp. 7–9.

775 Schwenzer, Ingeborg, in Collaboration with Dimsey, Mariel, Model Family Code From a Global Perspective, 2006, Arts. 1.22 and 1.27.

776 Schwenzer, Ingeborg, in Collaboration with Dimsey, Mariel, Model Family Code From a Global Perspective, 2006, p. 5.

problems and financial injustice when such relationships end, because the couples have not formalized their relationship by marrying or safeguarded both partners' equal rights through agreements. The legislator's response has been to intervene in the couple's private relationship through the cohabitee regulation, for the purpose of creating a certain level of social protection, equality and fairness upon dissolution of the relationship. This "welfare function" of the Cohabitees Act is still relevant in Sweden, even if it is smaller today than when the Act was adopted.

If future research should indicate that there is a need for a registration model for unmarried cohabitees in Sweden, such a model should not replace the Cohabitees Act but supplement it. However, the issue of whether or not a supplementary registration procedure should be introduced will not be further developed within the framework of this thesis.[777] If an unmarried couple wishes to formalize the relationship through a registration, the institution of marriage is available. In the Netherlands, as will be discussed in chapter 7, the Registered Partnership Act, accessed through a formalized registration ceremony, appears to function as a "marriage lite" to couples who do not want to marry.

5.4.3. LEGAL EFFECTS OF COHABITATION WITHOUT MARRIAGE: THE ACT OF 2003

5.4.3.1. Division of Property

In 2003, the title of the Cohabitees Act was changed from "the Cohabitees Joint Homes Act" to the "Cohabitees Act". This terminological change can be criticized for creating confusion concerning the scope of the Act, falsely indicating that the scope of the Act changed from only encompassing the joint home to being more extensive. However, the Cohabitees Act of 2003 is still – like its predecessor – limited to providing rules on the division of the joint dwelling and household goods, acquired for the purpose of the cohabitees' joint use. The Act does apply, however, to property (home or chattels) which has been acquired by one partner with money gained prior to the cohabitation. Property primarily used by one cohabitee, as well as property used for leisure purposes, is not covered by the Act (Sections 6 and 7). Moreover, a dwelling or property acquired before the parties began living together is not covered by the Act, neither is private property acquired through inheritance or as a gift (Section 4).[778]

---

777 A few more observations in this respect are made in section 5.4.3.3 below.

778 Also property which has replaced property acquired through inheritance, will or as a gift, with the condition that it should be the receiver's private property, is excluded from the Act (Section 4).

The Act becomes applicable when the cohabitation ends, provided that one cohabitee (or both) makes use of the possibility to request a division of property. Unless otherwise agreed by the cohabitees, the net value of the cohabitees' joint dwelling and household goods is to be divided equally between them. It should be emphasized that cohabitation – like marriage – does not change the ownership conditions; it only creates a latent claim to a net value realizable upon dissolution of the cohabitation. It is irrelevant if property qualifying as cohabitee property is owned by one cohabitee. The value is still subject to division, if it was acquired for the purpose of joint use. In the Act of 2003, for reasons of clarity, a one-year time-limit was introduced within which a request for division of cohabitee property must be made.

The cohabitees are free to enter into an agreement which excludes division of property.[779] This possibility was slightly broadened in the Act of 2003 (Section 9). Thus the cohabitees can agree to exclude certain – not necessarily all – property otherwise covered from a future division. Such an agreement, which must be in writing and signed by both cohabitees (or future cohabitees), can be adjusted by the Court, provided that the Court finds the result unreasonable (Section 9).

Yet not all aspects of the Cohabitees Act can be set aside through an agreement. The social protection concerning the right to take over the joint home upon dissolution of the cohabitation is indispensable. It applies irrespective of whether or not the dwelling is classified as "cohabitee property" (the equivalence to marital property).[780] Conversely, if the joint home is not cohabitee property, the right to take over the home only applies to tenancy contracts and tenancy owner rights – not to real estate (Section 22).

5.4.3.2. Joint "Caveat" Ownership

The doctrine of so-called caveat ownership, developed in case law, can be used to avoid some unfair results when a cohabitee relationship ends. By claiming caveat ownership, official titles to property excluded from the scope of the Cohabitees Act – such as summer homes, motor vehicles, etc. – are challenged. This way a cohabitee's "hidden" title to property can be made overt. According to these rules, spouses and cohabitees are in principle treated equally.[781]

---

779 Committee Report (SOU 1999:104), pp. 212 f. Government Bill (Prop 2002/03:80), pp. 33–35.

780 The term *samboegendom* (cohabitee property) is discussed in: Government Bill (Prop 2002/03:80), Ny sambolag, p. 33. This term was preferred to *samborättsgods* because the latter connotes marital property and, as pointed out by the Uppsala Law Faculty in the Government Bill of 2003, p. 33, in respect of cohabitation without marriage, unlike in respect of marriage, the division of property is, as a rule, not obligatory. However it should be kept in mind that when spouses have concluded a contract concerning property relations making all property private, there is no division of property when the marriage is dissolved.

781 Maarit Jänterä-Jareborg. See Rechtregeln für nichteheliches Zusammenleben in Schweden, 2009, pp. 222 f. See also Ryrstedt, Eva, Legal Status of Cohabitants in Sweden, 2004, pp. 429–431 and Ryrstedt, Eva, Delning mellan sambor i Sverige, 2000, pp. 378–380.

There are three requisites for caveat ownership: (1) that the property had been acquired for joint use by the couple, (2) that the spouse or cohabitee without the title to the property in question had made some financial contribution aiming at becoming a joint owner and (3) that the cohabitee with the title was aware of the aim of the other to become joint owner.[782] This case law is more relevant to cohabitees than to spouses, since the marital property regime, as a main rule, includes all property, whereas the property covered by the Cohabitees Act is more limited.[783]

5.4.3.3. Proposals to Extend the Scope of the Act

When the 2003 Act was adopted, extending the scope of property included in property division was considered since cohabitation without marriage had become a common and socially accepted "life style".[784] More precisely, it was discussed whether also motor vehicles should be included, the idea being that the car is often just as economically and practically important to the couple as their joint home.[785] The government found, however, that such an extension demanded further investigation of its effects. Including motor vehicles, it was held, might not best serve the purpose of protecting the weaker party.[786] No enactment has been proposed in respect of motor vehicles since the Act of 2003 was adopted.

Although excluding motor vehicles, in my opinion, may not be the most conspicuous shortcoming of the Act, keeping in mind the examples discussed in section 5.4.1.3, it is noteworthy that further extending the scope of the Cohabitees Act has been subject to discussion. This discussion suggests that also other issues could be subject to division in the future. Another question, which appears to be more urgent than whether or not to include motor vehicles, is if succession rules

---

782 See Brattström, Margareta, The Protection of a Vulnerable Party when a Cohabitee Relationship Ends, 2006, p. 350.

783 This has been pointed out by Maarit Jänterä-Jareborg. See Rechtregeln für nichteheliches Zusammenleben in Schweden, 2009, p. 223.

784 Government Bill (Prop 2002/03:80), p. 25.

785 Government Bill (Prop 2002/03:80), p. 31. Including motor vehicles as equivalent to household goods, was proposed when the Cohabitees Act of 1987 was enacted, in Committee Report (SOU 1981:85). The proposal, which was not endorsed, was that spouses' as well as cohabitees' property, including motor vehicles, should be owned jointly. Since the proposal was not carried out in respect of spouses, it was not carried out in respect of cohabitees either. It can be noted that including motor vehicles in the cohabitee regulation has been discussed for some time. See Government Bill (Prop 2002/03:80), p. 31.

786 The government pointed out that there are often two cars in a household, one of which might be a company car. In such cases a division of property would only include the joint car – not the company car – and this would, perhaps, be disadvantageous for the weaker party. Although the government found that it is likely that the protection of the weaker party demands an extended application of the Act, the achievement of this might not be best served through the proposal concerning motor vehicles and the issue should therefore be further investigated. See Government Bill (Prop 2002/03:80), pp. 31 f.

should be applied to unmarried cohabitees, in line with the Norwegian or Danish legal developments. In Norway cohabitees were granted succession rights in 2009.[787] In Denmark, a proposal to introduce succession rights for cohabitees was rejected in 2007. However, a possibility for a cohabitee to protect the interests of a surviving cohabitee through a special will, a "cohabitation will", was introduced. Thus it is possible for unmarried cohabitees to establish a will stating that they shall inherit one another as if they were married.[788] In my opinion, which is also the opinion of Margareta Brattström, the possibility of introducing such rules also in Sweden should be considered.[789]

5.4.4. DISSOLUTION OF COHABITATION WITHOUT MARRIAGE

5.4.4.1. Substantive Content of the Rules

A significant clarification achieved through the 2003 Act was the introduction of an explicit statutory provision for the determination of when a cohabitee relationship ends. Until 2003 there was no explicit provision defining when a cohabitee relationship ended. Instead principles established in case law were guiding in this respect.[790] Grey zones could still arise and require a court decision on whether or not the cohabitation had ended. For instance, in 1994 the Supreme Court clarified that a cohabitee moving to a nursing facility, for some time or permanently, did not necessarily mean that the cohabitation had ended.[791]

According to the Cohabitees Act of 2003, a cohabitee relationship ends if (1) the couple (or one of them) contracts a marriage,[792] (2) if they move apart or (3)

---

787 See Norwegian Government Bill, Ot.prop. no. 73, 2007–2008.

788 Lov nr. 515 og 516 af 6. juni 2007, which entered into force on 1 January 2008.

789 Brattström, Margareta, The Protection of a Vulnerable Party when a Cohabitee Relationship Ends, 2006, p. 353. See also section 5.4.1.3.

790 Government Bill (Prop 2002/03:80), p. 28. See also Committee Report (SOU 1999:104) pp. 212 f. Government Bill (Prop 2002/03:80), pp. 210–212, with reference to case law.

791 See decision by the Supreme Court, NJA 1994 p. 61. In the case, a man had suffered brain damage after a severe accident and was living in a nursing facility. The question whether or not the cohabitation had ended was raised when the man's administrator applied for a division of property, which the other cohabitee contested. The administrator was considered authorized to demand a division of property, but the Court, nevertheless stated that the parties' intentions as a rule should be taken into account in situations when the cohabitees no longer live together, for instance because of hospitalization. The Court of Appeals came to the same conclusion in a similar case. See RH 1997:98. See also Government Bill (Prop 2002/03:80), p. 46.

792 It was discussed in the Government Bill whether or not it was necessary to include a clarifying statement in the Act, laying down that it did not apply to spouses or registered partners, but this was considered self-explanatory and well-known to the general public. See Government Bill (Prop 2002/03:80), p. 28.

if one of them dies. Moreover, a cohabitee relationship ends (4) if a cohabitee (or both of them) applies to the district court for the appointment of a property distributor, for entitlement to reside alone in the joint home until the division of property is completed, or for the right to take over the joint home (Section 2).

The Cohabitees Act is centered on the dissolution of the relationship as a requisite for application and does not create any financial legal effects between the couple during the relationship. This is a significant difference compared to the marriage regulation, which is based on the idea that the spouses should live on the same financial standard during marriage. A cohabitee relationship does not create maintenance obligations between the parties. Cohabitees are able to enter into various legal agreements regulating their relationship. How extensive such agreements can be is unclear, although it is, most likely, not possible to agree that *all* legal effects of marriage should apply to the cohabitee relationship.[793]

5.4.4.2. Dissolution Because of the Death of a Cohabitee – A Few Comments

Unlike spouses, cohabitees do not inherit from each other unless there is a will. Succession law is based on the idea that a deceased person's assets should be distributed in accordance with his or her wishes or assumed wishes. When a couple has refrained from marrying, and from writing a will on behalf of each other, it has been considered incorrect to assume that the deceased person would have wanted inheritance rights to apply in respect of his or her surviving cohabitee.[794]

Certain limited survivor benefits nevertheless apply to unmarried cohabitees pursuant to the Cohabitees Act of 2003. The surviving cohabitee can demand a division of property and be granted a certain sum (two basic amounts)[795] from the estate of the deceased cohabitee, as his or her share in the division, before the estate is distributed among the heirs (Section 18, Para. 2).[796] The heirs have no right to receive such a sum, and they have no right to demand a division of property. Furthermore, a surviving cohabitee, who is the financially stronger of the two, can choose not to demand a property division, and instead keep his or her share, if it amounts to more than half of the net value of the couple's joint

---

793 Committee Report (SOU 1981:85), p. 252. See also Agell, Anders, Brattström, Margareta, Äktenskap, samboende, partnerskap, 2008, p. 254, with reference to a decision by the Supreme Court, NJA 1985 p. 172.

794 See Agell, Anders, Familjebegrepp och lagstiftningsideologi i svensk rätt, 1993, p. 43. It can be mentioned that a surviving cohabitee can sometimes be awarded compensation from the deceased cohabitee's life insurance.

795 In Swedish: *prisbasbelopp*, a fixed monetary amount established in the law and raised annually, lag (1962:381) om allmän försäkring. In 2010, one basic amount was 42 400 SEK. See also Government Bill (Prop 2002/03:80) p. 39 and Committee Report (SOU 1999:104), pp. 234 f. This rule does not apply if a cohabitee dies after separation but before the property has been divided.

796 See Agell, Anders, Legal Issues of the late 1990's, 1999, Vol. 38, p. 200.

home and chattels. This right only applies to the surviving cohabitee – not to the heirs of the deceased (Section 18, Para. 1).

According to the main rule, when a *spouse* dies without leaving a will on behalf of a third party and without leaving behind children from a previous relationship, the entire estate goes to the surviving spouse. *Cohabitees*, on the contrary, as mentioned above, do not inherit from each other, unless there is a will which secures the surviving cohabitee's financial situation. As pointed out by Margareta Brattström, cohabitees' ability to secure each other's financial situation upon the death of one of them through a will is limited.[797] For instance, unmarried cohabitees are not able to conclude an agreement stating that the succession rules applicable to spouses shall apply to their informal cohabitation.[798] The rules concerning succession law will not be further discussed here.[799]

5.5. SUMMARIZING ANALYSIS – THE IMPACT OF COHABITATION WITHOUT MARRIAGE ON THE INSTITUTION OF MARRIAGE

Above it has been claimed that all three Cohabitee Acts were adopted to solve practical problems relating to couples' choice to cohabit instead of marrying. The first Cohabitees Act – the 1973 Act – only solved the most essential problems, by providing, on certain conditions, the cohabitee with the greatest need of the couple's joint home with the right to take over the joint home upon separation. The second and the third Cohabitee Acts were extended to also include rules on division of the joint dwelling and household goods acquired for the purpose of joint use. An outspoken aim in the Swedish preparatory work has been to avoid creating a "second-class marriage" which would compete with marriage.[800] In fact, the fear of undermining marriage has prevented the adoption of a more extensive regulation, even if such regulation could well be claimed to increase the level of fairness upon dissolution of a cohabitee relationship.[801] One can argue that in spite of this legislative caution, cohabitation without marriage has come to function as a second-class marriage in Sweden, through the application of property division rules inspired by the rules applicable to marriage.

---

797 Brattström, Margareta, The Protection of a Vulnerable Party when a Cohabitee Relationship Ends, 2006, p. 352.

798 See decision by the Supreme Court, NJA 1985 p. 172. See also Agell, Anders, Brattström, Margareta, Äktenskap, samboende, partnerskap, 2008, pp. 254 f.

799 See Brattström, Margareta, Singer, Anna, Rätt arv, Fördelning av kvarlåtenskap, 2007.

800 Government Bill (Prop 1986/87:1), p. 40 and Government Bill (Prop 2002/03:80), pp. 25 and 27.

801 Government Bill (Prop 2002/03:80), Ny sambolag, p. 25.

On the other hand, the Cohabitees Act is much more limited in scope than the marriage regulation, which decreases its connotations of marriage. Then again, the scope of the Act is not necessarily decisive when analyzing whether or not a "second-class" marriage has been created. As discussed above, cohabitation without marriage under the Cohabitees Act can be described as having certain "status features".[802] For example, it can be claimed that being "cohabitees" under the Swedish Cohabitees Act, connotes a certain level of stability and commitment in respect of the relationship, which the reference to one's partner in the terms of "boyfriend" or "girlfriend" lacks. In other words, in contrast to marriage, cohabitation without marriage is not an independent civil status, but it has nevertheless "status-like" traits, which connote a certain level of stability and public recognition of the relationship.

The impact of the cohabitee enactments on the institution of marriage can be regarded from different perspectives. One can argue that the institution of marriage has been weakened or even threatened by the Cohabitee Acts. On the other hand, one can also argue that these regulations have in fact strengthened the institution of marriage. Through the Cohabitee Acts of 1987 and 2003, "marriage-like" rules on division of property have been extended to a broader category of people through application by default to couples who have chosen not to marry.

In this author's opinion, it is time to abandon the concerns of undermining marriage through cohabitee enactments. Cohabitation without marriage has become a legally recognized popular cohabitation model, which is not likely to disappear in society. Against this background, contributing to creating fairness when a cohabitee relationship ends ought to be the primary interest and the main goal of the Cohabitees Act – not retaining a clear distinction between cohabitation without marriage and marriage.[803] In other words, the issues of if cohabitation without marriage has threatened the institution of marriage and whether or not cohabitation without marriage should be classified as a "second-class marriage" are irrelevant from a legal point of view. The relevant issues are what kind of regulation unmarried cohabitees need today, in order to safeguard a high level of fairness upon dissolution of the cohabitee relationship, and how the interests of children are best protected.

---

802 See section 5.3.1.

803 This line of argument was also applied in 2006, in an extensive consultation paper by the English Law Commission, investigating cohabitation without marriage. The Law Commission, Consultation Paper No. 179, Cohabitation: The Financial Consequences of Relationship Breakdown, A Consultation Paper, published 31 May 2006. Fairness has been discussed in section 5.4.1.4.

6. TOWARD GENDER-NEUTRAL MARRIAGE – PRECEDING DEVELOPMENTS

"What's in a name? that which we call a rose
By any other name would smell as sweet."[804]

6.1. WHAT'S IN A NAME?

Opening up marriage to persons of the same sex has been called "one of the greatest family law controversies of our time".[805] This also applies to the Swedish enactment. In fact, the Swedish gender-neutral marriage regulation of 2009, like the Registered Partnership Act of 1994, proved to be so controversial that the government failed to present a bill to the Swedish Parliament. Instead the Registered Partnership Act was, in the end, based on a proposal by Parliament's own Committee on Civil Affairs.[806]

Why was adopting a gender-neutral marriage concept controversial in Sweden, where the basic idea since the 1970s has been to avoid moral input in family law legislation as far as possible? Adopting a gender-neutral marriage concept was irrelevant from a strictly legal point of view, since couples of the same sex already had access to a marriage-like civil status through the Registered Partnership Act and the same legal effects as those attached to marriage. Why was registered partnership not an adequate legal institution for same-sex couples in Sweden, and how did the institution of marriage become a symbol of full equality between same-sex and different-sex couples? What's in a name?

---

804 Quote from Romeo and Juliet, by William Shakespeare. The rose metaphor appears popular to use when discussing registered partnership. See, for instance, Curry-Sumner, Ian, All's well that ends registered? pp. 3–5.

805 Antokolskaia, Masha, Harmonisation of Family Law in Europe, 2006, p. 310.

806 Report of the Committee on Civil Affairs, (Civilutskottet) (2008/09:CU19).

6.2. LEGAL STRATEGIES AND APPROACHES TO HOMOSEXUALITY IN SWEDEN

6.2.1. THE POINT OF DEPARTURE

The 2009 enactment, which opened up marriage to two men or two women wishing to formalize their relationship, appears to have challenged certain fundamental core values attached to marriage. For centuries, the purpose of marriage was procreation and all sexual activity was to take place within marriage. As shown in chapter 2, sexual relations outside of marriage were criminalized and viewed as a threat to the fundamental components of society, marriage and the family.[807] Against this background, sexual acts between two persons of the same sex were also criminalized and condemned as immoral by both the state and the church. It was not until the 1970s, when the values concerning sexual relations changed, that the prerequisites for homosexual relationships in Swedish society changed.[808]

6.2.2. HOMOSEXUALITY AS A CRIMINAL OFFENSE: 1734–1944

According to the provincial laws, in force prior to the Code of 1734, fornication involving animals (bestiality), as well as persons of the same sex (sodomy), was forbidden on pain of death, with reference to the Bible.[809] It is noteworthy that these two crimes were dealt with in the same provision, treated as examples of "unnatural" sexuality.[810] In the Bible, bestiality and homosexual sexual acts can also be understood as addressed at the same time, which might explain why the two in the past became interchangeable.[811]

The Code of 1734 did not contain any provision in criminal law *explicitly* prohibiting sexual acts between persons of the same sex. Only fornication with

807 Coester-Waltjen, Dagmar, Coester Michael, International Encyclopedia of Comparative Law, Vol. IV, Persons and Family, Chapter 3, Formation of Marriage, 1997, p. 50. Also Vagn Greve, from a Danish perspective, notes that only married couples were allowed to have a sexual relationship and, as a consequence, it was self-evident to criminalize extra-marital sexual relations. See Hvornår er bigami strafbart? 2009, p. 93.

808 See section 4.3.1.

809 See Silverstolpe, Fredrik, Praxis och teori 1726–1864, Sympatiens hemlighetsfulla makt, 1999, p. 36.

810 This is also noted by: Rydström, Jens, Sinners and Citizens, 2001, p. 39.

811 King James Bible, Roman 1:23 and 1:26–27. This has been criticized as the result of a false interpretation of the scripture, the intention being to condemn sexual assault, not consenting sexual acts between two adult homosexual persons. See Nilsson, Gert (Editor) En fråga om kärlek, 1988, p. 26 and pp. 46 f. See also sections 6.5.3.2 and 6.5.3.3.

animals was mentioned in the criminal law.[812] However, this did not mean that homosexuality was tolerated. It was left to the individual judge's own discretion to impose a proper punishment on an individual basis when such a case appeared.[813] Publicity was thought to increase the unwanted behavior from society's point of view, rather than deterring such behavior.[814] Neither did the Criminal Code of 1864 include an explicit prohibition against same-sex sexual acts. A possible explanation for this might be that homosexuality was not considered as appalling as bestiality, which was explicitly criminalized, since bestiality – unlike homosexuality – was thought to lead to monstrous offspring.[815]

In the Criminal Code of 1864, Chapter 18, Section 10, a more general formulation was chosen, criminalizing "fornication against nature" without specifying the types of acts covered. The prohibition could be applied to homosexual acts: "Anyone who commits fornication against nature with another person, and anyone who commits fornication with animals shall be sentenced to up to two years' hard labour."[816] In theory, also "unnatural sexual behavior" between persons of different sex was included in the general prohibition and could be prosecuted, although this was rarely done.[817] The wording of the provision did not exclude sexual acts between two women. This was unusual from a European perspective.[818] However, it appears that that sexual acts between two women were in practice generally not prosecuted.[819] It can be noted that homosexual sexual acts were punished as "a grave offence to common civil order and good morality" – not as crimes against an individual.[820]

---

812 Fornication with animals seems to have been considered as a more severe offence than sexual acts between two persons of the same sex, capital punishment being the sanction for fornication with animals, whereas capital punishment for "fornication" between persons was normally not imposed. See Committee Report (SOU 1935:68), p. 72. For more information on the early criminal law, see Law Commission Report of 1832, (1832:1,2).

813 Silverstolpe, Fredrik, Praxis och teori 1726–1864, Sympatiens hemlighetsfulla makt, p. 36. Even judgments were short in order to keep a silent approach and not tempt the public to experience the forbidden sin, see p. 37. Capital punishment for crimes of fornication were in principle not executed after 1778, see p. 38.

814 Rydström, Jens, Sinners and Citizens, 2001, p. 41.

815 Rydström, Jens, Sinners and Citizens, 2001, p. 41.

816 Chapter 18, Section 10 of the Criminal Code of 1864. As translated by: Rydström, Jens, Sinners and Citizens, 2001, p. 39.

817 Rydström, Jens, Sinners and Citizens, 2001, p. 39. See also Nilsson, Gert (Editor) En fråga om kärlek, 1988, p. 44.

818 Rydström, Jens, Sinners and Citizens, 2001, p. 39. One explanation why sexual acts between two women traditionally have not been prosecuted is that the immoral aspect had to do with "wasting seed", sexuality primarily belonging to marriage for the purpose of reproduction. See Nilsson, Gert (Editor) En fråga om kärlek, 1988, p. 44.

819 According to statistics from 1913–1932, only one woman was prosecuted but it is unclear if she was prosecuted for fornication with another woman or with an animal. No difference between these crimes were made in the statistical compilation referred to. See Committee Report (SOU 1935:68), p. 73.

820 Rydström, Jens, Sinners and Citizens, 2001, p. 49.

6.2.3. DECRIMINALIZATION OF HOMOSEXUALITY

Decriminalization of homosexuality in 1944 is often mentioned as a landmark event toward legally recognizing same-sex relationships. In the early twentieth century, homosexuals opposing the prohibition against sexual acts between two persons of the same sex started to make themselves heard in the Swedish debate.[821] Political initiatives toward decriminalization, however, were not taken until 1933, when the first motion to Parliament demanding decriminalization was presented.[822] The main argument in the motion was that homosexuality in most cases was a condition caused by biological factors.[823] If homosexuality was a congenital condition, it was argued, criminalization of homosexuality as being "against nature" was a contradiction in terms: "[...] Acting in accordance with a person's own natural instincts cannot be to act "against nature". Rather this expression could be used if a homosexual e.g. had married and was forced to have sexual intercourse with his wife."[824]

The motion to Parliament was followed by several investigations resulting in committee reports dealing with the decriminalization issue.[825] The view of homosexuality as a congenital condition, supported by medical research, was endorsed by the legislator and eleven years after the first motion to Parliament homosexual sexual acts were decriminalized.[826]

The 1944 decision to decriminalize was not an expression of approval of homosexual behavior, but rather a matter of political strategy. It was the result of a shift in focus from regarding homosexuality as moral decadence to treating it as a genetic condition.[827] In other words, homosexuality was seen as a medical problem instead of a criminal problem. In the Government Bill, a general

821 Silverstolpe, Fredrik, Praxis och teori 1726–1864, Sympatiens hemlighetsfulla makt, 1999, p. 164.

822 Motion no 1, 1933, Motioner i Andra Kammaren, av herr Lundstedt, om upphävande av 18 kap. 10 § strafflagen m.m.

823 Motion no 1, 1933, Motioner i Andra Kammaren, av herr Lundstedt, om upphävande av 18 kap. 10 § strafflagen m.m., p. 6.

824 "[...] Att handla i enlighet med sin drift kan icke vara att handla "mot naturen". Snarare skulle detta uttryck kunna användas, ifall en homosexuell t.ex. gift sig och nödgar sig till könsumgänge med sin hustru." Motion no 1, 1933, Motioner i Andra Kammaren, av herr Lundstedt, om upphävande av 18 kap. 10 § strafflagen m.m., p. 6. Author's translation.

825 Committee Report (SOU 1935:68), Committee Report (SOU 1941:3) and Committee Report (SOU 1941:32).

826 Committee Report (SOU 1935:68), p. 82. Much consideration was paid to the findings of *Medicinalstyrelsen*, a civil service department, which existed in Sweden 1877–1967. In 1935 it presented its results (statement 24 October 1935) as regards homosexuality, supporting the view of homosexuality as a biological, innate condition, see pp. 78–81. In Government Bill (Prop 1937 nr. 187), the proposal to abolish 18:10 was rejected, homosexuality being considered a danger to society despite biological explanations. It was held that also social factors contributed to the occurrence of homosexuality and, thus, decriminalization was not desirable, see pp. 91 f. In Government Bill (Prop 1944 nr 13), pp. 44–58.

827 Committee Report (SOU 1935:68), pp. 6 f.

distinction was made between so-called "congenital homosexuals" (homosexuals from birth due to biological reasons) and other persons who acquired homosexuality by early exposure to a deviant lifestyle.[828] It was considered necessary to actively work against "the spreading of homosexual habits".[829] Young persons were considered to be in special need of protection from exposure to homosexual behavior, an established conviction being that homosexual experiences in early ages could in fact make a person homosexual. In addition, homosexual acts between two adults were thought to risk "contagion" if given publicity.[830]

Decriminalization as such did not lead to any immediate recognition of same-sex relationships, neither by the authorities nor in society.[831] In Swedish society in the 1950s, attitudes toward homosexuality remained negative. In fact, decriminalization was even in some quarters interpreted primarily as an efficient and strategic way of coming to terms with the issue of homosexuality as a public danger.[832] Once homosexuality was treated as a medical condition, caused by genetic factors, it became urgent to find medical treatment for those concerned.[833] Nevertheless, decriminalization and focusing on medical aspects appear more humane than speaking in terms of crime and punishment. The classification as a disease by the Swedish National Board of Welfare was repealed in 1979.[834]

6.2.4. A TURNING POINT: OFFICIAL ACCEPTANCE AND LEGAL RECOGNITION

6.2.4.1. Background

In the rapid Swedish legal development several key "events" can be discerned as especially relevant in the process of improving the situation of homosexuals in society. From the perspective of homosexuals and lobby groups pressuring for legal change, each of these events meant another step toward legal and societal recognition of homosexual relationships, breaking with a long tradition of disapproval. The first legal recognition of same-sex cohabitee relationships was achieved through the Homosexual Cohabitees Act of 1987. This Act was the

828 Government Bill (Prop 1944 nr 13), p. 13. The expression was used by Professor Petrén in the Report of 1935.

829 Government Bill (Prop 1944 nr 13), p. 46. Author's translation.

830 Government Bill (Prop 1944 nr 13), utdrag av protokollet över justitiedepartementsärenden, hållet inför Hans Maj:t Konungen i statsrådet å Stockholms slott den 5 november 1943, p. 45.

831 Andreasson, Martin, Samhällsfara eller samhällsgrupp? 2000, p. 37.

832 See Söderström, Göran, En aktiviströrelse växer fram, Sympatiens hemlighetsfulla makt, 1999, p. 399, footnote 9.

833 For an account of efforts to "cure" homosexuals, see Tripp, C.A., Homosexualitet, 1981, pp. 251–267. (Original title: The Homosexual Matrix, 1975.).

834 Committee Report, (SOU 1984:63), p. 33.

result of an extensive investigation of homosexual individuals' conditions of life in different sections of Swedish society, presented in the form of a committee report in 1984.[835] Thereafter, equal treatment of same-sex and different-sex couples became a prioritized political goal, resulting in the Registered Partnership Act in 1994, and access to marriage in 2009.

6.2.4.2. A Lesbian Mother Awarded Child Custody in 1955

When discussing legal incidents that have contributed to strengthening the legal rights of homosexual persons in Swedish society, a ruling by the Supreme Administrative Court, delivered already in 1955, is often mentioned as an early example. It should be kept in mind that homosexuality was still classified as a disease at this point in time and a special concern was to protect children from being exposed to a homosexual lifestyle.

In the mentioned case, the court ruled in favor of a lesbian mother in a custody dispute.[836] A question for the court to determine was whether or not the mother's homosexuality made her unfit to be the legal guardian of her daughter. In the court's opinion, the mother's homosexuality in itself did not necessarily disqualify her as the legal guardian of her child. The court held that: "[E]vidence has not been shown that [the mother], as a result of her homosexuality or due to psychological characteristics, would be incapable of caring for the daughter adequately."[837] Moreover, the Supreme Court found that young children, especially girls, were in special need of a close relationship with their mother. Based on these concerns, the court granted the mother custody of the child. It should be clarified that the child's father was not found unsuitable as a parent by the court, but at this time joint custody was not an available legal option.[838]

Keeping in mind that the 1955 precedent was delivered in a time when homosexuality was classified as a disease, and attitudes in society toward homosexual persons were generally disapproving, the outcome of the case was remarkable. The judgment of the first instance trying the case, the district court, which ruled in favor of the father, can be seen as a reflection of the prevailing negative attitudes toward homosexuality: "It appears [...] that the environment in a home where [the daughter] lives alone with [the mother] might harm her, partly by affecting her own natural instincts and partly by being influenced by

835 Committee Report, (SOU 1984:63), Homosexuella och samhället.

836 Judgment of the Supreme Court, NJA 1955 p. 63. For more explanations, see also Rydström, Jens, Sinners and Citizens, 2001, p. 41.

837 Judgment of the Supreme Court, NJA 1955 p. 63. Author's translation.

838 When the judgment was delivered, the 1949 Code on Parents and Children applied, according to which child custody after divorce could only be awarded to one of the parents – so-called sole custody. Through a reform in 1976, which entered into force in 1977, a legal possibility for both parents to have joint custody of a child after divorce was introduced. See Government Bill (Prop 1975:76:170).

[the mother's] disharmony, which as a result of her [the mother's] sexual preference, will surely mark her." The Court of Appeal, however, ruled in favor of the mother, rejecting the ruling of the District Court: "A woman's ability to create a good and safe environment for a child may not be dependent on if she lives alone with the child or if she remarries, and a woman's harmony is definitely not dependent on whether she is homosexual, heterosexual or bisexual."

This case should not necessarily be seen as a shift toward a more positive attitude toward homosexual individuals in Swedish society. The ruling might in fact say more about gender roles than about homosexuality. The outcome was in line with the predominating traditional division of duties between men and women in the 1950s, when women were the primary caretakers of children, while men provided the main income in the family. The Supreme Court underlined that a young child – a girl in particular – was especially dependent on her mother's daily care. It appears that the interest in defending the view of the mother as the most suitable parent was given priority to the view of homosexuality, as an undesirable lifestyle. In other words, the mother was granted custody *despite* her homosexuality, because she was the girl's mother. Nevertheless, the fact that the lesbian mother was considered more suitable than the father – who was not found unsuitable – makes the case worth mentioning as a step away from a categorical disapproval of homosexuality.

6.2.4.3. A Perfectly Acceptable Form of Family Life from Society's Point of View

In 1973, the Parliament's *lagutskott* (Law Commission), while drafting the Act on the Joint Dwelling of an Unmarried Couple (applicable to different-sex couples), for the first time in positive terms commented on cohabitation between a couple of the same sex. The Parliament's Law Commission stated that "[...] cohabitation between two persons of the same sex is a perfectly acceptable form of family life from society's point of view."[839] The statement was a response to a motion to Parliament, which was put forth by the Left Party[840] in 1973, advocating that the "sexually deviant" (the expression used in the motion) should be granted access to a registered form of cohabitation.[841] The Law Commission objected to the term "sexually deviant" as an inappropriate term with negative connotations.[842] Instead the commission proposed using the term "homosexual cohabitees," when referring to two men or two women cohabiting as a couple.[843]

---

839 "[...] en samlevnad mellan två parter av samma kön är från samhällets synpunkt en fullt acceptabel samlevnadsform" Law Commission Report (LU 1973:20), p. 116. Author's translation.

840 In Swedish this party went by the name *Vänsterpartiet kommunisterna*, later shortened to just *Vänsterpartiet*, losing its communist appendix (kommunisterna).

841 Motion to Parliament (1973:1793) Hermansson m. fl. (vpk).

842 Law Commission Report (LU 1973:20), p. 116.

843 Law Commision Report (LU 1973:20), p. 116.

The quoted statement of Parliament's Law Commission has attracted international attention for expressing an early acceptance of homosexuality, and significant weight has been laid on it. For instance, Masha Antokolskaia has pointed out that through this statement, Sweden became the first country in the world to officially declare its acceptance of same-sex partnerships.[844] However, the importance of the statement by Parliament's Law Commission in 1973 might be overrated. The statement was given more or less in passing in a rather "radical" setting, namely in Parliament's Law Commission Report, following the 1972 Committee Report, which contained the proposals to abolish the marriage ceremony, i.e. the ceremonial aspects surrounding the conclusion of a marriage.[845] The statement was consistent with the general policy to aim to avoid expressing moral values in family law legislation,[846] but same-sex couples were not subject to any of the progressive proposals in the 1972 Report. The statement concerning same-sex couples was clearly a side track mentioned briefly. No statutory law enactment granting same-sex couples mutual rights and duties was proposed at that time. Against this background, the statement was most likely not intended as the starting signal toward legally recognizing same-sex relationships. The Law Commission of Parliament could not possibly foresee how often this statement would be quoted in the future, as an illustration of how "progressive" Sweden was in 1973 in respect of acceptance of homosexuals.

Although no proposals to introduce family law provisions governing same-sex cohabitation were presented in the Committee Report of 1972, the official standpoint of the Parliament's Law Commission appears to have had an impact on the political discussions under the years to come. The Law Commission acknowledged that there might be a need to introduce family law legislation for same-sex couples, but found it suitable to first analyze homosexual couples' conditions of life separately.[847] This resulted in the appointment of another commission, in 1978, which was given the task to investigate the conditions of life of homosexuals in society. The commission presented its results in 1984, in an extensive report containing, inter alia, a proposal to introduce the Homosexual Cohabitees Act, which was finally adopted in 1987. These events and connected enactments will be further analyzed below.[848]

It has been pointed out in the literature that the official standpoint of Parliament's Law Commission in 1973 might have encouraged the Swedish Federation for Lesbian, Gay, Bisexual and Transgender Rights (RFSL) to become

---

844 Antokolskaia, Masha, Harmonisation of Family Law in Europe, 2006, p. 408.

845 See section 4.2.2.4.

846 See section 4.2.1.

847 The Law Commission referred to the statements of, inter alia, the Swedish National Board of Health and Welfare (Socialstyrelsen), pointing out the fact that same-sex couples living together appeared to be treated in an unfair manner compared to cohabitees of different sex. Law Commission Report (LU 1973:20), p. 116 and Government Bill (Prop 1973:32), p. 214.

848 See section 6.4.1.

more active in its work to convey politicians and authorities to focus on gay rights.[849] From this point of view the position taken that homosexual cohabitation was an acceptable form of family life can be connected to the future enactments concerning same-sex relationships and can be claimed to have paved the way for their adoption.

6.3. THE CHURCH OF SWEDEN – RESPONSES TO THE LEGAL DEVELOPMENT AND BIBLICAL PERSPECTIVES ON HOMOSEXUALITY

6.3.1. THE POINT OF DEPARTURE

For a long time the Church of Sweden was the most influential source of morality in matters relating to sexual relations, and the Bible was the ideological basis for criminalizing homosexuality. The Church of Sweden was the state church in Sweden until the year 2000, and remains significant in Sweden since then as the "Folk Church". A great number of marriages are annually solemnized by the Church of Sweden. In 2008, 44 percent of all marriages were concluded by the Church of Sweden.[850] Although the church's influence in society has decreased considerably since the eighteenth and nineteenth centuries, it has remained a relevant body participating actively in connection with reforms dealing with marriage. These factors, as well as the historical description in chapter 2, account for the central position of the Church of Sweden in Swedish society, and explain why the Church of Sweden has been chosen for closer analysis here, whereas other religious communities have been excluded.[851]

In the Government Bill of 1987, containing the proposal for the Homosexual Cohabitees Act of 1987, it was stated that the opinions expressed by the religious communities with regard to homosexuality had great impact on the basic values in society affiliated with this topic.[852] It is likely that the Church of Sweden's concept of marriage as a union reserved for one man and one woman for the purpose of having and raising children still influences the basic values connected to marriage in Sweden. Signs of this can be found in the church's argumentation in connection with the gender-neutral marriage reform of 2009. Also a comparison between the words spoken during the civil marriage and partnership ceremonies (applicable until 2009) indicates a presence of values deriving from the church's conception of marriage as a union including one man and one woman for the purpose of procreation. One can speculate that these values

---

849 See Andreasson, Martin, Samhällsfara eller samhällsgrupp? 2000, p. 45. The RFSL was founded in 1950.

850 www.svenskakyrkan.se. Accessed 20 September 2010.

851 When the term "church" is used here, the Church of Sweden is intended.

852 Government Bill (Prop 1986/87:124), p. 13.

contributed to reinforce previous conceptions that there is a relevant difference between marriage and registered partnership.

However, it should be kept in mind that a strong minority within the Church of Sweden was in favor of introducing a gender-neutral marriage concept. Once the marriage concept of the Marriage Code had been extended to cover same-sex couples, also a corresponding proposal for the church to officiate at same-sex marriages within the church was passed at the Church Assembly in October 2009 with a clear majority.[853]

6.3.2. SAME-SEX PARTNERSHIPS AND THE CHURCH OF SWEDEN: RESPONSES TO THE LEGAL DEVELOPMENT

6.3.2.1. Decriminalization of Homosexuality

When homosexuality was decriminalized in 1944, the bishops of the church officially took a joint position against the repeal, in a letter addressed to the ministers of the Church of Sweden.[854] In the letter, homosexuality was described as a sin and it was found urgent that medical science prioritized finding a cure for this "abnormal drive". Also the risk of a homosexual person seducing young persons was considered impending. Under no circumstances, it was stated in the letter, should the decriminalization of homosexual acts be used to support an outlook on such acts as ethically justifiable in society.[855]

The argumentation by the bishops appears to correspond, more or less, with the generally prevailing view on homosexuality in Sweden following the decriminalization, although more outspoken by the bishops. The bishops were concerned with what they called the "sexual problem" and the connected tendency to focus on individual pleasure and happiness, at the expense of biblical norms regulating cohabitation.[856] According to the bishops, homosexuality was an example of such a tendency to disregard biblical principles in favor of individual happiness.[857]

---

853 The Church Assembly of 2009 official website: www.svenskakyrkan.se/default.aspx?di=252610. 176 voted in favor of the Church of Sweden marrying same-sex couples, 62 voted against and 11 members refrained from voting. Accessed 20 September 2010.

854 Ett brev i en folkets livsfråga, 1951. The document was addressed to the ministers of the Church of Sweden from the bishops, dealing with different aspects of sexuality: Divorce, extra-marital relations, prevention of pregnancy, abortion, sterilization, artificial procreation and homosexuality.

855 Ett brev i en folkets livsfråga, 1951, p. 14.

856 Ett brev i en folkets livsfråga, 1951, p. 3.

857 Ett brev i en folkets livsfråga, 1951, pp. 14–16.

6.3.2.2. Officially Accepting "Genuine" Homosexuality

In 1972, a church investigation aimed to improve the situation of homosexual members was initiated, to be carried out by a psychologist and a chief physician.[858] This was in fact six years before the government appointed a commission with a corresponding societal purpose. The result of the investigation was presented in 1974 in the book *De homosexuella i kyrkan* (the homosexuals in the church[859]). In this study a "u-turn" was made in respect of homosexuality, the conclusion being that the church should accept *genuine* homosexuality, interpreted as long-term stable relationships – but not homosexuality exercised as occasional sexual contacts.[860] The state church of Sweden adopted the same standpoint as the state in this question. The study emphasized that it was desirable that homosexual persons were able to have durable and stable relationships.[861] Although the idea of allowing same-sex marriages was rejected as contrary to the Bible, it was suggested that some form of church blessing – without legal implications – for same-sex relationships could be considered.[862] These statements appear quite radical for the 1970s, expressed in a time when homosexuality was still classified as a disease in Sweden.

In the Committee Report of 1984, in which the situation of homosexuals in Swedish society was analyzed, it was stated that: "[...] [I]t is clear that the opinions of the Christian communities are still important to the standpoint taken by many people toward homosexuality."[863] As a result, it was desirable that the Church of Sweden participated in a public debate on homosexuality, instead of secluding the ethical discussions to the church internally.[864]

6.3.2.3. The Registered Partnership Act

When the institution of registered partnership was introduced in Sweden, the Church of Sweden was faced with same-sex couples' request for a ceremonial church blessing of their union. Unlike a different-sex couple, a same-sex couple was unable to choose a legally binding ceremony, since registered partnership could only be concluded in the civil form. The Church of Sweden's controversial

---

858 The appointed investigators, the psychologist Bengt Haglund and the chief physician Herman Hedqvist, presented their results in the book called: De homosexuella och kyrkan, 1974.

859 Author's translation.

860 De homosexuella och kyrkan, 1974, p. 152.

861 De homosexuella och kyrkan, 1974, p. 157.

862 De homosexuella och kyrkan, 1974, p. 164.

863 "[...] [D]et är klart att de kristna samfundens uppfattning alltjämt har betydelse för många människors ställningstaganden när det gäller homosexualitet." Committee Report (SOU 1984:63), p. 57. Author's translation.

864 Committee Report (SOU 1984:63), p. 59.

response[865] was to offer a couple of the same sex a church blessing of their registered partnership as a part of the "pastoral care".[866]

In 2005, the Church Assembly decided to amend the Church Order to include an official service for the blessing of same-sex couples who had registered their partnership.[867] It should be emphasized that this service had no legal effects for the couple concerned, since registered partnership could only be concluded in the civil form. The church representative officiating at the blessing was given the right to, in consultation with the partners, freely compose the service. However, the following elements were mandatory: (1) Introductory words about the gift of love and responsibility, (2) reading of the Bible, (3) intercession, (4) the Lord's Prayer and (5) the blessing.[868]

6.3.2.4. The Gender-Neutral Marriage Concept

The Church of Sweden was a reference group when the 2009 reform was being prepared. Other religious communities were also represented.[869] During the preparations of the enactment, the Church of Sweden was of the opinion that registered partnership was adequate for same-sex couples. The church suggested a change in the law which would make it possible to register legally binding partnerships in the form of a church ceremony, but requested that the word marriage be reserved for couples of different sex. However, once the new marriage concept had been adopted in the revised legislation, without regard to the church's opposition, the Church of Sweden reconsidered its position in compliance with the state's definition of marriage and declared – among the first religious communities in the world – that it was willing to legally marry couples of the same sex.[870]

---

865 See, for instance, Svenska Dagbladet, a leading Swedish newspaper: www.svd.se/opinion/brannpunkt/artikel_471557.svd. Accessed 20 September 2010. The proposal to introduce a special act for blessing registered partnerships resulted in a public appeal open for signatures of those against a special blessing.

866 Pastorala råd angående förbön för dem som ingått partnerskap, utgivna 1994 och reviderade 1999. This service was offered when at least one of the partners was a member of the church. The same criterion regarding membership applies to marriage.

867 The Worship Commission's Report (2005:2), Cohabitation issues, see also motions no 40 and 105, opposing that such a ceremony be introduced.

868 (In Swedish: Inledningsord om kärlekens gåva och ansvar, Bibelläsning, Förbön, Herrens bön, Välsignelsen.) Author's translation. See General Instructions, Blessings of Registered Partnerships, Experimental Order, Accepted by the Church Board 6 December 2006. (Kyrkostyrelsen) p. 3. www.svenskakyrkan.se/Sve/Dokument/Dokumentfiler/A6161ABF-CA24–4F31-AE40–08447B44D818.pdf. Accessed 20 September 2010.

869 Committee Report (SOU 2007:17).

870 This decision was reached at the General Synod in October 2009. The statistics on the number of marriages concluded by the Church of Sweden can be found at www.svenskakyrkan.se. Accessed 20 September 2010.

The introduction of a gender-neutral marriage concept in the Marriage Code proved to be problematic and divisive for the Church of Sweden. Masha Antokolskaia discusses legal recognition of same-sex partnerships in terms of countries being divided between two camps: a "progressive" and a "regressive".[871] The same division can be observed within the Church of Sweden. There is a struggle between a progressive and a regressive (conservative) side within the church, representing opposing views on how the Bible should be interpreted and how the church should respond to changing societal values. Nevertheless, the Church of Sweden has profiled itself as quite progressive, through the decision to marry couples of the same sex. Although this study only focuses on the response by the Church of Sweden, it should be pointed out that most other religious communities still apply a traditional interpretation of the concept of marriage. However, the Swedish *Missionskyrkan* (Mission Church) – along with a few other congregations – has also opened up for same-sex marriages, by leaving it up to each congregation to decide whether or not to celebrate such marriages.[872]

6.3.3. HOMOSEXUALITY AND THE BIBLE: DIFFERENT INTERPRETATIONS

Different interpretations of certain biblical passages are the basis for the opposing views on homosexuality and same-sex partnerships within the Church of Sweden. This also applies to other religious communities. For centuries, the Bible was the basis for condemning and criminalizing homosexual behavior.[873] Considering the extensive historical impact of the Church of Sweden on the moral climate in society and on the values reflected in the law, it is understandable that rethinking the attitude toward same-sex relationships and the meaning of the connected biblical passages have proven difficult. In section 6.4 it will be suggested that religious values can sometimes be discerned as general values in society, not only in religious contexts.[874] Against this background it is relevant to study what the Bible says about homosexuality. Certain passages in the Bible can be claimed to support the idea of homosexuality as a sin.[875]

---

871 Antokolskaia, Masha, Harmonisation of Family Law in Europe, 2006, p. 435.

872 On 21 November 2009, Svenska Missionskyrkan opened up for same-sex marriages, if the congregations so wished. http://missionskyrkan.se/Svenska-Missionskyrkan/Missionskyrkan/Enstaka/En-kyrka-med-sjalvstandiga-forsamlingar---brev-till-forsamlingar-och-pastorer/. Accessed 13 September 2010. See section 1.4.2.

873 See section 6.2.1. The Bible and homosexuality is discussed in: De homosexuella och kyrkan, 1974, pp. 92–106.

874 See section 6.4 and subsections.

875 It should be clarified that the account of relevant biblical references to homosexuality is not intended to be exhaustive. The references have been selected here because they appear frequently in the debates.

6.3.3.1. *"Contra Naturam": Sexuality and Reproduction*

"Thou shalt not lie with mankind, as with womankind: it [is] abomination."[876]

In the Bible, the Old Testament in particular, certain passages appear to support the idea of homosexuality as a sin and a perversion.[877] The primary biblical source cited to support this view is found in the quote from Leviticus rendered above. However, different interpretations of the cited passage are possible, depending on what "camp" of opinions relating to homosexuality one belongs to. When the passage from Leviticus is used to express disapproval of same-sex partnerships or homosexual relations, homosexuality is regarded as "*contra naturam*" – against nature and the biblical Creation story.[878] Also, according to this view, the purpose of sexuality is procreation, which requires that the persons are married and of different sex.[879]

In the 2009 Report of the Church Board, it was pointed out that the creation story of the Bible does not necessarily contradict the idea of same-sex marriage. In fact, the story of the Creation can also be claimed to support same-sex marriage.[880] The close link between marriage and procreation has been weakened during the last century, in pace with changing gender-roles and sexual behavior. Today marriage and sexual relations can be seen as serving a broader purpose than producing joint offspring, namely to function as a basis for intimacy, enjoyment and solidarity between the spouses. This can also apply to same-sex relationships.[881] Furthermore, it was added in the report, although same-sex couples cannot procreate jointly, they do in practice raise children together. Thus same-sex couples participate in "procreation" in a wide sense.[882] From this point of view, allowing same-sex marriages does not appear to be contrary to the Creation story.

Moreover, a contextual perspective can be applied when interpreting the Bible today, which necessitates taking into to account the prevailing values in society when the text was written and making certain adjustments to suit contemporary conditions. The Bible does not contain one universal definition of marriage. In the Old Testament, polygamy is frequent. In the New Testament, life-long monogamous marriage is the norm.[883] The cited passage above can be

---

876 King James Bible, Leviticus, Chapter 18, Verse 22.

877 For an account of biblical passages dealing with homosexuality, see, for instance, En fråga om kärlek, 1988, pp. 37–56.

878 Committee Report (SOU 1993:98), p. 86.

879 King James Bible, Genesis 1:27, 1:28 and 2:24. Mathew 19:4–6 and Ephesians 5:31–32. These passages in the New and the Old Testament focus on the relationship between one man and one woman. The purpose of their union is procreation.

880 Report of the Church Board, Kyrkostyrelsens skrivelse 2009:6, p. 52.

881 Report of the Church Board, Kyrkostyrelsens skrivelse 2009:6, p. 50 and 52.

882 Report of the Church Board, Kyrkostyrelsens skrivelse 2009:6, p. 52.

883 Report of the Church Board, Kyrkostyrelsens skrivelse 2009:6, p. 46.

interpreted from a contextual point of view, as dealing with gender roles during the sexual act – not with homosexuality – prescribing that the man should be the active and the woman the passive party. This hierarchical view on the sexual act appears difficult to combine with modern societal values, more precisely the political strivings in Sweden since the 1920s to treat men and women equally.[884]

It can be noted that only sexual acts between two men – not sexual acts between two women – appear to be mentioned in the biblical passage quoted above. This has been seen as a result of the link between sex and reproduction, creating a moral prohibition against wasting a man's "seed".[885] This appears to be in compliance with the prescribed gender roles during sex described above, the man being the active and superior party.

Finally it can be mentioned that also 1 Corinthians is often claimed to express condemnation of homosexuality:

> "Know ye not that the unrighteous shall not inherit the kingdom of God? Be not deceived: neither fornicators, nor idolaters, nor adulterers, nor effeminate, nor abusers of themselves with mankind,"[886]

This passage can also be interpreted as dealing with the question of the active and passive roles during heterosexual intercourse, rather than sexual acts between two persons of the same sex. It has also been interpreted as prohibiting mature men from having sex with young boys.[887]

6.3.3.2. The Story of Sodom

> "For this cause God gave them up unto vile affections: for even their women did change the natural use into that which is against nature:
> And likewise also the men, leaving the natural use of the woman, burned in their lust one toward another; men with men working that which is unseemly, and receiving in themselves that recompence of their error which was meet."[888]

Another biblical passage often interpreted as dealing with sexual acts between persons of the same sex is the story of Sodom, found in Romans cited above. In the story of Sodom, the city was, in the end, burned down as a result of its sinfulness. The men of the City of Sodom demanded that men who were visiting

---

884 See, for instance, www.bibelsajten.nu/fragelada/117-homosexualitet-/11445-homosexualitet-i-bibeln. The reply to the Biblical question was written by Anders Tingström, parish teacher in the Church of Sweden. Accessed 13 June 2009.

885 Nilsson, Gert (Editor) En fråga om kärlek, 1988, pp. 42 f.

886 King James Bible, 1 Corinthians, Chapter 6, Verse 9.

887 See, for instance, www.bibelsajten.nu/fragelada/117-homosexualitet-/11445-homosexualitet-i-bibeln. The reply to the Biblical question was written by Ander Tingström, parish teacher in the Church of Sweden. Accessed 13 June 2009.

888 King James Bible, Romans, Chapter 1, Verses 26–27.

the city be brought to them for the purpose of "getting to know them", a phrase which was generally used when referring to sexual acts.[889] The story of Sodom can be seen as expressing a negative view on sexual acts between two persons of the same sex. However, other possible explanations have also been presented in the literature.

It has been underlined that the concept of homosexuality as the expression of genuine feelings linked to a person's identity did not exist at the period of time described in the Bible, more than 2000 years ago.[890] If a contextual approach is applied to the story of Sodom, it can be seen as prohibiting sexual assault and inhospitable attitudes in general – not same-sex sexual acts. The story of Sodom has also been interpreted as denouncing sexual acts involving children, in other words pedophile sexual acts, where a grown man takes advantage of a young boy sexually.[891]

6.3.3.3. *The Song of Solomon*

> "Set me as a seal upon thine heart, as a seal upon thine arm: for love is strong as death; jealousy is cruel as the grave: the coals thereof are coals of fire, which hath a most vehement flame.
>
> Many waters cannot quench love, neither can the floods drown it: if a man would give all the substance of his house for love, it would utterly be condemned."[892]

Some Christians regard the message of love in the Song of Solomon, cited above, as being of superior significance when interpreting the Bible. The quote above from the "Song of Solomon" has given rise to various interpretations dealing with love between two persons of the same sex. Some interpret the quoted verse cautiously, as an argument against excluding homosexuals from the congregation, but without tolerating homosexual behavior. From this point of view, it can be considered to be the religious congregation's duty to help and encourage homosexuals to a life of celibacy and friendship.[893]

However, the quoted verse has also been interpreted, in other religious circles, as supporting the view that the message of love in the Bible is superior to a literal interpretation of the Bible. From this viewpoint homosexuality is acceptable also from a biblical perspective without preventing the recognition of stable same-sex unions.[894]

---

889 Nilsson, Gert (Editor) En fråga om kärlek, 1988, p. 41.
890 Nilsson, Gert (Editor) En fråga om kärlek, 1988, p. 26.
891 Nilsson, Gert (Editor) En fråga om kärlek, 1988, p. 46.
892 King James Bible, Song of Solomon, Chapter 8, Verses 6–7.
893 Committee Report (SOU 1993:98), Partnerskap, Part A, p. 86. This attitude is the main line in the Catholic Church in Sweden. See Carlberg, Axel, Ekumeniska perspektiv, Homosexuella i kyrkan – en katolsk respons, 2004, pp. 203–210.
894 Committee Report (SOU 1993:98), p. 86.

The purpose here is not to reach any conclusion as to what the preferred interpretation of the Bible in respect of homosexuality should be. The theological deliberations and interpretations will be left to theologians. However, it can be noted that focusing on the message of love as a superior value and all-encompassing purpose is in line with the principle of equality, which has justified legal recognition of same-sex unions.[895]

6.3.4. THE IMPACT OF RELIGIOUS VALUES RELATING TO MARRIAGE IN THE TWENTY-FIRST CENTURY

Historically the disapproval of homosexuality was motivated with reference to the Bible. Also in present time, it is possible that the criticism toward legally recognizing the rights and duties of same-sex partners in Sweden partly can be traced back to biblical values relating to sexual relations and married life, as interpreted by the Church of Sweden. For centuries the church conveyed the idea that marriage was the only accepted cohabitation model, and procreation was the primary purpose of marriage. From this point of view, marriage was a prerequisite for sexual relations, and sexual relationships between couples who could not marry – such as same-sex couples – were not allowed. The view which prevailed for centuries, that two persons of the same sex were not permitted to have a sexual relationship with each other, has been abandoned in legislation. Nevertheless, the deeply rooted conception of marriage as a cornerstone of society, guaranteeing the survival of the species through its reproductive function, most likely lives on, especially in ecclesiastical circles, and might have colored the debates preceding the gender-neutral marriage enactment in Sweden.

In section 6.6.1 it will be claimed that values which can be traced back to a religious conception of marriage can be discerned, for instance, in a comparison between the registered partnership ceremony and the civil marriage ceremony. Until these ceremonies merged into one gender-neutral marriage ceremony in 2009, the civil marriage ceremony linked marriage to reproduction and caring for children, whereas the registered partnership ceremony focused on making same-sex couples visible in society.[896] It could be that religiously based values, sometimes unconsciously, form the basic point of departure for the traditional or "conservative" defenders of the concept of marriage – in the literature called the "regressive" camp – when opposing enactments to strengthen the legal position of same-sex couples.[897] This can be seen as contrary to the ambition to

[895] Committee Report (SOU 1993:98), p. 87.
[896] See section 6.4.1.
[897] The division between a progressive and a regressive camp is illustrated by: Antokolskaia, Masha, Harmonisation of Family Law in Europe, 2006, p. 435.

keep family law free from moral values promoting one cohabitation form to another, which has been a point of departure in Swedish family law reforms since the late 1960s.[898]

To a foreign observer it might appear inconsistent with Sweden's "secular" reputation that religious communities participated in the legal discussions when the gender-neutral marriage enactment was prepared. In the Netherlands, as will be discussed in chapter 7, the religious communities have no legal authority to officiate at marriages and were, as a result, not directly involved in the preparations of the same sex marriage enactment. Thus, the Dutch same-sex marriage enactment does not appear to have given rise to the same intense discussions on the essence of marriage as the Swedish enactment did.

6.4. FAMILY LAW ENACTMENTS RECOGNIZING SAME-SEX COUPLES

6.4.1. THE HOMOSEXUAL COHABITEES ACT OF 1987

Adopting statutory law provisions, which recognized the rights and duties of cohabiting persons of the same sex, was a significant event that strengthened the legal position of these couples in Sweden. In 1978, the government appointed a commission to investigate, from a legal perspective, homosexual individuals' conditions of life and the occurrence of unmotivated differential treatment based on sexual orientation in various sections of society.[899] The commission's extensive report was presented six years later; covering the situation of homosexuals not just in the field of family law, but in various sections of society, such as the labor market, housing market, military and schools. Introducing a special cohabitees act for same-sex cohabiting couples was proposed in the report.[900] The commission stated that: "[...] the only certain difference between homosexuals and heterosexuals is that homosexuals are emotionally drawn to persons of the same sex. In the light of this it is self-evident that homosexuals shall not be discriminated against."[901]

Once the commission had come to the conclusion that a family law enactment on same-sex cohabitation should be introduced, several options were discussed: (1) allowing same-sex couples to contract a formal marriage, (2) introducing a

898 See section 4.2.1.

899 Directive of December 8, 1977. The Commission was appointed on 17 January, 1978, and given the name: utredningen om homosexuellas situation i samhället.

900 Committee Report (SOU 1984:63).

901 "[...] den enda skillnaden mellan homosexuella och heterosexuella är att homosexuella känslomässigt dras till personer av samma kön. Mot denna bakgrund är det självklart att homosexuella inte skall diskrimineras." Committee Report (SOU 1984:63), p. 19. Author's translation.

special registration procedure for same-sex couples or (3) making the rules referring to "marriage-like" relationships (the Cohabitees Act) applicable also to same-sex couples.[902] The idea of introducing a special registration model for couples of the same sex was rejected in the report. In the opinion of the commission, a registration procedure, available only for same-sex couples would risk creating unnecessary focus on the couples' sexual orientation and fortify existing prejudices instead of reducing them.[903] At the same time, the commission also dismissed the idea of opening up the institution of marriage to same-sex couples, the main reason being that such a reform would risk being discriminatory to same-sex couples, since same-sex could not be given access to a church marriage ceremony.[904]

In the end, the commission decided on the third option – drafting rules corresponding to those attached to heterosexual cohabitees. As a result, the Homosexual Cohabitees Act of 1987 was adopted by Parliament.[905] Through this enactment, Sweden was the first country in the world to adopt statutory family law provisions legally recognizing same-sex couples.[906] In its proposal the commission had emphasized that such an enactment could be expected to help homosexual individuals accept their sexual orientation and in this way reduce their feeling of alienation in society, through recognition of their relationships.[907]

Technically, the Homosexual Cohabitees Act consisted of one single provision, which referred to the Cohabitees Joint Homes Act of 1987 and other enactments dealing with the situation of unmarried cohabiting persons.[908] In spite of this technical simplicity, the Act can be seen as a substantive as well as a symbolic breakthrough for same-sex couples. The Act did not apply the term "marriage-like" cohabitation directly to same-sex couples. However, through the reference to the "Heterosexual Cohabitees Act", same-sex couples – until then excluded from all legal effects of marriage – can be seen as indirectly qualifying as "marriage-like".

902 Committee Report (SOU 1984:63), p. 94.
903 Committee Report (SOU 1984:63), pp. 98 f.
904 Committee Report (SOU 1984:63), p. 98.
905 Government Bill (Prop 1986/87:124).
906 This has also been noted by Agell, Anders, The Legal Status of Same-Sex Couples in Europe – A Critical Analysis, 2003, p. 126.
907 Committee Report (SOU 1984:63), p. 93.
908 The provision in the Homosexual Cohabitees Act read: "If two persons live together in a homosexual relationship, what applies in relation to cohabitees in the following enactments shall also apply to the homosexual cohabitees [...]" Author's translation. The Act continued with an enumeration referring to 21 different Acts and provisions which apply also to homosexual cohabitees.

6.4.2. THE GENDER-NEUTRAL COHABITEES ACT OF 2003

In 2003, the two "Cohabitee Acts" were merged into one through the gender-neutral Cohabitees Act.[909] The first initiative to apply the same enactment to heterosexual and homosexual cohabitees was presented in a motion to Parliament in 1991, which criticized the two separate regulations and the differences in treatment between same-sex and different-sex cohabitees for being discriminatory.[910]

In the 1999 Committee Report, it was pointed out that the Homosexual Cohabitees Act, because of the legislative technique used, had resulted in unmotivated legal differences between same-sex and different-sex cohabitees.[911] In the Government Bill, the interest in avoiding unmotivated legal differences between same-sex and different-sex cohabitees was emphasized as the main reason for adopting the gender-neutral Cohabitees Act of 2003.[912] The noted differential treatment was not called "discriminatory" in the bill. Instead structural advantages with introducing one act were emphasized.[913] In my opinion, this was correct. It appears rather far-fetched to refer to the Homosexual Cohabitees Act as being "discriminatory", if one keeps in mind that it was a pioneering act when it was adopted in 1987. Moreover, adopting two different sets of rules for same-sex and different-sex couples generally appears to have functioned as a first step toward adopting one gender-neutral enactment; this also took place in respect of registered partnership and gender-neutral marriage. In section 5.4.1.1 the symbolic value of applying the same Cohabitees Act to same-sex and different-sex couples has been discussed. The Act contained few novelties as regards substance.[914]

It can be noted that the term "marriage-like conditions" was abandoned in the 2003 Act, without much discussion on this topic in the preparatory work. In the Government Bill of 2002, it was held that an independent definition of "cohabitees", instead of speaking in terms of "marriage-like conditions", clarified the Act's terms of application. It was also considered necessary to use a "neutral" terminology, which also included same-sex couples.[915] Same-sex couples did not have access to marriage in 2002. The Registered Partnership Act had been introduced in 1994 for the purpose of providing same-sex couples with a legal status equivalent to the legal status attached to marriage. The abolishment of the term "marriage-like" from the cohabitee regulation can be seen as a result of the controversy surrounding

---

909 Sambolag (2003:376). The Cohabitees Act of 2003 entered into force on 1 July 2003.

910 Motion 1991/92:L408. Thereafter, Parliament's Law Commission held that an evaluation of the existing legislation was necessary, Law Commission Report (1991/92:LU32), requiring that Parliament made the government aware of the findings of the Law Commission. This was done in rskr. 1991/92:236. See also Committee Report (SOU 1999:104), p. 172.

911 Committee Report (SOU 1999:104), p. 260.

912 Government Bill (Prop 2002/03:80), p. 1.

913 Government Bill (Prop 2002/03:80), pp. 27 f.

914 See section 5.4 and subsections.

915 Government Bill (Prop 2002/03:80), pp. 27 f.

the idea of calling a same-sex relationship "marriage" (or even "marriage-like"). On the other hand it can also be argued that the terminology was imprecise and that a definition facilitated identifying the Act's scope of application.

6.4.3. THE REGISTERED PARTNERSHIP ACT

6.4.3.1. Background and Substantive Content

In the early 1990s, soon after unmarried cohabitation between two persons of the same sex had been legally recognized in Sweden, demands for additional rights and, thus, for increased recognition through a legal institution resembling marriage, were made by proponents of gay rights issues. Denmark and Norway had recently adopted family law enactments on registered partnership and in 1994 also Sweden, having investigated the issue thoroughly, was ready to introduce the new institution reserved (as in Denmark and Norway) for same-sex couples.[916] The enactment of the Swedish Registered Partnership Act was turbulent. The sitting government could not agree on a bill to be presented to Parliament. Instead Parliament took the matter into its own hands and voted on the basis of a bill prepared by its Law Commission, contrary to the opinion of the Council on Legislation.[917]

The Registered Partnership Act of 1994, like its Nordic counterparts, enabled two men or two women to formalize their relationship. In the first provision of the Registered Partnership Act it was laid down that: "Two persons of the same sex may request the registration of their partnership".[918] Registered partnership was reserved for same-sex couples, but it was not required that the couple in fact was homosexual, or had a sexual relationship with one another. Prescribing criteria dealing with sexual orientation in the Registered Partnership Act would have been inconsistent, since there are no corresponding criteria applicable to marriage, demanding that the couple is in fact heterosexual.[919] The impediments to registered partnership corresponded to those applicable to spouses.[920]

---

916 Denmark's enactment was made in 1989 (Act on Registered Partnership No. 372, 7 June 1989) (and Norway's in 1993 (Act on Registered Partnerships, No. 40, 30 April 1993). The Acts were translated in Legal Recognition of Same-Sex Couples in Europe, 2003.

917 *Lagrådet* (the Council on Legislation) is a state body assigned to give a guiding opinion on law proposals before they are passed in Parliament. For instance, when a proposed reform has to do with the individual's freedom, rights and obligations, the Council is normally requested to give a statement. Also changes in the Constitution, as a rule, should be subject to the Council's scrutiny. In its statement the Council takes into account factors such as how a proposal relates to the Constitution and how it impacts on legal security. Obtaining the Council's opinion is not mandatory but recommended. See www.lagradet.se/index.htm.

918 As translated in: Legal Recognition of Same-Sex Couples, 2003, p. 220.

919 Committee Report (SOU 1993:98), Partnerskap, p. 98.

920 See the Registered Partnership Act, Chapter 1, Section 4 and.

The partnership registration ceremony was equal to the registration procedure which applied to civil marriage, but couples of the same sex could not choose to celebrate their partnership with legal effects through a religious ceremony. Thus the partnership ceremony was concluded by an appropriate civil official, not by a minister of the church.[921] However, two men or two women who wished a more ceremonial setting could have an additional church blessing of their partnership, conducted by a minister of the church. A church blessing could be of religious and emotional significance for the couple, but had no legal implications. Until 2005, access to such a blessing depended on the individual minister's willingness to contribute. In 2005, the Church Order was amended with an official service for the blessing of a registered partnership, which establishes that the Church of Sweden welcomes same-sex couples to the church for a religious blessing of their union.[922]

The rules concerning dissolution of registered partnership were the same as those laid down in the Marriage Code. Even the six-month period of reconsideration, established in the Marriage Code was made applicable to registered partnerships.[923] A reconsideration period is mandatory either if only one partner wishes to dissolve the relationship or if the partners have children under the age of 16 living with them. In this author's opinion it appears inconsistent that a reconsideration period was applied to registered partners before their de facto family ties in respect of children were legally recognized. On the other hand, this indicates that there was a political willingness to recognize and protect existing same-sex family constellations from hasty break-ups through the period of reconsideration. At the same time, however, existing social ties within the family of the registered partners were not recognized in the law. In the preparatory work to the Registered Partnership Act application of the reconsideration period in respect of registered partners was motivated with reference to the interests of children already living in homosexual family constellations.[924]

The legislative technique used in the Registered Partnership Act was simple: With certain exceptions, the rules applicable to a marriage were stated to be applicable to a registered partnership. The exceptions originally concerned specific gender-related provisions,[925] provisions based on international

921 The Church of Sweden is intended here, but the line of reasoning applies, in principle, to all religious communities.

922 The Worship Commission's Report (2005:2) Cohabitation issues. See also motions no 40 and 105, opposing that such a ceremony is introduced.

923 The Registered Partnership Act, Chapter 2, Section 2.

924 Law Commission Report (1993/94:LU28), p. 21. Author's translation.

925 These were provisions using the terms "husband" or "wife" or defining a spouse by sex. Such provisions exist in social welfare legislation (pension rights, etc.), but are few in number and of diminishing importance. Also rules on establishment of fatherhood, the presumption that the mother's husband is the father of a child born to married parents, were excluded through this exception.

treaties[926] and provisions on parenthood. When the gender-neutral marriage enactment entered into force, on 1 May 2009, the Registered Partnership Act was repealed. However, it continues to give rise to legal effects in respect of couples who have chosen not to transform their existing registered partnership into a marriage. The substantive content of the Registered Partnership Act will only be summarized briefly here to illustrate the development toward equalizing the registered partnership rules with the marriage regulation.[927]

6.4.3.2. *Subsequent Amendments to the Act*

6.4.3.2.1. Adoption of Children

After the 1994 enactment of the Registered Partnership Act, the differences between registered partners and spouses relating to legal parenthood were done away with through subsequent amendments to the Registered Partnership Act. On 1 February 2003, a possibility for registered partners to jointly adopt children in Sweden, as well as children from abroad, was introduced.[928]

The decision to include adoption of children from abroad in the 2003 enactment was considered motivated for reasons of principle. It was not expected to be of practical relevance in the near future. The authorized Swedish adoption agencies have no cooperation with states of origin which accept registered partners as adoptive parents.[929] The states of origin have a unilateral right to choose and approve of the adoptive parents in each single adoption case, thereby being able to avoid, for instance, same-sex adoptive parents. The states of origin also have the right to terminate an ongoing adoption procedure if circumstances become known which the state of origin does not approve of.[930] Keeping this in

---

926 An inter-Nordic convention from 1931 was excluded, regulating private international law in the fields of marriage, adoption and guardianship. An exception was motivated since not all Nordic countries had registered partnership acts originally. Moreover, no acute problems were created later on because of the exception. See Jänterä-Jareborg, Maarit, Registered Partnership in Private International Law: The Scandinavian Approach, 2003, p. 139. Moreover, a general rationale is that no state can on its own motion extend the scope of an existing international Treaty concerning marriages or the rights of spouses to cover also registered partners. See Jänterä-Jareborg, Maarit, Sörgjerd, Caroline, The Experiences with Registered Partnership in Scandinavia, 2004, pp. 578.

927 The legal effects of registered partnership in the Nordic countries, as well as the gradual abolishment of differences compared to marriage, have been accounted for elsewhere. See Jänterä-Jareborg, Maarit, Sörgjerd, Caroline, The Experiences with Registered Partnership in Scandinavia, 2004, pp. 577–597. Jänterä-Jareborg, Maarit, Parenthood for Same-Sex Couples, 2006, pp. 75–91. Jänterä-Jareborg, Maarit, Registered Partnerships in Private International Law: The Scandinavian Approach, 2003, pp. 137–158.

928 Committee Report (SOU 2001:10), Parts A and B. See also Government Bill (Prop 2001/02:123).

929 Jänterä-Jareborg, Maarit, Registered Partnership in Private International Law: The Scandinavian Approach, 2003, p. 155.

930 Government Bill (Prop 2001/02:123), p. 29.

mind, it is understandable that until now, no Swedish same-sex partners have received a child from abroad for joint adoption.[931]

So-called second-parent adoptions, where one partner adopts a child born of or previously adopted by the other partner, were also made possible.[932] In this situation the reform has been of practical relevance in Sweden. According to an uncertain estimate made in the Committee Report of 2001, there were approximately 40 000 children living in de facto family constellations consisting of one or two homosexual parents.[933] A goal was to grant these children, through the proposed extended outlook on parenthood, the same economical and emotional security as children with parents of different sex.[934] Yet another exception which was abolished in 2003 was that registered partners and same-sex couples could be appointed as special guardians of a child, if the child's parents were unsuitable or otherwise incapable of being guardians.[935]

6.4.3.2.2. Assisted Procreation Methods

On 1 July 2005, lesbian couples were granted access to assisted procreation methods: insemination as well as in vitro fertilization (IVF).[936] The Swedish rules governing assisted reproduction, as well as establishment of legal parenthood for the female partner of the biological mother, only apply when treatments take place at a public hospital in Sweden. According to the 2005 enactment, legal parenthood can be established for the birthmother's partner along with the birthmother, provided that the former has confirmed that she consented to the fertility treatment of her partner.[937] Treatments which take place abroad or through private arrangements are not included. In such situations, adoption is necessary in order for the birthmother's partner to become a legal parent to the child together with the birthmother.[938] Establishing legal

---

931 This information was provided by Marie Alm at the Swedish Intercountry Adoptions Authority, 25 November 2010.

932 This possibility exists regardless of whether the child of one partner had previously been adopted from abroad.

933 Committee Report (SOU 2001:10), p. 73. This figure is not based on statistics, but on presumptions and is, as a result, not certain. There are no statistics or registers available showing how common it is for children to have homosexual parents.

934 Committee Report (SOU 2001:10), p. 331.

935 Government Bill, (Prop 2001/02:123), pp. 31 f.

936 Memorandum of the Ministry of Justice, (Ds 2004:19), Föräldraskap vid assisterad befruktning för homosexuella. See also Government Bill (Prop 2004/05:137).

937 The Code on Parents and Children, Chapter 1, Section 9. Oral consent is sufficient in this context. According to Lag (2006:351) om genetisk integritet, Chapter 6, Section 1, the partner's consent must be in writing. It can also be mentioned that in the memorandum of the Ministry of Justice (Ds 2004:19), the term "mother" was proposed for both parents. In the end, however, it was considered necessary to distinguish between the birthmother and the consenting mother, which is why the term "parent" was used to describe the latter. Government Bill (Prop 2004/05:137), p. 55.

938 Lag (2006:351) om genetisk integritet, Chapter 6, Section 2.

parenthood based on consent of the birthmother's partner when a child has been conceived at a clinic abroad was proposed in 2007,[939] but no Government Bill had been presented on the topic by May 2010.

6.4.4. GENDER-NEUTRAL MARRIAGE

Once almost all legal differences between spouses and registered partners had been abolished, the two institutions were nearly identical and the question of whether it was motivated to retain two separate sets of rules for heterosexual and homosexual couples arose. In 2005, a special commissioner, assisted by two reference groups and several experts, was appointed to review certain aspects of the existing marriage regulation.[940] Their main task was to investigate if marriage should be made available to couples of the same sex.[941] The assignment also included investigating if the possibility to choose between a *civil* and a *religious* legally binding marriage ceremony – the double track system – should be maintained, or if a *civil* marriage procedure should be made the only option available. In the Committee Report of 2007 the necessity of changing the law so that it reflects the values in society was underlined: "A particular perception or definition of a social phenomenon cannot last forever, even if it has very deep roots. Social progress takes place and new values and opinions may have to be given space also in respect of fundamental issues."[942]

However, again the issue of introducing a gender-neutral concept of marriage was too politically sensitive for the sitting government to be willing to present a bill to Parliament, as had been the case when the Registered Partnership Act was enacted. Instead the Committee on Civil Affairs drafted the proposal, which Parliament adopted on 1 April 2009.[943] In fact, there was wide support for the enactment in Parliament: out of the Parliament's 349 members only 22 voted against it and 16 refrained from voting.[944]

---

939 Committee Report (SOU 2007:3).

940 Directive (Dir 2005:6). The reference groups comprised the Swedish Parliament and representatives of religious communities. The Catholic Church requested that the commission be parliamentary, see Yttrande från trossamfundet Romersk-Katolska kyrkan over äktenskaps- och partnerskapsutredningens betänkande (SOU 2007:17), dnr Ju2007/3311/L2.

941 Their task was also to investigate and report on private international and procedural law issues relating to same-sex marriage and to propose solutions to problems encountered.

942 "En viss uppfattning om eller definition av en samhällsföreteelse [kan] inte för alltid vara bestående även om den har mycket djupa rötter. Samhällsutvecklingen går framåt och nya värderingar och åsikter kan behöva ges utrymme också då det gäller grundläggande uppfattningar." Committee Report (SOU 2007:17), p. 230. The Author's translation has been inspired by the summary on p. 33.

943 Report of the Committee on Civil Affairs, (Civilutskottet) (2008/09:CU19).

944 Protocol 2008/09:95

Just like the two cohabitee enactments had been merged into one in 2003, on 1 May 2009 the two "marriage regulations" were molded into one through the inclusion of same-sex couples in the Marriage Code. At the same time the Registered Partnership Act was repealed. However, couples already living in a registered partnership were given the option of either remaining registered or converting their registered partnership into a marriage. The latter could be realized either through a marriage ceremony or by an application to the Swedish Tax Agency, in charge of the population records of the county. The Registered Partnership Act continues to apply to those couples who wish to stay registered.[945]

The double track system with a possibility to choose between a religious and a civil marriage ceremony was retained, leaving it up to each religious community to determine if they wish to officiate at marriages between persons of the same sex. In the Committee Report it was underlined that introducing an obligation for religious communities, with authorization to officiate at marriages, to also marry same-sex couples would risk violating their freedom of religion.[946] As a result, an explicit clarification was included in the Marriage Code, Chapter 4, Section 3, stating that there is no obligation for authorized religious communities or their authorized marriage officials to officiate at marriages.[947] In the 2007 Committee Report, a fear was expressed that taking away the freedom to choose between a religious and a civil marriage ceremony might in fact increase the disapproval of same-sex couples, the fear being that same-sex couples might be blamed for this.[948] Strengthening the negative attitudes toward homosexuals in society would be contrary to the Instrument of Government, which contains an obligation to counteract discrimination on the basis of sexual orientation.[949]

---

945 Committee Report (SOU 2007:17) and Government Bill (Prop 2008/09:80). See also Report of the Committee on Civil Affairs (Civilutskottet) (2008/09:CU19), based on a Motion to Parliament: Motion (2008/09:C454).

946 Committee Report (SOU 2007:17), pp. 275 f.

947 Government Bill (Prop 2008/09:80), p. 22.

948 Committee Report (SOU 2007:17), p. 26.

949 The Instrument of Government (Regeringsformen), Chapter 1, Section 2. Committee Report (SOU 2007:17), p. 33. The constitutional protection against discrimination will be discussed in section 6.5.4.

6.5. REGISTERED PARTNERSHIP AND SAME-SEX MARRIAGE: IDEOLOGY, SYMBOLISM AND CONSTITUTIONAL ASPECTS

6.5.1. THE REGISTERED PARTNERSHIP ACT: IDEOLOGICAL FOUNDATION AND THE HUMAN RIGHTS DISCOURSE

The proposal to adopt a special act for couples of the same sex, based on the registration of their relationship, was justified in the following words by the commission appointed by the government to investigate the issue:

> "Our standpoint has an ideological foundation, based as it is on human equality, both as between individuals and under the law. We acknowledge homosexual love as equal in value to heterosexual love. We affirm, we do not deny, love between persons. Love is an important driving force of both personal and social development.
> From this point of view we do not feel it to be incumbent on society to have viewpoints concerning the way in which people choose to live together. Society's tasks ought instead to be that of enabling people to live in accordance with their own preferences and personalities, not preventing them from doing so, so long as this does not cause harm to others.
> We wish to accommodate the desire of homosexual couples for a valuable setting for their relations, as a way of manifesting their love. We also wish to accommodate the need of homosexual couples for economic and legal security in their relations. We wish to create greater awareness of, understanding for and openness concerning homosexuality and homosexual relations. One important way of achieving this, in our belief, is by establishing, as far as possible, legal parity between homosexual and heterosexual cohabitation."[950]

This statement of the commission encompasses several different motivations for the proposal and, indirectly, also for the enactment (once adopted) as such. It is openly declared that the proposal rests on an ideological foundation. The key concept here is human equality, and it is explicitly stated that heterosexual and homosexual love are equally valuable. This part of the ideological standpoint, permeated by emotional emphasis and the reference to human equality, connotes human rights issues. The commission was well aware of the similarities to human rights documents and even argued that adopting a registered partnership act was in line with the underlying intentions of international instruments such as the UN Declaration of Human Rights and the European Convention for the Protection of Human Rights and Fundamental Freedoms.[951]

---

950 Committee Report (SOU 1993:98), Part A, p. 21.
951 Committee Report (SOU 1993:98), Part A, p. 33.

The increased impact of human rights instruments, focusing on different aspects of gender equality, most likely contributed to a political interest in introducing a special registration model for same-sex couples in Sweden. Improving the legal situation of same-sex couples has become widely recognized as a matter of human rights.[952] However, the topic remains sensitive on a general European level and no consensus has been reached among the Member States.[953]

The Registered Partnership Act aimed to promote the recognition of same-sex relationships in Swedish society, using legislation as a tool to reach this goal. In the last part of the quote above, the wish to meet the demands from same-sex couples for a legal framework recognizing their relationships was emphasized, as well as the aim to promote a greater understanding in society of homosexual relationships. This in fact qualifies the Registered Partnership Act as a modern example of social engineering in the spirit of equality. As has been described above, during the course of the 1900s, legislation has in Sweden regularly been used as a tool for promotion of equality, between men and women in particular, through intervention in family law issues.[954] Eliminating inequalities between men and women is an essential component of the creation of what David Bradley has referred to as an "egalitarian society".[955] From this point of view, promoting the principle of equality one step further by focusing on homosexuals as a "disfavored" group in need of legal protection can be claimed to be an almost self-evident development, in particular with regard to the dynamic development of human rights aspects of family law.

In addition, taking public opinion into account has been significant in all contexts when the legal situation of homosexuals in society has been in focus. When same-sex couples' access to marriage was discussed in the early 1980s in Sweden, the commission in charge dismissed this option on the ground that such

952 This is, for instance, pointed out by Bonini-Baraldi, Matteo, Variations on the Theme of Status, Contract and Sexuality: An Italian Perspective on the Circulation of Models, 2003, p. 321.

953 Masha Antokolskaia has pointed out that legal recognition of same-sex unions has proven to be much more divisive in Europe than, for instance, legally recognizing the rights of children born to unmarried parents compared to children born within marriage. Issues relating to strengthening the position of children born outside of marriage are characterized by a general uniformity and have not given rise to much political controversy, much thanks to the impact of the ECHR. See Antokolskaia, Masha, Harmonisation of Family Law in Europe, 2006, p. 448. However, this could also be a result of same-sex marriage being a comparatively recent issue compared to recognition of the rights of children born to unmarried parents. Legal development and the task of changing attitudes take time. However, during the past few years, a European "trend" to legally recognize same-sex couples in special family law acts has become visible. See Boele-Woelki, Katharina, The Legal Recognition of Same-Sex Relationships Within the European Union, 2007–2008, pp. 1949–1981 and Saez, Macarena, Same sex marriage, same sex cohabitation, and same sex families around the world: Why "same" is so different? 2010, pp. 1–49.

954 The impact of the social engineers in Sweden is discussed in section 3.7 and subsections. See also Bradley, David, Family Law and Political Culture, 1996, pp. 10 and 275.

955 Bradley, David, Family Law and Political Culture, 1996, p. 275.

a reform would be contrary to public opinion.[956] By 2007, however, when the gender-neutral marriage provisions were under investigation, it was observed that attitudes in society toward same-sex couples and homosexual individuals had become much more positive.[957]

In fact, a survey presented in 2005 indicated that society had become much more open toward homosexuals and homosexual relationships.[958] A majority (46 percent) of the Swedish population could be estimated to be in favor of allowing same-sex marriage, whereas 31 percent were negative and the remaining 23 percent were "neither positive nor negative" to such a reform.[959] It is likely that the Registered Partnership Act had succeeded in promoting a greater openness in society and had contributed to making homosexuality less stigmatized. It follows that the enactment had succeeded in what it aimed to achieve.[960]

6.5.2. REGISTERED PARTNERSHIP: EQUALITY IN RIGHTS – NOT IN DIGNITY?

Soon after the Registered Partnership Act had been adopted, additional law reform to abolish the substantive legal differences between registered partnership and marriage were initiated. This process was characterized by rapidness and progressive legal solutions, for instance regarding joint legal parenthood for same-sex couples.[961] When all relevant substantive differences compared to a marriage had been erased, the next step on the "equality agenda" was to abolish the institution of registered partnership and introduce a gender-neutral marriage concept.

---

956 Committee Report (SOU 1984:63), p. 98.

957 Committee Report (SOU 2007:17), pp. 17 and 206 f. See also Föreställningar/vanföreställningar, Allmänhetens attityder till homosexualitet, Study conducted by Östermalm, Torsten, p. 46. It should be kept in mind, however, that according to statistics homophobic hate crimes appear to have increased. See Rapport 24 July, 2008, Hatbrotten mot homosexuella ökar, https://svt.se/svt/jsp/Crosslink.jsp?d=62242&a=1201620&lid=senasteNytt_793033&lpos=rubrik_1201620. See also Dagens Nyheter, 29 November, 2005, Antalet brott mot homosexuella ökar, www.dn.se/DNet/jsp/polopoly.jsp?d=147&a=495316. Both Accessed 12 September 2010.

958 Committee Report (SOU 2007:17), p. 207. The survey was carried out by the Swedish National Institute of Public Health (Folkhälsoinstitutet). The Institute has measured attitudes toward homosexuals since the end of the 1990s and has published several reports (in 2000, between 1998 and 2000, as well as in 2004 and 2005) showing that attitudes have become more positive. See Committee Report (SOU 2007:17), pp. 206 f.

959 In 1999, the percentage of persons answering that they found the proposed reform (to allow same-sex couples to marry one another) desirable amounted to 18 percent. In 2005 the figure had increased to 26 percent. See Committee Report (SOU 2007:17), p. 207.

960 See section 6.4.1.1, where the ideological foundation of the Registered Partnership Act is analyzed, the motivation to change attitudes in society in particular.

961 See section 6.4.3.2 above.

Why was registered partnership not an adequate alternative to marriage, once all relevant differences in respect of legal effects had been abolished? The fact that same-sex couples' demands for access to marriage remained, even after all the substantive differences had been done away with, illustrates that the gender-neutral marriage reform was not about legal effects, but about something else, namely access to the symbolic values of the institution of marriage and of the civil status it entails. Defending and challenging the label "marriage" as reserved for different-sex couples appears to have been a core issue causing debates in connection with the 2009 reform, especially from the perspective of the Church of Sweden.[962] The Church of Sweden showed a willingness to officiate at legally binding registered partnership ceremonies in the church, and not only at (legally irrelevant) "blessings", as long as the word "marriage" was reserved for different-sex couples. This suggests that marriage has a historical and religious symbolic dimension, which the institution of registered partnership could not match.

The different symbolic value of registered partnership compared to marriage has been observed by the previous Swedish Ombudsman against Discrimination on Grounds of Sexual Orientation, Hans Ytterberg. He claimed that the Act created equality in rights but not in dignity, which he found inconsistent with the UN Declaration of Human Rights, Art. 1, according to which the point of departure is that "All human beings are born free and equal in dignity and rights".[963] Ytterberg claimed further that the Registered Partnership Act was comparable to the racist "separate but equal doctrine" established by the Supreme Court of the United States in 1896.[964] The terminology "separate but equal" has also been used by Masha Antokolskaia when discussing registered partnership compared to marriage.[965]

The legislative technique used in the Registered Partnership Act – to refer to the Marriage Code and enumerate the exceptions – underlined what the registered partnership *was not* – i.e. a marriage – instead of laying down what it *was*. This technique might have created negative connotations to registered partnership as an institution inferior to marriage – a "second-class marriage" (or a union "separate but equal" to marriage), which offers a possible explanation for why the number of registrations remained low in Sweden.[966]

---

962 Committee Report (SOU 2007:17), p. 248. See section 6.3.2.4 above.

963 Ytterberg, Hans, All Human Beings Are Equal, but Some Are More Equal than Others, 2003, p. 8.

964 Ytterberg, Hans, All Human Beings Are Equal, but Some Are More Equal than Others, 2003, p. 8.

965 Antokolskaia, Masha, Harmonisation of Family Law in Europe, 2006, pp. 402 f.

966

Year	1995	1996	1997	1998	1999	2000	2001	2002	2003	2004	2005	2006	2007	2008	**Total**
Men	498	201	158	158	154	18	95	212	240	285	244	278	262	311	**3414**
Women	167	118	104	92	133	139	186	210	257	282	349	382	388	503	**3310**
Total	665	319	262	250	287	357	381	422	497	567	593	660	650	814	**6724**

The Swedish Registered Partnership Act created equality in rights between same-sex and different-sex couples. The explanation that the Act did not stop the demand for access to marriage on the basis that registered partnership was of lower "dignity" compared to marriage, is an example of how concepts, charged with positive values directly connected to human rights law, were used to motivate reform in the context of legal recognition of same-sex unions.[967] However, as will be analyzed in chapter 7, in respect of the Dutch and the Spanish legal developments, the legislative technique used when adopting a registration scheme for same-sex couples does not appear to be decisive for the legal development. Same-sex couples have demanded access to marriage irrespective of the legislative technique used and the legal effects included in the previous enactment.

6.5.3. SAME-SEX MARRIAGE: VALUE-CHARGED CONCEPTS AS THE BASIS FOR REFORM?

The human rights features of the same sex marriage enactment can be observed at different stages of the legislative process. Before the Swedish government endorses a bill, the proposal concerned is circulated for comments among concerned authorities, municipalities and organizations. The idea is to investigate if there is support for the planned reform, and to provide those concerned with a possibility to state their opinion; consulted government authorities and other public bodies are in fact obliged to comment.

In respect of the gender-neutral marriage reform, a majority of the bodies consulted supported the enactment, but some religious communities, churches and organizations were opposed.[968] Also an individual is free to, on his or her own accord, comment on a proposed reform in connection with the circulation of comments. When the gender-neutral marriage proposal was circulated for comments, the family law expert Anders Agell took the opportunity to deliver comments of his own, in which he objected to the proposed reform.[969] Agell claimed that the statistical support in favor of adopting the gender-neutral Marriage Code was a result of connotations to feminism and sexual liberalism as something desirable, in contrast to the undesirable conjectural conservatism. In other words, in Agell's opinion, concepts charged with positive values, such as "equality" and "rights", were perceived as generally attractive features in a democratic and progressive country.[970]

---

967 See section 6.4.2.

968 See Government Bill (Prop 2008/09:80), pp. 13 f.

969 Individual statement by Anders Agell, No 120, 28 January, 2008, Ju2007/3311/L2, circulation for comments regarding Report (SOU 2007:17).

970 Statement by Anders Agell regarding Report (SOU 2007:17), p. 3.

Agell's observation that certain concepts are linked with positive connotations, which have made them generally perceived as something desirable and "modern" makes a point. Also his observation that the argumentation supporting a gender-neutral marriage concept was built on the idea of equal treatment as a human right is accurate. Equality issues relating to the individual are a part of the prevailing human rights discourse, which has a clear impact on the ongoing legal development, in Sweden as well as at European level, influenced not least by the case law following the ECHR. It has been pointed out that this has also contributed to the Swedish course of events dealing with legal recognition of same-sex couples.

Masha Antokolskaia also attaches weight to contrasts and positive connotations. She has held that there is a "progressive – conservative" division in Europe, which is not expected to vanish.[971] In fact, Antokolskaia argues that such a division can even be observed within a nation, creating subcultures, which either defend or oppose reforms which aim to improve the legal situation of same-sex couples.[972] This division, visible as a pan-European trend, can explain the national controversy of the enactments on same-sex couples. The division between the two camps dates back to the Age of Enlightenment when the "progressive camp" in Europe sought to modernize family law and the "regressive camp" opposed modernization in the name of traditional family values."[973]

Antokolskaia has pointed out that, in Sweden, as well as in many other countries in the forefront in respect of legally recognizing same-sex unions, significant family law enactments in this field have been enacted by political parties on the left wing, belonging to the "progressive camp" supporting modernization.[974] David Bradley and Katharina Boele-Woelki have also underlined the decisive role that political composition plays in this context.[975] From this point of view it could be argued that the Registered Partnership Act of 1994, and the at that time radical standpoint that joint adoption of children by two persons of the same sex is in compliance with the child's best interest, were more concerned with maintaining Sweden's vanguard position in the field of family law, than with expressing a deeply rooted engagement in protecting the rights of same-sex couples.

971 Antokolskaia, Masha, Harmonisation of Family Law in Europe, 2006, p. 441. This has been touched upon in section 1.3.1. and 6.3.2.4.

972 Antokolskaia, Masha, Family Law and National Culture, Arguing against the cultural constraints argument, 2009, p. 43. This division, visible as a pan-European trend can explain the national controversy over the enactments on same-sex couples.

973 Antokolskaia, Masha, Family Law and National Culture, Arguing against the cultural constraints argument, 2009, p. 43. See also section 2.2.3.

974 See Antokolskaia, Masha, Harmonisation of Family Law in Europe, 2006, p. 438.

975 Bradley, David, Family Law and Political Culture, 1996, pp. 34–45. Boele-Woelki, Katharina, The Legal Recognition of Same-Sex Relationships Within the European Union, 2007–2008, pp. 1961.

In the case of Sweden, the progressive legal development concerning same-sex couples is most likely a combination of a desire to appear progressive in an international perspective and a genuine interest in the principle of equality. It should be kept in mind that Sweden appointed a law commission already in 1978 for the purpose of investigating the conditions of life of homosexuals in Sweden. The commission worked on the report for six years and produced a thorough analysis covering many sections of Swedish society. In 1984 – five years prior to the Danish Registered Partnership Act – the commission even considered (but dismissed) the idea of introducing a registration model, or opening up marriage to same-sex couples. Moreover, the Swedish Registered Partnership Act, as well as the subsequent amendments dealing with assisted reproduction and adoption by same-sex couples, was thoroughly prepared through costly and time-consuming research. The investment of resources in these enactments signals a genuine political interest in Sweden to improve the conditions of life of same-sex couples.

Furthermore, it can be noted that defending values such as equal treatment, personal freedom and individuality fits well in with the ideals of the social welfare state, making Sweden a suitable environment for cultivating and marketing "progressive" family law values as something positive.[976] The goal of equal treatment is not a novelty in Swedish family politics. In the previous chapters it has been illustrated that different aspects of the principle of equality have been the target of political interest in Sweden since the 1920s, more precisely gender-equality, equality between the rich and the poor, equality between unmarried and married couples and equality between same-sex and different-sex couples. In the 1960s, when the social welfare state was well-established, a political interest in strengthening the individual's autonomy in the name of equality arose in Sweden. The social welfare state had provided a social security network which made such a focus on the individual possible.[977] It is likely that this historical focus on the individual and the principle of equality paved the way and set the basic political "tone" in respect of legal recognition of homosexual individuals and couples in Swedish society.

6.5.4. CONSTITUTIONAL PROTECTION AGAINST DISCRIMINATION – BASIC PROVISIONS RELATING TO SAME-SEX UNIONS

The human rights of homosexual individuals and same-sex couples are protected in Swedish constitutional law. The point of departure in the Swedish *Regeringsformen* (RF) (Instrument of Government), laid down in Chapter 1, Section 2, is that "Public power shall be exercised with respect for the equal

[976] See section 3.7 and subsections.
[977] See sections 3.7.1.1–3.7.1.4.

worth of all and the liberty and dignity of the private person".[978] This provision can be seen as the foundation for the Swedish legal order and the starting point for the rights enumerated in Chapter 2 of the Instrument of Government.[979] Furthermore, Section 2 establishes that the public institutions are obliged to promote democracy and protect a person's private and family life. The protection of a person's family life includes a right to marry.[980] A duty to combat discrimination, inter alia on the ground of sexual orientation, is also explicitly laid down in the same provision. The principle of the equal value of all human beings is also expressed in Chapter, 1, Section 9, laying down that courts of law performing tasks within the public administration shall treat everybody equally and observe objectivity and impartiality.

Chapter 2 of the Instrument of Government contains a catalogue of individual rights in relation to public institutions. Some of these rights are absolute in the sense that they cannot be limited without first changing the Constitution, whereas other rights can be infringed through general law amendments. Chapter 2, Section 15 contains a prohibition against unfavorable treatment in the law of a citizen because he or she belongs to a minority group by reason of race, color, or ethnic origin. It can be noted that sexual orientation is not mentioned as a ground in this section.[981]

The Instrument of Government does not contain any specific provision dealing with the right to marry. However, Chapter 2, Section 23 refers to the European Convention for the Protection of Human Rights and Fundamental Freedoms (ECHR) and prohibits the adoption of rules which conflict with the Convention. In Art. 12 of the ECHR, the right to marry and form a family is established. As will be further elaborated on in chapter 8, it has not been found discriminatory to exclude same-sex couples from the right to conclude a marriage.

Finally a few additional developments can be mentioned. Since 2006, sexual orientation is included in Chapter 16, Section 8 of the Criminal Code as a ground of "agitation against a national or ethnic group". In 2008, civil law enactments dealing with discrimination issues were merged into one discrimination act.[982] It can also be mentioned that the right to marry is protected in the UN-Declaration on Human Rights of 10 December, 1948 and in the UN

978 Translation retrieved at the Swedish Parliament website: www.riksdagen.se/templates/R_PageExtended____6309.aspx. Accessed 12 September 2010.

979 Committee Report (SOU 2007:17), p. 73.

980 Committee Report (SOU 2007:17), p. 73.

981 A proposal to include sexual orientation in Chapter 2 Section 15 was rejected in the Government Bill of 1987. In the bill the necessity of constitutional stability was stressed as a reason why homosexuals were not included in the provision as a minority group. The Constitution should not easily be changed and it should not be too detailed, it was argued. See Government Bill (Prop 1986/87:124), p. 32 f.

982 Government Bill (Prop 2007/08:95). The Act entered into force on 1 January 2009.

International Covenant on Civil and Political Rights of 19 December, 1966. However, the UN instruments are not directly legally binding.[983]

6.6. LINGUISTIC PERSPECTIVES ON MARRIAGE AND REGISTERED PARTNERSHIP

6.6.1. THE PARTNERSHIP CEREMONY – DIFFERENCES AND SIMILARITIES COMPARED TO CIVIL MARRIAGE

When the Registered Partnership Act was repealed in 2009, the possibility to register a partnership disappeared in Sweden and was replaced by a possibility for couples of the same sex to contract a marriage. Along with this change came a new ceremony, linguistically and substantively adjusted to a gender-neutral concept of marriage. Nevertheless, studying the wording of the old ceremonies applicable to the conclusion of marriage compared to the conclusion of registered partnership adds to our understanding of what the registered partnership symbolized in Sweden and how it could be claimed to be different "in dignity" compared to a marriage.

The two versions of the partnership ceremony were modeled on the two versions of the marriage ceremony, following the same basic procedure as a civil marriage ceremony. Thus, the partners had to appear simultaneously before the officiating person and confirm that they wished to be pronounced as registered partners. Thereafter, the official was to confirm the couple's legal status as registered partners. Certain differences between civil marriage and registered partnership indicate that the institutions were based on different values and served different purposes.[984] There are two different versions available, both for registered partnership and for marriage, here called "the longer" and "the shorter".[985] The couple was free to choose between the two versions based on personal preferences. Passages containing differing values have been marked with bold letters.

---

983 Coester-Waltjen, Dagmar, Coester Michael, International Encyclopedia of Comparative Law, Vol. IV, Persons and Family, Chapter 3, Formation of Marriage, 1997, p. 13.

984 Rydström, Jens has also compared the wording of the two ceremonies. See Tvåsamhetens brunn: Registrerat partnerskap i Norden, 2005, pp. 325–329.

985 The ceremonies can be found in Decree (Förordning) 2006:214, med närmare föreskrifter om vigsel och registrering av partnerskap som förrättas av domare eller särskilt förordnad förrättare. Author's translation.

6.6.1.1. *The Longer Versions of the Ceremonies*

Civil Marriage (until 2009)	**Registered Partnership (until 2009)**
The purpose of marriage is the well-being of the individual and the **upholding of society.** You have declared that you wish to marry each other.	Registered partnership means that the partners, before each other and to the outside world, **show their solidarity.** You have requested the registration of your partnership. This registration gives you rights and obligations toward one another and society.
Do you N.N. take this N.N. as your lawful wedded wife, to love her for better or for worse?	Do you N.N. take this N.N. as your partner, to love for better or for worse?
(Answer: Yes)	(Answer: Yes)
Do you N.N. take this N.N. as your lawful wedded husband, to love him for better or for worse?	Do you N.N. take this N.N. as your partner, to love for better or for worse?
(Answer: Yes)	(Answer: Yes)
Give each other your hand in confirmation of this.	Give each other your hand in confirmation of this.
(Before the handshake, the man may give the woman a ring.)	(Before the handshake, the partners may give each other a ring.)
I now pronounce you husband and wife.	You are now registered partners.
Never forget the promise of faithfulness that you have confessed to. Live with each other in mutual respect, love and confidence, **in consideration of generations to come.** May unity and happiness prevail in your marriage and in your home	Never forget the promise of faithfulness that you have confessed to. Live with each other in mutual respect, love and confidence. May unity and happiness prevail in your partnership and in your home.

The wording and structure of the civil marriage ceremony and the registered partnership ceremony were similar. Except for evident terminological differences, such as the use of the word "partner" instead of "husband/wife", certain traits of symbolic relevance can be observed. The marriage ceremony has certain characteristics, without counterpart in the partnership ceremony, such as the reference to the upholding of hierarchical traditions, where the man is the first person the official turns to, asking if he wishes to marry the woman. There is no equivalence to such hierarchical structures in the partnership ceremony, because of its gender-neutral composition.

6.6.1.2. Upholding of Society as the Purpose of Marriage

The most significant symbolic difference between the two ceremonies is laid down in the very beginning and the very end of the marriage ceremony, signaling that marriage is the suitable institution for having children.[986] In the first sentence of the marriage ceremony, a main purpose of marriage is defined as: *"the well-being of the individual and the upholding of society."* In the end of the ceremony, the spouses are reminded to live *"in consideration of generations to come"*.

There was no corresponding reference to children or future generations in the partnership ceremony. Instead a main purpose of registered partnership was expressed as "showing solidarity" toward one another, as well as to the outside world. The latter probably aimed at making same-sex relationships more visible in society. The goal to create visibility of same-sex unions was expressed in the preparatory work to the Registered Partnership Act as a wish to "create greater awareness of, understanding for and openness concerning homosexuality and homosexual relations. One important way of achieving this "[...] is by establishing, as far as possible, legal parity between homosexual and heterosexual cohabitation".[987] The symbolic value of signaling to the world that same-sex partnerships are acceptable was central.

The overall impression from comparing the two ceremonies is that a main purpose of marriage according to the wording of the ceremony was connected to children (generations to come), whereas the registered partnership focused on legal and societal recognition of a new civil status. These different purposes can be challenged, particularly the linking of marriage to procreation. In fact, marriage was disconnected from procreation in Sweden already in 1972, through an enactment allowing transsexuals who had undergone gender reassignment surgery to marry a person of their opposite assigned sex, irrespective of the couple's biological incapacity to reproduce jointly.[988] Today not all married couples have children and many women marry after having passed a "fertile" age. Children are furthermore born of unmarried and single parents, and cohabiting unmarried couples and registered partners have access to medically assisted fertilization methods. Keeping this in mind, it is thought-provoking that the *civil* marriage ceremony, applicable until 2009, defined the purpose of marriage as procreation.

---

986 Rydström, Jens, Tvåsamhetens brunn: Registrerat partnerskap i Norden, 2005, p. 327.

987 As translated in Committee Report (SOU 1993:98), Part A, p. 21.

988 Bradley relates this to the enactment of a liberal statute on transesxualism in 1972. This statute disconnected marriage from procreation since actual biological capacity to bear children was abandoned. See Bradley, David, Family Law and Political Culture, 1996, p. 67.

In the religious marriage service of the Church of Sweden, however, the view that sexual acts should take place within marriage for the purpose of reproduction is more expected and in compliance with Christian tradition.[989] In the Church Handbook of 1987, which still applies in 2010, the minister introduces the service with the following words:

> "Marriage is a gift of God instituted for the upholding of society and as a source of help and joy for man and woman, for their mutual support and deeper communion in times of darkness and of light. To live together as husband and wife is to live in confidence and love, and to take responsibility for one another and for the home (to receive and nurture children together) and faithfully to stand at each other's side."[990]

It is likely that a couple choosing the civil form of concluding a marriage instead of the religious wishes to avoid religious elements in their ceremony. From this point of view the wording of the civil ceremony is highly questionable. The comparison between the civil marriage ceremony and the registered partnership ceremony provides an example of how values based on a *religious* perception of marriage defined also *civil* marriage. It is likely that the deeply rooted link between marriage and procreation was a factor which contributed to the controversy concerning the gender-neutral marriage concept in Sweden, on a conscious, as well as a subconscious level.

6.6.1.3. The Shorter Versions of the Ceremonies

It should be mentioned that couples – of the same sex as well as of different sex – have the option of choosing a shorter version of the ceremony. This simplified version of the marriage ceremony was introduced in the 1970s.[991] Against this background the short version can be seen as a compromise. The ceremonial and oral formalities were kept, which implicitly can be regarded as upholding the traditional values of marriage, but the words spoken, as well as value-based statements, were reduced to a minimum. The shorter versions basically consist of

---

989 Opponents to legally recognizing same-sex partnerships within the Church of Sweden as well as elsewhere often base their argumentation on the fact that a same-sex couple cannot produce joint offspring and, as a result, should not be given access to marriage (or registered partnership). See, for instance, Committee Report (SOU 2007:17), p. 223–225. See also the discussions in Svenska kyrkans utredningar 2005:1, Kärlek, samlevnad och äktenskap, Rapport från en offentlig hearing den 6–9 september 2004, Svenska kyrkans teologiska kommitté.

990 Kyrkohandboken, 1986. English translation available at www.svenskakyrkan.se/gudstjanstbanken/service_book/20Vigsel.htm.Accessed 13 September 2010. The term "upholding of society" has been used instead of "sustenance of community" when translating the Swedish phrase *samhällets bestånd*. There is an alternative, longer wording in the handbook with more references to God and the religious aspects of marriage.

991 At this point in time replacing the oral ceremony with a registration procedure was discussed but in the end not found possible. See also Government Bill (Prop 1973:32), pp. 101 f. See also Government Bill (Prop 2008/09:80), p. 10.

the questions by the official to the couple, followed by a declaration by the official that the couple is married or registered.[992]

Short Civil Marriage Ceremony (applicable until 1 May 2009)	Short Registration Ceremony (applicable until 1 May 2009)
You have declared that you want to marry each other.	You have requested the registration of your partnership.
Do you N.N. take this N.N. as your wife?	Do you N.N. take this N.N. as your partner?
(Answer: Yes)	(Answer: Yes)
Do you N.N. take this N.N. as your husband?	Do you N.N take this N.N as your partner?
(Answer: Yes)	(Answer: Yes)
I now pronounce you husband and wife.	You are now registered partners.

The mere existence of a shorter ceremony, which resembles a simple contract, appearing to be free from values and declarations about the purpose of marriage, does not justify the wordings in the two longer ceremonies, or bring the two institutions on the same symbolic level.

When analyzing the symbolic differences between marriage and registered partnership, it appears remarkable that the longer civil marriage form, applicable until 2009, defined a main purpose of marriage as having children. It is equally remarkable that no corresponding reference to future generations existed in the long partnership ceremony, keeping in mind that same-sex partners can also explicitly according to the law adopt children jointly and that lesbian couples have been granted access to medically assisted fertilization methods in Sweden. In the redrafted gender-neutral version of the marriage ceremony, no differences are made on the basis of the spouses' sex.

6.6.1.4. Gender-Neutral Marriage – the Civil Ceremonies

Since 1 May 2009 a gender-neutral marriage ceremony applies, the wording of which has replaced the ceremonies cited above. The system with two alternative versions of the civil ceremony, a short and a long version, has been retained. The new versions of the marriage ceremony read as follows.[993]

---

992 See Government Decree (Förordning 2006:214), med närmare föreskrifter om vigsel och registrering av partnerskap som förrättas av domare eller särskilt förordnad förrättare, provisions 5 and 7.

993 Government Decree (Förordning 2009:263), om vigsel som förrättas av särskilt förordnad vigselförrättare, provision 5. Author's translation.

Gender-Neutral Marriage Ceremony
Short (primary)
Civil Version

You have declared that you wish to marry each other.

Do you N.N. take this N.N. as your wife/husband? (Answer: Yes)

Do you N.N. take this N.N. as your wife/husband? (Answer: Yes)

I now pronounce you spouses.

Gender-Neutral Marriage Ceremony
Long (supplementary)
Civil Version

You wish to marry each other. Marriage is based on love and trust. Through marriage you promise to respect and support each other.

As spouses you are two independent individuals who can gather strength from your community.[994]

Since you have declared that you wish to marry each other, I pose the question:

Do you N.N. take this N.N. as your wife/husband to love her/him for better or for worse?

(Answer: Yes)

Do you N.N. take this N.N. as your wife/husband to love her/him for better or for worse?[995]

(Answer: Yes)
(The couple can now exchange rings)

I now pronounce you spouses.[996]

When you now go out in life and back to the daily round, remember your desire for community, the love to each other and the respect for each other that you have felt in this moment and that have brought you here.[997]

Let me wish you happiness and prosperity in your marriage.’

994 “Ni vill ingå äktenskap med varandra. Äktenskapet bygger på kärlek och tillit. Genom att ingå äktenskap lovar ni att respektera och stötta varandra. Som makar är ni två självständiga individer som kan hämta styrka ur er gemenskap.” Author’s translation.

995 “Vill du N.N. ta denna/denne N.N. till din hustru/man att älska henne/honom i nöd och lust?”

996 “Jag förklarar er nu för äkta makar.” Author’s translation.

997 “När ni nu går ut i livet och åter till vardagen så minns den vilja till gemenskap, den kärlek till varandra och den aktning för varandra som ni känt i denna stund och som lett er hit.” Author’s translation.

In substance, the shorter version is more or less unaltered compared to its predecessor, except for the obvious fact that there is no longer a given order in the ceremony, establishing that the husband should be the first to be requested to state his consent to the marriage.

A significant difference between the longer civil marriage ceremony and its predecessor is that the new ceremony does not mention faithfulness. The couple's "community" is emphasized, as a source of strength for the individual spouses to lean on.[998] Moreover, there is no reference to children or the "upholding of society" with reference to future generations in the new ceremony. In other words, marriage appears in legislation to have been disconnected from reproduction.

The gender-neutral marriage ceremony, applicable to persons of the same sex as well as persons of different sex, focuses on love and trust as the basis of marriage: *"Marriage is based on love and trust. Through marriage you promise to respect and support each other."* Thereafter, an "individualist component" is added: *"As spouses you are two independent individuals who can gather strength from your community".* After the questions have been posed and answered affirmatively, the officiating person finalizes the ceremony by declaring the couple as spouses, and by reminding them to hold on to the feeling of togetherness when they go back to daily life: *"remember your desire for community, the love and the respect for each other that you have felt in this moment and that has brought you here".*

An overall impression is that the gender-neutral ceremony is not less "value-based" than its predecessors. However the values reflected in the ceremony are formulated differently. Individualism, love, trust and mutual respect are expressions of values, "updated" to meet the needs and conditions of life in Swedish society in the twenty-first century. From this point of view, the new ceremony can be seen as a more accurate illustration of the "essence" of marriage in the twenty-first century. Analyzing the different purposes in respect of marriage and registered partnership, expressed in the two ceremonies prior to the law revision of 2009, suggests that the two institutions, although providing the same legal effects, were symbolically different to some extent. It is possible that these symbolic differences were a reason why the registered partnership was not considered as equal to the institution of marriage.

Finally it should be noted that the order of the short and the long versions of the ceremony has been reversed. The short version applies now as the primary version, whereas the longer is available as an alternative. The couple is free to choose either ceremony, but if no choice is made the shorter ceremony applies. No explanation for why the order of the two versions has been changed is to be

[998] Eva Ryrstedt has analyzed the contradiction between the individualistic and the community function of marriage. See Ryrstedt, Eva, Bodelning och bostad, 1998.

found in the travaux préparatoires and no oral explanation could be given from the Ministry of Justice upon my request.[999]

The reversed order of the ceremonies can be interpreted as in line with the general ambition to avoid moralizing in the private family sphere, which has predominated in Swedish family law since the 1970s and has been discussed in previous chapters. Form this point of view, making the short version of the ceremony the primary version can be seen as making marriage more "contract like", toning down the symbolic and value-based dimension of marriage discussed above. It is also possible that swapping the order of the two versions of the ceremony was done in haste without thoroughly reflecting on the possible impact on the essence of marriage. The practical effect of the reversed order, however, is most likely limited since, a majority of the couples can be assumed to make an active choice between the two.

6.6.1.5. Gender-Neutral Marriage – the Religious Service

Once the Church of Sweden had decided to officiate at same-sex marriages, it became clear that there was wide support within the Church of Sweden for adopting one marriage service for all couples, irrespective of their sex.[1000] Nevertheless, critical opinions were raised within the Church of Sweden against the wording of the new marriage liturgy, more precisely for playing down the significance of marriage as a social institution, and for instead focusing on the individual and private features of marriage.[1001]

Since 1 November 2009, the marriage liturgy in the Church Handbook of 1986 applies also to couples of the same sex, with a slightly modified wording in a few places. The alternative wording only applies to marriages between two persons of the same sex. However, this appears to be a temporary solution. In October 2010, a revision of the Church Handbook by an internal working group of the Church of Sweden is in progress for the purpose of updating the liturgy, including the marriage liturgy. A proposal for a new Church Handbook is expected to be presented in 2014.[1002] Until then, linguistic alterations of the applicable marriage service have been made to include also couples of the same sex, for instance, in the initial praise:

---

999 This information was given to me through e-mail correspondence with Sofia Jungstedt, legal counselor at the Department of Justice, the Division for Family Law and the Law of Contracts, Torts and Personal Property, 22 September 2009.

1000 Report by the Church Board, Kyrkostyrelsens skrivelse 2009:6, p. 27.

1001 Report by the Church Board, Kyrkostyrelsens skrivelse 2009:6, p. 26.

1002 See Directive from the Church Board, 19 April 2006, Fortsatt arbete med översyn av Den svenska kyrkohandboken.

"Wonderful are your works, Lord our God wonderfully have you created man and woman **alt. the human being.** We live by your love. We praise you for the gift of life that is continually renewed."[1003]

In the wording of the marriage service applicable to different-sex couples, the minister is to turn to the man first and ask him if he wishes to marry the woman and then turn to the woman and ask the same. In respect of couples of the same sex, however, it is stated that: "The minister asks [...] in agreed order the spouses-to-be". After the questions, the minister announces that they are "spouses" (the term "husband and wife" is used for different-sex couples.)

The wording of the religious marriage service applicable when the Marriage Code of 1920 was adopted was criticized for being outdated in section 3.4.4. Since the 1920s, the wording of the religious marriage service has been made more equal, based on the parties' joint responsibilities, rather than laying down the traditional duties of man and wife respectively. However, the retained order where the minister addresses the man first and asks if he wishes to marry the woman can be seen as a remnant of values which conflict with the principle of gender equality. In the gender-neutral civil ceremony, the order of the questions is optional. This aspect will most likely be taken into account in the ongoing revision of the Church Handbook, as a part of the commission, laid down in the directive to the working group, to "adapt the liturgical formulations for the purpose of finding a more inclusive language".[1004]

6.6.2. SEMIOTIC REFLECTIONS

6.6.2.1. The Word "Marriage" as a Source of Conflict

Critics to opening up marriage to same-sex couples – the religious communities in particular – were opposed to applying the term "marriage" to same-sex unions. From their point of view the word marriage was an emotive term and a significant component of their religious beliefs, which should be reserved for different-sex couples.[1005] Instead the religious communities with the Church of Sweden in the forefront argued that the state should replace the term (civil) "marriage" (for all couples regardless of sexual orientation) with a new term. The word "marriage" should from their point of view be used exclusively by the

1003 Den svenska kyrkohandboken, 1986. Translation (which does not take into account the new wording – in bold – since 1 November 2009, including same-sex couples, has been found at www.svenskakyrkan.se/gudstjanstbanken/service_book/20Vigsel.htm. Accessed 13 September 2010. The complete Swedish version can be found at www.svenskakyrkan.se/default.aspx?di=310232&ptid=0. Accessed 13 September 2010.

1004 Directive from the Church Board, 19 April 2006, Fortsatt arbete med översyn av Den svenska kyrkohandboken, p. 1.

1005 Committee Report (SOU 2007:17), pp. 33 f. and pp. 232 f.

religious communities in their religious contexts.[1006] In other words, granting same-sex couples the legal effects of a marriage was not the problematic issue causing the debates. The problem was calling this union "marriage".

The commission considered overriding reasons to speak against abolishing the civil use of the term "marriage". In the committee report, the difficulties in respect of coming up with an alternative name for (civil) marriage were underlined. The commission acknowledged that changing the terminology might be inconvenient and awkward to spouses, who suddenly would consider themselves living in a "new" union. Also international difficulties connected to abolishing an established legal term such as "marriage" were pointed out in the report.[1007]

A similar line of argument, on the topic of creating a new union, can be applied by opponents to the gender-neutral marriage concept. According to the Norwegian scholar Helge Johan Thue, from a symbolic perspective, remoulding marriage into a gender-neutral concept, through the law reform carried out in Norway in 2008, affected the values attached to marriage so fundamentally that the reform should be seen as the abolishment of marriage and the introduction of a new marital institution.[1008] Including persons of the same sex in this new marriage concept, Thue emphasized, was a conceptual change so essential that it required the consent of couples already married. Thue further argued that many couples married prior to the reform for religious, cultural or historical reasons might not have contracted a marriage today on these new gender-neutral premises. In other words, Thue claimed that extending the concept of marriage to encompass same-sex couples retroactively changed the basic prerequisites for the marital "contracts" concluded by couples prior to 2009. He even questioned if a couple was still necessarily bound by the marriage contract, or if the marriage could be seen as invalid as a result of lacking consent to be bound by a union encompassing same-sex spouses.[1009]

Furthermore, according to Thue it is unfair that registered partners have the option of transforming their partnership into a marriage or to remain registered partners, whereas there is no corresponding option for couples married prior to the gender-neutral marriage concept to remain in the "older-version" of (heterosexual) marriage or to opt into the new marriage regime.[1010] Thue's reasoning highlights the symbolism attached to the concept of marriage and the

1006 Committee Report (SOU 2007:17), p. 232.

1007 Committee Report (SOU 2007:17), pp. 232 f.

1008 Thue, Helge, Gift uten samtykke, 2009, pp. 68 f.

1009 In Norway, there is a group of couples married prior to 2009 who are preparing to bring the question of the validity of the Norwegian same-sex marriage act before the Strasbourg Court. See www.dagenmagazinet.no/Nyheter/Innenriks/tabid/248/Default.aspx?articleView=true&ModuleId=69289. Accessed 24 November 2010.

1010 Thue, Helge, Gift uten samtykke, 2009, p. 68 f.

controversy connected to the topic of gender-neutral marriage and legal recognition of same-sex partnerships.

However, as illustrated in this thesis, marriage is no fixed concept with one clear meaning, unaffected by societal changes and changing values over time. On the contrary, marriage in the Nordic countries has undergone significant changes, particularly during the last century and proven to be quite "elastic".[1011] If major changes in the marriage regulation, with an impact on the symbolic meaning of marriage, are seen as the abolishment of marriage and the introduction of a new marriage, this has happened many times before. Examples in Sweden of previous fundamental challenges of the concept of marriage is the abolishment of the husband's legal guardianship over his wife, as well as the introduction of equal rights and duties regarding distribution of property upon marriage dissolution through the deferred community of property regime in 1920, and the introduction of a unilateral no-fault divorce in 1973, which took the concept of marriage as a voluntary union an additional step further.

In connection with the Swedish 2009 marriage law reform, the term marriage was kept and extended also to couples of the same sex, despite the opposition by the religious communities. The commissioner pointed out that the religious communities are not bound by the terminology used by the legislator, and they are not obligated to interpret terms in exactly the same way as the legislator does.[1012] Hence, the *legal* use of terms does not necessarily have to be problematic for the religious communities, provided that no obligation to marry same-sex couples is imposed on them. They are free to choose not to marry same-sex couples and continue to interpret the concept of marriage as a union reserved for a man and a woman. Moreover, it was underlined in the committee report that the symbolic value of the word "marriage" from the point of view of same-sex couples should not be forgotten:

> "The legal effects of registered partnership do not differ significantly from those of marriage. However, [...] marriage may be deemed to have a higher symbolic value. [...] Although society's development has resulted in a somewhat different view on marriage, registered partnership does not have the same connotations as marriage in the general public consciousness. For homosexuals, marriage is important as a standard of values, for their own relationships as well as for the attitudes of those around them."[1013]

1011 This will be further developed in section 9.4.2.

1012 Committee Report (SOU 2007:17), p. 233.

1013 Committee Report (SOU 2007:17), p. 16. The translation on p. 32 has been used as a basis, the author taking the liberty to make a few strictly linguistic alterations.

6.6.2.2. Focusing on Differences

The symbolic value of marriage compared to registered partnership can also be discerned by studying the terminology used and the negative connotations attached. In other words, saying what something *is* at the same time reveals what it *is not.*[1014] The symbolic dimension of the word "marriage" appears more striking in Swedish than in English: the Swedish terms *äktenskap* (marriage) and *äkta make* (spouse) literally imply that marriage is the *genuine* (*äkta*) institution. When the institution of registered partnership is placed next to the (genuine) institution of marriage, the symbolism is brought to a head; a registered partnership is *not* a marriage, but simply a formalized partnership and therefore not as "genuine" as a marriage, literally speaking.

Focusing on the differences between the two institutions instead of the similarities is not far-fetched, but a consequence of retaining two separate names, as well as two sets of rules for, in practice, the same union, depending on the sex of the couples – registered partnership for same-sex couples and marriage for different-sex couples. From this perspective, registered partnership might not be perceived by people in general as equal to marriage on a symbolic level, despite the substantive legal equivalence.

Moreover, the symbolic difference between the two institutions could be a factor contributing to why the figures on partnership registration remained comparatively low. Perhaps same-sex couples in general considered the institution of registered partnership to be a second-class marriage of lower dignity than a "real" marriage and not worth contracting into.[1015] It is likely that the term "marriage" is important also to same-sex couples, as a result of the symbolic meaning of marriage.[1016] In Spanish legal doctrine, the pursuit of the term marriage has been summarized accordingly: "Gay people wanted not only material and legal equality (same rights and duties) but symbolic equality too".[1017] Another way of expressing this is that same-sex couples wanted equality not only in rights but also in dignity.[1018]

1014 Inspiration to focusing on differences and negative connotations attached to words has been found in, Andersson, Håkan, "Barthesianska meditationer", 2003, especially pp. 83 ff.

1015 An international comparison will shed light on this aspect. See chapter 7.

1016 See Gårdfeldt, Lars, Äkta vill jag också vara, 2007, pp. 367–386. The title of the essay translates: "I too wish to be genuine", which illustrates the symbolic significance of words.

1017 Pichardo Galán, José Ignacio, Same-Sex Marriage in Spain, 2005, p. 7.

1018 See section 6.5.2.

6.7. SUMMARIZING ANALYSIS

6.7.1. GENDER-NEUTRAL MARRIAGE: UNDERMINING MARRIAGE?

Has the introduction of a gender-neutral marriage concept undermined marriage in Sweden? The answer to this question appears to depend, at the outset, on whom one asks. Proponents of the reform will most likely find the question without relevance, emphasizing that there is no reason to make any difference between spouses of the same sex and spouses of different sex, as regards issues of relevance to marriage such as emotional commitment and community. The twosome intimate relationship is still the target of marriage regulation, although extended to encompass couples of the same sex. The concept of marriage is still intended for long-term unions with far-reaching legal effects. From this point of view, the concept of marriage appears to remain the same, and is not threatened by the extension to encompass same-sex couples.

In my opinion, opening up marriage to couples of the same sex can even be claimed to strengthen the institution of marriage, by keeping it à jour with modern values and attitudes in society. For instance, in the revised gender-neutral marriage ceremony hierarchical features have been abolished, as well as references to values linking marriage to procreation. These changes may have the potential of making marriage instead more attractive to couples, who, totally independent of their sexual orientation, might otherwise have considered marriage to represent a patriarchal and outdated institution, incompatible with contemporary values. At least there is less ground to attack marriage on the basis of outdated symbolism.

Critics to adopting a gender-neutral marriage concept, on the contrary, may find that the symbolic impact of allowing two persons of the same sex to marry each other is so significant that marriage is no longer the same institution after such a reform. As described above, Helge Johan Thue has claimed that the symbolic and value-based effects of including two men or two women in the concept of marriage fundamentally altered the prerequisites for the marital contracts already concluded.[1019] According to his line of reasoning, couples already married cannot be assumed to have consented to such an essential change in basic conditions. Consequently the state has, through the new legislation, broken a valid agreement between two persons (the marriage contract concluded by the spouses). A counter-argument, well-known to any conflicts of law scholar, is that parties to a legal relationship do not have the right to "petrify" the contents of the applicable law. Law changes, and with this change the applicable rules change as well, irrespective of whether the parties wish it or not.[1020]

1019 See section 6.4.2.1.

1020 See decision by the Supreme Court, NJA 1968 p. 126.

These conflicting views illustrate that, regardless of whether or not we regard the gender-neutral marriage concept to undermine marriage or to modernize it to suit contemporary values, adopting a gender-neutral marriage concept in Sweden was a challenge for the legislator, touching upon values that extend beyond the legal sphere. The cultural and religious values attached to marriage are not easy to control through legislation.

6.7.2. WHY MARRIAGE?

The institution of marriage in the twenty-first century can be seen as having two primary functions, as a *contract* between the adults concerned and as a *civil status*. The Registered Partnership Act was equal to marriage in respect of the contractual side, gradually providing the same legal effects. However, the civil status as "registered partners" does not appear to have been equal on a *symbolic level* to the civil status as "married", which can explain why the Registered Partnership Act only became an interim legal solution in Sweden. The assumption that marriage has a higher symbolic value than registered partnership has been illustrated with a linguistic analysis, emphasizing the differences between the two institutions.[1021] The higher value of marriage compared to registered partnership was also explicitly mentioned in the committee report of 2007, as an argument supporting opening up marriage to couples of the same sex.[1022]

The marriage enactments of the 1970s, analyzed in chapter 4, emphasized the contractual side of marriage in the spirit of avoiding mandatory normative features in marriage law. The previously central function of marriage as creating a fundamental civil status in society was downplayed, most likely because this understanding of marriage was perceived as outdated in a society where individual freedom and autonomy were political concerns. Furthermore, practical reasons were given as the main motive for the enactments concerning cohabitation without marriage. The Registered Partnership Act, on the contrary, appears to have highlighted the symbolic "status function" of marriage and toned down the practical and non-intervening approach to legislation. In Sweden, the same sex marriage reform was not about acquiring mutual legal rights and duties, but about acquiring the *legal status* of marriage and the symbolic value attached to the concept of marriage. The Registered Partnership Act already provided same-sex couples with access to the contractual side of "marriage". Legally recognizing the rights of same-sex couples – the goal being full equality

1021 See section 6.6.2.2.

1022 Committee Report (SOU 2007:17), p. 16. See also section 6.5.2.1.

between same-sex and different-sex couples – has been turned into a human rights issue in Sweden, as well as in Spain and the Netherlands.[1023]

Protecting the human rights of the individual is of central political interest, not only in Sweden, but also in other parts of the Western world and at European level.[1024] As described in chapter 4, the Swedish welfare reforms provided a basis for improving the legal position of the individual and for creating equality between men and women, starting already in the 1930s. In the 1980s, the rights of homosexual individuals and same-sex couples were acknowledged and subject to legislation in the field of family law. In the preparatory work to the Swedish Registered Partnership Act, parallels were explicitly drawn to human rights documents, as a motivation for the enactment. In fact, the symbolic value of equal treatment and the ambition to counteract negative attitudes toward homosexuals in society were expressly emphasized as primary motivations for the enactment.[1025]

Once legal recognition of same-sex couples had been shaped into a human rights issue, demands for full equalization with heterosexual couples through access to marriage was a development close at hand. This trend has been visible not only in Sweden, but in many parts of the Western world.[1026] A contributing factor in this context is, most likely that at European Union level, and in the interpretations by the Strasbourg Court regarding the European Convention on Human Rights, a person's civil status as married is significant for exercising certain rights of the Convention, and for the right to move freely within the European Union.[1027] This has most likely also contributed to an increased focus in general on the status function of marriage in European countries.

Another example of the increasing significance of the status function of marriage is that gender-neutral marriage enactments have been adopted in several European states, without including all of the legal effects of a marriage. For instance, some marriage enactments allow same-sex couples to marry and call their union a marriage, but the marriage does not create any – or all – of the legal consequences in respect of children.[1028] This can be claimed to support the theory that being able to call a union "marriage" and acquiring the legal status as "married" has a special value, even without access to the full "contractual deal",

1023 See chapter 7.
1024 See chapters 7 and 8.
1025 See section 6.5.1.
1026 For current updates on the legal status of same-sex couples, see the homepage of ILGA Europe at www.ilga-europe.org/home/issues/families/recognition_of_relationships/legislation_and_case_law/marriage_and_partnership_rights_for_same_sex_partners_country_by_country. Accessed 13 September 2010.
1027 See chapter 8.
1028 This is the case for instance in Portugal. See compilation of states and legal effects of registration and marriage enactments for same-sex couples by: Saez, Macarena, Same sex marriage, same sex cohabitation, and same sex families around the world: Why "same" is so different? 2010, pp. 1–49. See also section 9.1.1.

which is available to spouses of different sex. On the other hand, access to marriage without all legal effects of marriage risks connoting a "second-class" marriage, which is regarded as less valuable than a "real" marriage. This might, in turn, make same-sex couples less inclined to marry. Furthermore, from a human rights perspective, full equality in legal rights must be regarded as the goal.[1029]

On reflection, returning to the rose metaphor cited initially, what something is called does appear to matter a great deal on a symbolic level. In Sweden, registered partnership became gradually equal to marriage in respect of legal rights and duties attached, but not on a symbolic level. The tension concerning the introduction of a gender-neutral marriage concept boiled down to being about the label of "marriage". In other words, the "rose" simply did not smell as sweet when called a "carnation", irrespective of how quite similar the two different flowers may have appeared at first glance.

1029 This will be further developed in the following chapters. See, for instance, section 8.4.

PART III

INTERNATIONAL AND EUROPEAN OUTLOOKS

7. LEGAL RECOGNITION OF SAME-SEX COUPLES – SPAIN AND THE NETHERLANDS

7.1. RECAPITULATION AND CHOICE OF JURISDICTIONS

The question of whether or not to permit same-sex couples access to a formalized union is not unique to Sweden. It is a topical and controversial issue in many other European countries as well. More than two-thirds of the Member States of the EU have adopted, or are preparing, statutory registration schemes which include same-sex couples.[1030] The number is expected to continue to increase.[1031] The Netherlands and Spain are two examples of jurisdictions that have enacted far-reaching regulations on same-sex relationships. Both of these jurisdictions have, like Sweden, adopted a registration scheme for same-sex couples, as well as a gender-neutral marriage concept.

In the previous chapters the essence of marriage in Sweden and the changing prerequisites for the individual in Swedish society have been analyzed. It has been illustrated that since the 1920s, the principle of equality has been a key component of the Swedish legal development concerning marriage; it has been visible in the ideology of the Swedish welfare state and in various legislative projects. The target areas of enactments to achieve equality have shifted from focusing on equality between husband and wife, to equality between different cohabitation models and to equality between same-sex couples and different sex couples.

It has been argued that the enactment of a gender-neutral marriage concept in Sweden highlighted the symbolic dimension of marriage, by in a sense challenging the moral foundation of society, more precisely, the deeply-rooted and religiously-based idea of marriage as a union between a man and a woman

1030 In 2008, Katharina Boele-Woelki counted that 17 out of the 27 EU Member States had either adopted a registration scheme or had a pending proposal. Boele-Woelki, Katharina, The Legal Recognition of Same-Sex Relationships Within the European Union, 2007–2008, pp. 1960 f. Boele-Woelki holds that most Member States are expected to legislate on same-sex unions. Updated information about the legal status of same-sex couples in the world can be found at CBC News: www.cbc.ca/world/story/2009/05/26/f-same-sex-timeline.html. Accessed 20 September 2010.

1031 Boele-Woelki, Katharina, The Legal Recognition of Same-Sex Relationships Within the European Union, 2007–2008, pp. 1960 f.

for the purpose of procreation. Despite the political aim to eradicate moral values from family law legislation – a Swedish goal pronounced in the 1970s – it has been suggested that moral values based in religion appear to have lingered on in Sweden and re-emerged in connection with the 2009 gender-neutral marriage enactment, which can explain why introducing same-sex marriage was controversial.[1032]

In the present chapter, the Swedish legal development regarding same-sex partners will be contrasted with two jurisdictions with similar legislation but different societal, historical and religious backgrounds. In Spain, the Catholic Church strongly criticized the same-sex marriage reform of 2005 and the church has been unwilling to solemnize a marriage between two men or two women. Although 76 percent of the Spanish population define themselves as Catholic,[1033] there appears to have been support in Spanish society to open up marriage to same-sex couples. Furthermore, a political interest in supporting enactments perceived as "progressive", such as the gender-neutral marriage enactment can be discerned.[1034]

In respect of the Dutch legal development, it has been observed that primarily secular and rational arguments of equality and non-discrimination – not religious arguments – were brought into play when the gender-neutral marriage enactment of 2001 was prepared.[1035] This appears to be in line with the fact that civil marriage is the only legally valid form of concluding a marriage in the Netherlands.[1036] Celebrating a religious marriage prior to the civil ceremony is criminalized and officials from the religious communities who disregard this prohibition can face a pecuniary fine.[1037] However, the fact that secular arguments predominated in political quarters in connection with the Dutch same-sex marriage reform does not per se necessarily mean that Dutch society is in fact more "secularized" than Swedish society, or that the same-sex marriage reform was less controversial in the Netherlands than it was in Sweden. As will be illustrated below, there was political opposition to opening up marriage to same-sex couples in the Netherlands as well, in particular within the Christian Party, and adopting the act was time-consuming partly because of this.[1038]

1032 See section 6.3.4.

1033 CIS Barometer, July 2009, www.cis.es/cis/opencm/ES/2_barometros/depositados.jsp. Accessed 14 September 2010.

1034 See section 7.3.1.

1035 Antokolskaia, Masha, Harmonisation of Family Law in Europe, 2006, p. 295.

1036 Article 30, Section 2 of Book 1 of the Dutch Civil Code. Civil marriage as the only legally valid form of concluding a marriage in the Netherlands is the result of the influence of Napoleon.

1037 Curry-Sumner, Ian, Private International Law Aspects of Homosexual Couples, 2007, p. 5.

1038 See section 7.2.5.1. See also Antokolskaia, Masha, Harmonisation of Family Law in Europe, 2006, p. 35, where Antokolskaia notes that during the parliamentary debates even the Christian Democrats "kept within the rational discussion and did not put forward any theological arguments". Only the small, strictly Protestant parties represented in the Dutch Parliament did so.

In Sweden, a double track system for conclusion of marriage applies, according to which a legally valid marriage can be celebrated either in the religious or the civil form. Unlike in the Netherlands, in Sweden theological arguments were openly discussed in connection with the same-sex marriage reform. Several religious communities in Sweden constituted a reference group in connection with the enactment of the gender-neutral marriage legislation. Although initially critical, in the end the Church of Sweden, the largest religious community, decided to marry also same-sex couples. However, most other religious communities in Sweden still defend a "traditional" conception of marriage as a union between a man and woman, and do not officiate at marriages between persons of the same sex.[1039]

It is worth emphasizing once again that my aim is not to provide an extensive legal comparison between the three jurisdictions – Sweden, Spain and the Netherlands – but to focus on why legally recognizing same-sex partnerships has been on the political "agendas" in two additional European countries, and illustrate how these enactments and the course of events compare to the Swedish. Also the legal development concerning same-sex relationships in the Nordic countries will be touched upon briefly in the end of this chapter.

7.2. THE NETHERLANDS

7.2.1. FREEDOM OF CHOICE – VARIOUS ALTERNATIVE REGULATIONS

Since 1998, Dutch law provides same-sex couples with a possibility to register a partnership and obtain legal effects similar to those attached to marriage.[1040] The Dutch Registered Partnership Act applies also to couples of different sex. In 2001, the Dutch legal development was taken one step further when the Netherlands became the first country in the world to adopt a gender-neutral marriage concept.[1041] There is also a third option available for Dutch couples wishing in some sense to formalize their relationship and acquire mutual rights and duties, namely to conclude a cohabitation agreement which regulates their

1039 However, *Missionskyrkan* (the Swedish Mission Church) has decided that it is up to each congregation to decide whether or not to celebrate same-sex marriages. By June 2010, however, no such marriages had been reported. See Jänterä-Jareborg, Maarit, The Same-Sex Marriage Reform with Special Regard to Concerns of Religion, 2010, p. 1507. See also Section 1.4.2.

1040 The Dutch Civil Code – Book 1, Title 5a: Registered Partnerships – 1 January 1998, Art. 80.

1041 The bill was introduced by the government on 8 July 1999, passed by the lower house on 12 September 2000, passed by the upper house on 19 December 2000 and, finally, signed by queen Beatrix on 21 December 2000. The Act entered into force on 1 April 2001. See, for instance, Waaldijk, Kees, Small Change: How the Road to Same-Sex Marriage Got Paved in the Netherlands, 2001, p. 437. The Dutch course of events is also described in Committee Report (SOU 2007:17), pp. 160–165.

property relations.[1042] More than half of all Dutch unmarried couples living together have signed such a cohabitation agreement.[1043]

According to Dutch law, all these options – marriage, registered partnership and a cohabitation agreement – are "gender-neutral", i.e. available to couples of the same sex as well as to couples of different sex. The legislative technique to not create separate institutions for couples of the same sex originally distinguished the Netherlands from Sweden.

In chapter 6, it has been suggested that the Swedish Registered Partnership Act was valued less than a "real" marriage by homosexual couples, partly because of the Act's structure and connotations of an institution separate, yet legally equivalent, to marriage, and exclusively available to same-sex couples.[1044] In respect of the Dutch institution of registered partnership, the risk of registered partnership signaling differential treatment instead of equal treatment can be claimed to appear less imminent, because the Act is open to same-sex as well as different-sex couples. In other words, the Dutch Registered Partnership Act does not appear to "point out" same-sex couples in a manner which might create negative connotations to preferential – possibly discriminatory – treatment. Furthermore, the Dutch Registered Partnership Act appears more independently structured than the Swedish Act, enumerating applicable rights and duties, instead of referring in an abstract manner to exceptions from the regulation governing marriage without laying down what rules do in fact apply. These features suggest that the Dutch institution of registered partnership might, more clearly than the Swedish institution of registered partnership, serve a purpose of its own, by avoiding a legislative technique which focuses on establishing what a registered partnership is *not*.[1045]

Nevertheless, the Dutch registered partnership, irrespective of its "autonomous features", was not the same as a marriage, and like in Sweden, the pressure for a gender-neutral conception of marriage remained. In 2001, the Dutch institution of marriage was extended to encompass couples of the same sex. The Swedish Registered Partnership Act was repealed when the gender-neutral marriage enactment entered into force on 1 May 2009, but it continues to give rise to legal effects in respect of same-sex couples who registered their partnership prior to the 2009 law reform and have not transformed their

---

1042 A Dutch cohabitation agreement must be drawn up by a notary and is limited to covering issues that the couple agrees to include. Moreover, it only applies to the couple's mutual relationship and has no validity toward a third party. Critics have emphasized the need of action from the legislator in respect of the growing tendency of couples to live together without being married. See Boele-Woelki, Katharina, Registered Partnership and Same-Sex Marriage in the Netherlands, 2003, p. 41, with reference to critical legal doctrine on this subject matter.

1043 Statistics Netherlands, www.cbs.nl/en-GB/menu/themas/bevolking/publicaties/artikelen/archief/2010/2010-3044-wm.htm?Languageswitch=on. Accessed 20 September 2010.

1044 See section 6.5.1.

1045 See section 6.6.2.2.

registered partnership into a marriage. In the Netherlands, registered partnership has been retained as a generally available optional legal institution after the same-sex marriage reform. This further illustrates that the Dutch registered partnership has become an independent institution distinct from marriage, whereas the Swedish registered partnership turned out to be no more than a substitute – an interim legal solution – only retained while awaiting "the real thing", i.e. access to marriage by same-sex couples.[1046]

7.2.2. EQUAL TREATMENT – THE BASIS FOR THE DUTCH COURSE OF EVENTS

7.2.2.1. The Dutch Concept of Discrimination

> "All persons in the Netherlands shall be treated equally in equal circumstances. Discrimination on the grounds of religion, belief, political opinion, race or sex or on any other grounds whatsoever shall not be permitted."[1047]

An explanation for Dutch couples' freedom to choose between three different sets of rules, lies in a wide interpretation of the concept of equality. The primary aim of introducing same-sex marriage in the Netherlands was to achieve equal treatment in accordance with the quoted section of the Dutch Constitution. In fact, the idea of equal treatment has been called "the foundation stone of the Act opening marriage to same-sex couples" and "the core objective at the heart of its enactment."[1048] What constitutes discrimination according to the Dutch Constitution? In the Criminal Code, Art. 90 (quarter), discrimination is defined accordingly:

> "The term 'discrimination' or 'to discriminate against' is to be taken to mean any form of differentiation, any act of exclusion, restriction or preference, that intends or may result in the destruction or infringement of the recognition, enjoyment or equal exercise of human rights and fundamental freedoms in the field of politics or economics, in social or cultural matters or any other area of social life."[1049]

1046 See section 6.6.2.2, for semiotic reflections on the concept of marriage in Sweden. The symbolic difference between marriage and registered partnership in the Netherlands will be discussed in section. 7.2.6.1.

1047 Article 1 of the Dutch Constitution, as translated by Waaldijk, Kees, Universiteit Leiden, July 2001. See www.law.leiden.edu/general/img/Translation%20of%20Dutch%20laws%20against%20sexual%20orientation%20discrimination_tcm19-55182.pdf. Accessed 20 September 2010.

1048 These expressions were used by the research team evaluating the reform of 2001. See Boele-Woelki, K, Curry-Sumner, I, Jansen M, Schrama W, Evaluatie 'Wet openstelling huwelijk' en van het geregistreerd partnerschap, 2006, p. 252.

1049 As translated by Waaldijk, Kees, Universiteit Leiden, July 2001. See www.law.leiden.edu/general/img/Translation%20of%20Dutch%20laws%20against%20sexual%20orientation%20

As the quote illustrates, the Dutch definition of discrimination is wide-ranging, including all forms of differentiation, exclusion, restriction and preference, which – intentionally or unintentionally – violate human rights. It appears that, in order to live up to this obligation, it was found necessary to introduce a gender-neutral marriage concept.[1050] However, at the outset, just like in Sweden, it was found motivated to retain certain distinctions between same-sex couples and different-sex couples when the Dutch Registered Partnership Act was introduced, primarily in the field of legal parenthood. Thus the same institution – marriage – was made available to all couples regardless of sex, but the legal effects applicable to a married couple of the same sex were not *exactly* the same as the legal effects of a married couple of different sex.[1051] The presumption of parenthood applicable to different-sex spouses was not applied to spouses of the same sex, and only second-parent adoption – not joint adoption of a child from abroad – was included in the reform. Abolishing these exceptions is currently being considered in the Netherlands.[1052]

The general impression is that the idea of what constitutes discrimination under Dutch law seems to have changed rapidly. The Dutch legislator appears to have challenged the remaining differences in treatment between same-sex and different-sex couples step by step, for the purpose of achieving equality (and decreasing the risk of discrimination). This course of events, reforms dealing with same-sex couples taking place one small step at a time,[1053] has not been secluded to the Netherlands, but has a counterpart in many other countries as well.[1054] From this point of view, the institution of registered partnership was an

---

discrimination_tcm19–55182.pdf. Accessed 20 September 2010.

1050 Boele-Woelki, K, Curry-Sumner, I, Jansen M, Schrama W, Evaluatie 'Wet openstelling huwelijk' en van het geregistreerd partnerschap, 2006, p. 252.

1051 The symbolic impact of applying different legal effects to a marriage depending on the sex of the spouses will be discussed in section 9.1.1.

1052 See section 7.2.4.3.

1053 Kees Waaldijk speaks about a "small change theory", according to which: "Any legislative change advancing the recognition and acceptance of homosexuality will only be enacted, if that change is either perceived as small, or if that change is sufficiently reduced in impact by some accompanying legislative 'small change' that reinforces the condemnation of homosexuality. See Waaldijk, Kees, Small Change: How the Road to Same-Sex Marriage Got Paved in the Netherlands, 2001, p. 440. The theory has been criticized for not being equally suitable for analysis of, for instance, the English course of events in the field of same-sex relationships. In England, pressure from the European Court of Justice, as well as the European Court of Human Rights, has been claimed to have played an important role in the legal development, not just changes in society influencing how people conceive reforms. See Sumner, Ian, Going Dutch? 2002, pp. 52–56. Kees Waaldijk disagrees, considering the English development to fit into the second aspect of the theory, i.e. the idea that decriminalization is followed by stricter prohibitions against, for instance, public homosexual behavior. See Waaldijk, Kees, Small Change: How the Road to Same-Sex Marriage Got Paved in the Netherlands, 2001, p. 441.

1054 In fact, in all Nordic countries, the same course of events can be observed, i.e. homosexual individuals and same-sex couples gaining legal recognition gradually, one step at a time. See section 7.4 and subsections.

important step on the way toward granting same-sex couples access to marriage.[1055]

Applying a wide interpretation of the concept of equality can give rise to unexpected results. The decision to include different-sex couples in the Registered Partnership Act can be seen as an expression of a far-reaching interpretation of the concept of equality under Dutch law.[1056] Including different-sex couples was not expected to be of any considerable practical significance, the presumption being that only a small number of different-sex couples would make use of this possibility.[1057] Same-sex couples, who could not marry at that point in time, were the primary target group of the legislation. The outcome of the reform was unexpected: one third of all couples registering a partnership when the Act entered into force in 1998 were of different sex.[1058]

The great number of different-sex couples choosing registered partnership instead of marriage, it will be suggested below, contributed to marking the Dutch institution of registered partnership as an independent cohabitation model – an option to marriage. It does not appear to be a "second-class" marriage of lower dignity than a "real" marriage, which the Swedish Registered Partnership Act was called by critics,[1059] but an institution of its own. The Dutch decision to include different-sex couples in the Registered Partnership Act, in the spirit of equality, would turn out to be decisive for the decision to retain the institution, also after the gender-neutral marriage enactment had been adopted in 2001. By then registered partnership had become an established institution in Dutch society, particularly popular among different-sex couples, which was quite contrary to the original intention of the Dutch legislator. This made it difficult to abolish the institution of registered partnership.[1060]

7.2.2.2. "Discrimination" – Different Approaches in Sweden and the Netherlands

Differences between same-sex and different-sex couples in the Netherlands have largely been challenged and eliminated as a means of avoiding discrimination in the wide sense of the concept discussed above.[1061] It can be noted that in Sweden, a special discrimination act was adopted in 2008 and entered into force on 1 September 2009.[1062] This Act aims to counteract discrimination and promote equal rights irrespective of, inter alia, sexual orientation. The Act replaced several

---

1055 Boele-Woelki, K, Curry-Sumner, I, Jansen M, Schrama W, Evaluatie 'Wet openstelling huwelijk' en van het geregistreerd partnerschap, 2006, p. 252.

1056 However, the idea was also to signal that the two institutions were equal in value. Schrama, Wendy, Registered Partnership in the Netherlands, 1999, p. 323.

1057 Schrama, Wendy, Registered Partnership in the Netherlands, 1999, p. 323.

1058 Schrama, Wendy, Registered Partnership in the Netherlands, 1999, p. 323.

1059 See sections: 6.5.1 and 6.6.2.2.

1060 See section 7.2.6.1.

1061 See section 7.2.2.1.

1062 Government Bill (Prop 2007/08:95).

different enactments dealing with discrimination issues, collecting them in one statute and widening the level of protection. The prohibition against discrimination applies to various sections of Swedish society, such as education, employment and membership in certain organizations.[1063] Furthermore, there is constitutional protection against discrimination under Swedish law.[1064] Thus, the level of protection against discrimination appears far-reaching also in Sweden.

The Swedish legal scholar Anders Agell recommended a cautious approach in general to the legal concept of discrimination. He emphasized that not all differential treatment constitutes discrimination, arguing that the word "discrimination" is often used in an unclear manner by advocates for legal change in the field of sexual orientation law.[1065]

In section 6.5.1, I have pointed out that in connection with the enactment of the Swedish Registered Partnership Act, references to human rights issues were made in the committee report of 1993.[1066] However, in the following Law Commission Report, (which was the basis for the enactment since no Government Bill was presented) same-sex couples' practical need of legal rules governing their relationship was expressed as the main reason for reform – not achieving equal treatment and preventing discrimination.[1067] When the Swedish Registered Partnership Act was amended with rules on legal parenthood for partners of the same sex, this was motivated with reference to the best interests of the child.[1068] When the same-sex marriage enactment of 2009 was adopted, ideological reasons for reform were taken into account by the Law Commission. At the same time, however, the ideas that the law should primarily provide solutions to practical problems and aim to avoid expressing moral values were underlined.[1069]

It appears that the idea of striving for neutrality in the context of Swedish family law reforms, discussed in chapter 4, continues to motivate a practical approach to legislation.[1070] This policy might be a reason why the Swedish legislator appears to be less inclined than the Dutch to speak openly in terms of

1063 Chapter 2 of the Swedish Discrimination Act of 2008.

1064 The Instrument of Government (Regeringsformen, RF) RF 1:2, RF 1:9, RF 2:15, 16, 22, 23 and RF 11:9. See also section 6.5.4 above.

1065 Agell, Anders, The Legal Status of Same-Sex Couples in Europe – A Critical Analysis, 2003, pp. 123 f.

1066 Committee Report (SOU 1993:98), Part A, p. 21.

1067 Law Commission Report (1993/94:LU28), Registrerat partnerskap, m.m.

1068 The extensive investigation of the situation of children in same-sex families was presented in: Committee Report (SOU 2001:10), Parts A and B, The task of the Committee was also to determine if the distinction made between registered partners and spouses in respect of adoption was justified.

1069 Report of the Committee on Civil Affairs, (Civilutskottet) (2008/09:CU19), p. 10. This has been a recurring theme in the preparatory work since the 1970s. See chapters 4 and 5.

1070 See sections: 4.2.1 and 5.2.3.

equality and non-discrimination. On the other hand, as argued in chapter 4, creating equality has been an omnipresent political goal also in Sweden, since the establishment of the welfare state. It appears that, whereas equality in a sense "goes without saying" in Sweden, in the Netherlands, it is explicitly "said".

In summary, equality and non-discrimination have been important concerns of both the Dutch and the Swedish legislators in connection with reforms to improve the legal situation of same-sex couples. Both in Sweden and in the Netherlands, far-reaching protection against discrimination is provided through legislation. However, the Dutch approach to non-discrimination and equality appears more direct and explicit than the more cautious Swedish approach, which – in accordance with the guiding Swedish policy since the 1970s – tends to focus primarily on practical reasons for reform. However, as illustrated in chapter 6, the Swedish Registered Partnership Act and the same-sex marriage enactment were not just practical legal solutions, but at the same time ideological statements of legal recognition.

7.2.3. LEGAL APPROACHES TO HOMOSEXUALITY: POLICIES AND KEY ENACTMENTS

7.2.3.1. Background

Homosexual sexual acts were decriminalized already in 1811 in the Netherlands, which was then a part of the French Empire.[1071] However, it should be underlined that decriminalization in itself – like in Sweden in the 1940s – did not mean that homosexuality was socially acceptable in the Netherlands. In 1911, the age of consent to same-sex sexual acts was established at 21 years, which was a significant sharpening compared to the age-limit for heterosexual sexual acts, set at 16.[1072] Six decades later, however, in 1971, the Netherlands became the first European country to equalize the age of consent between homosexual and heterosexual sexual acts.[1073] During the 1970s, homosexual orientation ceased to be considered an obstacle to child custody or visitation rights after divorce.[1074] Unlike in Sweden, it has not been forbidden in the Netherlands for medical clinics

1071 France had decriminalized homosexuality already in 1791. See Waaldijk, Kees, Small Change: How the Road to Same-Sex Marriage Got Paved in the Netherlands, 2001, p. 438.

1072 Sumner, Ian, Going Dutch? 2002, p. 32.

1073 As pointed out by Waaldijk, Kees, unequal age-limits had never existed in Turkey, Italy or Poland. See Small Change: How the Road to Same-Sex Marriage Got Paved in the Netherlands, 2001, p. 438.

1074 Waaldijk, Kees, Small Change: How the Road to Same-Sex Marriage Got Paved in the Netherlands, 2001, p. 441. The 1955 decision by the Swedish Court in which a lesbian mother was granted custody of her daughter, has been accounted for in section 6.2.3.1.

to offer assisted procreation treatments to same-sex couples, but in practice many clinics have in the past refused to offer their services to two women.[1075]

Another key event toward legal recognition of same-sex couples was a decision by the Dutch Supreme Court in 1982, according to which discrimination on the basis of sexual orientation in the armed forces was considered unlawful.[1076] Furthermore, discrimination on the grounds of sexual orientation was criminalized in the Netherlands in 1992.[1077] It can also be mentioned that the Dutch Homosexual Movement (COC), founded in 1973, is well-established in the Netherlands, as a body with legal personality receiving financial aid from the Dutch government.[1078] In 2008, the COC, together with the State Federation of Lesbians, Gays, Transsexuals and Bisexuals of Spain (FELGTB), became the first gay organization to be granted consultative status in the United Nations.[1079]

7.2.3.2. Court Interpretations of Same-Sex Marriage

In 1990, the question of whether denying a same-sex couple the possibility to conclude a legally valid marriage constituted unlawful discrimination was dealt with in two cases: firstly, by a district court in Amsterdam and secondly, by the Dutch Supreme Court. Both courts ruled against the petitioners.[1080] The Supreme Court stated that:

> "Civil marriage is since time immemorial understood to be an enduring bond between a man and a woman to which a number of legal consequences are attached, which partly relate to the difference in sex and the consequences connected therewith for the descent of children. Marriage has these characteristics not only in the Netherlands but in many countries. Moreover, it cannot be said that the general opinion in the legal community has developed such that the considerations just mentioned do not justify the distinction in treatment on the grounds of sexual

---

1075 Waaldijk, Kees, Small Change: How the Road to Same-Sex Marriage Got Paved in the Netherlands, 2001, p. 442 (especially note 21).

1076 See Waaldijk, Kees, Small Change: How the Road to Same-Sex Marriage Got Paved in the Netherlands, 2001, p. 442.

1077 Waaldijk, Kees, Small Change: How the Road to Same-Sex Marriage Got Paved in the Netherlands, 2001, pp. 438 f. This appears rather late compared to the Scandinavian countries, where criminalization took place in Norway in 1981, Denmark in 1987, Sweden in 1987 (partially) and in 1999 (completely), and Finland in 1995. See p. 438. For an account of the legal development as regards anti-discrimination law, see also Waaldijk, Kees, "Civil Developments: Patters of Reform in the Legal Position of Same-Sex Partners in Europe, 2000, pp. 75–79.

1078 Schrama, Wendy, Registered Partnership in the Netherlands, 1999, p. 317, note 24. It can be mentioned that also the corresponding Swedish organization – the RFSL – receives financial aid from the state.

1079 See www.ilga-europe.org/home/issues/beyond_europe/united_nations/consultative_status_in_the_economic_and_social_council_ecosoc_of_the_united_nations/more_lgbt_groups_gain_consultative_status_with_un. Accessed 20 September 2010.

1080 Curry-Sumner, Ian, All's well that ends registered? 2005, p. 118.

orientation, which can manifest itself in the impossibility to enter a relationship like marriage with a person of the same sex as oneself."[1081]

Although the Supreme Court underlined that excluding same-sex couples from access to marriage did not constitute unlawful discrimination, the court pointed out that denying same-sex couples access to the legal effects of marriage might be discriminatory.[1082] The Supreme Court thereby "passed the ball" to the Dutch legislator.

7.2.4. REGISTERED PARTNERSHIP

7.2.4.1. The First Kortmann Committee

As a result of the statement by the Supreme Court in 1990, the first "Kortmann committee" was formed.[1083] In 1991, the committee delivered its initial report, proposing that a formalized relationship scheme should be introduced for same-sex couples who could not marry, as well as for different-sex couples who did not wish to marry.[1084] Including different-sex couples in the Act proved controversial, and the bill to Parliament, submitted in 1994, only included same-sex couples.[1085] While the Registered Partnership Act was being prepared, the political pressure for legal recognition of same-sex couples made some city councils take the matter into their own hands. Registers were created for same-sex couples and non-binding registration ceremonies were performed for the purpose of demonstrating the urgency of reform. These registers, although without legal significance, signaled to politicians that the law should be changed.[1086] As a result of a memorandum published in 1995, different-sex couples were once again included in the registration scheme.[1087]

1081 Hoge Raad, 19 Oktober 1990, (1992), p. 192, as translated by Maxwell, Nancy G, Opening Civil Marriage To Same-Gender Couples, 2001, p. 147.

1082 Hoge Raad, 19 October 1990 (1992). See Sumner, Ian, Going Dutch? 2002, p. 33.

1083 It was a committee formed for the purpose of advising the Dutch government in respect of marriage regulation and propose necessary reforms.

1084 In its report "Leefvormen" (Lifestyles) the Committee presented two types of registrations, one dealing with public law effects, to be carried out at the local municipal administration, and a second one providing almost the same legal effects as a marriage, to be carried out in the civil status register. The former was not endorsed by the government. See Schrama, Wendy, Registered Partnership in the Netherlands, 1999, pp. 317 f.

1085 Schrama, Wendy, Registered Partnership in the Netherlands, 1999, p. 317.

1086 Curry-Sumner, Ian, All's well that ends registered? 2005, p. 120. Also in Spain symbolic registrations were carried out, for instance in Vitoria as a means of pressuring politicians to adopt a registration scheme. See section 7.3.2.1.

1087 Schrama, Wendy, Registered Partnership in the Netherlands, 1999, p. 317. See also Sumner, Ian, Going Dutch? 2002, pp. 33 f.

The Dutch Registered Partnership Act was adopted in 1997 and entered into force on 1 January 1998.[1088] As mentioned above, the Act was applicable to same-sex couples as well as different-sex couples. Wendy Schrama has pointed out that legally recognizing same-sex couples was the primary aim of the legislator – not providing a legal framework for unmarried cohabitees of different sex. According to Schrama, also different-sex couples were in the end included in the Registered Partnership Act for the purpose of underlining that registered partnership was indeed *equal* to marriage and not a "second-class marriage", which according to the Dutch government would have been the main impression, had same-sex couples been dealt with separately.[1089] As mentioned above, it was quite unexpected from the point of view of the Dutch legislator that a significant number of different-sex couples made use of the institution of registered partnership.[1090]

According to Ian Curry-Sumner's interpretation, the decision to include different-sex couples in the Registered Partnership Act can also be seen as an attempt to silence the Dutch homosexual movement's demand for access to marriage.[1091] Including different-sex couples in the Dutch Registered Partnership Act appears to have created an institution largely independent of marriage, serving a purpose of its own, namely to provide an option for *different-sex* couples who do not want to marry. However, the Dutch Registered Partnership Act did not silence the demands by same-sex couples for access to marriage.

In fact, while the Registered Partnership Act was prepared, the demands by same-sex couples for access to marriage intensified in the Netherlands, and the institution of registered partnership was criticized by the Dutch homosexual movement for being a "second-class" marriage.[1092] The lower Chamber of Dutch Parliament also pushed for the introduction of a gender-neutral marriage concept.[1093] Opponents to the same-sex marriage enactment, however, pointed out that allowing same-sex couples access to marriage would create difficulties, especially if same-sex marriage was combined with a presumption of parenthood in respect of children born into the marriage.[1094] Moreover, opponents feared that same-sex marriage, if combined with a right to adopt children, would discourage foreign countries from placing children in Dutch adoptive families, which would be detrimental to childless Dutch couples of different sex.[1095]

1088 The Dutch Civil Code, Title 5a: Registered Partnerships.

1089 Schrama, Wendy, Registered Partnership in the Netherlands, 1999, p. 323.

1090 Schrama, Wendy, Registered Partnership in the Netherlands, 1999, p. 323. See section 7.2.2.1.

1091 Curry-Sumner, Ian, All's well that ends registered? 2005, p. 119.

1092 Sumner, Ian, Going Dutch? 2002, p. 34.

1093 Maxwell, Nancy G, Opening Civil Marriage To Same-Gender Couples, 2001, p. 151.

1094 Maxwell, Nancy G, Opening Civil Marriage To Same-Gender Couples, 2001, pp. 151 f. This critique was held by the Dutch Cabinet.

1095 Maxwell, Nancy G, Opening Civil Marriage To Same-Gender Couples, 2001, p. 152.

In the legal literature the opposition toward the same-sex marriage reform in the Netherlands has been described as comparatively limited.[1096] However, as will be discussed in section 7.2.5.2, adopting a gender-neutral marriage concept in the Netherlands was time-consuming and not without ideological obstacles. It appears that adopting a gender-neutral marriage concept challenged traditional conceptions and values attached to marriage in the Netherlands, just like in Sweden, although theological arguments put forth by religious communities were not given much room in the preparations of the Dutch enactment. Instead human rights arguments concerning equality and non-discrimination were in the forefront.

7.2.4.2. The Forms and Conditions of Registered Partnership – Similarities and Differences Compared to Marriage

7.2.4.2.1. Impediments

Impediments to marriage signal which relationships are undesirable in a society, by excluding certain couples from access to marriage. However, impediments to marriage do not prohibit couples from cohabiting outside of marriage. In the Netherlands – just like in Sweden – unmarried cohabitation is a wide-spread habit which is socially accepted. Since impediments to marriage no longer prevent couples from living together without being married, the general trend in many European countries has been to reduce the impediments to marriage.[1097] Nevertheless, as discussed above in respect of Sweden, certain impediments have been found justified to retain, even in a country with Sweden's "liberal" reputation.[1098] Not everybody has access to the institution of marriage – or to the institution of registered partnership.

Under Dutch law, the impediments to registered partnership have from the beginning largely corresponded with the impediments to marriage, and there is no difference in respect of impediments between a same-sex marriage and a different-sex marriage.[1099] The first impediment deals with exclusivity: registered partnership can only be concluded by two persons and only one formalized relationship can exist at a time. Polygamous marriage and polygamous registered partnership are criminalized.[1100] Moreover, a person registering a partnership may not at the same time be married, and a person concluding a marriage may not be in a registered partnership.[1101]

1096 See section 7.2.5.2.
1097 See section 4.2.2.1.
1098 See section 4.2.2.1.
1099 Marriage in the Netherlands, Report at the request of the Swedish Marriage and Partnership Inquiry Commission, 19th January 2006, 14.00–17.00, p. 7.
1100 Curry-Sumner, Ian, All's well that ends registered? 2005, p. 122.
1101 Curry-Sumner, Ian, All's well that ends registered? 2005, p. 122.

The second category of impediments deal with prohibited degrees of relationships: relatives in the direct descending or ascending line, or brothers and sisters, are not allowed to marry each other or conclude a registered partnership with each other.[1102] The third impediment governs the minimum age for conclusion of marriage or registered partnership; like a couple wishing to marry, a couple wishing to register their partnership must have reached the age of 18. Younger persons must have parental consent and apply for special dispensation at the Ministry of Justice.[1103] The fourth category of impediments deals with residency criteria, more precisely private international law provisions on connection requirements, which will not be further analyzed here.[1104]

The overall impression is that the relationships found worth socially sanctioning through access to a formalized union covered by family law rules, appear quite "traditional", and are limited to encompassing the committed, intimate (often sexual) relationship between two adults who are not related to each other. In this respect, the Dutch and the Swedish views on formalized unions correspond. However, if registered partnership in the Netherlands in some sense is perceived as the "non-symbolic" alternative to marriage – in contrast to the symbolic institution of marriage[1105] – then why restrict access to registered partnership through application of the same impediments to registered partnership as to marriage? Why not let any two – or three or four – persons who wish to be covered by the legal package of rules attached to registered partnership conclude the partnership "contract"?

In chapter 6, it has been claimed that the idea of marriage as a monogamous relationship between a man and a woman for the purpose of procreation is based on Christian values, which came to the surface in connection with the Swedish same-sex marriage reform. Against this background, it can be noted that also in the Netherlands the impediments to registered partnership and marriage reflect these "traditional" values.[1106]

1102 Article 1:41 of the Dutch Civil Code, which applies to registered partnership according to Art. 80a, Section 6. However, the Minister of Justice may allow exceptions as regards adoptive brothers and sisters if significant reasons exist. See Curry-Sumner, Ian, All's well that ends registered? 2005, p. 125, with further references.

1103 Curry-Sumner, Ian, All's well that ends registered? 2005, p. 123. As regards rules on competency to marry and register partnership, it can be mentioned that those under guardianship due to mental disorder must obtain permission to marry from the sub-district court judge. See p. 125.

1104 See for instance, Curry-Sumner, Ian, All's well that ends registered? 2005, pp. 123 f.

1105 This will be further developed under section "B. The Ceremony" below.

1106 See section 9.2.2.

7.2.4.2.2. The Marriage Ceremony

Civil marriage is the only legally recognized form of concluding a marriage in the Netherlands, for different-sex couples and for same-sex couples.[1107] The partnership registration ceremony closely resembles that of a civil marriage, including witnesses and the oral declaration of the parties that they wish to become registered partners.[1108] The officials authorized to marry and register partnerships are the same: Registrars of Births, Deaths, Marriages and Registered Partnerships.[1109]

However, the Dutch partnership registration ceremony includes an additional element, absent in the marriage ceremony, namely that the couple signs a registered partnership certificate. There is no valid registered partnership without the couple's signatures.[1110] In 2006, when the Registered Partnership Act and the same-sex marriage enactment were evaluated, an observation made was that registered partnership was regarded more as "a business arrangement whilst the reasons for choosing to marry lie more embedded in the symbolic and emotional sphere".[1111] According to my opinion, one can speculate that the requirement that the couple sign the partnership certificate added to the registered partnership's connotations of a contract, resembling any contract in the field of law of obligations, lacking the symbolic connotations of marriage.[1112] Also in Finland a registered partnership is established through the signatures of the couple on the registration document, in the presence of the official - not through an oral procedure of consent. In Finnish legal literature, the absence of an oral statement of consent as the constituting factor for registration of partnership has been criticized as an indication that a formal same-sex

1107 Thus it is stated in Art. 30, Section 2 of Book 1 of the Dutch Civil Code, that "The rules laid down in this Book only extend to the civil effects of marriage." This provision as well as the Registered Partnership Act is translated in: Legal Recognition of Same-Sex Couples, 2003, pp. 231–234.

1108 There can be a minimum of two and a maximum of four witnesses over the age of 18. See Committee Report (SOU 2007:17), p. 161.

1109 Officials appointed before 2001 are not also obliged to marry same-sex couples, if the municipality can find a suitable alternative official. Officials appointed after 2001, however, are obliged to marry all couples, irrespective of the sex of the couple. See Marriage in the Netherlands, Report at the request of the Swedish Marriage and Partnership Inquiry Commission, 19th January 2006, p. 8.

1110 Curry-Sumner, Ian, All's well that ends registered? 2005, p. 128.

1111 Boele-Woelki, K, Curry-Sumner, I, Jansen M, Schrama W, Evaluatie 'Wet openstelling huwelijk' en van het geregistreerd partnerschap, 2006, p. 254.

1112 According to Katharina Boele-Woelki, however, the signing of the certificate in connection with partnership registration has not been controversial in the Netherlands. Information concerning Dutch law, provided on my request by Katharina Boele-Woelki, 19 November 2010.

relationship in the eyes of society is not "equally valuable and acceptable as a marriage."[1113]

The Dutch civil marriage and partnership ceremonies can be combined with a church blessing, but only after the civil ceremony. This additional religious blessing is irrelevant from a legal point of view, but can be of significance for the couple from a religious or emotional point of view.[1114] There is no obligation to offer such a blessing. It is up to each religious community to decide if and under what conditions blessings should be offered.[1115] Some protestant religious communities in the Netherlands perform blessings of same-sex relationships.[1116]

In the Netherlands, the roles of the state and the religious communities appear more clearly distinguished than in Sweden, because of the Dutch tradition with civil marriage as the only legally valid form of concluding a marriage. The Dutch Registered Partnership, with the element of the signing of the partnership certificate, can be seen as an attempt to further emphasize that concluding a registered partnership, like concluding a marriage, is a civil matter, not to be confused with the additional religious marriage blessing. However, below it will be suggested that also in the Netherlands the same-sex marriage enactment disclosed certain values which can connote religious interpretations of marriage.[1117]

7.2.4.3. Legal Effects of Registered Partnership

In the Netherlands, like in many other countries, the Registered Partnership Act originally provided less extensive legal effects than the marriage regulation. Gradually, however, the differences compared to marriage were abolished through subsequent amendments. Today, the legal effects of registered partnership are in principle the same as those of a marriage.

1113 Savolainen, Matti, The Finnish and Swedish Partnership acts – Similarities and Divergences, Legal Recognition of Same-Sex Couples, 2003, pp. 30 f. See section 7.4 and subsections below for an account of the Nordic registered partnership acts. In the Finnish Government Bill, however, symbolic reasons were not in focus. Instead the motivation for the written procedure was that the official can certify by reading the summary of the rights and duties connected to registered partnership that the couple fully consents to the registration (and know what they are consenting to). See Government Bill (HE 200/2000 vp), p. 16.

1114 Future registered partners can choose if they want to have the church blessing prior to or after the legal registration ceremony at Civil Hall. Future spouses, however, may not celebrate the religious ceremony prior to the civil ceremony. See Schrama, Wendy, Registered Partnership in the Netherlands, 1999, p. 319. In fact, having a religious marriage ceremony prior to the civil marriage ceremony is criminalized according to Art. 449 of the Dutch Criminal Code. This article does not apply to registered partnership.

1115 Marriage in the Netherlands, Report at the request of the Swedish Marriage and Partnership Inquiry Commission, 19th January 2006, p. 3.

1116 Committee Report (SOU 2007:17), p. 161.

1117 See section 7.2.5.2.

When the Registered Partnership Act was adopted in 1998, no rules on legal parenthood in respect of same-sex couples were included. In 2001, when the gender-neutral marriage concept was introduced, so-called second parent adoption, as well as adoption of Dutch children was made available to registered and married couples of the same sex. In the Swedish adoption reform of 2001, adoption of children from abroad was included, as well as adoption of children within Sweden and so-called second parent adoption.[1118] It could be argued that the Swedish legislator through the decision to include adoption of children from abroad made a more far-reaching interpretation of the concept of equality than the Dutch legislator. The decision to include international adoption in the reform was a value-based signal of equality between same-sex and different-sex couples – quite contrary to Sweden's officially stated practical approach to legislation since the 1970s. Sweden does not cooperate with states of origin, which approve of adoptive parents of the same sex. Thus the adoption reform has been primarily a matter of political ideology in Sweden and not so much of practical importance.[1119] In 2009, the Dutch adoption law was revised in relation to same-sex couples, for the purpose of including joint adoption by same-sex couples of children from abroad.[1120]

Since 2002, the Netherlands has a law which directly gives registered partners as well as spouses of the same sex shared "parental authority" over a child born into the registered partnership or the marriage. However, this presupposes that the child does not have legal ties to another parent.[1121] Parental authority entails an obligation to raise and care for the child, but it is not the same as legal parenthood.[1122] Parental authority does not, e.g. create inheritance rights between the child and the parent exercising parental authority and, if the partners separate before the birth of the child, the presumption ceases to apply. There is no presumption of parenthood (or possibility to establish parenthood based on consent) when a child conceived through assisted procreation methods is born into a same-sex registered partnership or marriage.[1123] As a result, in a lesbian relationship dissolved before the birth of the child, the non-biological parent will have no obligation to raise and care for the child, not even an obligation to pay child support. A Government Bill is pending in the Netherlands, which contains a proposal to introduce a possibility for the partner of the

---

1118 See section 6.4.3.2.

1119 See section 6.4.3.2.

1120 The Dutch Ministry of Justice press release: http://english.justitie.nl/currenttopics/pressreleases/archives-2008/new-acts-as-from-1-january-2009.aspx. Accessed 20 September 2010.

1121 Vonk, Machteld, One, Two or Three Parents? 2004, p. 105.

1122 In Swedish: rättsligt föräldraskap.

1123 See European Family Law in Action, Vol. III: Parental Responsibilities, 2005, p. 271. Dutch Report written by: Boele-Woelki, Katharina, Schrama, Wendy and Vonk, Machteld, and available at www.ceflonline.net/. See also Vonk, Machteld, The role of formalised and non-formalised intentions in legal parent-child relationships in Dutch law, 2008, p. 132 f.

birthmother to legally recognize a child conceived through assisted procreation methods.[1124]

In the Netherlands, assisted procreation methods are not restricted to married couples. Before the Registered Partnership Act was adopted, also single couples and cohabiting unmarried couples of the same sex or of different sex had access to these techniques. But before the adoption enactment of 2001, a lesbian couple could not establish joint legal parenthood in respect of children born into their relationship.[1125]

Finally it can be briefly mentioned that the same default property regime applies to spouses and registered partners – namely the Dutch universal community of property regime.[1126] In short, the regime means that all assets and debts of the couple, acquired before or after the marriage, fall within the community and can be subject to division upon dissolution. The community even includes gifts and inherited assets, unless the donor or testator has specifically excluded them.[1127] Moreover registered partnership gives rise to the same legal effects as a marriage in respect of pensions,[1128] legal transactions and inheritance rights.[1129]

7.2.4.4. Dissolution of Registered Partnership

7.2.4.4.1. Registered Partnership: Easier to Dissolve than a Marriage

As illustrated above, today the Dutch marriage and registered partnership regulations, in respect of impediments and legal effects, are in principle the same. The differences between the two institutions in respect of legal effects have diminished gradually since the Registered Partnership Act was adopted in 1998. However, the rules governing dissolution of registered partnership differ from the rules governing dissolution of marriage. As will be developed below, this difference might have contributed to turning registered partnership into an institution of its own, independent of marriage and with a distinct function.

1124 See www.internetconsultatie.nl/ouderschapduomoeder. Accessed 29 November 2010.

1125 See Curry-Sumner, Ian, All's well that ends registered? 2005, p. 147.

1126 This regime has applied since 1938. In fact, the Netherlands is the only country applying a universal matrimonial property regime as a default regime. See Antokolskaia, Masha, Boele-Woelki, Katharina, Dutch Family Law in the 21st Century: Trend-Setting and Straggling Behind at the Same Time, 2002, p. 9.

1127 Article 1:94 (7) of the Dutch Civil Code. As regards the universal community of property regime, see Curry-Sumner, Ian, All's well that ends registered? 2005, pp. 135–137.

1128 Upon the death of a registered partner, the pension received by the surviving partner may be smaller than the pension received by a surviving spouse. See Curry-Sumner, Ian, All's well that ends registered? 2005, p. 130.

1129 Boele-Woelki, Katharina, Registered Partnership and Same-Sex Marriage in the Netherlands, 2003, p. 43. For a brief description of inheritance law, see Curry-Sumner, Ian, All's well that ends registered? 2005, pp. 137 f.

An administrative divorce – without a judicial procedure – is available to registered partners in the Netherlands, but not to spouses.[1130] A registered partnership can be dissolved during the partners' lifetime through an administrative procedure, provided that the partners are in agreement to dissolve their partnership. The registered partners must draw up a declaration, stating that they are in agreement to dissolve their partnership, and declare that the registered partnership has irretrievably broken down. The agreement has to be signed by the partners and a notary or a lawyer.[1131] If the partners are *not* in agreement in this respect, court proceedings are required.[1132] However, Dutch law does not permit dissolution of marriage without a judicial procedure. Divorce by consent does not exist as an autonomous ground for divorce under Dutch law, the absence of which has been criticized as inconsistent with the liberal views expressed elsewhere in the law, for instance in respect of legal recognition of same-sex relationships.[1133] Divorce can be granted upon the common request of the spouses, based on their mutual agreement that the marriage has irretrievably broken down, but only registered partners can do this through an administrative procedure, i.e. without involving a court.[1134]

Another difference between dissolution of registered partnership and dissolution of marriage is that the Dutch rules on legal separation do not apply to registered partners. Religious objections to divorce are the most common motivation for requesting a legal separation decree, and the Dutch government did not believe registered partners in general had such religious convictions. This assumption has been questioned in the Dutch legal literature.[1135] Moreover, as Ian Curry-Sumner has pointed out, legal separation affects certain provisions dealing with children, maintenance and the use of the spouses' home.[1136] These areas are relevant also for registered partners. When Registered Partnership was introduced in the Netherlands, the motivation for making registered partnership easier to dissolve than a marriage was that registered partnership did not create filiations to children.[1137] This argument no longer holds valid, as adoption rights fully apply also to registered partners.

1130 See section 4.4.2.2.

1131 Art. 1:80c/c of the Dutch Civil Code. The agreement is also to contain provisions on related issues such as maintenance, use of marital home, division of assets and pension rights. See Boele-Woelki, Katharina, Registered Partnership and Same-Sex Marriage in the Netherlands, 2003, pp. 48 f.

1132 Curry-Sumner, Ian, All's well that ends registered? 2005, p. 149.

1133 Boele-Woelki, Katharina, Registered Partnership and Same-Sex Marriage in the Netherlands, 2003, p. 48.

1134 Boele-Woelki, Katharina, Registered Partnership and Same-Sex Marriage in the Netherlands, 2003, p. 48.

1135 Curry-Sumner, Ian, All's well that ends registered? 2005, p. 148, with futher references to Dutch literature on this subject.

1136 Curry-Sumner, Ian, All's well that ends registered? 2005, p. 148.

1137 Antokolskaia, Masha, Boele-Woelki, Katharina, Dutch Family Law in the 21st Century: Trend-Setting and Straggling Behind at the Same Time, 2002, p. 7.

In chapter 4, it has been claimed that in Sweden, liberalizing the divorce regulation through the 1973 enactment enhanced the contractual function of marriage and toned down its status function. Also the simplified dissolution procedure attached to the Dutch Registered Partnership Act can be seen as enhancing the institution of registered partnership as more "contractual" than the institution of marriage. However, it appears that same-sex couples in the Netherlands – just like Swedish same-sex couples – wanted access to more than a legal contract, namely to the *symbolic* dimension of the institution of marriage.[1138]

7.2.4.4.2. The Conversion Mechanism

When the gender-neutral marriage concept was introduced in the Netherlands in 2001 it was considered necessary to provide registered partners with a possibility to easily convert their partnership into a marriage, instead of obliging the couple to first dissolve their partnership on the ground of irretrievable breakdown, and then conclude a marriage.[1139] As a result, a conversion mechanism was introduced in the law in 2001. More precisely, a possibility to transform a marriage into a registered partnership and vice versa was introduced.[1140] The decision to allow conversions, not only from registered partnership to marriage, but also from marriage to registered partnership, appears to be an example of the previously mentioned far-reaching interpretation of the concept of equality under Dutch law, which has resulted in an inclination to avoid *all* differential treatment in respect of cohabitation models.[1141]

Transformation from marriage to registered partnership was in practice frequently (ab)used as a means of bypassing the divorce regulation for the purpose of obtaining a "lightning divorce".[1142] The Dutch government was criticized for underestimating the risk that this would happen.[1143] Through the conversion mechanism it became possible for a married couple to – at least in theory – obtain a divorce within 24 hours.[1144] The rule enabling conversion from

---

1138 The symbolic dimension of marriage is discussed in section 9.2.2.

1139 Boele-Woelki, Katharina, Registered Partnership and Same-Sex Marriage in the Netherlands, 2003, p. 49.

1140 Article 1: 149 of the Dutch Civil Code. For English translation, see Sumner, Ian, Warendorf, Hans, Family Law Legislation of the Netherlands, A Translation Including Book 1 of the Dutch Civil Code, 2003, p. 80.

1141 See section 7.2.2.1.

1142 Boele-Woelki, Katharina, Registered Partnership and Same-Sex Marriage in the Netherlands, 2003, p. 49. Moreover, spouses can easily change their property regime by transforming their marriage into a registered partnership, dissolving it and then remarrying again with a prenuptial agreement choosing another matrimonial regime, see p. 50.

1143 See Antokolskaia, Masha, Boele-Woelki, Katharina, Dutch Family Law in the 21st Century: Trend-Setting and Straggling Behind at the Same Time, 2002, pp. 7 f.

1144 Antokolskaia, Masha, Boele-Woelki, Katharina, Dutch Family Law in the 21st Century: Trend-Setting and Straggling Behind at the Same Time, 2002, p. 8.

marriage to registered partnership was repealed in 2008.[1145] Conversion from registered partnership to marriage, however, has been retained.[1146]

The readiness of the Dutch legislator to facilitate for registered partners to transfer their partnership into a marriage, and the fact that this option has been retained when conversion from marriage to registered partnership has been abolished, signals that the Dutch legislator is not indifferent to if couples marry.

7.2.5. GENDER-NEUTRAL MARRIAGE

7.2.5.1. The Second Kortmann Committee

In 1996, the second Kortmann committee was appointed by the Dutch government. The main question for the committee to decide was if denying same-sex couples the right to marry constituted unlawful discrimination.[1147] Like in Sweden access to marriage was primarily a symbolic issue in the Netherlands, in the sense that registered partnership already provided same-sex couples with access to legal rules equivalent to the rules attached to marriage. The second Kortmann committee published its report in 1997, shortly after the enactment of the Registered Partnership Act. A majority of the committee supported the introduction of a gender-neutral marriage concept. Regulation of parenthood, however, was excluded from the committee's proposal. In the majority's opinion concerns of equality motivated introducing same-sex marriage:

> "[S]ame-sex couples can only be afforded equal treatment if they are allowed to enter into civil marriages. These members [of the committee] do not view the new type of marriage as a break with tradition; after all, marriage has always been a flexible institution which has kept pace with changes in society. They feel that their proposal represents a step towards recognizing homosexual relationships, and might in fact inspire other countries to extend proper recognition to homosexual couples."[1148]

1145 The original provision permitting conversion of a marriage into a registered partnership was found in Art. 1:77a of the Dutch Civil Code. It was repealed by Staatsblad 2008, 500, on the basis of parliamentary documentation: Kamerstukken II, 2008–2009, 30145. The repeal came into force on 1 March 2009.

1146 The rules on conversion have been described by Ian Curry-Sumner. See Dissolution of Registered Partnerships: Excursion in Conversion! 2004, pp. 213–237.

1147 Schrama, Wendy, Registered Partnership in the Netherlands, 1999, p. 318. See also Sumner, Ian, Going Dutch? 2002, p. 34.

1148 As translated by: Maxwell, Nancy G, Opening Civil Marriage To Same-Gender Couples, 2001, p. 154. Words in brackets added. It can be noted that the Dutch committee spoke in terms of "they" when referring to themselves. The Swedish committee used the word "we" to underline the desirability of reform. See Committee Report (SOU 1993:98), Part A, p. 11.

It appears that the symbolic value of achieving equal treatment of different-sex and same-sex couples and signaling official approval of same-sex relationships to Dutch society and the rest of the world were the main motivations for the Dutch gender-neutral marriage reform. Also in Sweden, the institution of marriage was used for the purpose of signaling official approval of same-sex couples. In other words, the signal sent was that same-sex couples were considered worthy of social recognition and of serving the purpose of marriage.[1149] However, there is not just one clear definition of what the purpose of marriage is. Interpretations in this respect are based on moral values which differ depending on beliefs and conceptions. In section 9.2.2.1 it will be held that religious values came to the surface in connection with the Swedish same-sex marriage reform, according to which marriage is a monogamous, lifelong and heterosexual union for the purpose of procreation, in compliance with the story of the Creation in the Bible.

Also when the Dutch gender-neutral marriage regulation was enacted, values connoting Christian views on morality and marriage can be detected. A minority of the committee, which was opposed to same-sex marriage, argued that a relationship between two persons of the same sex was similar, but not equal to, a relationship between two persons of different sex. More precisely, a significant difference between same-sex and different-sex couples, which the minority emphasized, was that the same-sex couples had a biological inability to reproduce jointly on their own.[1150] The minority questioned if the institution of marriage should be open for reinterpretation, since reproduction was seen as an essential function of marriage, which a same-sex couple could not fulfill.[1151]

The Dutch same-sex marriage proposal was rejected at first, but after the election of 1998 it was endorsed by the subsequent government.[1152] The bill was presented to Parliament in 1999 and approved by the cabinet late in December of that year, as what appears to have been a last minute effort of the liberal/social democratic/labor coalition government to live up to its election promise.[1153]

The gender-neutral marriage regulation entered into force 1 April 2001.[1154] Two couples transformed their registered partnerships into marriages when the

---

1149 See sections 9.2.2.1 and 9.2.2.2.

1150 Maxwell, Nancy G, Opening Civil Marriage To Same-Gender Couples, 2001, pp. 154 f.

1151 The minority also underlined certain international difficulties that extending the concept of marriage to same-sex couples risked creating. See Maxwell, Nancy G, Opening Civil Marriage To Same-Gender Couples, 2001, pp. 154 f.

1152 Sumner, Ian, Going Dutch? 2002, p. 37. As a result of the election, the mandates of the Labor Party, the People's Party for Freedom and Democracy and the Democrats were renewed without the Christian Democratic Appeal, the absence of which appears to have been decisive for the legal development in this respect. See p. 37.

1153 Maxwell, Nancy G, Opening Civil Marriage To Same-Gender Couples, 2001, p. 155. The coalition had declared as an election promise to introduce a bill to open civil marriage to same-sex couples before 1 January 1999, see p. 155. The coalition has been called "the Purple Coalition" with reference to the mixture of political colors.

1154 Maxwell, Nancy G, Opening Civil Marriage To Same-Gender Couples, 2001, p. 158.

clock struck midnight on 1 April 2001.[1155] During the first month, almost 400 same-sex marriages were concluded.[1156] The gender-neutral provision in the Dutch Civil Code, Art. 30 of Book 1 reads:

1. A marriage can be contracted by two persons of different sex or of the same sex.
2. The law only considers marriage in its civil relations.[1157]

The second paragraph of the Civil Code establishes that civil marriage is the only legally valid form of concluding a marriage in the Netherlands. An additional religious marriage ceremony has no legal relevance. This principle clearly distinguishes between the functions of the religious communities on the one hand, and the functions of the state on the other hand. The state only deals with marriage from a strictly legal perspective and leaves all religious aspects to the religious communities. In Sweden, such a strict distinction between the state's and the religious communities' functions is not upheld. The religious communities' can be authorized to conclude legally valid marriages and the opinions of the main religious communities in Sweden were taken into account in connection with the gender-neutral marriage reform.

7.2.5.2. Why Was the Netherlands First?

The Netherlands was the first jurisdiction in the world to allow marriages between two men or two women. Masha Antokolskaia has pointed out that it might appear puzzling that the Netherlands was first, since the Netherlands (unlike the Nordic countries) has no long tradition of liberal family law legislation.[1158] There was no break with a recent political regime (like in Spain), and there was no clear break with religious views, which might explain the liberal marriage enactment of 2001. To cap it all, according to Antokolskaia, the enactment of a gender-neutral marriage concept in the Netherlands did not give rise to heated debates, neither in Parliament nor in the society in general.[1159] The absence of "commotion", according to Antokolskaia, can be viewed either as a sign of indifference, or as an expression of tolerance by the Dutch population. Antokolskaia has claimed that either way, the general public in the Netherlands was not *against* the gender-neutral marriage enactment.[1160]

1155 Waaldijk, Kees, Small Change: How the Road to Same-Sex Marriage Got Paved in the Netherlands, 2001, p. 453.

1156 Lahey, Kathleen A, Alderson, Kevin, Same-Sex Marriage, The Personal and the Political, 2004, p. 43. It can be noted that, most likely, conversions are included in this figure.

1157 This translation is found in: Maxwell, Nancy G, Opening Civil Marriage To Same-Gender Couples, 2001, p. 156, with reference to the translations made by Waaldijk, Kees.

1158 Antokolskaia, Masha, Harmonisation of Family Law in Europe, 2006, p. 294.

1159 However, religious perspectives were ventilated, to some extent, in the media. See Antokolskaia, Masha, Harmonisation of Family Law in Europe, 2006, p. 295.

1160 Antokolskaia, Masha, Harmonisation of Family Law in Europe, 2006, p. 295.

However, the road toward opening up the institution of marriage to couples of the same sex was not without obstacles in the Netherlands. It took six years for the Netherlands to adopt its Registered Partnership Act. The first Kortmann committee delivered its report in 1991, and the Act was finally enacted in 1997. Moreover, the introduction of the Registered Partnership Act did not silence the demands for a gender-neutral marriage concept. These factors suggest that adopting a gender-neutral marriage concept faced a certain amount of political resistance also in the Netherlands.

Nevertheless, opening up marriage to couples of the same sex may have faced more resistance in Sweden than in the Netherlands, as a result of the retained Swedish double track system for concluding a marriage. Moreover, in Sweden, there is a legal tradition to take into account the opinions of the Church of Sweden in connection with enactments dealing with marriage – in its capacity as state church (until the year 2000) and "Folk Church".[1161] When the gender-neutral marriage act was enacted in the Netherlands, where civil marriage is the only legally valid form of concluding a marriage according to the Civil Code, importance was not openly attached to religious arguments. As Masha Antokolskaia has put it: "Once the idiom of religion was dismissed, it became very difficult to reject same-sex marriage on the basis of rational arguments".[1162]

It can be claimed that the distinction between the religious and the civil marriage concepts in the Dutch Civil Code contributed to enhancing the image of civil marriage in the Netherlands as being more of a "contract" than civil marriage is in Sweden, where the religious and the civil conceptions of marriage are more intertwined, as a result of the Swedish double track system for conclusion of marriage. One can speculate that this, in turn, is a reason why the Netherlands was the first jurisdiction in the world to adopt a gender-neutral marriage concept. However, marriage appears to be a value-charged and symbolic concept also in the Netherlands, and legally recognizing same-sex marriages was a process which took time.[1163] Legally recognizing same-sex couples was a topical and politically prioritized issue in many European countries at the dawn of the twenty-first century. Against this background it appears rather random that the Netherlands were the first country to adopt a gender-neutral marriage concept.

1161 See Report of the Church Board, Kyrkostyrelsens skrivelse 2009:6, The role of the Folk Church is analyzed by Bäckström, Anders et al., Religious Change in Northern Europe, 2004. The term "People's Church" is another possible translation. See Hadenius, Stig, Swedish Politics During the 20th Century, 1988.

1162 Antokolskaia, Masha, Harmonisation of Family Law in Europe, 2006, p. 295. See also Waaldijk, Kees, Small Change: How the Road to Same-Sex Marriage Got Paved in the Netherlands, 2001, p. 453, where he points out that problems related to the position of the religious communities could be left out of the Dutch discussion, which, most likely, contributed to the Dutch becoming pioneers with a gender-neutral marriage enactment.

1163 See section 7.2.6.2.

7.2.6. REGISTERED PARTNERSHIP AND MARRIAGE IN THE NETHERLANDS AS TWO PARALLEL INSTITUTIONS – COMPARISONS WITH SWEDISH DISCUSSIONS

7.2.6.1. Dutch Registered Partnership: Marriage without Its Symbolism?

The Dutch registered partnership was intended to be a "marriage-like" institution with implications on family life, which is underlined by the placing of the Registered Partnership Act in the first book of the Dutch civil code, dealing with family law and the law of persons.[1164] The Act was designed primarily with same-sex couples in mind, but also different-sex couples were in the end included to underline that registered partnership was indeed *equal* to marriage and not a "second-class marriage."[1165] However, registered partnership does not appear to have been regarded as equal to marriage, since the Dutch Registered Partnership Act did not silence the demands by same-sex couples and their spokespersons for access to marriage.

When same-sex marriage was introduced in the Netherlands, the future of the institution of registered partnership was discussed, and it was decided that it should be retained during a five-year trial period. Thereafter, the system was to be evaluated. However, because the Dutch government found it appropriate to evaluate the Registered Partnership Act and the same-sex marriage enactment at once, the evaluation of the institution of registered partnership was delayed until 2006.[1166] In its report, the evaluation team, commissioned by the Dutch Ministry of Justice, pleaded for the repeal of the institution of registered partnership, for the purpose of simplifying the legal system.[1167] The evaluation group pointed out that maintaining two legal institutions – registered partnership and marriage – with the same legal effects, risked creating limping relationships, recognized in one country but not in another. The dual system also contributed to making the legal effects of each union unclear to people in general. On the other hand, it was pointed out by the evaluation team, retaining both institutions could be a means to offer a formalized type of union *without the symbolism of marriage*.[1168] The Registered Partnership Act was kept in the Netherlands. According to Katharina Boele-Woelki, who was on the evaluation team, by 2006 it was probably already too late to abolish registered partnership.[1169] The institution had become an

1164 Curry-Sumner, Ian, All's well that ends registered? 2005, p. 122.
1165 Schrama, Wendy, Registered Partnership in the Netherlands, 1999, p. 323.
1166 Boele-Woelki, K, Curry-Sumner, I, Jansen M, Schrama W, Evaluatie 'Wet openstelling huwelijk' en van het geregistreerd partnerschap, p. 251.
1167 Information provided by Katharina Boele-Woelki to the author, 19 November 2010.
1168 Boele-Woelki, K, Curry-Sumner, I, Jansen M, Schrama W, Evaluatie 'Wet openstelling huwelijk' en van het geregistreerd partnerschap, 2006, p. 255.
1169 Information provided by Katharina Boele-Woelki to the author, 19 November 2010.

established option to marriage, which continued to be chosen by a small but not insignificant group of couples.[1170]

In the Netherlands, registered partnership appears to function as a "marriage lite", quite contrary to the aim of the legislator when the Registered Partnership Act was introduced in 1998. The intention of the Dutch legislator was to create an institution equal to marriage, with same-sex couples as the main target group.[1171] The interest shown by different-sex couples in the institution of registered partnership was unexpected.[1172] During 1998, 30 percent of all registered partnerships were concluded by different-sex couples.[1173] Since the same-sex marriage reform, different-sex couples are totally dominating in the number of partnership registrations.[1174] In Sweden, registered partnership was never intended to be an alternative to marriage. Only same-sex couples had access to the Swedish institution, and the ideological aim was to provide these couples with an institution equal in value to marriage and as similar as possible to marriage in respect of legal effects.[1175] From the ideological "declaration" by the Swedish 1994 committee, quoted in section 6.5.1, one could claim that deliberate attempts were made to fill the Swedish institution of registered partnership with a value equal to the symbolic dimension of marriage, signifying something more than just an agreement between the couple to be covered by legal rules. However, also in Sweden the demands for access to marriage remained after the introduction of registered partnership.

In summary, access to marriage appears to have remained a central goal in Sweden and the Netherlands, irrespective of whether the Dutch or the Swedish registered partnership "model" was chosen. The experiences with registered partnership in the Netherlands and Sweden illustrate that marriage has a special value for many couples, same-sex couples in particular, and registered partnership could not match the symbolic values attached to the label "marriage".

7.2.6.2. Hierarchical and Patriarchal Connotations Attached to Marriage: A Few Reflections

The idea that Dutch unmarried couples, primarily different-sex couples according to the statistics, wanted access to more of a "contractual version" of marriage

1170 Boele-Woelki, K, Curry-Sumner, I, Jansen M, Schrama W, Evaluatie 'Wet openstelling huwelijk' en van het geregistreerd partnerschap, 2006, p. 254.

1171 Schrama, Wendy, Registered Partnership in the Netherlands, 1999, p. 323.

1172 Schrama, Wendy, Registered Partnership in the Netherlands, 1999, p. 323. During 1998, 30 percent of all registered partnerships were concluded by different-sex couples.

1173 www.cbs.nl/. Accessed 30 November 2010.

1174 The number of different-sex couples only amounts to a few hundred couples each year, whereas the number of different-sex couples, since 2004 has amounted to between 8000 and 10 000 annually. See www.cbs.nl/.

1175 See section 6.4.1.1.

without the symbolism of marriage has been discussed above. Also, at the outset, the rules on conversion from marriage to registered partnership, abolished in 2009, contributed to making registered partnership especially popular among different-sex couples. Many registrations were "short-lived" converted marriages on the way to divorce.[1176]

Another explanation why registered partnership is a popular alternative to marriage, among different-sex couples in particular, which will only be mentioned here, could be a wish to avoid marriage because of unwanted negative connotations to marriage as a hierarchical institution. In chapter 2 the institution of marriage in Sweden has been described from a historical perspective as an unequal union, with the husband as the master of the house and the legal guardian of his wife. It is not impossible that connotations of the spouses' past unequal conditions may lie behind a general disinclination to marry in several countries today, including Sweden and the Netherlands. Internationally, certain feminists have argued along these lines, claiming that the equal-treatment focus of interest groups – be it women's rights or gay rights organizations – falls short with regard to questioning the normative group and their values, i.e. men and patriarchy.[1177] From this point of view, registered partnership might appear to be an appealing practical solution, which provides the necessary legal rules without the negative connotations to marriage as a hierarchical institution. On the other hand, the registered partnership regulation is modelled on the marriage regulation and contains basically the same legal effects. As a result, to the most critical opponent to marriage, registered partnership might be found to represent similar historical associations to hierarchy between spouses.

There has been opposition to same-sex marriage from certain feminist circles, primarily in the United States, arguing that marriage as such promotes neither equality nor freedom.[1178] It can be mentioned that in the feminist debates in the United States there appears to be more room for diversity than in the Dutch and the Swedish discussions. For instance, the "gay community" in the United States appears to be regarded as a part of the multicultural society, as a minority group with a culture of its own.[1179] From this point of view, diversity is generally perceived as something positive in a society, worth protecting, be it cultural

1176 Boele-Woelki, Katharina, Registered Partnership and Same-Sex Marriage in the Netherlands, 2003, p. 48.

1177 In Spain this focus on similarities, rather than differences, is called "identity politics". Raquel Méndez, Intersecting Gender and Sexual Orientation, 2007, p. 579. It can be mentioned that queer studies as a research field can be seen, somewhat simplified, as focusing on the right to be different, rather than trying to fit into the heterosexual traditional system and patterns. For an easy introduction to the conception of "queer", see, for instance, Ambjörnsson, Fanny, Vad är queer?, 2006.

1178 Cooper, Davina, "Like Counting Stars?: Re-Structuring Equality and the Socio-Legal Space of Same-Sex Marriage", 2001, p. 75, with further references.

1179 For a discussion on the term "multiculturalism", see Modood, Tariq, Multiculturalism, A Civic Idea, 2007, pp. 1–5 in particular.

diversity because of religious faith or because of a homosexual orientation. Preserving this diversity might require tailor-made legal solutions.

In Sweden, the political goal during the 1990s and beginning of the twenty-first century has been quite the opposite, namely to strive toward treating homosexuals exactly the same as heterosexuals in the field of family law. Arguments focusing on the patriarchal features of marriage from a historical perspective have not been common. Introducing a gender-neutral marriage concept – in Sweden as well as in the Netherlands – has become a symbol of full equality between couples of different sex and couples of the same sex. It can be noted, however, that notwithstanding the Swedish legislator's "assimilation approach" to same-sex couples, homosexuals in Sweden enjoy special protection as a group in the provision of the Criminal Code prohibiting "agitation against a national or ethnic group".[1180]

The Swedish sexual orientation reforms are based on the assumption that heterosexual and homosexual couples need the same kind of regulation. In the Swedish Committee Report of 2007, it was emphasized that the only difference between homosexuals and heterosexuals is that "homosexuals are emotionally drawn to persons of the same sex."[1181] Also in the Netherlands, as described above, the gender-neutral marriage concept was a matter of achieving equality. Anders Agell criticized the Swedish legislator for neglecting to investigate same-sex couples' need of regulation. Agell suggested that same-sex couples might have different needs than couples of different sex, and that applying rules designed for spouses of different sex might not take into account the needs of same-sex couples.[1182]

Also Eva Ryrstedt has questioned if applying rules modeled on the marriage regulation laid down in the Registrered Partnership Act was the best legal solution for same-sex couples in Sweden.[1183] The property division rules in the Marriage Code were created to avoid unjust results because men and women traditionally have different roles and fields of responsibility in a marriage. Such gender related aspects, Ryrstedt pointed out, are often connected to the couple having children, and since same-sex couples cannot reproduce jointly, the same concerns do not necessarily apply to same-sex couples. Thus, Ryrstedt suggested in 1998, instead of introducing the Registered Partnership Act, which was modeled on marriage, it might have been more appropriate to have designed a

---

1180 The Criminal Code, Chapter 16, Section 8.

1181 "[...] den enda skillnaden mellan homosexuella och heterosexuella är att homosexuella känslomässigt dras till personer av samma kön." Committee Report (SOU 1984:63), p. 19. Author's translation.

1182 Agell, Anders, The Legal Status of Same-Sex Couples in Europe – A Critical Analysis, 2003, p. 127.

1183 Ryrstedt, Eva, Bodelning och bostad, 1998, p. 407.

new cohabitation model for same-sex couples, which departed from same-sex couples' specific needs.[1184]

Ryrstedt's observations were made in her doctoral thesis in 1998, i.e. before the Registered Partnership Act had been amended by rules enabling adoption by same-sex partners and providing these couples with access to assisted procreation methods. These reforms have reduced the differences between same-sex and different-sex couples and have, in my opinion, weakened the argument that same-sex couples are essentially different from different-sex couples and in need of "tailor-made" rules to suit their specific situation.

Returning briefly to Dutch couples' reasons for registering a partnership instead of marrying, it appears that the couples who choose registration instead of marriage because of the latter's hierarchical connotations, if there in fact are such couples, most likely constitute a limited group of people. Dutch sociological and legal researches have indicated that registered partnership is generally perceived as less symbolic than marriage and more as a "business arrangement" between the contracting parties.[1185] In 2006, the Dutch research team, which evaluated the institutions of registered partnership and marriage in the Netherlands, pointed out that a basic symbolic distinction between registered partnership and marriage was generally perceived by same-sex as well as different-sex couples.[1186] The simplified divorce rules attached to registered partnership compared to marriage most likely contributed to this conception, signaling that registered partnership entailed less of a commitment by the couple than a marriage, since it was easier to dissolve than a marriage.

7.2.6.3. Secular and Religious Values Relating to Marriage

The institution of marriage appears to be charged with special connotations and values also in the Netherlands. The gender-neutral marriage concept was a symbolic enactment, which signaled to same-sex couples, and to the general public, that homosexual relationships from a legal perspective are equally valuable as heterosexual relationships.[1187] In fact, the second Kortmann committee explicitly stated that denying couples of the same sex access to marriage might signal that same-sex relationships were of lesser value, than heterosexual relationships.[1188] It appears that neither in the Netherlands nor in

---

1184 Ryrstedt, Eva, Bodelning och bostad, 1998, p. 385.

1185 Boele-Woelki, K, Curry-Sumner, I, Jansen M, Schrama W, Evaluatie 'Wet openstelling huwelijk' en van het geregistreerd partnerschap, 2006, p. 248.

1186 Boele-Woelki, K, Curry-Sumner, I, Jansen M, Schrama W, Evaluatie 'Wet openstelling huwelijk' en van het geregistreerd partnerschap, 2006, p. 254.

1187 Antokolskaia, Masha, Harmonisation of Family Law in Europe, 2006, p. 295.

1188 Antokolskaia, Masha, Harmonisation of Family Law in Europe, 2006, p. 295, with reference to the second Kortmann Committee's statement in Explanatory note. Second Chamber, 1998/1999, 26 672, No. 3.

Sweden could registered partnership match the symbolic value of marriage. Why is this so?

It is possible that in the Netherlands, just like in Sweden, the symbolic dimension of marriage is to some extent connected to values originating in religion, signaling a life-long commitment and durability of the relationship – resting on the idea that "God has brought together man and woman, so that no man can put them asunder".[1189] From this point of view it would not have been far-fetched to openly have taken religious viewpoints into account, in addition to secular and rational arguments, when the Dutch gender-neutral marriage concept was enacted.[1190]

However, it can be claimed that in the Netherlands, the interest in promoting a "secular" interpretation of marriage in general has in certain respects outweighed the interests of the religious communities, which can be attributed to their religious practice. For instance, the religious communities are prevented by law from celebrating religious marriages before the mandatory civil marriage ceremony has been officiated. Religious marriages have no legal relevance, since civil marriage is the only legally recognized form under Dutch law. Individual ministers can even be fined for performing religious blessings before the civil marriage ceremony has been officiated.[1191] In Germany, a corresponding prohibition against celebrating a religious marriage without first having a civil ceremony was recently abolished as contrary to the freedom of religion.[1192] In Sweden, the religious communities were involved in the preparations of the same sex marriage enactment and able to present their arguments, even though their objections to applying the word marriage to same-sex relationships were in the end disregarded by the commissioner.

It can be added that allowing the religious communities to participate, for instance, in the enactment of a gender-neutral marriage act, does not necessarily mean that the enactment will be "obstructed". The Swedish experiences with including the Church of Sweden in the preparations of the 2009 Act resulted in the Church of Sweden deciding to legally marry same-sex couples. However, most other religious communities in Sweden continue to interpret marriage as a union reserved for a man and a woman and do not officiate at same-sex marriages.

1189 "dher Gud man och qwinna så hafwer sammanfogat, at ingen menniska them åtskilia kan." See Handbok, ther vti är författat, huruledes gudstiensten med christelige ceremonier och kyrckioseder, 1693, p. 109. Author's translation. See sections 9.2.2.1 and 9.2.2.2.

1190 See section 7.2.5.2.

1191 Curry-Sumner, Ian, Private International Law Aspects of Homosexual Couples, 2007, p. 5.

1192 See Koch, Elisabeth, Das Verbot der kirchlichen Voraustrauung – politische Hintergründe und historische Entwicklung, 2010, pp 135 f. See also the Bundestag's printed papers, BT-Drucks, 16/1831, pp. 66 f. The enactment entered into force on 1 January 2009.

7.3. SPAIN

7.3.1. PROGRESSION AS A MEANS OF REINFORCING DEMOCRACY

A gender-neutral marriage concept was adopted in Spain on 30 June 2005.[1193] Spain was under the dictatorship of General Franco between 1939 and 1975, and during this time period homosexuality was criminalized and homosexual individuals risked persecution.[1194] In 1978, the importance of creating a more equal society was underlined in the new Spanish Constitution, which laid the foundation for establishing equal rights and duties for men and women during marriage.[1195]

From a political point of view the introduction of same-sex marriage has been explained as a way of compensating homosexual citizens for their exclusion from society and prosecution during the dictatorship.[1196] In Spanish preparatory work to the gender-neutral marriage enactment it was explicitly stated that: "[...] History bears witness to a long path of discrimination based on sexual orientation, a discrimination which the legislator has decided to eliminate."[1197]

Another key "driving force" for adopting laws which appear progressive relative to earlier values is the European Union, of which Spain became a member in 1986. In "post-dictatorship times", Spain appears to have been eager to prove that it had become "modern" in a European Union context.[1198] In other words, legally recognizing the rights of same-sex couples was a demonstrative method of enforcing democratic values based on equality in Spain. The political strategy for gaining support for the enactment was to link it to the fundamental human rights laid down in the Spanish Constitution, namely the right to freely develop one's personality and the right to non-discriminatory treatment.[1199]

1193 Ley 13/2005, de 1 julio, por la que se modifica el Código Civil en material de derecho a contraer matrimonio.

1194 Pichardo Galán, José Ignacio, Same-Sex Marriage in Spain, 2005, p. 1. See also section 7.3.4.1.

1195 Pichardo Galán, José Ignacio, Beyond Marriage: LGTB Families in Spain, 2008. See also section 3.7.2.2.

1196 See section 7.3.4.1.

1197 Official Journal of the Spanish government, Boletín Oficial del Estado, BOE, 157, 2 July, 2005. The Prime Minister José Luis Rodríguez Zapatero, during the plenary session of congress, also emphasized that allowing same-sex marriage was a way to compensate for the wrongs of the past: "Today, Spanish society is responding to a group of people who for years have been humiliated, whose rights have been ignored, their dignity offended, their identity denied and their freedom restricted."
See www.nytimes.com/2005/06/30/international/europe/30cnd-spain.html. Accessed 22 November 2010. The translation has been modified slightly by the author.

1198 Platero Méndez, Raquel, Intersecting Gender and Sexual Orientation, 2007, where the membership of the European Union is pointed out as an important explanatory factor in the speedy legal development in the field of same-sex relationships.

1199 González Beilfuss, Cristina, Private international law aspects of homosexual couples, 2006, p. 2.

Same-sex couples do not constitute the only group which has been subjected to progressive family law legislation in Spain. In 2007, far-reaching Spanish family law legislation was adopted to improve the situation for transgender persons.[1200] More precisely, an enactment which entitled transgender persons to change their first names in the national register, without first having to go through gender reassignment surgery, was adopted.[1201] Later on, other European countries, e.g. Sweden, have followed suit in this respect.[1202]

The support from the general public in Spain of the enactments dealing with homosexuals, sexual minorities and same-sex couples has been strong. In fact, 64 percent of the Spanish population were in favor of the 2005 gender-neutral marriage enactment.[1203] Same-sex marriage, as will be suggested below, was openly dealt with as a human rights issue in Spanish politics, and protecting human rights is an essential component of a democracy. It is likely that the general public in Spain had a special interest in strengthening the democratic principles in the country, and that this contributed to the wide support for the gender-neutral marriage enactment. Yet the public support for the enactment does not mean that it was not – and still is in some quarters – controversial in Spain. The Catholic Church, which retains a central position in Spanish society, has from the beginning been strongly opposed.[1204]

7.3.2. BACKGROUND – LEGAL STRATEGIES AND APPROACHES TO SAME-SEX UNIONS

7.3.2.1. Toward Legal Recognition of Same-Sex Couples

Homosexuality was decriminalized in Spain in 1975, at the end of the Franco regime.[1205] Like in the other jurisdictions studied here, decriminalization did not equal tolerance toward homosexuals. At the time of decriminalization, homosexuals were still considered a social danger according to a law from 1970.[1206] In the late 1970s, two Amnesty processes were pending, dealing with

[1200] Platero, Raquel, Outstanding Challenges in a Post-Equality Era: The Same-Sex Marriage and gender identity Laws in Spain, 2008, p. 45.

[1201] Law 3/2007 of March 15th, regulating the rectification of the register with regard to a person's sex, BOE 65, March 16th 2007 p. 11251.

[1202] See decision by the Supreme Administrative Court, no 2893–09, 28 September 2009.

[1203] This will be further discussed in section 7.3.4.3.

[1204] See section 7.3.4 and subsections.

[1205] Inspired by the French initiative to decriminalize homosexual behavior in 1791, this was partially done in Spain in 1822. However, in Spain a provision against "serious scandal and indecency" was retained and used to punish homosexual acts. Waaldijk, Kees, Civil Developments: Patterns of Reform in the Legal Position of Same-Sex Partners in Europe, 2000, p. 68.

[1206] The Law on Social Danger (LRPS, 1970). See Platero Méndez, Raquel, Intersecting Gender and Sexual Orientation, 2007, p. 578.

the fact that homosexuals were incarcerated in Spain, while political prisoners taken during the dictatorship were being released. The first gay rights organization was established in 1980, in response to these processes. In 1979 "the social danger law" of 1970 was made inapplicable to homosexual behavior.[1207] In 1995, discrimination based on a person's sexual orientation, inter alia in the field of employment, was criminalized in Spain.[1208]

During the 1990s, same-sex couples' need of legal rules attracted political attention in Spain. In 1994, a registration office performing registrations without any legal implications was set up in the region Vitoria-Gasteiz as a political statement to the effect that introducing a registration scheme for same-sex couples was urgently needed. This registration granted same-sex couples visibility and recognition, but no legal rights and duties toward each other.[1209] In 1998, Catalonia was the first of the Spanish autonomous communities to introduce the institution of stable unions – "uniones estables de pareja" – granting unmarried cohabiting couples legal protection and recognition of their relationships.[1210] By including also same-sex couples in this enactment, Catalonia became the first predominantly Roman Catholic region in the world to systematically regulate relationships between two persons of the same sex.[1211]

Other autonomous communities have followed suit, introducing regulation inspired by the Catalan Act.[1212] However, the substantive content and details of these enactments will not be accounted for here. Instead focus is on the gender-neutral marriage enactment adopted at the federal level in Spain.[1213] The Catalan Act is only dealt with here to illustrate the course of events preceding the gender-neutral marriage enactment of 2005. Since the introduction of a gender-neutral marriage regulation in Spain, the regional enactments have lost a significant part

---

1207 Platero Méndez, Raquel, Intersecting Gender and Sexual Orientation, 2007, p. 578.

1208 Cánovas, Pérez Nicolás, Spain: The Heterosexual State Refuses to Disappear, 2001, p. 494. The prohibition against discrimination on grounds of sexual orientation also applied in respect of the rights guaranteed by the Constitution. In military law, the development was slower, discrimination in military law remaining until 1999, see p. 494.

1209 Tobío, Constanza, Marriage, Cohabitation and the Residential Independence of Young People in Spain, 2001, p. 76.

1210 Ley 10/1998 de 15 julio de Uniones Estables de Pareja, amended in 2005, Ley 3/2005, de 8 abril. The instiution is sometimes called "parejas de hecho". See also González Beilfuss, Cristina, Parejas de hecho y matrimonios del mismo sexo en la unión Europea, 2004.

1211 Jaurena i Salas, Francesc, The Law on Stable Unions in the Catalonia Autonomous Community of Spain, 2001, p. 506.

1212 Aragon (1999), Navarra (2000), Valencia (2001), Madrid (2001), Balearic Islands (2001), Asturias (2002), Castile and Leon (2002), Andalusia (2002), Canary Islands (2003), Extremadura (2003), Basque Country (2003) and Cantabria (2005). Only Aragon, Navarra, Balearic Islands and the Basque Country have legislative power in the field of family law. See Martín-Casals, Miquel, Family Law of Spanish Autonomies: Following a Similar Pattern? 2007, p. 72.

1213 The autonomous enactments have been discussed by inter alia Roca, Encarna, Same-Sex Partnerships in Spain: Family, Marriage or Contract? 2001, pp. 365–382.

of their function and sometimes "lag behind" the developments at the federal level.[1214]

7.3.2.2. *Competence to Legislate: The Federal State and the Autonomous Communities*

After the Franco regime, Spain was organized into 17 autonomous communities, and in 1978 six of these communities recovered the power to develop their own civil law regulation; a power historically attributed to these autonomous communities.[1215] The six autonomous communities with civil legislative power of their own are: Aragon, the Basque Country (Alava and Biscay) the Balearic Islands, Catalonia, Galicia and Navarre.[1216] The legislative power in the field of civil law is divided between, on the one hand, the six autonomous communities with such power and, on the other hand, the federal Spanish state. In family law matters, the authority of the six autonomous communities mentioned above is extensive, but they cannot pass family law rules regarding conclusion of marriage.[1217] Only a small area of competence is reserved for the federal Spanish state exclusively, namely "civil relations arising from the forms of marriage".[1218]

However, rules establishing the legal effects of marriage are not covered by the federal state's exclusive authority to legislate, for instance, in respect of the regulation on the spouses' property relations, and can thus be adopted at the regional level in the six autonomous communities with capacity to legislate in the field of civil law.[1219] The distinction is sometimes unclear between the federal Spanish state's power to legislate and the legislative power of the autonomous communities. Several Spanish autonomous communities have enacted laws

---

1214 The content of the autonomous regulations on stable unions are likely to be revised as a result of the 2005 marriage act, taking into account, for instance, that rules on legal parenthood for same-sex spouses have been introduced at the federal level. For instance, a bill proposing major reforms of Catalan family law is presently pending in the Catalan Parliament, as a response to the federal decision to open up marriage to couples of the same sex. See Government Bill to the Catalan Parliament, Butlletí Oficial del Parlament de Catalunya, 19 January 2009, Number 284. See especially Arts 234.1–14.

1215 In the codification process in nineteenth century Spain, it was not possible to enact one unifying civil law for the entire state. See Martín-Casals, Miquel, Family Law of Spanish Autonomies: Following a Similar Pattern? 2007, p. 63. See also Martín-Casals, Miquel, Same-Sex Partnerships in the Legislation of Spanish Autonomous Communities, 2003, p. 54.

1216 Even during the dictatorship some of this legislative power was preserved. Martín-Casals, Miquel, Same-Sex Partnerships in the Legislation of Spanish Autonomous Communities, 2003, p. 54.

1217 Martín-Casals, Miquel, Family Law of Spanish Autonomies: Following a Similar Pattern? 2007, p. 63.

1218 Martín-Casals, Miquel, Family Law of Spanish Autonomies: Following a Similar Pattern? 2007, p. 64.

1219 See for instance in respect of Catalonia: European Family Law in Action, Volume IV: Property Relations between Spouses, 2003, question 2, pp. 51 f. Spanish National Report written by, González Beilfuss, Cristina.

which touch upon substantive civil law aspects under the "disguise" of social welfare regulation.[1220]

7.3.2.3. Why was Catalonia First?

The fact that Catalonia was the first autonomous Spanish community to introduce an act on stable unions has been explained with reference to the inclusive nature of the region's civil society, with the first gay rights organizations, a strong feminist movement and extensive gay activist networks.[1221] Moreover, a regional program was created in Catalonia in 1994, administered by influential persons, for the purpose of introducing inclusive policies for homosexual persons in all governmental bodies.[1222] This environment appears to have provided a favorable base for cultivating the rights of the individual, the legal recognition of same-sex couples included.

Anther explanatory factor to why Catalonia was first is that the political situation in Catalonia differs from the rest of Spain. In the regional election of 1996, the conservative party – the PP[1223] – became only the third biggest party, with about 18 percent of the votes. The majority party was the socialist party – the PSOE[1224] – with 39 percent of the votes, followed by the (comparatively liberal) Christian party – the CiU[1225] – with approximately 30 percent.[1226] This result was quite different from the situation at the Spanish federal level, where the PP had majority in 1996 with 39 percent, and the PSOE was the second biggest political party with 38 percent of the votes.[1227]

The political color of the government appears to be a significant factor in the context of legal recognition of same-sex couples in many European countries.[1228] In general, political parties on the left have taken the initiative to reforms to strengthen the legal position of same-sex couples.[1229] In 2005 the Spanish socialist party (the PSOE) made the introduction of same-sex marriages an

---

1220 Martín-Casals, Miquel, Family Law of Spanish Autonomies: Following a Similar Pattern? 2007, pp. 63–77.

1221 See Platero Méndez, Raquel, Intersecting Gender and Sexual Orientation, 2007, pp. 579 and 585.

1222 This regional, inclusive program was unique for Catalonia, other regions choosing the path of creating specific services for homosexuals in society. See Platero Méndez, Raquel, Intersecting Gender and Sexual Orientation, 2007, p. 588, particularly footnote 20.

1223 El Partido Popular.

1224 El Partido Socialista Obrero Espagñol.

1225 Convergència i Unió. This is a Catalan party which does not operate at the federal level in Spain.

1226 Election resources on the internet: http://electionresources.org/es/congress.php?election =1996&community=09. Accessed 3 November 2010.

1227 Election resources on the internet: http://electionresources.org/es/congress.php?election= 1996. Accessed 3 November 2010.

1228 See section 7.3.3.1.

1229 See section 7.3.3.

electoral promise, which was kept when it seized the government power at the federal level in Spain. The fact that the conservative party (the PP) had a comparatively weak position in Catalonia when the 1998 Catalan Act was adopted can explain why Catalonia became the first Catholic region in the world to legally recognize same-sex couples in statutory law.

Furthermore, one can speculate that the Catholic Church might be less influential in Catalonia than elsewhere in Spain, and that this facilitated introducing the 1998 Act in the region. Since the support for the conservative party is weak in Catalonia, support for the traditional (conservative) family values as interpreted by the Catholic Church may also be weaker in Catalonia than elsewhere in Spain.[1230] In section 6.3.4 it has been suggested that religiously-based values sometimes form the basic point of departure for the "traditional" or "conservative" defenders of the concept of marriage. Likewise, in Sweden in the past, representatives of the Church of Sweden have periodically opposed law reforms which, for instance, were aimed to create equality between men and women and thus represented values perceived as conservative compared to the "liberal" values promoted by the legislator.[1231] Since the Church of Sweden decided to marry same-sex couples, however, the church has appeared quite progressive, whereas the Catholic Church, as will be illustrated below, continues to defend traditional family values.

According to Professor Cristina González Beilfuss, the Catholic Church is not particularly weak in Catalonia compared to other Spanish regions. However, González Beilfuss points out that there are ideological differences between the conservative parties in Spain, which can explain why Catalonia could adopt a formalized relationship scheme for same-sex couples already in 1998.[1232] More precisely, the CiU, which only operates in Catalonia and not at the federal level in Spain, is a conservative party, but it nevertheless represents more liberal views on family law matters than the PP does, which operates both at the regional and the federal level.[1233]

7.3.2.4. *Two Key Cases from the Spanish Constitutional Court*

The Catalan Act on Stable Unions did not originally set out to legally recognize *same-sex couples*. Unmarried *different-sex couples* were the main political target of interest in Catalonia. The starting point for adopting special rules for unmarried couples was two cases concerning the legal status of unmarried couples, decided in 1994 by the Spanish Constitutional Court (Tribunal

1230 See section 7.3.4.

1231 Bäckström et al., Religious Change in Northern Europe, 2004, pp. 142.

1232 Information provided by Professor Cristina González Beilfuss to the author, 10 November 2010.

1233 Information provided by Professor Cristina González Beilfuss to the author, 10 November 2010.

Constitucional). The first case dealt with the legal position of cohabiting couples of different sex and the second with unmarried same-sex cohabitees in particular.

7.3.2.4.1. Unmarried Cohabitees' Legal Position

The political interest in adopting statutory rules on heterosexual cohabitation without marriage was connected to a case decided by the Spanish Constitutional Court in 1994, which attracted public attention.[1234] The case dealt with an unmarried different-sex couple's legal position in respect of pension rights. The couple concerned had deliberately chosen *not* to marry, due to personal convictions.[1235] When, upon the death of the man, the woman was denied widow's pension, the general public found this unreasonable.[1236] At that point in time, the Catalan Ministry of Justice was drafting a Family Code and the ministry took the opportunity of dealing with the situation of unmarried couples in that context instead of in separate enactments.[1237] Revolutionary, in a sense, was that when the Catalan Act of 1998 was enacted it also included same-sex couples. To understand why such a progressive law could be passed in Catalonia, we need to look at the second decision by the same Court.

7.3.2.4.2. The Legal Position of Same-Sex Couples

Another relevant court decision preceding the Catalan enactment was delivered in 1994, also by the Spanish Constitutional Court. The key issue for the court to decide was whether a surviving male partner was entitled to widower's pension upon the death of his male partner. The court did not rule in favor of such benefits, but nevertheless opened up for adopting registration schemes in Spain. It can be noted that in Spain, like in the Netherlands, the legal development toward legal recognition of same-sex couples started through insinuations in court jurisprudence. The court stated that:

> "[P]ublic authorities may grant a privileged treatment to the family union consisting of a man and a woman compared with a homosexual union. This does not preclude the legislator from establishing an equivalent system permitting homosexual

1234 Martín-Casals, Miquel, Same-Sex Partnerships in the Legislation of Spanish Autonomous Communities, 2003, p. 58, with reference to the case: STC 66/1994, de 28 febrero, Sala Segunda, Ponente Luís López Guerra, BOE núm. 71, 24.3.1994.

1235 Martín-Casals, Miquel, Same-Sex Partnerships in the Legislation of Spanish Autonomous Communities, 2003, p. 58, with reference to the case: STC 66/1994, de 28 febrero, Sala Segunda, Ponente Luís López Guerra, BOE núm. 71, 24.3.1994.

1236 Martín-Casals, Miquel, Same-Sex Partnerships in the Legislation of Spanish Autonomous Communities, 2003, p. 58.

1237 Martín-Casals, Miquel, Same-Sex Partnerships in the Legislation of Spanish Autonomous Communities, 2003, p. 58.

cohabitants to enjoy the full rights and benefits of marriage, as proposed by the European Parliament."[1238]

Legislation concerning conclusion and dissolution of marriage belongs to the exclusive legal authority of the federal Spanish state. However, adopting formalized relationship schemes – which were not defined as marriage regulations – applicable to unmarried couples was not seen as infringing on the federal state's exclusive field of legal competence. In other words, a prerequisite for adopting regulation on "stable unions" was that such unions were not marriages.

This was not merely a linguistic issue. Also substantively there are significant differences between a stable union and a marriage. It can be noted that same-sex couples and different-sex couples are treated differently under the Catalan Act, in the sense that a stable union between a different-sex couple can be established either by default after two years of cohabitation, or through registration. In respect of same-sex couples, however, registration is the only way to establish a stable union.[1239] In short, a Catalan stable union is basically an agreement – concluded orally or in writing by means of a public deed – which establishes the legal effects of the union.[1240] The Catalan Act contains rules on financial compensation to a partner, who as a result of working in the home without adequate compensation from the other partner, has suffered financially. Moreover, the Act can provide compensation to a party in the form of maintenance, during a maximum of three years, or longer if the parties have a common under-age child.[1241] The overall impression is that the Catalan Act is much less comprehensive in scope than the marriage regulation, and it does not compare with the Swedish and Dutch institutions of registered partnership in respect of the legal effects attached.

A result of the distinction made by the court between a marriage and a stable union is that, unlike a marriage, a stable union does not enjoy constitutional

1238 TC 222/1994 (11 July), as translated and quoted by: Cánovas, Pérez Nicolás, Spain: The Heterosexual State Refuses to Disappear, 2001, p. 494.

1239 A period of cohabitation is not required if the different-sex couple has a child. However, since same-sex couples could not marry when the act was adopted, succession rules apply to same-sex unions and not to different-sex unions. See Martín-Casals, Miquel, Family Law of Spanish Autonomies: Following a Similar Pattern? 2007, p. 71. In the bill pending in the Catalan Parliament, however, abolishing these differences is proposed.

1240 The legal effects of a stable union are described by Martín-Casals, Miquel, Same-Sex Partnerships in the Legislation of Spanish Autonomous Communities, 2003, pp. 58–64.

1241 For instance, in the Catalan Act of 1998, there is no requirement of an oral procedure of consent. Instead a stable union between two persons of the same sex is established by means of a jointly executed deed, which is officially registered. In the other autonomous communities a stable union between two persons of the same sex can also be established by default after a period of cohabitation. Moreover, a stable union pursuant to the Catalan Act is not an impediment to marriage. However the Catalan Act is currently being revised by the regional government to comply with the federal marriage enactment of 2005.

protection.[1242] The court's statement in this respect was received critically by proponents of gay rights. The main criticism was that without constitutional protection the level of legal protection of same-sex couples – once a registration scheme had been adopted – was made dependent on the prevailing political ideology in the region, which might shift or be replaced by other political goals.[1243] Since 2005, marriage has been opened up to same-sex couples in Spain,[1244] but the constitutionality of the enactment remains unclear, because it has been challenged by the PP. In October 2010, this case was still pending before the Spanish Constitutional Court.[1245]

7.3.3. GENDER-NEUTRAL MARRIAGE

7.3.3.1. The Impact of Politics

A gender-neutral marriage concept was introduced at the federal level in Spain on 30 June 2005. Through this enactment a married couple of the same sex was granted in principle the same legal effects as those obtained by spouses of different sex.[1246] During the 1990s, adopting special family law rules creating rights and duties for same-sex unions became topical in Spain. The introduction of same-sex marriage in Spain coincided with a shift in political power in 2004, whereby a socialist government replaced the conservative government, which until then had been in office without interruption since 1996. An electoral promise of the socialist government (the PSOE), which was kept, was to introduce marriage for same-sex couples.[1247] The political color of the government has been significant for the interest in improving the legal position of same-sex couples also in Sweden and the Netherlands.[1248] According to Katharina Boele-Woelki, Spain offers the most explicit example of the decisive role of a country's political developments in respect of the development toward legal recognition of

1242 Martín-Casals, Miquel, Same-Sex Partnerships in the Legislation of Spanish Autonomous Communities, 2003, pp. 57 f.

1243 Cánovas, Pérez Nicolás, Spain: The Heterosexual State Refuses to Disappear, 2001, p. 497.

1244 Ley 13/2005, de 1 julio, por la que se modifica el Código Civil en material de derecho a contraer matrimonio.

1245 See section 7.3.3.2 below.

1246 Ley 13/2005, de 1 julio, por la que se modifica el Código Civil en material de derecho a contraer matrimonio. Some differences remained, mainly in the field of parenthood. This will be further developed below.

1247 Martín-Casals, Miquel, Same-Sex Partnerships in the Legislation of Spanish Autonomous Communities, 2003, p. 57.

1248 In the Netherlands, same-sex marriage was introduced by the so-called purple coalition, and in Sweden the "conservative" government failed to present a bill on registered partnership to Parliament. In the end Parliament voted on the basis of a proposal drafted by its Legislative Committee. The same thing happened in Sweden in connection with the same-sex marriage enactment, i.e. no bill could be presented to Parliament.

same-sex relationships in statutory law.[1249] Boele-Woelki finds politics to be much more decisive in this respect than religion and culture.[1250]

The gender-neutral marriage concept appears to have faced opposition in ecclesiastical circles, as well as in conservative realms of the Spanish society, represented by the Conservative Party (the PP), which in the general elections became the second biggest political party with 38 percent of the votes.[1251] In the 2003 regional election of the City of Madrid, a political party called "Family and Life"[1252] was established, which was opposed to the idea of opening up marriage to same-sex couples, as well as the idea of allowing adoption of children by same-sex couples. However, the party only received 0.18 percent of the votes in the 2003 elections in the region.[1253]

7.3.3.2. Constitutional Aspects of a Gender-Neutral Marriage Concept

The introduction of a gender-neutral marriage concept enabling same-sex marriage did not require extensive revision of the wording of the Spanish Civil Code of 1978. Before the reform, the Civil Code did not define marriage as a union *between* a man and a woman, although this had been the predominating interpretation before the reform of 2005, but simply stated that: "man and woman have a right to contract a marriage."[1254] This can be claimed to have opened up for introducing a gender-neutral marriage regulation, since the wording does not necessarily mean that the man and the woman had to contract a marriage *with each other.* In other words, since the Code did not explicitly limit this right to applying *between* man and woman, a free interpretation could read out from the wording of the Code a woman's right to marry another woman, as well as a man's right to marry another man.[1255] This interpretation of the

1249 Boele-Woelki, Katharina, The Legal Recognition of Same-Sex Relationships Within the European Union, 2007–2008, p. 1961. Also Masha Antokolskaia and David Bradley underline the importance in general of the color of the political government when it comes to adopting registration schemes for same-sex couples. See section 6.4.1.3.

1250 Boele-Woelki, The Legal Recognition of Same-Sex Relationships Within the European Union, 2007–2008, pp. 1961. The impact of politics as well as the political role of the gay movement in Spain is discussed by Calvo, Kerman, Sacrifices that Pay: Polity Membership, Political Opportunities and the Recognition of Same-Sex Marriage in Spain, 2007, pp. 295–314.

1251 Election Resources on the Internet: http://electionresources.org/es/congress.php?election=2004. Accessed 21 September 2010.

1252 In Spanish: Familia y Vida. www.partidofamiliayvida.es/sitio/index.php. Accessed 1 December 2010.

1253 Pichardo Galán, José Ignacio, Same-Sex Couples in Spain, 2004, p. 161. For election results, see Wikipedia: http://en.wikipedia.org/wiki/Municipal_elections_in_Madrid. Accessed 21 September 2010.

1254 The Spanish Civil Code, Art. 44.

1255 This constitutional interpretation was made prior to the enactment by Martín-Casals, Miquel, Same-Sex Partnerships in the Legislation of Spanish Autonomous Communities, 2003, p. 57. The same discussion has arisen in connection with the interpretation of Art. 12 of the ECHR. See section 8.3.3.1.

wording of the Constitution in relation to same-sex couples, however, was and still is debated in the literature, and the marriage act of 2005 has been challenged as unconstitutional on several occasions since the enactment. So far however, the challenges have been rejected by the Constitutional Court.[1256] As mentioned above, a constitutionality challenge raised by the PP has been pending since 2005, but in September 2010, the Constitutional Court had not yet ruled on this matter.

The gender-neutral marriage concept was introduced without a constitutional amendment.[1257] Instead a provision was added in the Civil Code (paragraph 44), clarifying that the rights and obligations of marriage are the same regardless of the sex of the spouses. Also a few linguistic alterations were required, such as changing the words "wife" and "husband" into gender-neutral terminology.[1258]

The semantically small adjustments of the Spanish law to include same-sex couples were described accordingly by the Prime Minister: "It is just a small change to the legal text, adding but a paragraph, in which we establish that marriage will have the same requirements and the same rights, irrespective of whether the couple is of different sex or of the same sex. It is a small change in the letter of the law that creates an immense change in the lives of thousands of our fellow citizens."[1259]

Clearly the same-sex marriage enactment had an important political dimension. Legally recognizing the rights of same-sex couples was used in Spain by political parties on the left to appear "progressive" and "modern" in a European context. However, the political focus on opening up marriage to same-sex couples also contained a symbolic dimension. The reference to same-sex marriage being "an immense change in the lives of thousands of fellow citizens" most likely did not only refer to the legal effects attached to marriage, but also to the value of signaling to society that same-sex couples were worthy of serving the purpose of marriage in the eyes of the federal Spanish state. From this point of view, the same-sex marriage reform was more than an expression of a political

---

1256 Martínez de Aguirre Aldaz, Carlos and De Pablo Contreras, Pedro, Four years of Same-Sex Marriage in Spanish Law, 2010, pp. 1–15. On 21 July 2005, a judge, who refused to issue a marriage license to a female couple, filed a constitutional challenge against the same-sex marriage enactment. In August the same year, another judge filed a corresponding challenge. The Constitutional Court rejected the challenges.

1257 Martín-Casals, Miquel, Same-Sex Partnerships in the Legislation of Spanish Autonomous Communities, 2003, p. 57. The constitution is not amended easily or frequently. However, it was amended to allow citizens of the European Union the right to active and passive suffrage in local elections, Art. 13.2, title 1. The family is protected in Art. 39.1 of the Constitution.

1258 Official Journal of the Spanish government, Boletín Oficial del Estado, BOE, 157, 2 July, 2005.

1259 Speech delivered by the President José Luis Rodríguez Zapatero, during the plenary session of Congress, supporting reform of the Civil Code to allow same-sex marriage, 30 June 2005. Translation found at www.buddybuddy.com/zapat-01.html. Accessed 15 September 2010. The translation has been modified by the author.

willingness to appear progressive. It was also an illustration of the symbolic dimension of marriage.[1260]

7.3.3.3. Legal Parenthood for Same-Sex Couples: Adoption and Assisted Procreation Methods

Assisted procreation methods have been legal in Spain since 1988, available to spouses, single persons and to unmarried couples. The rules on establishment of legal parenthood have been revised several times. In 2005, when the gender-neutral marriage regulation was enacted, a law on reproduction techniques was also adopted.[1261] The Act introduced a possibility for lesbian partners to become joint legal guardians of a child conceived through assisted procreation, by means of so-called second parent adoption.

In 2007, the law was revised again and a possibility for the lesbian partner of the biological mother to be recognized as the legal parent of the child without an adoption procedure was introduced. Legal parenthood was established based on the "co-mother's"[1262] consent to the assisted reproduction.[1263] From a comparative point of view, basing the establishment of parenthood for same-sex couples when a child is born during the marriage on a presumption of parenthood – equivalent to the "*pater est*" presumption that applies to different-sex spouses – is progressive and in the forefront of any trends in this direction. In Sweden, such a proposal is pending, and in the Netherlands the introduction of rules on establishing legal parenthood for the lesbian partner of the birthmother based on a presumption of parenthood is being considered.[1264] However, neither the Dutch nor the Swedish law proposals had been endorsed by the national Parliaments by September 2010.

Single persons – irrespective of sexual orientation – are allowed to adopt a child in Spain. Since the introduction of same-sex marriage in 2005, federal

---

1260 See in particular section 9.2.2.

1261 Law of Assisted Reproduction Techniques (45/2003, 21 November).

1262 For lack of a better term, "co-mother" is used here in respect of the consenting partner of the birthmother. In Sweden this term was considered but dismissed as unsuitable in connection with the 2005 enactment on assisted procreation methods. See Memorandum of the Ministry of Justice, (Ds 2004:19), p. 52. In the memorandum using the term mother for both women was advocated. However, distinguishing between the woman giving birth and her partner was found adequate for practical reasons in the following bill, using the terms "mother" and "parent". The term co-mother, however was thought to signal that both parents were not equal. See Government Bill (Prop 2004/05:137), pp. 43 f.

1263 Pichardo Galán, José Ignacio, Beyond Marriage: LGTB Families in Spain, 2008, p. 9. See also Platero, Raquel, Outstanding Challenges in a Post-Equality Era, 2008, p. 44, with reference to: Boletín Oficial del Estado, BOE 65, 16 March, 2007, p. 11253.

1264 Swedish Committee Report (SOU 2007:3). In respect of the Dutch legal development: See Vonk, Machteld, The role of formalised and non-formalised intentions in legal parent-child relationships in Dutch law, 2008, p. 132.

Spanish law allows same-sex spouses to adopt a child jointly.[1265] Also joint adoption of children from abroad is possible according to the Spanish enactment.[1266] Including international adoption in the reform was a political statement of equality without practical relevance, since the states of origin which Spain cooperates with do not accept adoptive parents of the same sex.[1267] However, in respect of joint adoption of children within Spain – national adoption – there appears to be a number of children available for adoption, also by same-sex couples. In 2006, media reported of the first case of adoption by a same-sex couple, which took place in Catalonia.[1268]

7.3.3.4. What Difference in Treatment Is Left?

As a result of the 2005 gender-neutral marriage enactment, almost all the legal effects of marriage apply also to spouses of the same sex. However, there may still be slight regional variations between cohabiting same-sex and different-sex couples in the different enactments on stable unions in Spain. These will not be accounted for here.

A significant remaining difference between same-sex and different-sex couples in Spain relates to the marriage ceremony. Like Swedish couples, Spanish couples have the possibility to choose between a legally binding religious and a civil marriage ceremony. In practice, however, only civil marriage is available to same-sex couples, since the Catholic Church, which is the largest religious denomination in Spain, is unwilling to marry two persons of the same sex. The official standpoint taken by the Catholic Church toward the legal recognition of same-sex couples will be further discussed below.

1265 It can also be mentioned that a right for same-sex couples to adopt jointly already existed in four autonomous regions in Spain prior to the reform of 2005. Pichardo Galán, José Ignacio, Same-Sex Marriage in Spain, 2005, p. 2. Moreover, it should be emphasized that there is no right for adults to adopt children, but merely a possibility to be evaluated as prospective adoptive parents. Prior to 2005, adoption was possible by one homosexual person, but not jointly by a homosexual couple. See www.typicallyspanish.com/news/publish/article_6619.shtml. Accessed 29 November 2010.

1266 The reform of 2005 was aimed at placing same-sex couples on equal footing with different-sex couples. The aspects of the reform dealing with children were, allegedly, more controversial than the ones dealing with whether or not marriage should be made available to same-sex couples. See, for instance, Pichardo Galán, José Ignacio, Same-Sex Marriage in Spain, 2005, p. 4.

1267 El Mundo, 30 September, 2004, "Los matrimonios homosexuales no podrán adoptar niños extranjeros." www.elmundo.es/elmundo/2004/09/30/sociedad/1096545670.html. Accessed 15 September 2010. It is pointed out that South Africa accepts same-sex couples as adoptive parents, but that Spain did not cooperate with South Africa in adoption cases. See also section 6.4.3.2.

1268 See www.typicallyspanish.com/news/publish/article_6619.shtml. Accessed 29 November 2010.

7.3.4. THE CATHOLIC CHURCH AND GENDER-NEUTRAL MARRIAGE

7.3.4.1. The Franco-Regime and the Sacramental Nature of Marriage in the Catholic Faith

During the political regime of General Franco, 1939–1975, the position of the Catholic Church was cemented in Spanish society and protected in constitutional law.[1269] Catholicism was made the official religion and the Catholic faith enjoyed state protection.[1270] Other religions appear to have been tolerated to some extent when exercised, but it was criminal for non-Catholic groups to gather in private and discuss the Bible. Moreover, possession of non-Catholic books and magazines could be a criminal offense.[1271] As a rule, religious marriage was mandatory for Catholics, whereas civil marriage was available to non-Catholics who could not marry in the church.[1272]

The Spanish situation in respect of religion resembles the situation in Sweden between 1593 and 1809, when religious unity in accordance with the Evangelist-Lutheran faith prevailed in Sweden. As pointed out by Maarit Jänterä-Jareborg, the religious unity meant that Swedish nationals were expected to lead a religiously active life under the supervision of the state church.[1273] This role of religion in Sweden, as interpreted by the Lutheran state church of Sweden, appears similar to the role of religion in Spain during the Franco regime, although Catholicism was the state religion in Spain – not Lutheranism.

A traditional division of duties was encouraged during the Franco regime, in the sense that the wife cared for children and performed household chores, while the husband provided financially for the family. In capacity of housewife, however, the woman was allowed to make purchases concerning ordinary household matters.[1274] The wife was obliged to obey her husband, who, in turn, was responsible for protecting his wife. The wife had to follow her husband to whatever residence he chose, at least within Spain, and she was unable to have gainful employment without his permission.[1275]

When the dictatorship ended upon the death of General Franco in 1975, democracy was re-established, and in 1978 a new Spanish Constitution was adopted.[1276] The Spanish Constitution of 1978 was the starting point for the new

---

1269 Combalía, Zoila, Roca, María, Religion and the Secular State of Spain, 2010, p. 630.

1270 On the topic of National Catholicism in Spain, see Payne, Stanley G, The Franco Regime, 1987, pp. 362–369.

1271 Combalía, Zoila, Roca, María, Religion and the Secular State of Spain, 2010, p. 630.

1272 Platero, Raquel, Love and the State: Gay Marriage in Spain, 2007, p. 332.

1273 See Jänterä-Jareborg, Maarit, Religion and the Secular State, 2010, p. 671.

1274 Glendon, Mary Ann, Rheinstein, Max, International Encyclopedia of Comparative Law, Vol. IV, Persons and Family, Interspousal Relations, 2007, p. 6.

1275 Glendon, Mary Ann, Rheinstein, Max, International Encyclopedia of Comparative Law, Vol. IV, Persons and Family, Interspousal Relations, 2007, p. 6.

1276 Combalía, Zoila, Roca, María, Religion and the Secular State of Spain, 2010, p. 631.

"secular" Spain, establishing that there can be no official state religion.[1277] However, this did not mean that the Spanish legislator was against religion and religious communities. On the contrary, a principle was laid down in the Constitution, which requires that "[t]he public authorities shall take into consideration the religious creeds in Spanish society and shall maintain the ongoing cooperative relations with the Catholic Church and the other faiths".[1278] This principle – in the literature referred to as "the principle of cooperation" – obliges the federal Spanish state to communicate with the religious communities in Spain and to recognize their religious autonomy. In other words, the cooperation principle aims to safeguard the freedom of religion. The principle is also connected to the bilateral agreements between the state and some of the religious communities, regulating issues of mutual interest, for instance authority to conclude legally valid marriages.[1279] Also in Sweden the state cooperates with religious communities, and a religious community which is registered and contributes to the maintenance and development of fundamental values in Swedish society can be granted state subsidies.[1280]

During the Franco-regime, divorce was banned from the legal system. Legal separation was available only upon the request of an innocent spouse, as a sanction against the other spouse's reprehensible conduct. After the reestablishment of democracy, however, divorce was introduced in the Spanish Constitution and enactments were made to achieve equality in the law between husband and wife, for instance by assigning an economic value to household work in the context of rules dealing with spouses' property relations.[1281]

The Catholic Church's opposition to allowing two men or two women to marry each other is closely connected to its interpretation of marriage as a sacrament. According to the view of the Catholic Church, marriage is a life-long union between a man and a woman, for the purpose of procreation.[1282] The Catholic conception of marriage is that dissolution can only be obtained through

---

1277 Article 16, Paragraph 3 of the Constitution. See Glendon, Mary Ann, Rheinstein, Max, International Encyclopedia of Comparative Law, Vol. IV, Persons and Family, Interspousal Relations, 2007, p. 62.

1278 Combalía, Zoila, Roca, María, Religion and the Secular State of Spain, 2010, p. 632. As translated by: Glendon, Mary Ann, Rheinstein, Max, International Encyclopedia of Comparative Law, Vol. IV, Persons and Family, Interspousal Relations, 2007, p. 62.

1279 Combalía, Zoila, Roca, María, Religion and the Secular State of Spain, 2010, p. 632. As pointed out by Cristina, Gonzáles Beilfus, however, the agreement with the Holy See, was negotiated in 1978, which means that this particular agreement is not directly based on the Constitution. Information concerning Spanish law, provided on my request by Professor Cristina González Beilfuss, 10 November 2010.

1280 See Jänterä-Jareborg, Maarit, Religion and the Secular State, 2010, p. 678.

1281 See section 3.7.2.3.

1282 Pichardo Galán, José Ignacio, Same-Sex Couples in Spain. Historical, Contextual and Symbolic Factors, 2004, p. 166, with reference to canon 1055§ 1: "The marriage covenant, by which a man and a woman establish between themselves a life-long partnership, ordered by its nature for the good of the spouses and the procreation and education of offspring, has been raised by Christ the Lord to the dignity of a sacrament between the baptized."

the death of a spouse, as divorce is not recognized by the Catholic Church.[1283] Annulment of marriage is also a way out of a "dysfunctional" marriage, the basic idea being that there has never been a valid marriage in the first place.[1284]

Under the Catholic notion of marriage, a marriage is not valid until it has been consummated. The consummation of a Catholic marriage occurs when the man and the woman become "one flesh" during the conjugal act – i.e. through sexual intercourse.[1285] A marriage without sexual intercourse, due to for instance impotence, can be nullified.[1286] The Catholic Church's strict focus on the conjugal act and on reproduction as a basis for marriage have been regarded as difficult to apply to same-sex couples, who are unable to reproduce jointly on their own.[1287] This position can be compared with that of the Church of Sweden, which has theologically found it possible to promote a wider interpretation of marriage, including also same-sex couples. On the other hand, the Church of Sweden remains rather alone with this approach also among the Christian protestant churches in the world.[1288]

7.3.4.2. A "Virus" Destroying the Family?

The introduction of a gender-neutral marriage concept conflicted with the Catholic faith and values, and the critical responses of the Catholic Church in

---

1283 Cohabitation presupposes marriage. Adultery is no ground for separation, the basic idea being that the adulterous party should be forgiven and conjugal life continued. Separation does not break the marital bond. See Katolska kyrkans Katekes, 1996, Paras. 1649–1650, 2236 and 2380–2381. See also Codex Iuris Canonici, canon 1152 § 1: "Although it is earnestly recommended that a spouse, moved by Christian charity and concerned for the good of the family, not refuse forgiveness to an adulterous partner and not disrupt conjugal life, nevertheless, if the spouse did not condone the fault of the other expressly or tacitly, the spouse has the right to sever conjugal living unless the spouse consented to the adultery, gave cause for it, or also committed adultery." See www.vatican.va/archive/ENG1104/__P45.HTM. Accessed 15 September 2010.

1284 See sections 2.7 and 3.4.2.2.

1285 Codex Iuris Canonici, canon 1061 § 1: "A valid marriage between the baptized is called ratum tantum if it has not been consummated; it is called ratum et consummatum if the spouses have performed between themselves in a human fashion a conjugal act which is suitable in itself for the procreation of offspring, to which marriage is ordered by its nature and by which the spouses become one flesh." See www.vatican.va/archive/ENG1104/__P3V.HTM. Accessed 15 September 2010.

1286 See Katolska kyrkans Katekes, 1996, Paras. 1628–1629, with reference to Codex Iuris Canonici. 1095–1107. See also canon 1084 § 1: Antecedent and perpetual impotence to have intercourse, whether on the part of the man or the woman, whether absolute or relative, nullifies marriage by its very nature." See www.vatican.va/archive/ENG1104/__P3Y.HTM. Accessed 15 September 2010.

1287 Pichardo Galán, José Ignacio, Beyond Marriage: LGTB Families in Spain, 2008, Slovenia, p. 3.

1288 See section 6.3 for an account of the responses of the Church of Sweden to the legal recognition of same-sex couples in Sweden.

Spain to the enactment were expected.[1289] It appears that the Catholic Church has come to symbolize the "regressive camp"[1290] in Spain, and that there is a tendency to connote all forms of regression to the Franco regime. Challenging traditional Catholic values concerning marriage has also been considered to be a means for the Spanish state to break with the past and live up to European Union's democratic and human rights standards.[1291] From the point of view of the Catholic Church, the gender-neutral marriage concept was most likely seen as a provocative "attack" on the teachings of the Church. The Spanish Catholic Church responded with outspoken disapproval, as the following quote by the President of the Pontifical Council for the Family illustrates:

> "Same sex 'marriage' is another step towards the total destruction of the institution of the family, the most valuable heritage of all peoples and all humanity. [...] [Adoption by same-sex couples] would destroy the child's future. [It] would be an act of moral violence against the child."[1292]

In the opinion of the Catholic Church, members of the Roman Catholic Church should refuse to cooperate with the new law, when confronted with issues relating to it in their line of work, referring to the pending gender-neutral marriage bill as "iniquitous".[1293] The church's opposition gave rise to spectacular publicity in international media. An example is an interview with the archbishop of Barcelona, in which he compared officials who were against same-sex marriage, but refused to follow the law and marry same-sex couples, with Nazis at Auschwitz, who "believed that they had to obey the laws of the Nazi government before their own conscience."[1294] A spokesman for the Roman Catholic bishops referred to same-sex marriage as "a virus": "It would impose on society a virus, something false, which will have negative consequences for social life."[1295]

1289 See Katolska kyrkans Katekes, 1996, Paras. 2357–2359.

1290 See section 6.4.1.3, where a distinction between a so-called regressive and a progressive camp has been discussed.

1291 See, for instance, Platero Méndez, Raquel, Intersecting Gender and Sexual Orientation, 2007, where the membership of the European Union is pointed out as an important explanatory factor in the speedy legal development in the field of same-sex relationships.

1292 Interview with Cardinal Alfonso López Trujillo, President of the Pontifical Council for the Family, published at www.fides.org/eng/news/2005/0505/02_4784.html. Accessed 15 September 2010.

1293 Times Online, "Vatican attack on Spain's gay marriage law, 22 April 2005. www.timesonline.co.uk/tol/news/world/article384255.ece. Accessed 14 September 2010.

1294 New York Times, 30 June, 2005. www.nytimes.com/2005/06/30/international/europe/30cnd-spain.html. Accessed 14 September 2010.

1295 Statement by Juan Antonio Martinez Camino, spokesman of the Roman Catholic bishops. See http://news.bbc.co.uk/2/hi/europe/3695748.stm. Accessed 14 September 2010.

7.3.4.3. *The Catholic Church's Impact on Spanish Society Today*

Although Catholic values no longer permeate all aspects of Spanish society, which largely appeared to have been the case during the dictatorship,[1296] the Catholic Church continues to be important in Spanish society.[1297] In 2009, 76 percent of the Spanish population defined themselves as Catholic.[1298] When Swedes were asked the question if they believe in God, only 23 percent answered affirmatively.[1299] These figures are not equivalent or comparable, but they nevertheless say something about the role of religion in these societies. Furthermore, the Catholic Church comes in contact with a significant number of Spaniards at mass, which 15 percent of the population (almost 7 million people) attends on a weekly basis in Spain,[1300] and has a possibility to influence their moral values relating to the family. Moreover, in 2007, 50 percent of all marriages were officiated by the Catholic Church, a figure which corresponds to the Swedish context.[1301]

Against this background it is noteworthy that various polls from 2004 indicated that as many as 64 percent of the Spanish population supported the introduction of same-sex marriage, whereas only 26 percent were opposed to the idea of such a reform.[1302] This suggests that the popularity of church marriage – and a high number of persons who define themselves as Catholic – does not necessarily contradict a progressive view on family law related issues in general. In fact, also in Sweden, which is generally regarded as one of the most secular countries in the world, more than 40 percent of all marriages in 2009 were officiated in accordance with the ordinance of the Church of Sweden.[1303] It can be noted that the number of Spaniards who define themselves as Catholic is much higher than the number that attends mass regularly. In 2009, 58.2 percent stated that they almost never attend mass or religious services other than weddings, communions or funerals.[1304] In Sweden this figure is even lower. Only

---

1296 See section 7.3.4.1.

1297 The Roman Catholic Church has been called: "the smallest great power in the world". See Dagens Nyheter, 26 March, 2005, "Nya vindar sveper in i Vatikanen".

1298 CIS Barometer, July 2009, www.cis.es/cis/opencm/ES/2_barometros/depositados.jsp. Accessed 14 September 2010.

1299 Jänterä-Jareborg, Maarit, Religion and the Secular State, 2010, p. 669.

1300 CIS Barometer, July 2009: www.cis.es/cis/opencm/ES/2_barometros/depositados.jsp. Accessed 15 September 2010.

1301 Instituto Nacional de Estadística, www.ine.es.

1302 See José Ignacio Pichardo Galán, Beyond Marriage: LGTB Families in Spain, 2008, p. 3. See also CBS News, Spain Close On Same-Sex Weds, Madrid, 21 April 2005. www.cbsnews.com/stories/2005/04/21/world/main689929.shtml?source=search_story. Accessed 14 September 2010.

1303 Jänterä-Jareborg, Maarit, Religion and the Secular State, 2010, p. 672.

1304 Combalía, Zoila, Roca, María, Religion and the Secular State of Spain, 2010, p. 629.

two percent of the members of the Church of Sweden state that they attend religious services on a regular basis.[1305]

The wide support for same-sex marriage in Spain – 64 percent according to the poll mentioned above – reflects a social disconnection from traditional Catholic morality among the Catholic population in Spain, in favor of a more modernized view on sexual relations and the family.[1306] This appears to be especially visible among the young adults in Spain, in respect of which demographic research has indicated that church attendance and conformity with Catholic views on family life are low compared to older generations.[1307] According to a survey in 2004, about 90 percent of the young adults stated that they never follow the recommendations of the Catholic Church in respect of sexual relations and cohabitation prior to marriage.[1308]

Another dimension to take into account when analyzing the "progressive" attitude in Spain in connection with the introduction of same-sex marriage is that strict "conventional" Catholicism most likely reminds people of the dictatorship, during which Catholicism permeated law and society. With the recent experiences of the dictatorship in mind – during which the law subordinated women to men in a strictly patriarchal context – a conformist Catholic approach might appear unattractive to people in general.[1309]

In summary, the "battle" of introducing same-sex marriage in Spain was in a certain sense fought at two levels. It was a battle to enforce human rights and give homosexuals restitution for the oppression during preceding decades. It was also an opportunity for the state to claim the power to determine sexual morality and family values from the Catholic Church, and thus to "secularize" the law. Also, other aspects of marriage regulation were "modernized" in 2005. For instance, a unilateral right to divorce was introduced.[1310]

1305 Jänterä-Jareborg, Maarit, Religion and the Secular State, 2010, p. 669.

1306 Domínguez, Marta, Castro Martín, Teresa and Mencarini, Letizia, European Latecomers: Cohabitation in Italy and Spain, First Draft, March 2007, Prepared for the 2007 Annual Meeting of the Population Association of America, New York, Session 71, Cohabitation, p. 8. See also Bäckström, Anders, et al., Religious Change in Northern Europe, 2004, pp. 87–98, where the changing function of religion and the use of religious "rites" are discussed, the marriage ceremony being an example of a "rite" which culturally unites a country.

1307 Domínguez, Marta, Castro Martín, Teresa and Mencarini, Letizia, European Latecomers: Cohabitation in Italy and Spain, 2007, pp. 7 f.

1308 Domínguez, Marta, Castro Martín, Teresa and Mencarini, Letizia, European Latecomers: Cohabitation in Italy and Spain, First Draft, March 2007, Prepared for the 2007 Annual Meeting of the Population Association of America, New York, Session 71, Cohabitation, p. 8.

1309 This perspective has been emphasized by José Ignacio Pichardo Galán, Beyond Marriage: LGTB Families in Spain, 2008, p. 3.

1310 This has been discussed in section 4.4.2.

7.4. REGISTERED PARTNERSHIP AND SAME-SEX MARRIAGE – DRIVING FORCES TO LEGISLATE IN THE NORDIC COUNTRIES

7.4.1. THE NORDIC ENACTMENTS[1311]

During 1989–2001, all Nordic countries enacted legislation on registered partnership. This development started with the Danish Registered Partnership Act in 1989,[1312] and was rapidly followed by corresponding enactments in Norway in 1993,[1313] Sweden in 1994,[1314] Iceland in 1998[1315] and Finland in 2001.[1316] The Nordic enactments follow the same basic approach and structure. The registered partnership "Nordic style" is a marriage-like union exclusively available to persons of the same sex. The legal effects of a registered partnership are, as a rule, the same as those of a marriage. The same legislative technique was used in all of the Nordic Acts: with certain exceptions, the rules applicable to marriage – which were originally reserved for different-sex couples – apply to a registered partnership.[1317] All Nordic Registered Partnership Acts aim explicitly, according to the preparatory work, to make same-sex couples visible and accepted in society, by granting them almost equal legal rights to those enjoyed by spouses.[1318] Most exceptions from marriage originally enumerated in the different registered partnership acts have been abolished through subsequent amendments.[1319]

In Sweden, Norway and Iceland the Registered Partnership Acts have been repealed and replaced by a gender-neutral marriage concept. With regard to the history of harmonization of marriage laws in the Nordic countries, which will be described below, it is not unlikely that Finland and Denmark will eventually

---

1311 The legal development regarding same-sex partnerships has been accounted for separately by Jänterä-Jareborg, Maarit and Sörgjerd, Caroline in: The Experiences with Registered Partnership in Scandinavia, 2004, pp. 577–597. See also Jänterä-Jareborg, Maarit, Registered Partnerships in Private International Law, 2003, pp. 137–158 and Jänterä-Jareborg, Maarit, Parenthood for Same-Sex Couples, Liber Memorialis Petar Sarcevic, Universalism, Tradition and the Individual, 2006, pp. 75–91.

1312 Act on Registered Partnership (No. 372, 7 June 1989). The Act entered into force on 1 October 1989 and was implemented in Greenland on 26 April 1999.

1313 Act on Registered Partnerships (No. 40, 30 April 1993). The Act entered into force on 1 August 1993.

1314 The Registered Partnership Act (1994:1117, 23 June 1994). The Act entered into force on 1 January 1995.

1315 Act on Registered Partnership (No. 87, 12 June 1996). The Act entered into force on 27 June 1996.

1316 Act on Registered Partnership (950/2001). The Act entered into force on 1 March 2002.

1317 Jänterä-Jareborg, Maarit, Sörgjerd, Caroline, The Experiences with Registered Partnership in Scandinavia, 2004, pp. 577 f.

1318 Jänterä-Jareborg, Maarit, Sörgjerd, Caroline, The Experiences with Registered Partnership in Scandinavia, 2004, p. 578.

1319 Jänterä-Jareborg, Maarit, Parenthood for Same-Sex Couples, 2006, pp 79–82.

adopt a gender-neutral marriage regulation just like their Nordic neighbors. It can be mentioned that a bill containing a proposal for a gender-neutral Cohabitees Act is currently pending in Finland.[1320] The bill was endorsed by Parliament on 24 November 2010.[1321] Adopting a gender-neutral cohabitee regulation might be a step toward adopting a gender-neutral marriage concept as well.

7.4.2. NORDIC LEGAL COOPERATION IN THE TWENTIETH CENTURY

During the first half of the twentieth century, Nordic legal cooperation for the purpose of harmonizing marriage laws was a prioritized political goal. This has been discussed in section 3.2.2. In 1952, the Nordic Council was founded.[1322] It consisted of members from the Swedish, Danish, Icelandic and Norwegian national Parliaments, meeting once a year, inter alia, to discuss questions of harmonization in different fields of law. Finland joined in 1955. The Council's first agreement concerned the introduction (in 1955) of a common labor market, social security and free movement across borders without passports, visas or work permits for the citizens of the Nordic countries.[1323]

Between the 1920s and 1970s, family law legislation in the Nordic countries was closely harmonized in the field of marriage law.[1324] In the 1970s, however, this started to change, in pace with changing cohabitation patterns in society. For instance, the Swedish cohabitee regulation was not copied in the other Nordic countries.[1325] However, the legal situation of unmarried couples has been subject to legislation recently in some other Nordic countries. As mentioned above, the Finnish Parliament has recently passed a bill on cohabitation without

1320 Government Bill (RP 37/2010 rd).

1321 Http://web.eduskunta.fi/Resource.phx/riksdagen/index.htx.

1322 See www.norden.org. Accessed 14 September 2010.

1323 See www.norden.org/da/nordisk-raad/om-nordisk-raad/nordisk-raads-historie/1953–1971. Accessed 14 September 2010.

1324 Other areas of Nordic cooperation were the Acts on Sales and on Contracts (introduced in Sweden in 1905 and 1914). See Agell, Anders, Is There One System of Family Law in the Nordic Countries? 2001, pp. 313–330. As regards family law cooperation on registered partnerships, see e.g. Jänterä-Jareborg, Maarit, Registered Partnerships in Private International Law: The Scandinavian Approach, 2003, pp. 137–158, where she speaks of an "inter-Scandinavian Lacuna" of rules on registered partnership, p. 149. See also Kangas, Urpo, Divorce System and Maintenance of Former Spouses in Scandinavian Countries, 2007, pp. 37 f, where he points out that when examined closely the Nordic marriage regulations differ at the "micro structure" level.

1325 Agell, Anders, Is There One System of Family Law in the Nordic Countries? 2001, p. 317. In 1968, a bill on stable cohabitee relationships was presented in Denmark. In the end the bill was not endorsed. The Bill has been called a result of the Danish socialists wishing to compete with the Swedish in radicalism. See Sundberg, Jacob, Marriage or No Marriage in Swedish Law, 1971, pp. 238.

marriage, which contains rules which to some extent resemble the Swedish model of cohabitation without marriage.[1326] Norway has introduced rules on inheritance for unmarried cohabitees with children. The new rules entered into force 1 July 2009.[1327] Denmark has introduced a possibility for unmarried couples to conclude a "cohabitation will".[1328]

It can be discussed whether or not the tradition of Nordic legal cooperation has remained a prioritized political goal in the twenty-first century. The Swedish legal scholar Kjell Å Modéer has claimed that "the Nordic co-operation model within family law [...] is dead", and he links this to the development of the Nordic countries from homogenous and monolithic into heterogeneous, multicultural societies.[1329] Another factor worth mentioning in this context is that the influence of the European Union has decreased the role of the Nordic Council, since EU law has among the Member States of the Union replaced certain Nordic agreements.[1330] Also in respect of Norway and Iceland, which are not part of the EU, EES agreements have decreased the role of the Nordic Council.[1331] According to Maarit Jänterä-Jareborg, the legislative activities of the EU have made the Nordic countries realize the value of their own harmonization achievements. Jänterä-Jareborg holds that this insight has created a renewed interest among the Nordic countries in legal cooperation in the field of family law.[1332] The quite similar Nordic Registered Partnership Acts can be seen as an example of a renewed – although short lived – focus on Nordic legal harmonization.[1333]

1326 Government Bill (RP 37/2010 rd).

1327 See www.nrk.no/nyheter/1.6673894. Accessed 14 September 2010. See also Norwegian Government Bill (Ot.prop.) no. 73 (2007–2008).

1328 Lov nr. 515 og 516 af 6. juni 2007, which entered into force on 1 January 2008.

1329 Modéer, Kjell Å, Secularization, Liberalization and Modernization: Family Law in Scandinavian Welfare States in the 1960s-1970s, 2009, p. 221.

1330 See, for instance, Jänterä-Jareborg, Maarit, Mot en europeisk (internationell) familjerätt, 2001/02 pp. 65 f, and idem in Jänterä-Jareborg, Maarit, En harmoniserad familjerätt för Europa? 2009, pp. 327 f.

1331 Norway became a part of the EES in 1992.

1332 Jänterä-Jareborg, Maarit, Unification of International Family Law in Europe – A Critical Perspective, 2003, p. 216. Furthermore, comparative Nordic legal research has been carried out in the early twenty-first century by legal experts from the different countries, commissioned by the Nordic Council. The research has been published in four volumes, dealing with child law, inheritance law and marriage law in the five Nordic countries. See Lødrup, Peter, Agell, Anders and Singer, Anna, Nordisk børneret I, 2003, and Danielsen, Svend, Nordisk børnret II, 2003. Lødrup, Peter, Nordisk Arverett, 2003 and Agell, Anders, Nordisk äktenskapsrätt, 2003. Modéer, Kjell Å, pointed out that by 2009, this comparative research had not given rise to legislative Nordic harmonization action. See Modéer, Kjell Å, Secularization, Liberalization and Modernization: Family Law in Scandinavian Welfare States in the 1960s-1970s, 2009, p. 221.

1333 For instance it can be mentioned that the Swedish double track system for conclusion of marriage was kept, inter alia, with reference to the fact that the Nordic countries had such a system. See Government Bill (Prop 2008/09:80), p. 19.

7.4.3. BEING THE MOST "PROGRESSIVE": A MOTIVATION ALSO IN THE NORDIC COUNTRIES

The Nordic countries and their enactments are influenced by each other. This applies not least in respect of marriage regulation. The accounts of the Spanish, Dutch and Swedish courses of events suggest that these countries take pride in advancing themselves as "progressive" or "liberal". For instance, the Dutch legal scholar Kees Waaldijk has referred to the Netherlands in terms of being "one of the most gay-friendly nations in the world".[1334] Adopting rules generally perceived as "progressive" – i.e. aimed to strengthen the human rights of the individual through focusing on equality and prohibiting discrimination – is a means to market a country as "modern" and "democratic".

Also in an "inter-Nordic" context, an ambition to be the most progressive Nordic country in respect of family law legislation in general can be discerned. Already in 1978, a parliamentary committee was appointed in Sweden to investigate the conditions of life for homosexuals in different sections of Swedish society.[1335] After six years, in 1984, the 568 page Committee Report was presented with proposals to eradicate all forms of social and legal unjustified differential treatment.[1336] In the Committee Report, different legal solutions for same-sex relationships were considered, i.e. including access to a registration procedure or to the institution of marriage. For reasons accounted for in section 6.3.1, the proposals were rejected in the Committee Report of 1984.[1337] Instead the Homosexual Cohabitees Act of 1987 was enacted. The extensive Swedish Committee Report of 1984, with its thorough analysis of a Nordic society, can in many ways be seen as a foundation for the Nordic registered partnership enactments of the 1990s.

In 1984, Denmark followed suit and appointed a parliamentary committee for the purpose of investigating homosexual couples' need of legal recognition, which resulted in the Registered Partnership Act of 1989.[1338] The Danish enactment contributed to inspiring Swedish legislative action on an issue rejected a few years earlier, namely the introduction of a formalized union for same-sex couples.[1339] Thus a second Swedish committee dealing with these issues was

---

[1334] Waaldijk, Kees, Small Change: How the Road to Same-Sex Marriage Got Paved in the Netherlands, 2001, p. 439.

[1335] Directive of December 8, 1977. The Committee was appointed on 17 January, 1978, and given the name: utredningen om homosexuellas situation i samhället.

[1336] Committee Report (SOU 1984:63), see section 6.3.1.

[1337] Committee Report (SOU 1984:63), pp. 94 and 98 f.

[1338] Nielsen, Linda, Family Rights and the Registered Partnership in Denmark, 1990, p. 297. See also Dupuis, Martin D, The Impact of Culture, Society, and History on the Legal Process: An Analysis of the Legal Status of Same-Sex Relationships in the United States and Denmark, 1995, p. 104.

[1339] The legal enactments – or the lack of such enactments – in the other Nordic countries dealing with same-sex unions was accounted for in the Swedish Committee Report of 1993, pp.

appointed in 1991, and the Registered Partnership Act was enacted in 1994. In the meanwhile, in 1993, the Norwegian legislature managed to pass a Registered Partnership Act modeled on the Danish Act.[1340] Iceland was also influenced by the Swedish and Norwegian courses of events.[1341] The Icelandic Act on Registered Partnership was enacted in 1996.[1342] Finland was the last Nordic country to adopt a formalized relationship scheme for same-sex couples. A registered partnership act was first considered in Finland in 1990, but could not be adopted until 2001.[1343]

Once most of the legal differences between marriage and registered partnership had been challenged and abolished one by one in the Nordic countries,[1344] the next issue that arose was whether or not it was motivated to retain two separate institutions based on the couples' sex, i.e. marriage for different-sex couples and registered partnership for same-sex couples. In 2005, Sweden was the first Nordic country to appoint a commissioner for the purpose of investigating the prospects of extending marriage legislation to same-sex couples. The Norwegian gender-neutral marriage enactment entered into force in 2008, while the Swedish proposal was still under consideration. The Swedish gender-neutral marriage regulation entered into force on 1 May 2009.

The mapping of the Nordic legislative initiatives and enactments above suggests that the Nordic countries have influenced each other, not only for the purpose of favoring the tradition of Nordic legal cooperation, but also as a means of appearing equally "progressive" and concerned with the principle of equality. This provides an example of how a broad understanding of the concept of equality has become a symbol of "progression", which in turn has become a value-based and politically desirable goal in the human rights discourse in Europe.[1345]

75–79.

1340 The proposal was presented in 1989 and the Act was adopted in 1993. The debates surrounding the Norwegian act are illustrated by Strandbakken, Asbjørn, Lov om registrert partnerskap, 1993, p. 319. It should be noted, however, that in the Swedish Committee Report of 1984, the Committee stated that the idea of introducing a registration procedure for couples of the same sex could be considered again later on when societal values had changed. Committee Report, (SOU 1984:63), p. 99.

1341 The issue of regulating same-sex relationships was first raised in 1985, when a group of members of the Icelandic Parliament proposed appointing a committee to investigate the conditions of life of homosexuals. The timing coincided with a growing visibility of homosexuals in Iceland, which already had led to the founding of an official gay movement in 1978. See Björk Eydal, Stefánsson, Kolbeinn, Restrained reform – Securing equality for same-sex couples in Iceland, 2003.

1342 Act on Registered Partnership, No. 87, 12 June 1996.

1343 Savolainen, Matti, The Finnish and Swedish Partnership Acts – Similarities and Divergences, 2003, pp. 26 f.

1344 The extensive Swedish Committee Report of 2001, (SOU 2001:10), parts A and B, is worth mentioning in this context, because of its through investigations leading to the radical conclusion that having two parents of the same sex can be in a child's best interests.

1345 Human rights aspects of same-sex relationships will be dealt with in chapter 8.

7.5. SUMMARIZING REMARKS: GENDER-NEUTRAL MARRIAGE AS THE TARGET OF PROGRESSION AND EQUALITY ACHIEVEMENTS

The account of foreign courses of events illustrates that the Swedish experiences with registered partnership and same-sex marriage are not unique, although differences between the jurisdictions studied can be observed, for instance in respect of legislative techniques used in the enactments, legal effects attached and political and historical backgrounds. In all three of the jurisdictions compared – Sweden, Spain and the Netherlands – the legal development, regardless of the road chosen, all end in the same place: gender-neutral marriage.

It has been claimed above that the legal development concerning same-sex relationships in the jurisdictions studied can be seen as driven by a twofold, and sometimes coinciding aim: to provide legal rules which create a civil status for same-sex couples, and to appear progressive from a European (and Nordic) perspective. Legal recognition of same-sex relationships in statutory law has been a way to compensate for condemnation of homosexuals, particularly in Spain. Strengthening human rights was most likely especially urgent in a country with a distressing political past from a human rights perspective. In Spain, same-sex marriage was also a means for the state to mark dissociation from traditional values, which to some extent the Catholic Church still represents.

The enactment of the institution of registered partnership did not silence the demands for access to marriage by same-sex couples in Sweden or the Netherlands, and neither did the "stable unions" in Spain. It does not appear to matter if the registered partnership act is "gender-specific" or not, i.e. if it includes same-sex as well as different sex couples, like in the Netherlands, or only same-sex couples, like in Sweden. The legislative technique used does not appear to have mattered either, i.e. whether the enactment refers to the legal effects of marriage or enumerates the rights and duties covered. A gender-neutral marriage concept has been adopted in the three jurisdictions, regardless of the structure and legislative techniques applied in the registered partnership enactment.

The examples of Sweden, Spain and the Netherlands support the assumption that the adoption of a gender-neutral marriage concept was not about legal effects, but about the symbolic dimension of marriage. Registered partnership could not provide an adequate civil status for same-sex couples, because these registration schemes, although providing largely equivalent legal effects as a marriage, were not labeled "marriage."

Access to marriage for couples of the same sex meant challenging the Christian churches' interpretation of marriage as a union between a man and a woman, based on the story of the Creation in the Bible.[1346] It appears that traditional Christian values have continued to play a role in all three societies (Sweden, Spain and the Netherlands), for instance the view of marriage as a life-long union of a man and a woman for the purpose of the upholding of society. Even in the Netherlands, where a clear distinction between the state and the church is maintained through the "civil marriage tradition", such values might have contributed to making the gender-neutral marriage act politically controversial.

Generally, religious communities tend to be associated with disapproval of homosexuality, based on biblical interpretations of homosexuality as a sin.[1347] The religious communities have had a considerable impact on determining values dealing with marriage and sexual relationships. This makes the institution of marriage – central in the Protestant faith and a sacrament in the Catholic faith – an excellent arena for the legislator to challenge traditional religious values perceived as "outdated", by using the principle of equality as a tool. The leading churches in Spain and in Sweden respectively have responded differently to this challenge. The Catholic church in Spain maintains its traditional view, whereas the Church of Sweden has gone in the opposite direction by officiating at same-sex marriages. In the Netherlands, some churches offer blessings to civil marriages.

[1346] See section 6.6.3.1.
[1347] See sections 6.3.2 and 7.3.4.

8. THE EUROPEAN UNION'S, COUNCIL OF EUROPE'S AND HUMAN RIGHTS' PERSPECTIVES ON CHANGING COHABITATION MODELS

8.1. THE POINT OF DEPARTURE

A decisive aspect of the legal development toward introducing a gender-neutral marriage concept in Sweden, Spain and the Netherlands has been the impact of human rights issues in Europe. Human rights focus on improving the situation of the individual by emphasizing the principle of equality and counteracting unlawful discrimination.

The European Court of Human Rights, situated in Strasbourg (the Strasbourg Court) is the primary actor on the European human rights arena. In its interpretations of the 1950 European Convention of Human Rights (ECHR) a change in the previously restrictive policy toward unmarried couples and same-sex couples is visible. So far the right to marry has been reserved for different-sex couples, but the Strasbourg Court has recently ruled that same-sex couples under Art. 8 of the ECHR enjoy protection of their *family life* – not only of their *private life* – which can be seen as a step toward recognizing a right for same sex couples to marry.[1348]

Successively, also at the European Union level, human rights issues have become increasingly relevant, not only for the purpose of facilitating the free movement of persons within the EU, but also as an independent goal. The EU is preparing accession to the ECHR, and has also drafted an instrument of its own with legally binding human rights – the Charter of Fundamental Rights of the European Union (the Charter). The Charter protects the rights of the individual in the exercise of rights protected by the EU Treaties in relation to the European Union.

Both EU law and the European Convention of Human Rights apply in Sweden and protect the rights and interests of the individual, when moving across borders, as well as when the individual exercises his/her protected rights within a Member State. However, different opinions prevail in the European Member States in respect of the sensitive questions of who should be legally

[1348] See sections 8.3.2.3, 8.3.4.2 and 8.3.4.3.

recognized as family and who qualifies for various rights. How has the European Union responded to the legal development of new cohabitation models in the Member States, and what protection do unmarried couples of the same sex as well as of different sex have under the ECHR?

8.2. EU LAW PERSPECTIVES: WHO ARE "FAMILY"?

8.2.1. FREE MOVEMENT OF PERSONS: THE REGULATION OF 1968

In 1958, when the European Economic Community (EEC) was established, the cooperation focused on economy and integration – not family definitions. However, the importance of the free movement of workers was an essential component of establishing a common European market.[1349] From this point of view, it was central that workers from one Member State were not deterred from working in another Member State, but treated as equals to the host state's own workers. In order to encourage the free movement of workers, defining who qualified as their accompanying "family member(s)" became relevant. The principle of free movement can be seen as the starting point for the process toward including family law in EU law.[1350]

Qualifying as "family" in the context of the free movement of workers is not only a question of being allowed to accompany the worker into the host state.[1351] It is also a question in a wider sense of being entitled to certain financial benefits, for instance access to the social security system of the host state, including, inter alia, child benefits, housing benefits and sickness benefits.[1352] Moreover, the emotional importance for a family member of being allowed to accompany the worker into the host state should not be underestimated.[1353]

1349 Stalford, Helen, Concepts of Family under EU Law – Lessons from the ECHR, 2002, p. 412.

1350 See Jänterä-Jareborg, Maarit, Mot en europeisk (internationell) familjerätt, 2001/02 pp. 48–74.

1351 Problems connected to free movement and same-sex couples have been thoroughly analyzed by Toner, Helen, Partnership Rights, Free Movement and EU Law, 2004. Toner points out that guaranteed immigration rights are reserved for spouses, most likely of different sex. Immigration rights for other partners, such as unmarried couples and registered partners depend on the standpoint taken in this regard by the Member States. The problem, according to her, is the greatest in respect of couples consisting of one partner who is not an EU national, since all EU nationals have the right to move freely within the Union, see p. 1.

1352 Jänterä-Jareborg, Maarit, Mot en europeisk (internationell) familjerätt, 2001/02 pp. 51 f.

1353 Family reunification is essential for the migrant's well-being and social adaption in the host state. See Toner, Helen, Partnership Rights, Free Movement and EU Law, 2003, pp. 2 f.

In a Regulation from 1968 (Art. 10.1), the Council of the European Union (the Council) launched a definition of a "family member,"[1354] for the purpose of facilitating workers' mobility across borders by clarifying which workers were entitled to benefits in respect of their accompanying "family members".[1355] A family member entitled to accompanying and installing themselves with a worker, who is a national of one Member State and employed in another, is defined as:

(a) [the worker's] spouse and their descendants who are under the age of 21 years or are dependents;
(b) dependent relatives in the ascending line of the worker and his spouse.

The definition of a "family member" according to the regulation is narrow, only including the worker's spouse and their joint children.[1356] In Art. 10.2, a possibility to slightly extend the family concept is established:

> Member States shall *facilitate* the admission of any member of the family not coming within the provisions of paragraph 1 if dependent on the worker referred to above or living under his roof in the country whence he comes.[1357]

In practice, however, Art. 10.2 did not strengthen the position of families falling outside of Art. 10.1. The terms "facilitate" and "family members" are not sufficiently clear, precise and unambiguous for the provision to have so-called direct effect.[1358] As a result, the article does not have supremacy over national law and cannot give rise to rights and duties in the individual case.[1359]

1354 Council Regulation 1612/68 of 15 October 1968 on freedom of movement for workers within the Community [1968/9] OJ Sp Ed (II) 475.

1355 Stalford, Helen, Concepts of Family under EU Law – Lessons from the ECHR, 2002, p. 412.

1356 Article 10, Regulation 1612/68. Stalford, Helen, Concepts of Family under EU Law – Lessons from the ECHR, 2002, pp. 412 f. See also Bell, Mark, We are Family? 2002, pp. 335 f.

1357 Article 10.2, Regulation (EEC) No 1612/68 of the Council of 15 October 1968 on freedom of movement for workers within the Community (emphasis added).

1358 The ECJ decides when the prerequisites for direct effect are fulfilled. A distinction is made between horizontal and vertical direct effect, the former meaning that the provision can give an individual certain rights in relation to other individuals, whereas the latter creates such rights between an individual and the Member State. See Toner, Helen, Partnership Rights, Free Movement and EU Law, 2003, p. 51. The criteria for direct effect were laid down in McCollum v. SSHD [2001] EWHCAdmin 40 [2001] Admin Ct Digest 58 (the term "facilitate) and Van Gend en Loos v. Nederlandse Administratie der Belastingen, C-26/62 [1963] ECR 1.

1359 Hartley, Trevor C., The Foundations of European Community Law, 2007, p. 224. The only exception to this rule is in respect of a provision in national law, necessary due to an obligation arising from a legal cooperation entered into before the relevant treaty was entered into. Moreover, it should be clarified that all Community law provisions, in Treaties, Regulations and Directives can have direct effect. This was, most likely, not the intention originally, at least not in respect of Directives. See Nilsson, Mattias, Lundberg, Jenny, Europarätten – en introduktion till EG-rätten och Europakonventionen, 2006, p. 41, with reference to the ruling in Van Gend en Loos v. Nederlandse Administratie der Belastingen C-26/62 [1963] ECR 1.

The Regulation of 1968 still applies but it has been slightly altered. The regulation is no longer limited to workers, but applies to all EU citizens with sufficient means to avoid becoming a financial burden on the host state.[1360]

8.2.2. "THE CITIZENS DIRECTIVE" OF 2004

8.2.2.1. *The "If-the-Host-State-So-Wishes-Approach"*

The right of family members to move freely within the European Union was not directly regulated in the EC-Treaty, which was renamed "Treaty on the Functioning of the European Union" (TFEU), through the ratification of the Treaty of Lisbon in 2009. However, preservation of the family unit is a common basic right in the constitutional traditions of the Member States, protected also in EU law and mentioned in the Charter.[1361] In some Member States the family enjoys special protection through an explicit provision in the state's Constitution, for instance in Spain.[1362] In Sweden, the interest in safeguarding the family unit is visible in the marriage regulation, for instance, in the retained period of reconsideration prior to divorce in certain situations and in the ethical provision on faithfulness between spouses.[1363] Furthermore, the individual's right to protection of his or her private life and family life is provided through the European Convention of Human Rights (the ECHR), which has a special legal status in Sweden. This will be further analyzed in section 8.3.1 below.

Although the Member States share an interest in safeguarding the family unit, the views on what types of relationships constitute a "family", and what "family members" should be protected, differ significantly within Europe and have resulted in different legal solutions. The diversity in respect of family definitions and policies toward same-sex couples in Europe can be seen as posing a risk to the free movement of persons across EU borders, because of uncertainty

1360 Corrigendum to Directive 2004/38/EC of the European Parliament and of the Council of 29 April 2004, on the right of citizens of the Union and their family members to move and reside freely within the territory of the Member States, amending Regulation (EEC) No 1612/68 and repealing Directives 64/221/EEC, 68/360/EEC, 72/194/EEC, 73/148/EEC, 75/34/EEC, 75/35/EEC, 90/364/EEC, 90/365/EEC and 93/96/EEC OJ L 158, 30.4.2004. Corrected version in OJ L 229, 29.6.2004. Official Journal L 204, 04/08/2007 P. 0028 – 0028. Moreover, the Regulation of 1968 has been amended by two regulations, which do not deal with the family concept, but with trade unions (Council Regulation (EEC) No. 312/76 and Regulation (EEC) No. 2434/92), which deals with, inter alia, mechanisms applicable for clearing vacancies and applications for employment.

1361 Government Bill (Prop 2005/06:77), p. 38.

1362 See section 7.3.3.2.

1363 See sections 4.3.3 and 4.2.2.3.

whether or not the family unit established and recognized in one country will be recognized also in the host state.[1364]

The European Commission has proposed extending the narrow "spouse-only" approach to the family concept, laid down in the 1968 Regulation, several times without success.[1365] In 2003, the Commission[1366] presented a proposal for a directive to the Council of Europe, which aimed at facilitating for citizens of the EU and their family members to move freely across EU borders – the so-called Citizens Directive.[1367] In the Directive, Art. 2.2, a family member of an EU citizen is defined accordingly:

Family Member means:

(a) the spouse;
(b) the partner with whom the Union Citizen has contracted a registered partnership, on the basis of the legislation of a Member State,[1368] if the legislation of the host Member State treats registered partnerships as equivalent to marriage and in accordance with the conditions laid down in the relevant legislation of the host Member State.

The merit of the Directive is that it expanded the principle of free movement from applying not only to workers (or students, retired persons and economically self-sufficient persons) to all EU citizens, hence the name "Citizens Directive". However, the Directive contains no particularly "progressive" family definition. It largely codified principles established in ECJ case law.[1369] There is no *obligation* to recognize registered partnerships pursuant to the Directive, and the Directive does not mention same-sex marriage. Instead it is left to the national courts to determine if same-sex couples should be recognized under the Directive.[1370]

1364 See, for instance, Toner, Helen, Partnership Rights, Free Movement and EU Law, 2003. This will be discussed in section 8.4.

1365 For a thorough account of the different proposals in this respect, see Toner, Helen, Partnership Rights, Free Movement and EU Law, 2003, pp 49–68.

1366 COM (2003) 199, Amended proposal for a Directive of the European Parliament and of the Council on the right of citizens of the Union and their family members to move and reside freely within the territory of the Member States (presented by the Commission pursuant to Art. 250 (2) of the EC-Treaty).

1367 Council Directive 2004/38/EC of 29 June 2004. The Directive expanded the principle of free movement from applying not only to workers (or students, retired persons and economically self-sufficient persons) to all EU citizens, hence the name "Citizens Directive". The proposal was adopted by the Council in December 2003, Directive 2004/38/EC on the right of citizens of the Union and their family members to move and reside freely within the territory of the Member States. See also Government Bill (Prop 2005/06:77), p. 38.

1368 Note that partnerships registered outside the EU appear to be excluded, see Toner, Helen, Partnership Rights, Free Movement and EU Law, 2003, p. 67.

1369 Government Bill (Prop 2005/06:77), p. 35.

1370 Toner, Helen, Partnership Rights, Free Movement and EU Law, 2003, p. 67.

Interest groups protecting the rights of homosexuals were disappointed with the final outcome of the prolonged discussions on redefining the family concept, arguing that an ideal opportunity to bring about changes in the recognition of same-sex couples had been missed.[1371] Compared to the Commission's original proposal, which distinguished between "married" and "unmarried partners" irrespective of their sex, the final result appears limited.[1372] However, as Helen Toner has pointed out, from the perspective of same-sex couples, not mentioning same-sex marriage was better than explicitly denying that the word "spouse" could encompass a same-sex couple, which had been considered and dismissed during the preparation of the Directive.[1373] Also Mark Bell, although he called the Directive "a failure by the Union to recognize changed social and legal realities", acknowledged that the very mention of registered partners in Union legislation was an "illustration of awareness that these families will move around and seek to have their statuses recognized."[1374]

Katharina Boele-Woelki has emphasized the urgency – from a human rights perspective and from the perspective of the free movement of persons – of making a person's civil status portable across EU borders.[1375] From the perspective of same-sex couples, it is problematic that the Directive makes recognition of same-sex relationships dependent on the host state's domestic family law regulation. If the host state does not have an equivalent registered partnership scheme,[1376] there is no obligation to recognize the same-sex couple as a "family". The need of protection and recognition in EU law can be claimed to be particularly urgent in Member States without regulation of same-sex relationships. Against this background the new provision has been criticized as insufficient and disappointing.[1377] It can be mentioned however, that the preamble of the Citizens Directive contains an admonition that "[...] Member States should implement this Directive without discrimination between the beneficiaries of this Directive on grounds such as [...] sexual orientation."[1378] The importance of the preamble lies in that it establishes the purpose of the enactment and provides general guidance for the ECJ, as well as for national courts and legislators when interpreting the family concept in individual cases.

Mark Bell has noted that the Directive has created two zones of migration for registered partners within the European Union, an "inner zone" consisting of

1371 Toner, Helen, Partnership Rights, Free Movement and EU Law, 2003, p. 68 with reference to ILGA-Europe Newsletter 3, 2002.
1372 Bell, Mark, Holding Back the Tide? 2004, p. 623.
1373 Toner, Helen, Partnership Rights, Free Movement and EU Law, 2003, p. 67.
1374 Bell, Mark, Holding Back the Tide? 2004, p. 631.
1375 Boele-Woelki, Katharina, The Legal Recognition of Same-Sex Relationships Within the European Union, 2007–2008, p. 1978.
1376 As illustrated in chapter 7, the name of the union creating a civil status for same-sex couples varies in the European states, as well as the legal effects attached.
1377 Toner, Helen, Partnership Rights, Free Movement and EU Law, 2003, p. 67.
1378 Directive 2004/38/EC, preamble (31).

jurisdictions which recognize the partnership, and an "outer zone" where such relationships are not legally recognized.[1379] The distinction between these two zones is sometimes unclear. The legal development concerning same-sex couples in Europe has taken place during a short time span, and the registration schemes adopted at national level differ in respect of the legal consequences attached. When national courts apply the 2004 Directive, the diversity in legal solutions dealing with same-sex couples can give rise to results which appear "random" and not well thought out. For instance it is unclear if the French "PACS" is equivalent to marriage, in the sense that places France in the "inner zone" pursuant to the Directive.[1380]

8.2.2.2. A Once Again Established Duty to Facilitate Entry

As mentioned above, in the context of the 1968 Regulation, the term "facilitate" is too vague to give rise to a direct effect. Nevertheless, the same term was chosen in the Citizens Directive. The Citizens Directive also includes an article (3.2) stating that:

> Without prejudice to any right to free movement and residence the persons concerned may have in their own right, the host Member State shall, *in accordance with its national legislation,*[1381] facilitate entry and residence for the following persons:
> (a) Any other family members, irrespective of their nationality, not falling under the definition in point 2 of Article 2, who in the country from which they have come, are dependents or members of the household of the Union citizen having the primary right of residence, or where serious health grounds strictly require the personal care of the family member by the Union citizen;
> (b) The partner with whom the Union Citizen has a durable relationship, duly attested.

An ambiguity of Art. 3.2 is that no explanation in respect of what constitutes a *durable relationship* is offered in the provision. The interpretation and implementation of the Directive is left to each Member State. As a result, various definitions of what constitutes a "durable relationship" exist. When the Directive was implemented in Sweden, it was found to be motivated to include unmarried cohabiting couples, falling under the Cohabitees Act.[1382]

The different interpretations at national levels of what constitutes a durable relationship can create difficulties for unmarried couples of the same sex, as well as of different sex, to foresee what rules will apply to them when moving from one EU State to another. According to Art. 3.2 (b), the relationship needs to be

[1379] Bell, Mark, Holding Back the Tide? 2004, p. 624.
[1380] Mark, Holding Back the Tide? 2004, p. 624.
[1381] Emphasis added.
[1382] Government Bill (Prop 2004/05:170), p. 71.

"duly attested". This means that a couple might need to present evidence that their relationship has existed for some time. Relationships which have lasted for several years with shared family responsibilities, for instance in respect of children, are likely to qualify as "durable".[1383] If a same-sex registration scheme does not qualify as equivalent to marriage pursuant to Art. 2.2, the union can enjoy a certain level of protection under 3.2 (b), prescribing "a duty to facilitate entry".[1384]

Another novelty in the Citizens Directive is an additional paragraph (Art. 3.2.2) stating that: "The host Member State shall undertake an extensive examination of the personal circumstances and shall justify any denial of entry or residence to these people". This obligation brings some clarity to the provision, but the article is, most likely, still not sufficiently clear, unambiguous and precise to be directly effective in the context of family reunification.[1385] Nevertheless, in the legal literature, the right of an EU citizen to have his or her request for entry and residency seriously considered, through an emphasis on procedural requirements, has been seen as an improvement of the individual's position.[1386] More precisely, the requirements that the personal circumstances must be investigated on an individual basis and that denial of entry or residence must be justified, have been interpreted as preventing a Member State from adopting a general policy denying same-sex couples entrance or residence. This interpretation is also supported by the Preamble, recital 31 of the Directive, which establishes that the Directive should be implemented without discrimination on grounds of, for instance sexual orientation.[1387]

The personalized assessment criterion – the requirement that the personal circumstances shall be examined – has also been seen as likely to result in an increased focus on concepts such as the right to a fair hearing or the right to the review of an initial decision.[1388] The extension of the definition of a "family member", which Art. 3.2 opened up for, and the sharpened procedural requirements established in Art. 3.2.2, were intended to safeguard the family unit in a broader sense than the traditional married couple, taking into account the legal development taking place in many Member States away from regarding marriage as the only socially and legally acceptable cohabitation model. In 2004, however, the legal situation and values concerning unmarried different-sex and same-sex couples varied greatly, and the EU could not impose on the Member States a uniform definition of the traditionally culturally significant concept of family. Since then, however, as will be illustrated below, legal recognition of

1383 Bell, Mark, EU Directive on Free Movement and Same-Sex Families, 2005, p. 8, published at www.rfsl.se/public/ilga_eudirektivfreedom.pdf. Accessed 20 September 2010.
1384 Government Bill (Prop 2005/06:77), p. 39.
1385 Toner, Helen, Partnership Rights, Free Movement and EU Law, 2003, p. 67.
1386 Bell, Mark, Holding Back the Tide? 2004, p. 625. In Sweden,.
1387 See Bell, Mark, Holding Back the Tide? 2004, p. 625.
1388 Bell, Mark, Holding Back the Tide? 2004, p. 625.

same-sex couples in particular has evolved rapidly in the direction toward a European consensus. Most Member States are today open toward some form of legal recognition.[1389]

8.2.3. THE PRINCIPLE OF NON-DISCRIMINATION

8.2.3.1. Non-Discrimination – A Fundamental Principle in EU Law

The principle of equality applies at different EU law levels: (1) as a general ground for review of Community action, (2) as a prerequisite for free movement, prohibiting discrimination of nationals and (3) as a fundamental right.[1390] In this context, the third level of equality is focused on – more precisely the aim to treat persons equally irrespective of civil status. This level is, nevertheless, often intertwined with the second level. It can be mentioned that the terms "non-discrimination" and "equality" are often used synonymously, for instance in ECJ case law.[1391] Sometimes, however, a slight distinction is made between the two.[1392] In the present chapter the terms are used interchangeably.

In the jurisprudence of the ECJ, non-discrimination on the basis of nationality – and most likely also on the basis of sex – has developed into a general principle of EU law, legally binding for the Member States' national courts.[1393] As an autonomous, fundamental principle of law, all-pervasive and operating at different levels in the EU, it prohibits differential treatment of individuals in comparable situations, on the basis of nationality, unless an objectively justified purpose so requires, i.e. if unequal treatment does not pursue a legitimate aim,

1389 Furthermore, it can be mentioned that the Commission is preparing a Green Paper on the right to family reunification, which aims at facilitating the free circulation of documents in the EU. The aim is to initiate a discussion among interested Member States on how to facilitate recognition of documents concerning, for instance, EU citizens' civil status within the EU. This Green Paper might contribute to facilitating the free movement of EU citizens within the EU, but still without forcing Member States to recognize a same-sex marriage or registered partnership as equal to marriage. See www.fra.europa.eu/fraWebsite/attachments/FRA-LGBT-report-update2010.pdf. (p. 51) Accessed 5 December 2010.

1390 Tridimas, Takis, The General Principles of EU Law, 2006, p. 60.

1391 Tridimas, Takis, The General Principles of EU Law, 2006, p. 64.

1392 This is the case, for instance, in the EU Charter of Fundamental Rights and in the 2004 proposal for an EU Constitution (Art. 2) – "equality" emphasizing the positive obligations, and "non-discrimination" the negative aspect of equal treatment claims. See Tridimas, Takis, The General Principles of EU Law, 2006, p. 64.

1393 This development has taken place based on Article 18, TFEU, where the prohibition against discrimination based on nationality is laid down. See also Tridimas, Takis, The General Principles of EU Law, 2006, p. 61, with reference to Milac, C-8/78 [1978] ECR 1721, Para. 8. Establishing a general principle of law appears to be deemed necessary due to matters of principle rather than practical necessity. See McCrudden, Christopher, The New Concept of Equality, 2003, p. 3. In respect of the principle of equality, however, also necessity was behind establishing a general principle of law, since equal treatment provisions in EU law do not apply to all situations, see Tridimas, Takis, The General Principles of EU Law, 2006, p. 41.

or if there is not reasonable proportionality between the means employed and the aim sought to be realized.[1394] The ECJ's case law concerning discrimination based on a person's sexual orientation will be further analyzed below.[1395]

In 2002, the ECJ laid down that the protection against discrimination on the basis of nationality (Art. 18 TFEU) also covered the right to be treated *differently*, for the purpose of safe-guarding diversity.[1396] In the case, the children concerned had dual citizenships (Belgian and Spanish) and the parents wished the children's surname to follow the Spanish rules, even though the family was habitually resident in Belgium.[1397] According to Spanish law, the mother's and the father's (paternal) surnames are to be combined. This request was denied by the Belgian authorities. The Belgian-Spanish children, habitually resident in Belgium, were in a different situation than Belgian children in Belgium. The ECJ found that this constituted discrimination on the basis of the children's nationality.[1398]

Protecting diversity in the Member States is an integral part of the EU. Without respect for diversity in the Member States – for instance, in respect of language, culture and religion, the Union would risk losing its legitimacy and be perceived as a "super state", posing a threat to its Member States' basic values.[1399] As the Swedish EU commissioner Cecilia Malmström has put it: "Diversity is part of the very essence of the Union".[1400]

Literally speaking, the interest in protecting diversity can be interpreted as denoting an obligation for the different Member States to respect each other's family law regulations – including a state's decision to not legally recognize same-sex couples through special family law enactments. However, it is problematic if the concept of diversity is used as an argument not to recognize the rights of same-sex couples, particularly since the Strasbourg Court, as will be developed below, has found such recognition to be a human right under the European Convention of Human Rights.[1401]

1394 Tridimas, Takis, The General Principles of EU Law, 2006, pp. 61 f, where he points out that the prerequisites of "objectively justified" have applied since 1977. See also the references to case law on p. 62, reference 17.

1395 See section 8.2.3.2.

1396 Carlos Garcia Avello v État belge, Case C-148/02.

1397 Carlos Garcia Avello v État belge, Case C-148/02, Para. 34.

1398 Carlos Garcia Avello v État belge, Case C-148/02, Para. 45. A different interpretation can be noted in Grunkin-Paul v Standesamt Niebüll, Case C-353/06. In that case, the ECJ held that the authorities of a Member State, where a child and its parents are nationals, cannot refuse to recognize the surname, which a child born in another Member State has received and has registered in that state. For further analysis concerning this case, see Bogdan, Michael, EG-domstolens och svensk rättspraxis i internationell privat- och processrätt 2006–2008, SvJT 2010, p. 40.

1399 This will be further analyzed in section 8.4.

1400 Cecilia Malmström, Presentation at the Conference "Youth Perspectives on Security, Peace and Democracy, Gothenburg, 25 May 2007. Retrieved at http://regeringen.se/sb/d/8603/a82935. Accessed 11 November 2010.

1401 See sections 8.3.2.1, 8.3.4.2 and 8.3.4.3. See also Jänterä-Jareborg, Maarit, Family Law in the European Judicial Space, 2009, p.53, where she noted that mainstream positions in the

8.2.3.2. *A Few Key Judgments by the ECJ*

A development toward an extended concept of family is visible in the jurisprudence of the ECJ. However, the idea here is not to provide a thorough analysis of the ECJ decisions. This has already been carried out in the legal literature,[1402] but to provide a brief summary of the relevant ECJ case law concerning the legal position of unmarried couples, same-sex couples in particular.

In 1968, in the case of Reed, the ECJ declared that unmarried *different-sex cohabitees* were not to be treated as "spouses" in the sense of the 1968 Regulation. In the case a female UK national had been denied the right to accompany her partner, a Dutch national of the opposite sex, when he moved to the Netherlands to work. A main motivation for the decision by the ECJ was that there was no "general social development which would justify a broad construction [of the term 'spouse']."[1403] The 1968 case of Reed established that the Regulation of 1968 only protected the free movement of spouses.

Thirty years later, in 1998, the situation of *same-sex cohabitees* was subject to legal scrutiny by the ECJ, in the case of Grant v. South West Trains Ltd. In this case, a woman residing in the United Kingdom, employed by a railway company, was refused travel benefits in respect of her female partner with whom she was cohabiting.[1404] Such benefits were granted to the husband or wife of the employee, or to unmarried cohabiting couples of *different sex*. The key question for the ECJ to decide was whether this difference in treatment constituted discrimination based on sex,[1405] in accordance with the aim of the principle of equal pay for men and women.[1406]

European Member States risk taking over, to the detriment of what she calls "modern diversity" in more progressive jurisdictions. However, she notes that the Maruko ruling marks an opposite position.

1402 See, for instance, Toner, Helen, Partnership Rights, Free Movement and EU Law, 2004, Tridimas, Takis, The General Principles of EU Law, 2006, Bell, Mark, Holding Back the Tide? 2004. See also the contributions in Legal Recognition of Same-Sex Partnerships, A Study of National, European and International Law, 2001, pp. 623–689.

1403 Netherlands v. Reed [1986], Para. 15.

1404 Grant v. South West Trains Ltd [1998].

1405 See also P v. S and Cornwall County Council [1996], in which dismissal because of gender reassignment by surgical operation was found to be sex discrimination. In the case, the Court clearly treated the principle of equality as a general principle of Community Law, superior to the provisions in national law. The case shows that the ECJ prioritizes human rights issues: "to tolerate such discrimination would be tantamount, as regards such a person, to a failure to respect the dignity and freedom to which he or she is entitled, and which the Court has a duty to safeguard." This case has been said to open a "Pandora's box" toward further extending the principle of equality to other groups, same-sex couples for instance. See Tridimas, Takis, The General Principles of EU Law, 2006, pp. 104 f.

1406 Such benefits had already been considered as "pay" according to the Court of Justice in Garland v. British Rail Engineering [1982], Para. 9. In the present case, the claim of sex discrimination was based on Art. 119 (now 141) of the EC Treaty. The Directive in question

The ECJ did not consider denying the same-sex cohabitee the (spousal) employment benefit to be sex discrimination, since "[...] travel concessions are refused to a male worker if he is living with a person of the same sex, just as they are to a female worker if she is living with a person of the same sex."[1407] Thus, the ECJ held, male and female employees were in fact treated equally by the railway company, and no sex discrimination was at hand.[1408] The ECJ also considered whether a stable relationship between two persons of the same sex could be considered equal to a stable relationship between a man and a woman. In the opinion of the applicant (Grant), same-sex and different-sex couples were being treated equally in many European jurisdictions, and the ECJ should, as a result, also treat them equally. Nevertheless, also in this respect the ECJ ruled against Grant and in favor of the railway company. More precisely, the ECJ held that only a few Member States had regulated same-sex partnerships in a manner equivalent to marriage. Instead most countries treated them as equivalent to unmarried cohabitee relationships to a limited extent, or did not recognize them at all. The ECJ also referred to decisions by the Strasbourg Court, according to which same-sex couples did not enjoy protection of their "family life". In summary, because of the lack of a general consensus among the Member States in respect of same-sex unions, employers were not obliged to treat same-sex and different-sex stable relationships equally in 1998.[1409]

The decision in the Grant case has been frequently discussed in the legal literature. Some have criticized the ECJ for its reluctance to recognize the rights of same-sex couples.[1410] Others find the outcome of the Grant Case motivated with reference to the lack of a general consensus in Europe.[1411] Another aspect to consider in this context is that the traditional scope of the EC law originally focused on economic cooperation – not fundamental rights. The EC Treaty did not start out as a human rights instrument and surely the drafters of the EC Treaty did not intend to include a prohibition against discrimination of same-sex couples. This might have contributed to making the ECJ disinclined to extend

was the European Directive No. 76/207 of 9 February 1976 on the equal treatment of men and women with regard to the working conditions.

1407 Grant v. South West Trains Ltd [1998], Para. 27.

1408 Grant v. South West Trains Ltd [1998], Para. 28.

1409 Grant v. South West Trains Ltd [1998], Paras 29–36.

1410 Toner, Helen, Partnership Rights, Free Movement and EU Law, 2004, p. 152, Koppelman, Andrew, The Miscegenation Analogy in Europe, or, Lisa Grant meets Adolf Hitler, 2004, p. 623 and Ytterberg, Hans, All Human Beings Are Equal, but Some Are More Equal than Others, 2003, p. 5.

1411 See, for instance, Terrett, Steve A Bridge too Far? 1998, p. 506, where he argues that although he regrets the outcome of the case, based on the idea that the ECJ could have found the case to fall within the scope of sex discrimination. Nevertheless, he points out that "it is submitted that it is not at Europe's doorstep that the ultimate culpability can be laid". Instead, the Member States are required to take action to prohibit discrimination.

the treaty's substantive scope in such a dynamic manner.[1412] It can be mentioned that, as a result of the debate and close media coverage of the case in Great Britain, South West Trains felt impelled to repeal the provision disfavoring same-sex couples, in spite of the fact that the European Court had ruled in their favor.[1413]

In 2001, for the first time, the ECJ was faced with problems relating to the institution of registered partnership. In the case, a Swedish official (D) who was working at the European Council had registered a partnership with another man in Sweden. When he applied for a household allowance, in accordance with the Council's Staff Regulations, his application was denied because such allowance was only granted to a married, widowed, divorced or legally separated official.[1414] It can be mentioned that also *unmarried* officials with family responsibilities could be granted the allowance, but D did not apply for the allowance as an unmarried official.[1415]

The question for the ECJ to decide was whether or not a partnership registered in Sweden should be considered equal to a marriage according to EU law in the context of the Staff Regulations.[1416] D argued that family law definitions fall within the Member States' exclusive field of competence and should, as a result, be determined according to national law – not according to autonomous interpretations of the EU.[1417] The ECJ did not agree and dismissed the appeal, having established that the term "marriage" (as opposed to registered partnership) in all Member States was defined as a relationship between a man and a woman.[1418] The ECJ based its ruling on the prevailing situation in the Member States seen as a whole, also meaning an autonomous understanding of the concept of marriage. From this point of view, registered partnership could not be considered equal to marriage.[1419]

1412 Koppelman, Andrew, The Miscegenation Analogy in Europe, or, Lisa Grant meets Adolf Hitler, 2004, p. 632. See also Helfer, Laurence, International Decisions: Grant v. Southwest Trains Ltd, 1999, p. 203.

1413 Pintens, Walter, Europeanisation of Family Law, 2003, p. 22.

1414 Article 1(2) of Annex VII to the Staff Regulations of Officials of the European Communities. See D and Kingdom of Sweden, [2001].

1415 Speculations have been made as to why D refrained from claiming allowance on this ground, one such idea being that the principle of the matter – gaining recognition of the registered partnership as equal to marriage – was the primary aim, not actually gaining the allowance. See Bogdan, Michael, Registered Partnerships and EC Law, 2003, pp. 171 f.

1416 The question of whether non-recognition of D's legal status was contrary to the principle of the free movement of workers was not answered, since this aspect was raised too late in the proceedings. Also the question of if denying the allowance was discriminatory as it obstructed the free movement of workers within the Union was raised too late in the proceedings and could, as a result, not be taken into account by the ECJ.

1417 D and Kingdom of Sweden, [2001], Para. 29. See also Bogdan, Michael, Registered Partnerships and EC Law, 2003, pp. 171 f.

1418 D and Kingdom of Sweden, [2001], Paras. 1 and 50–51.

1419 Bogdan, Michael, Registered Partnerships and EC Law, 2003, p. 173.

D also claimed that his right to the protection of his civil status had been violated in a way which constituted discrimination, through the so-called country of origin principle.[1420] According to him, the "country of origin principle" was to be interpreted to cover the civil status of the citizens, as established in national law, and his civil status should be respected at European level. The ECJ rejected this ground without further explanation. An explanation in this respect would have been clarifying.[1421] A policy to strive toward a "principle of recognition" in the union was adopted in 1999,[1422] and continues to have priority in regard to the Union's judicial cooperation in civil matters.[1423] D also argued that denying him the allowance was discriminatory as it contradicted the rules on equal pay for men and women. The Court found that no discrimination had taken place, since both men and women were eligible for the benefit.[1424] In the opinion of the Attorney General, married couples and registered partners were not comparable, as a result of the differences *"in nature"*.[1425]

The ECJ's interpretation of the principle of equal treatment in the context of sexual orientation has been criticized for being too narrow. It reflects the Member States' difficulties to agree on the scope of certain fundamental rights, especially when dealing with national perceptions of moral and cultural values.[1426] Autonomous interpretations by the ECJ therefore risk "stagnating" the legal development at the EU level, since such interpretations might be understood as an infringement of the Member States' national and cultural diversity.[1427] It can be mentioned that in 2004, the staff regulations were revised to include registered partnerships where permitted in the state's domestic law. D's situation was thus automatically covered.

In 2008, the ECJ delivered a ruling in the Maruko case, which most likely has made the principle issues in the D ruling outdated.[1428] In the new case, a surviving German "registered partner" had been denied occupational survivor's

---

1420 In Case C-120/78 (the Cassis de Dijon case) a general principle was established according to which goods allowed in one Member State shall also be allowed in the other Member States. In the Case of D and the Kingdom of Sweden, an attempt to apply this principle also to a person's civil status was made.

1421 This has been noted in the literature. See Bogdan, Michael, Registered Partnerships and EC Law, 2003, p. 173.

1422 COM (2004/0401) final, Communication from the Commission to the Council and the European Parliament – Area of Freedom, Security and Justice: Assessment of the Tampere programme and future orientations {SEC (2004)680 et SEC (2004)693}.

1423 COM (2005/0184) final, Communication from the Commission to the Council and the European Parliament – The Hague Programme: Ten priorities for the next five years The Partnership for European renewal in the field of Freedom, Security and Justice.

1424 D and Kingdom of Sweden, [2001], Para. 46.

1425 Opinion of Advocate General Mischo, delivered on 22 February 2001, D and Kingdom of Sweden v. Council of the European Union, Para. 87, with reference to the outcome of the Grant Case, where same-sex cohabitation was not considered as equivalent to marriage.

1426 Bell, Mark, Anti-Discrimination Law and the European Union, 2002, p. 22.

1427 See section 8.4.

1428 Tadao Maruko v. Versorgungsanstalt der deutschen Bühnen [2006].

pension in respect of his deceased male partner, since only spouses were included in the occupational scheme. The legal question for the ECJ to decide was whether or not this constituted sexual orientation discrimination as regards pay, in breach of the Employment Directive of 2000.[1429] The ECJ found that the pension benefit constituted "pay", and that treating registered partners differently than spouses constituted direct discrimination according to the Directive,[1430] provided that marriage and registered partnership were equivalent according to German domestic law.[1431] Whether or not this was the case in respect of survivor's pension was left to German courts to decide.

Because of the Maruko ruling, the Court's reasoning in the Case of D no longer seems to be relevant. The Maruko case clearly takes into account the legal position of same-sex unions in German domestic law. However, protection against discrimination according to the Maruko case still depends on the content of the legislation in the concerned Member State. Also the requirement, that the two institutions (marriage and the institution reserved for formalized same-sex unions) must be equivalent, might lead to difficulties in interpretation for national courts and the ECJ, as a result of the diversity which characterizes the different national registration schemes which encompass same-sex couples.[1432]

Pursuant to the Maruko ruling, a Swedish registered partnership would most likely be considered equivalent to a marriage in matters defined as "pay" under the EU Directive of 2000, since marriage and registered partnership are equivalent under Swedish law from a strictly legal point of view. On the other hand, at least in theory the ideological differences between marriage and registered partnership, discussed in the 2009 Report of the Committee on Civil Affairs, could be claimed to support the interpretation that registered partnership is distinct from marriage in Sweden.[1433] More precisely, in the 2009 report, a motive for opening up marriage to same-sex couples was that having a separate institution reserved for same-sex couples (registered partnership) risked giving the impression that there was a legal ground for treating same-sex and different

[1429] Directive 2000/78/EC of 27 November 2000, establishing a general framework for equal treatment in employment and occupation.

[1430] Directive 2000/78/EC of 27 November 2000, establishing a general framework for equal treatment in employment and occupation, Arts. 1 and 2. A more far-reaching conclusion would have been if the court had declared that denying a person access to a pension scheme was indirect discrimination given that the person could not marry according to substantive national law, which was the Court's reasoning in Case C-117/01. Indirect discrimination in the sense of the Directive is defined as: "the application of a uniform condition or requirement which has a disproportionate and unjustified adverse impact on one sex", see Para. 6. If such an approach had been chosen in the present case, any legal system without a special "marriage-like" institution for same-sex couples wishing to formalize their relationship could be guilty of indirect discrimination.

[1431] Tadao Maruko v. Versorgungsanstalt der deutschen Bühnen, [2006], Paras 60 and 72.

[1432] See Saez, Macarena, Same sex marriage, same sex cohabitation, and same sex families around the world: Why "same" is so different? 2010, pp. 1–49. See also section 9.1.1 below.

[1433] Report of the Committee on Civil Affairs, (Civilutskottet) (2008/09:CU19), 11.

sex formalized relationships differently.[1434] In other words, it could be argued that a couple choosing not to convert their partnership into a marriage has made a deliberate ideological choice to be registered partners and not spouses, and from this point of view, treating them differently than spouses under the Directive of 2000 does not constitute discrimination based on sexual orientation.

However, for the most part in Sweden, a registered couple who has not transformed their partnership into a marriage has most likely refrained from doing so primarily for practical reasons, and because they consider the two institutions to be equivalent, which they are from a legal point of view.[1435] Also the upheaval of the Registered Partnership Act can be seen as signaling that the aim of the Swedish legislator is to treat same-sex and different-sex formalized relationships equally, and not to create or maintain two separate legal institutions. In respect of couples who registered their partnership in Sweden prior to 1 May 2009, and who have chosen not to convert their partnership into a marriage, the Swedish Registered Partnership Act continues to give rise to the same legal effects as a marriage.

8.2.4. THE CHARTER OF FUNDAMENTAL RIGHTS OF THE EUROPEAN UNION

8.2.4.1. Background – Drafting and Promulgation

The European Union was established in 1992, through the enactment of the Treaty of Maastricht, which entered into force in 1993.[1436] Along with the Treaty of Maastricht came the three-pillar system. Issues previously covered by the EC Treaties (the EEC and EURATOM Communities) were sorted under the first pillar, the most comprehensive and "supranational" one.[1437] The second and third pillars were based on interstate cooperation in fields such as foreign security policies, police matters, criminal law, civil law and private international law. Three treaties of special interest here have been adopted since the establishment of the European Union, namely the Treaty of Amsterdam in 1997,[1438] the Treaty of Nice in 2000[1439] and the Treaty of Lisbon in 2009.[1440]

1434 Report of the Committee on Civil Affairs, (Civilutskottet) (2008/09:CU19), 11.

1435 Jänterä-Jareborg, Maarit, Sweden: The Same-Sex Marriage Reform with Special Regard to Concerns of Religion, 2010, p. 1508.

1436 The Maastricht Treaty, Provisions amending the Treaty establishing the European Economic Community with a view to Establishing the European Community, 7 February 1992.

1437 Jänterä-Jareborg, Maarit, Mot en europeisk (internationell) familjerätt, 2001/02 pp. 48–74 (p. 50 in particular). The term "supranational" is here used to describe situations when decisions are made by the international institutions, not the individual Member States as such.

1438 The Treaty of Amsterdam, amending the Treaty on European Union, the Treaties Establishing the European Communities and Certain Related Acts, Amsterdam, 2 October 1997.

1439 The Treaty of Nice, amending the Treaty on European Union, the Treaties establishing the European Communities and Certain Related Acts, Nice, 26 February 2001. The Treaty of Nice entered into force on 1 February 2003.

1440 The Treaty of Lisbon amending the Treaty on European Union and the Treaty establishing the European Community, signed at Lisbon, 13 December 2007.

When the Treaty of Amsterdam was enacted, issues relating to judicial cooperation regarding civil matters in cross-border situations – including family law – were moved to the "supranational"[1441] first pillar, and were thus emphasized as a prioritized area from the perspective of the European Union.[1442]

In turn, the Treaty of Nice dealt primarily with institutional issues and reformed the decision making system, mainly in the Council, but also in other EU institutions. The Treaty of Nice was criticized for decreasing the democratic aspects of the Union because of complicated rules on decision making. To come to terms with this problem, in 2004, the Member States presented a proposal for a more efficient constitutional treaty, the so-called Treaty of Lisbon.[1443] The Lisbon Treaty was signed by the EU Member States on 13 December 2007 and entered into force on 1 December 2009. It placed human rights issues in a prominent position in the Union, by making the Charter of Fundamental Rights legally binding.[1444] The Charter establishes systematically the general principles of EU law, in a catalogue wider than the ECHR, through more detailed rights of integrity of persons.[1445] However, the EU has initiated negotiations with the Council of Europe on the issue of EU acceding to the ECHR as a contracting "State". Once this accession has been finalized, EU citizens will be able to initiate proceedings against European Union bodies on alleged violations of the ECHR.[1446]

1441 The term supranational means that decisions are made by the international institutions, not the individual Member States.

1442 Stalford, Helen, Concepts of Family under EU Law, 2002, p. 410. The Treaty of Lisbon abolished the three pillar system.

1443 The Treaty of Lisbon amending the Treaty on European Union and the Treaty establishing the European Community, signed at Lisbon, 13 December 2007. The Treaty took the work initiated by the Treaties of Amsterdam and Nice one step further, enhancing the democratic principles of the Union by introducing more qualified majority voting in the Council, and increased the participation of the European Parliament in the legislative process, by introducing more co-decision making between the Council and the Parliament. Moreover, the three pillar structure was abolished.

1444 However, the Charter does not apply fully to the United Kingdom, Poland, and the Czech Republic, who have "opted-out" of it.

1445 Hartley, TC, The Foundations of European Community Law, 2007, p. 143. The Charter, more precisely, aims at strengthening the position of the individual in relation to the EU institutions and decreasing bureaucracy. See also Sumner, Ian, The Charter of Fundamental Rights of the European Union and Sexual Orientation, 2004, p. 869. See also McCrudden, Christopher, The New Concept of Equality, 2003, p. 8.

1446 See COM (2010) final, communication form the Secretary-General of the European Commission to the Secretary-General of the Council of the European Union, 21 October 2010, 15319/10. (However, this can be expected to take several years).

8.2.4.2. Non-Discrimination and the Right to Marry and to Found a Family: The Charter and the ECHR Compared

The Charter contains a chapter (3), which is headed "Equality". In Art. 20 the general principle that "everyone is equal before the law" is laid down. The protection against discrimination is established in Art. 21, providing a prohibition against discrimination on numerous grounds.[1447] Unlike the ECHR (Art. 14), the Charter (Art. 21) explicitly mentions sexual orientation in the specified grounds, which offer protection when an individual exercises rights protected by the EU Treaties in relation to the European Union. As pointed out by Ian Curry-Sumner, Art. 21 of the Charter is the first provision, implemented at European level, which places discrimination on the basis of sexual orientation on an equal footing with other grounds for discrimination.[1448]

The Charter Art. 21: Prohibition of Discrimination	The ECHR Art. 14: Prohibition of Discrimination
"Any discrimination based on any ground such as sex, race, colour, ethnic or social origin, genetic features, language, religion or belief, political or any other opinion, membership of a national minority, property, birth, disability, age or sexual orientation shall be prohibited."	"The enjoyment of the rights and freedoms set forth in this Convention shall be secured without discrimination on any ground such as sex, race, colour, language, religion, political or other opinion, national or social origin, association with a national minority, property, birth or other status."

The right to marry and to found a family is protected under Art. 9 of the Charter and Art. 12 of the ECHR. In the wording of Art. 9 of the Charter, the distinction between, on the one hand, the right to marry and, on the other hand, the right to found a family is clarified compared to the wording in the ECHR. However, in the jurisprudence of the Strasbourg Court, marriage and procreation are also dealt with as two separate issues.[1449]

1447 Bell, Mark, Anti-Discrimination Law and the European Union, 2002, p. 24. The situation of same-sex couples is focused on.

1448 Sumner, Ian, The Charter of Fundamental Rights of the European Union and Sexual Orientation, 2004, p. 883.

1449 See section 8.3.3.2.

The Charter Art. 9	The ECHR Art. 12
"The right to marry and the right to found a family shall be guaranteed in accordance with the national laws governing the exercise of these rights."	"Men and women of marriageable age have the right to marry and to found a family according to the national laws governing the exercising of this right."

The revised wording of Art. 9 of the Charter (compared to the wording of Art. 12 of the ECHR) is not merely of linguistic significance, but also a deliberate liberalization aimed to cover situations when national law recognizes other arrangements than marriage as a basis for family formation.[1450] In spite of the more open wording of Art. 9 of the Charter, compared to Art. 12 of the ECHR, the Charter does not grant same-sex couples a right to marry. However, in the preamble to the Charter it is laid down that it is necessary to strengthen the protection of fundamental rights, taking into account, inter alia, changes in society, and the purpose is to open up for a wide scope of application, if the national law provides for this.[1451]

During the last decade, as will be illustrated below, a development toward recognizing same-sex couples' right to a formalized relationship scheme became visible in the jurisprudence of the Strasbourg Court. Against this background, including same-sex couples in human rights provisions under the Charter and the ECHR, dealing with the rights to marry and to found a family, may not be unrealistic a few years from now.

8.3. HUMAN RIGHTS PURSUANT TO THE ECHR

8.3.1. THE COURT AND THE CONVENTION IN BRIEF

The European Court of Human Rights, situated in Strasbourg (the Strasbourg Court) is an important actor on the European human rights arena, protecting the individuals' rights in relation to the state, through its interpretations of the 1950 European Convention of Human Rights (the ECHR or the Convention). The ECHR consists of the basic Convention and its seven additional Protocols.[1452]

1450 See, for instance, Christine Goodwin v. The United Kingdom, Strasbourg, 11 July 2002, Application no. 28957/95, where a reference was made to Art. 9 of the Charter.

1451 Draft Charter of Fundamental Rights of the European Union – Text of the explanations relating to the complete text of the Charter as set out in CHARTE 4487/00 CONVENT 50, see Para. 4.

1452 Protocol numbers: 1, 4, 6, 7, 11, 12 and 13 Most aspects of the additional protocols have been inserted in protocol 11. Full text available at www.echr.coe.int/NR/rdonlyres/D5CC24A7-

States that have chosen to accede to the ECHR – and to some or all of its additional Protocols – are obligated, according to international law, to respect the fundamental human rights of the Convention, not only in respect of the country's own citizens, but also in respect of foreign nationals abiding on its territory and belonging to its jurisdiction.[1453]

In Sweden, the obligation to respect the ECHR is laid down in the Instrument of Government.[1454] Thus the ECHR has special legal status in Sweden, meaning that no legislation which is in conflict with the Convention can be adopted.[1455] However, this does not mean that the ECHR should necessarily be given precedence over Swedish constitutional law, should a conflict of interests arise in this respect. However, in practice, the Swedish national courts have shown an inclination to give the Convention precedence.[1456] It can be noted that the ECHR will become directly applicable at EU level, in addition to the EU Charter, once the EU accedes to the Convention and the Convention enters into force in relation to the EU.[1457]

When studying a changing view on the family concept in the jurisprudence of the Strasbourg Court, three articles of the ECHR are of special interest, namely Art. 8 (the right to respect for private and family life), Art. 12 (the right to marry) and Art. 14 (the prohibition against discrimination).

8.3.2. THE RIGHT TO RESPECT FOR PRIVATE AND FAMILY LIFE (ART. 8)

1. *Everyone has the right to respect for his private and family life, his home and his correspondence.*
2. *There shall be no interference by a public authority with the exercise of this right except such as is in accordance with the law and is necessary in a democratic society in the interests of national security, public safety or the economic well-*

DC13-4318-B457-5C9014916D7A/0/EnglishAnglais.pdf. Accessed 20 September 2010. A varying number of States have chosen to accede to each additional Protocol.

1453 ECHR Art. 1.

1454 Regeringsformen Chapter 2, Section 23.

1455 Lag (1994:1219) om den europeiska konventionen angående skydd för de mänskliga rättigheterna och de grundläggande friheterna. Sweden ratified the ECHR in 1953, but no incorporation into Swedish law was made at that point in time, which gave rise to uncertainty among the Swedish courts in respect of the legal status of the Convention. See Danelius, Hans, Mänskliga rättigheter i europeisk praxis, 2007, p. 34.

1456 If the Convention needs to be incorporated into national law or applies directly depends on if the legal system is monistic or dualistic. About this distinction: See Danelius, Hans, Mänskliga rättigheter i europeisk praxis, 2007, pp. 33 f. See also the case of Åke Green, Decision by the Supreme Court, NJA 2005 p. 805, where EU law was given supremacy over national Swedish law.

1457 COM (2010) final, communication from the Secretary-General of the European Commission to the Secretary-General of the Council of the European Union, 21 October 2010, 15319/10.

being of the country, for the prevention of disorder or crime, for the protection of health or morals, or for the protection of the rights and freedoms of others.

8.3.2.1. *Private Life and Family Life – A Distinction*

Article 8 distinguishes between the concepts of "private life" and "family life". The protection of a couple's "family life" is more extensive than the protection of a couple's "private life".[1458] The distinction is of importance in discrimination cases. A same-sex couple enjoying "family life" would be comparable to a different-sex couple, and any differential treatment, as a result, would then risk being found discriminatory pursuant to Art. 14. This is not the case if the same-sex couple is merely enjoying "private life", since the situations are not "comparable".[1459]

How to define "family life" according to the ECHR, however, is up to the Strasburg Court to determine.[1460] It should be emphasized that the rights to family life and private life are not absolute, but can be interfered with if this is in accordance with the law and considered necessary in a democratic society (see Art. 8, Para. 2, quoted above).

Generally, the States' margin of appreciation is wide in respect of family law. The basic idea is that national courts often have more insight in the circumstances in the individual case and, as a result, are better equipped to deliver a fair judgment.[1461] Moreover, family law often deals with policy issues of special importance to the Member States' legal cultures and traditions.[1462] From this perspective, the margin of appreciation is a tool for respecting and safeguarding the diversity in the Member States. However, in respect of difference in treatment because of sex or sexual orientation, the Strasbourg Court has declared that the margin of appreciation afforded to the Member States is narrow. In these situations, the principle of proportionality requires that the measure chosen is suited for realizing the aim sought *and* that exclusion of a certain category of persons – for instance same-sex couples – is necessary to achieve that aim.[1463]

1458 See Toner, Helen, Partnership Rights, Free Movement and EU Law, 2004, p. 85.

1459 See X and Y v. United Kingdom, 1983, as analyzed by: Wintermute, Robert, Strasbourg to the Rescue? 2004, pp. 714 f. See also section 8.3.2.3 below.

1460 Many rights affect the private sphere, sometimes making different articles difficult to keep apart. Danelius, Hans, Mänskliga rättigheter i europeisk praxis, 2007, pp. 301 f.

1461 Danelius, Hans, Mänskliga rättigheter i europeisk praxis, 2007, p. 48.

1462 Danelius, Hans, Mänskliga rättigheter i europeisk praxis, 2007, p. 48.

1463 Karner v. Austria, 2003, Para. 41, and P.B. and J.S. v. Austria, 2010, Para. 42. See also section 8.3.4.1 below.

8.3.2.2. Unmarried Different-Sex Couples and Protection of Family Life

It is undisputed that *different-sex spouses* are included in the term "family life", irrespective of whether or not they are actually living together.[1464] In 1985, the Court found that *unmarried cohabiting couples* enjoyed protection of their "family life" in accordance with Art. 8.[1465] In the case, an Irish man was unable to marry the woman with whom he had been living the past 15 years, since he was already married to another woman and Irish marriage regulation did not permit divorce at that time. The couple even had a child together. The Strasbourg Court established that: "In the present case, it is clear that the applicants [...] constitute a "family" for the purposes of Art. 8. They are thus entitled to its protection, notwithstanding the fact that their relationship exists outside marriage."[1466] However, the Strasbourg Court underlined that: "Article 8 cannot be interpreted as imposing an obligation to establish a special regime for a particular category of unmarried couples".[1467] In other words, the unmarried family unit enjoyed protection in general and was entitled to the same social benefits as a married couple, but the Irish state was not obliged to legally recognize unmarried cohabitation in a special act.

Other factors which the Court has taken into account when determining if a relationship between two unmarried persons of different sex constitutes family life are the stability of the relationship and the intentions of the parties. In other words, Art. 8 (family life) is more likely to be found applicable if the relationship has lasted for a long time and if the couple has joint finances.[1468] *De facto* cohabitation is another important, but not necessarily decisive, factor when determining if an unmarried couple falls under the scope of Art. 8.[1469] A child born to unmarried cohabiting parents is *ipso jure* a part of the family from birth, irrespective of whether or not the parents are still together.[1470]

1464 Provided it is not a marriage of convenience, for the purpose of immigration, see Toner, Helen, Partnership Rights, Free Movement and EU Law, 2004, p. 80.

1465 Johnston and Others v Ireland, 1986. www.religlaw.org/template.php?id=173. Accessed 20 September 2010. See also Danelius, Hans, Reflections on some Important Judgments of the European Court of Human Rights Regarding Family Life, 2004, pp. 155 f.

1466 Johnston and Others v. Ireland, 1986, Para. 56.

1467 Johnston and Others v. Ireland, 1986, Para. 68.

1468 Toner, Helen, Partnership Rights, Free Movement and EU Law, 2004, p. 81. See also Sumner, Ian, The Charter of Fundamental Rights of the European Union and Sexual Orientation, 2004, p. 876 and Wintermute, Robert, Strasbourg to the Rescue? 2004, pp. 721–723.

1469 Toner, Helen, Partnership Rights, Free Movement and EU Law, 2004, p. 81, with reference to relevant case law on this topic.

1470 Holdgaard, Marianne, Family Life and Transsexuals, 2004, p. 283.

8.3.2.3. Same-Sex Partnerships: Family Life Instead of Private Life

In two cases in 2010, both involving complaints by same-sex couples against Austria, the Strasburg Court established that same-sex couples qualify as enjoying "family life" under Art. 8 of the Convention, namely in Schalk and Kopf v. Austria and P.B. and J.S. v. Austria.[1471] Before the judgment in Schalk and Kopf v. Austria, same-sex relationships had in the Court's jurisprudence only enjoyed protection as "private life" – not "family life."[1472]

As mentioned above, the distinction between family life and private life is essential for the level of protection guaranteed. Prohibitions against homosexual sexual acts in national legislation have been found to violate the protection of *private life*,[1473] but the right to respect for *family life* is much more far-reaching, inter alia encompassing a right for the family members to live together[1474] and an obligation for the national legislator to protect the family in domestic family law.[1475] Furthermore, the recognition of same-sex partners as a "family" pursuant to Art. 8 includes an obligation for the national legislators to guarantee the same social benefits as those applicable to unmarried cohabiting couples of different sex.[1476] These two cases and their impact on the legal development in respect of same-sex couples will be discussed in sections 8.3.4.2 and 8.3.4.3 below, when the right to marry and the prohibition against discrimination have been accounted for.

8.3.3. THE RIGHT TO MARRY AND FOUND A FAMILY (ART. 12)

> Men and women of marriageable age have the right to marry and to found a family, according to the national laws governing the exercise of this right.

8.3.3.1. Marriage: A Union Restricted to a Man and a Woman

The right to marry and found a family are closely connected to the right to family life, laid down in Art. 8. So far, the right to marry according to the ECHR has

1471 Schalk and Kopf v. Austria, 24 June 2010 and P.B. and J.S. v. Austria, 22 July 2010.

1472 See also Sumner, Ian, The Charter of Fundamental Rights of the European Union and Sexual Orientation, 2004, p. 876 and Wintermute, Robert, Strasbourg to the Rescue? 2004, pp. 714–718. In Karner v. Austria (in 2003), this question was left open.

1473 Dudgeon v. United Kingdom, 1981, Norris v. Ireland, 1988, Modinos v. Cyprus, 1993 and A.D.T. v. United Kingdom, 2000. See also www.homo.se/o.o.i.s/2711. Accessed 20 September 2010.

1474 However, Art. 8 does not guarantee rights of immigration, see Abdulaziz v. UK 1985. See also Wintermute, Robert, Strasbourg to the Rescue? 2004, p. 715.

1475 Danelius, Hans, Mänskliga rättigheter i europeisk praxis, 2007, p. 320.

1476 Danelius, Hans, Mänskliga rättigheter i europeisk praxis, 2007, p. 320.

been reserved for different-sex couples and has not included same-sex couples.[1477] Interpreting Art. 12 to include also same-sex couples has been claimed to contradict the wording of the article, which refers to "men and women".[1478] However, the wording as such, although the drafters only had different-sex couples in mind, does not necessarily exclude same-sex couples. The article establishes that men and women have the right to marry, without explicitly expressing the view that they have the right to marry *each other.*[1479] From this point of view and having regard to the dynamics of the Court's interpretations of the Convention in general, Art. 12 could be reinterpreted in the future to include same-sex relationships without changing its wording.

8.3.3.2. Christine Goodwin v. the United Kingdom

The "traditional" concept of marriage according to the ECHR has been challenged, for instance as a result of transsexuals claiming the right to marry a person of their opposite sex after a gender reassignment. In 2002, in Christine Goodwin v. the United Kingdom,[1480] the Strasburg Court stated that:

> "While it is for the Contracting State to determine inter alia the conditions under which a person claiming legal recognition as a transsexual establishes that gender reassignment has been properly effected [...] the Court finds no justification for barring the transsexual from enjoying the right to marry under any circumstances."[1481]

This statement can be seen as broadening the concept of marriage. The issue is whether it also could open up for a future extension of the right to marry to encompass same-sex couples. Before the judgment in the Goodwin case, the right to marry and found a family was interpreted as one entity according to the ECHR. This outlook on the family, connecting marriage to reproduction, has been challenged as too narrow and traditional. The Court was willing to alter it in order to include transsexuals in the right to marry; a development which, as will be elaborated in section 8.3.3.3, might favor also same-sex couples in future case law.

1477 Toner, Helen, Partnership Rights, Free Movement and EU Law, 2004, p. 87.

1478 See Danelius, Hans, Mänskliga rättigheter i europeisk praxis, 2007, p. 423. See also Christine Goodwin v. The United Kingdom, Strasbourg, 11 July 2002, Application no. 28957/95, Para. 100.

1479 Wintermute, Robert, Strasbourg to the Rescue? 2004, p. 728, where he stresses that without a "European consensus" to recognize same-sex relationships as marriages, the Court is not likely to make such an interpretation.

1480 Christine Goodwin v. The United Kingdom, Strasbourg, 11 July 2002, Application no. 28957/95.

1481 Christine Goodwin v. The United Kingdom, Strasbourg, 11 July 2002, Application no. 28957/95, Para. 103.

It should be underlined that the right to marry has only been applied to transsexuals wishing to marry someone of their *opposite* sex after a gender reassignment, provided that the gender reassignment is recognized under national law.[1482] The European Court of Human Rights has declared that transsexuals who have been assigned a new gender have the right to change the sex on their birth certificate, according to Art. 8. This contributed to increased recognition under national law and to providing access to marriage pursuant to Art. 12.[1483]

8.3.3.3. The Goodwin Case: Impact on Same-Sex Couples' right to Marry?

Extending the right to marry to also include transsexuals does not appear to have been as controversial and debated in the media as extending this right to same-sex couples generally. Why was this so? There are several possible explanations. One explanation is that a transsexual person, who has undergone a gender reassignment and thereafter wishes to marry someone of his or her assigned sex, is in fact complying with the "heterosexual norm" in society. As pointed out by Bea Verschraegen, unless one questions the gender reassignment as such, the marriage is not a deviation from the traditional concept of marriage, but simply a man marrying a woman or vice versa.[1484] From this perspective, allowing transsexuals the right to marry can in fact be seen as a drawback for same-sex couples, underlining the necessity of heterosexuality and thereby strengthening the "traditional" values connected to marriage.[1485]

Another explanation could be that the issue is less debated since the number of transsexuals who have undergone gender reassignment is much lower than the number of homosexuals, making the practical impact of the former more limited. However, in Sweden, a report published by *Socialstyrelsen* (the Swedish National Board of Health and Welfare) in 2010, showed that transgender persons constituted an exposed group in society, in need of various forms of legal

---

1482 Eriksson and Goldschmidt v. Sweden, 1989, a post-operative male to female transsexual was denied the right to marry another woman. It is likely that this standpoint would be upheld should a similar case arise today, same-sex couples still being excluded from the right to marry according to Art. 12.

1483 Sheffield & Horsham v. UK, 1998. See also Holdgaard, Marianne, Family Life and Transsexuals, 2004, pp. 285 and 288.

1484 Verschraegen, Bea, The Right to Private Life and Family Life, the Right to Marry and to Found a Family, and the Prohibition of Discrimination, 2003, p. 210. The same point was made by judge Malinverni, Joined by Judge Kovler, in their concurring opinion in the Schalk and Kopf-case.

1485 Verschraegen, Bea, The Right to Private Life and Family Life, the Right to Marry and to Found a Family, and the Prohibition of Discrimination, 2003, p. 210. Under the new case law (Goodwin v. UK) gender means social gender- not biological (chromosomal) gender, which stresses the importance of the spouses being of *different* sex.

protection.[1486] Hence, legally recognizing their right to marry under the Convention was not meaningless, irrespective of the relatively limited number of persons concerned. In my opinion the argument that a transsexual marrying someone of his or her opposite assigned sex is in fact not perceived to challenge the traditional notion of marriage is a more convincing explanation why the Court decided to apply Art. 12 of the Convention to this group of people in 2002. In other words, it appears to be the "heterosexual" characteristic of marriage that is found worth protecting. Therefore it could be claimed that, through the Goodwin case, the Court in fact only signaled that it recognized gender reassignment as such. This is further underlined by the fact that it has not been considered a violation of Art. 12 to require that a British married couple, who after a gender reassignment of one spouse had become a same-sex couple, divorce and then enter into a civil union with each other. Without this procedure, the assigned gender would not be registered in the UK.[1487]

However, the impact of the judgment in the Goodwin case should not be underestimated. It might also be a first step toward opening the door to recognition of same-sex marriages. In the Goodwin case the European Court of Human Rights stated that it "attaches less importance to the lack of evidence of a common European approach to the resolution of the legal and practical problems posed, than to the clear and uncontested evidence of a continuing international trend in favor not only of increased social acceptance of transsexuals but of legal recognition of the new sexual identity of post-operative transsexuals."[1488]

In other words, clear and uncontested evidence of a European trend to recognize the rights of transsexuals was not necessary for the outcome in the Goodwin case, which in fact contradicted the prevailing law in most European countries. The same line of argument could be applied to recognition of same-sex relationships in future case law based on the ECHR. In 2010, in Schalk and Kopf v. Austria, the Court for the first time declared that same-sex couples enjoy protection of their "family life" pursuant to Art. 8, without a general European consensus.[1489] It is likely that in the future, Art. 12 will also be found applicable, when more states have introduced a gender-neutral marriage concept and "uncontested evidence of a continuing international trend" in this respect is visible. According to the Goodwin case full consensus does not appear to be necessary.

1486 Report by the National Board of Health and Welfare, Transsexuella och övriga personer med könsidentitetsstörningar, rättsliga villkor för fastställelse av könstillhörighet samt vård och stöd. www.socialstyrelsen.se. Accessed 7 November 2010.

1487 Wena and Anita Parry v. United Kingdom, 2005, (declared inadmissible on 28 Nov. 2006.) Schalk and Kopf v. Austria, 2010, Para. 53. See also Wintermute, Robert, Written Comments of Fidh, ICJ, AIRE Centre & Ilga-Europe, concerning Shalk and Kopf v. Austria, Submitted on 26 June 2007, p. 8. The Strasbourg Court dismissed the complaints as manifestly ill-founded.

1488 Christine Goodwin v. The United Kingdom, 2002, Para. 85.

1489 See section 8.3.4.2. The same position was taken in P.B. and J.S. v. Austria, see section 8.3.4.3.

8.3.4. THE PROHIBITION AGAINST DISCRIMINATION (ART. 14)

The enjoyment of the rights and freedoms set forth in this Convention shall be secured without discrimination on any ground such as sex, race, colour, language, religion, political or other opinion, national or social origin, association with a national minority, property, birth or other status.

8.3.4.1. Prerequisites for Application

Firstly, it should once again be underlined that the prohibition against discrimination is not independent of the Convention and the rights protected there. Article 14 is limited to protecting individuals while enjoying their rights under the ECHR (or an additional protocol).[1490] In other words, an infringement of Art. 14 requires that it can be combined with a substantive right laid down in the Convention or in an additional protocol. Nevertheless, the prohibition against discrimination has certain "autonomous features". When Art. 14 is claimed to have been violated, in conjunction with another article in the Convention or one of its additional protocols, the other article does not need to have been infringed upon independently. It is enough that it is found applicable.[1491]

An autonomous prohibition against discrimination has been included in the Convention's twelfth additional protocol, but this has not yet been ratified by all Member States, Sweden for instance being reluctant to do so.[1492] Sweden's reluctance is explained by an ambition to include a general provision allowing differences in treatment as a means of promoting for instance gender-equality, but this aspect was not taken into account in the drafting of the protocol. Moreover, Sweden found the introduction of yet another additional protocol to be a cumbrous way of reaching the desired goal of improved protection against discrimination. Instead, Sweden prefers advocating the drafting of a separate interstate agreement in this respect.[1493] In 2010, the Swedish government declared in a special writ that it still does not intend to accede to the protocol.[1494]

1490 Cameron, Iain, Kirilova Eriksson, Maja, An Introduction to the European Convention on Human Rights, 1995, p. 105.

1491 Cameron, Iain, Kirilova Eriksson, Maja, An Introduction to the European Convention on Human Rights, 1995, p. 105.

1492 Danelius, Hans, Mänskliga rättigheter i europeisk praxis, en kommentar till Europakonventionen om de mänskliga rättigheterna, 2007, p. 437.

1493 Report by the Committee on Foreign Affairs, (2001/02:UU8) Mänskliga rättigheter m.m. länder, områden, enskilda folkgrupper och vissa FN-frågor. The Chamber decided in accordance with the committee report on 21 March 2002.

1494 Government Writ (Regeringens skrivelse) (2005/06:95), April 2010, p. 4. See also Government Bill (Prop 2007/08:95), p. 111, where it was stated that it might be of interest in the future to

The prohibition against discrimination in Art. 14 of the ECHR presupposes that the persons concerned, when claiming a specific ground for discrimination, are in fact in comparable situations with others, and that differential treatment is not found objectively and reasonably justified in the individual case.[1495] In other words: "treatment is discriminatory if it does not pursue a "legitimate aim" or if there is no "reasonable proportionality between the means employed and the aim sought to be realised".[1496] As mentioned above, in respect of discrimination based on, for instance, a person's sexual orientation, the margin of appreciation is narrow and the principle of proportionality requires that the measure chosen is suited for realizing the aim sought and that excluding same-sex couples in a certain context is necessary to achieve that aim.[1497]

The enumeration of grounds for discrimination in Art. 14 is according to its wording exemplifying – not exhaustive. Discrimination on the ground of sexual orientation is covered by the prohibition against discrimination, often in conjunction with Art. 8.[1498] Sexual orientation can also be a secondary issue in claims of discrimination on another ground, for instance on the ground of a person's sex. This was the case in 2003, when the European Court of Human Rights declared that upholding a higher age-of-consent for sexual acts between two men than for sexual acts between a man and a woman, or two women, was sex-discrimination.[1499]

As mentioned above, marriage is especially privileged as a family form under Art. 8, but also unmarried cohabitation can be granted protection as "family life" pursuant to the article. It has been considered legitimate to give spouses

investigate whether or not a general principle of equality should be introduced in Swedish law.

1495 Danelius, Hans, Mänskliga rättigheter i europeisk praxis, en kommentar till Europakonventionen om de mänskliga rättigheterna, 2007, pp. 438–440. The same criterion of "comparable situations" apply in the case law of the ECJ.

1496 E.B. v. France, January 22, 2008, Para. 91.

1497 Karner v. Austria, 2003, Para. 41, and P.B. and J.S. v. Austria, 2010, Para. 42. See section 8.3.2.1.

1498 However, jurisprudence on sexual orientation discrimination and Arts. 8 and 14 is rather uncertain. See Danelius, Hans, Mänskliga rättigheter i europeisk praxis, en kommentar till Europakonventionen om de mänskliga rättigheterna, 2007, pp. 449 f.

1499 L and V v. Austria, 2003. (Two separate violations of the Convention were dealt with in the same case by the Court.) The Court held that: "There is an ever growing European consensus to apply equal ages of consent for heterosexual, lesbian and homosexual relations." See Para. 50. It can be mentioned that the European Court of Human Rights, on the same day, delivered a ruling in a similar case, also dealing with sex-discrimination in respect of Austria. In this case, the man had not contravened the age-limit, but claimed that the age-limit as such had restricted him when exploring his sexuality as a young teenager. He was awarded damages since the age-limit was not objectively and reasonably justified: "What is decisive is whether there was an objective and reasonable justification why young men in the fourteen-to eighteen-year age bracket needed protection against any sexual relationship with adult men, while young women in the same age bracket did not need such protection against relations with either adult men or women." (Para. 41) This was not considered to be the case, the growing European consensus in this respect contributing to the outcome (Para. 42).

preferential treatment over other cohabitation models for instance in respect of inheritance issues as well as social and tax issues.[1500]

Article 14 applies to discrimination on the basis of a person's sexual orientation. There is an abundance of judgments made by the Strasbourg Court dealing with differential treatment because of sexual orientation.[1501] The aim is not to present a thorough analysis of all of these judgments, but to make selective down strokes and focus primarily on recent case law. It can be mentioned that in *Sagueiro da Silva Mouta v. Portugal*,[1502] refusing a father the custody of his daughter because of his sexual orientation was considered discriminatory, pursuant to Art. 14 in conjunction with Art. 8 (the right to private life). In *Karner v. Austria*,[1503] denying a homosexual cohabitee the right to take over a rental apartment upon the death of his partner was also considered as discrimination based on sexual orientation. In *E.B. v. France* it was established that French authorities' refusal to grant permission to a lesbian woman to adopt a child was discriminatory according to Art. 14, in conjunction with Art. 8.[1504]

8.3.4.2. Schalk and Kopf v. Austria

The tendency to protect same-sex relationships under Art. 14, often in conjunction with Art. 8, has been described as "evolving towards a general principle that all differences in treatment based on sexual orientation without a strong justification violate the Convention."[1505] In 2010, the Strasbourg Court took another step in this direction through its decision in Schalk and Kopf v. Austria.

In the case two men living together in a stable relationship in Austria had applied for the right to marry each other. Since same-sex marriage under Austrian law is null and void, their request, filed in 2002, was denied by Austrian authorities and courts. In the end they turned to the Strasbourg Court, claiming that they had been victims of unlawful discrimination because they as same-sex couple were denied the possibility to marry or to have their relationship otherwise recognized by law.[1506] Austria had not yet adopted special legislation

---

1500 Danelius, Hans, Mänskliga rättigheter i europeisk praxis, en kommentar till Europakonventionen om de mänskliga rättigheterna, 2007, pp. 448 f. It can be mentioned that treating two sisters living together differently than spouses or same-sex couples in respect of inheritance tax was not considered discriminatory. See Burden v. The United Kingdom, 29 April 2008 (application no. 13378/05).

1501 See for instance the contributions in: Legal Recognition of Same-Sex Partnerships, A Study of National, European and International Law, 2001, pp. 693–729.

1502 Salgueiro da Silva Mouta v. Portugal, (Application no. 33290/96), 21 December, 1999.

1503 Karner v. Austria (Application no. 40016/98), 24 July, 2003.

1504 E.B. v. France, January 22, 2008 (Application no. 43546/02), 22 January 2008. This Case has most likely overruled the Swedish Decision by the Supreme Administrative Court, RÅ 1993 ref 102.

1505 Wintermute, Robert, Strasbourg to the Rescue? 2004, p. 720.

1506 Schalk and Kopf v. Austria, 2010, Para. 3.

recognizing same-sex couples in 2002. The Austrian Registered Partnership Act was adopted in 2010.[1507]

In its decision, the Strasbourg Court noted that by June 2010, almost half of the Council of Europe's Member States had adopted some kind of registration scheme for same-sex couples.[1508] However, the legal effects attached to the different registration schemes differed in substance, from providing, in principle, the same legal effects as a marriage, to providing relatively limited rights.[1509] Only a handful of the States had gone as far as opening up marriage to same-sex couples. Thus the Court found that there was not yet a *European consensus* on the issue of same-sex marriage, and as a result, denying the same-sex couple access to marriage did not constitute discrimination pursuant to the ECHR.

However, the Court pointed out that the legal development in the field of legal recognition of same-sex couples is evolving rapidly in Europe, moving in the direction toward a European consensus.[1510] Nonetheless, for the time being excluding same-sex couples from the right to marry did not constitute unlawful discrimination, and keeping in mind the prevailing diversity in Europe in respect of the different legislative solutions chosen to recognize same-sex couples and the differences in the legal effects attached to these enactments, Austria should not be reproached for waiting until 2010 to introduce a registered partnership act.[1511] As a result, the claim was dismissed.

Irrespective of this outcome, this judgment established a new outlook, which confirmed for the first time that a stable relationship between two persons of the same sex enjoys protection as "family life" under Art. 8 of the ECHR – not just as "private life". The Court established that in view of the "evolution" that had taken place in the Member States, as well as within the EU, in respect of legal recognition of same-sex partnerships, it would be "artificial to maintain the view that, in contrast to a different-sex couple, a same-sex couple cannot enjoy "family life" for the purposes of Art. 8."[1512]

The recognition of same-sex couples as enjoying "family life" instead of "private life" does not mean that all Member States are required to adopt a gender-neutral marriage regulation. Still, by acknowledging a same-sex couple's right to family life, the Court also qualifies such a couple as family. The significance of qualifying as "family" has been discussed above.[1513] Furthermore, recognizing same-sex couples as family according to Art. 8 is, most likely, a first step toward requiring States to recognize same-sex marriage. Article 12 is closely

---

1507 The Registered Partnership Act (Eingetragene Partnerschaft – Gesetz – EPG), Federal Law Gazette (Bundesgesetzblatt) Part. I, no. 135/2009. The Act entered into force 1 January 2010.

1508 Schalk and Kopf v. Austria, 2010, Paras. 27–29.

1509 Schalk and Kopf v. Austria, 2010, Para. 31.

1510 Schalk and Kopf v. Austria, 2010. See also P.B. and J.S. v. Austria, 2010, Para. 94.

1511 Schalk and Kopf v. Austria, 2010. See also P.B. and J.S. v. Austria, 2010, Para. 106.

1512 Schalk and Kopf v. Austria, 2010, Paras. 93 and 94.

1513 See sections 8.3.2.1 and 8.3.2.3.

connected to the existence of "family life" pursuant to Art. 8, whereas "private life" is not.[1514] The Court found that there is not yet a European consensus on the issue of same-sex marriage. Thus access to marriage still falls within the Member States' margin of appreciation. On the other hand, the Member States' margin of appreciation in this respect will narrow down as the number of States with same-sex marriage regulation increases.

In its judgment in Schalk and Kopf, the Strasbourg Court referred to the Goodwin case, discussed above.[1515] In the Goodwin case, the Court reassessed the traditional notion of marriage so that it no longer had to be determined purely with reference to biology. The inability of a couple to conceive or parent a child – because one of them had undergone a gender reassignment surgery – could not per se motivate exclusion from the right to marry under Art. 12 of the Convention.[1516] In the Goodwin case, extending the right to marry to transsexuals, who after a gender reassignment wished to marry someone of their opposite assigned sex, was found possible because major social changes in the institution of marriage had taken place since the ECHR was adopted in 1950.[1517] A reference was also made to the gender-neutral terminology deliberately used in Art. 9 of the EU Charter, for the purpose of justifying a dynamic interpretation of the concept of marriage under the Charter.[1518] In the Goodwin case the Court observed that there was a continuing international trend toward legal recognition of transsexuals and widespread acceptance in society, thus excluding them from access to marriage violated Art. 12.

In the Schalk and Kopf case, the Court took another step away from the traditional notion of marriage, by acknowledging that a same-sex couple constitutes a family under Art. 8. In accordance with the Goodwin case, full consensus is not necessary in order to extend the definition of marriage in Art. 12. According to the outlook of the Strasbourg Court, the Convention is a living instrument which needs to be adjusted to present-day conditions.[1519] The Strasbourg Court has taken this task seriously. The right to marry pursuant to the EU Charter has been formulated in a gender-neutral manner to enable such an adjustment, and there is a clear trend in Europe to legally recognize same-sex couples, through access either to marriage or to a "marriage-like" institution.[1520]

1514 Verschraegen, Bea, The Right to Private Life and Family Life, the Right to Marry and to Found a Family, and the Prohibition of Discrimination, 2003, p. 206.
1515 Schalk and Kopf v. Austria, 2010, Paras. 51 and 52.
1516 Christine Goodwin v. The United Kingdom, 2002, Para. 98.
1517 Christine Goodwin v. The United Kingdom, 2002, Para. 100.
1518 See section 8.2.5.2 and Christine Goodwin v. The United Kingdom, 2002, Para. 100.
1519 E.B. v. France, 2008, Para. 92 and Christine Goodwin v. The United Kingdom, 2002, Paras. 74–75.
1520 Schalk and Kopf v. Austria, 2010, Paras. 27–34. See also Boele-Woelki, Katharina, The Legal Recognition of Same-Sex Relationships Within the European Union, 2007–2008, pp. 1956 f and Saez, Macarena, Same sex marriage, same sex cohabitation, and same sex families around the world: Why "same" is so different?, 2010, pp. 1–49. However, it can noted that in Bulgaria,

Against this background my prognosis is that it will only be only a matter of time before the Strasbourg Court will find Art. 12 applicable to same-sex couples.[1521]

8.3.4.3. P.B. and J.S. v. Austria

As mentioned above, in the Schalk and Kopf case, the Court established that a same-sex couple enjoys protection of their "family life" under Art. 8 of the Convention. However, in that case, no unlawful discrimination was established due to the fact that their family life could not be formalized through marriage. In P.B. and J.S. v. Austria, however, for the first time, violation of a same-sex couple's family life under Art. 8 was found to constitute unlawful discrimination and damages were awarded to the applicants.

In the case a homosexual man had been denied the right to be covered by his same-sex partner's sickness and accident insurance. According to Austrian insurance law, in force in 1997 when the couple's application was first made, only a close relative or a cohabitee of the opposite sex qualified for insurance coverage.[1522] In 2006, the Austrian insurance law was amended by an additional provision which made it possible for a same-sex couple to be included, either when the same- sex couple was raising a child together, or when one partner was nursing the other in the home. The requirement concerning children did not apply to a different-sex cohabiting couple under Austrian law. In 2007, the rules were amended once again so that the requirement concerning children was applied to different-sex couples as well.[1523]

In the P.B and J.S. case, the Strasbourg Court once again – like in Schalk and Kopf v. Austria – laid down that a same-sex relationship enjoys protection of their "family life" under Art. 8 of the Convention.[1524] In respect of the situation prior to 2006, a majority of the Court – five of the seven judges – found that the Austrian state had failed to present any circumstance which supported that treating same-sex and different-sex couples differently was necessary. As mentioned above, the criterion that the difference in treatment must be necessary is a limitation of the state's margin of appreciation. Since the State had not shown that treating same-sex and different-sex couples differently had been necessary,

---

Estonia and Romania it has been specified in the legislation that marriage is reserved for different-sex couples. See www.fra.europa.eu/fraWebsite/attachments/FRA-LGBT-report-update2010.pdf. (p. 8) Accessed 5 December 2010.

1521 The development in this direction is described by Wintermute, Robert, Written Comments of Fidh, ICJ, AIRE Centre & Ilga-Europe, concerning the Case of Shalk and Kopf v. Austria, Submitted on 26 June 2007, pp. 1–16. See also Wintermute, Robert, Strasbourg to the Rescue? 2004, p. 720.

1522 P.B. and J.S. v. Austria, 2010, Para. 17.

1523 P.B. and J.S. v. Austria, 2010, Paras. 18–20.

1524 P.B. and J.S. v. Austria, 2010, Paras. 28–30.

the same-sex couple in the case had been subject to discrimination on the basis of their sexual orientation.[1525]

The remaining two dissenting judges, however, found that no violation of Art. 14 in conjunction with Art. 8 had taken place prior to 2006, because only a few European jurisdictions had legally regulated same-sex relationships in 1997.

In respect of the situation between 2006 and 2007, although same-sex couples were no longer categorically excluded from insurance coverage, the Court unanimously found that there had been a violation of Art. 14 in conjunction with Art. 8, since different prerequisites applied to same-sex and different-sex couples, without establishing an objectively justifiable ground for the differential treatment.[1526] After 2007, however, when the scope of the insurance law was limited to couples with children only, without distinguishing between same-sex and different-sex couples, the Court unanimously found that the couple was no longer subject to unlawful discrimination, since also same-sex couples can raise children together and then be covered by the insurance law.[1527] The couple was granted compensation from the Austrian state for the violation of their right to protection of family life during 1997–2007.

When the European consensus increases, the States' margin of appreciation, in turn, decreases. As a result, differences based on sexual orientation require particularly weighty reasons in order to be deemed necessary.[1528] In PB v. JS, the same-sex couple was granted economic compensation for the time-period 1997–2007. According to my opinion, the two dissenting judges have a point in questioning whether the Austrian state can be reprimanded for failing to recognize the rights of same-sex couples in the 1990s. At that point in time, the Nordic countries, and a few others, had adopted registered partnership Acts. No State had opened up marriage to same-sex couples. As pointed out in Schalk and Kopf, most States have adopted their partnership laws during the last decade.[1529] It is only during this time that an increasing consensus toward legal rights for same-sex couples has developed, a circumstance which made it possible for the Court to include same-sex couples in the definition of "family life" under Art. 8 of the Convention. Just as the Strasbourg Court argued in the Schalk and Kopf case, it appears questionable to reprimand Austria for not being in the vanguard in the legal development toward recognizing same-sex couples, i.e. to award damages prior to 2006. By 2006–2007, however, as the Court also unanimously stated in its judgment, European consensus had grown strong enough for the Court to establish that the couple had been subject to unlawful discrimination.

1525 P.B. and J.S. v. Austria, 2010, Paras. 40–42.

1526 P.B. and J.S. v. Austria, 2010, Paras. 43–44.

1527 P.B. and J.S. v. Austria, 2010, Paras. 45–50.

1528 P.B. and J.S. v. Austria, 2010, Para. 38, with reference to Karner v. Austria, Para. 36.

1529 Schalk and Kopf, 2010, Para. 30. See for an account of the rapid legal development at national levels concerning same-sex couples, see also Saez, Macarena, Same sex marriage, same sex cohabitation, and same sex families around the world: Why "same" is so different? 2010.

The question remains unanswered as to whether or not the Member States, given the development toward a European consensus to legally recognize the rights of same-sex couples, should be obliged to provide a formalized union (or open up marriage) to same-sex couples. This question is likely to become subject to scrutiny by the Strasbourg Court in the foreseeable future. The fact that the Court in this case found that a violation of Art. 8 in conjunction with Art. 14 had taken place already in 1997 illustrates the above cited evolution "towards a general principle that all differences in treatment based on sexual orientation without a strong justification violate the Convention."[1530] In line with this "general principle", introducing a registration scheme for same-sex couples will most likely soon be required in order to protect the couple's family life under Art. 8.

It does not appear far-fetched to claim that a next step might well be that States will become obligated to grant same-sex couples access to a registration scheme. In such a scenario, the Court's impact on the harmonization of European laws will be considerable. A parallel can here be drawn to the effect that the Marx-case, decided by the Strasbourg Court in 1979, had on the harmonization of European laws, by establishing a new view on the legal position of children born "out of wedlock". Through this case law it was established that treating a child born to unmarried parents differently than a child born to married parents in respect of inheritance rights constituted a violation of Art. 14 in conjunction with Art. 8 of the Convention.[1531]

8.4. SUMMARIZING REFLECTIONS: ACHIEVING EQUALITY AND PRESERVING DIVERSITY – A CONTRADICTION

The rapid development toward legal recognition of same-sex couples that has taken place in Sweden, as well as in many other jurisdictions, is visible also on the EU level. Fundamental rights have been strengthened on the EU level, in particular since the EU Charter became legally binding. Furthermore, if the host state so wishes, the EU has opened up for including same-sex couples in the "family" definition applied to persons when moving across EU borders.

The Strasbourg Court, applied a dynamic interpretation of the family concept in its recent interpretation of Art. 8, in the Shalk and Kopf-case, by including same-sex couples in the notion of "family life", protected by the Convention. This was done without requiring full consensus among the Member States, based on

[1530] Wintermute, Robert, Strasbourg to the Rescue? 2004, p. 720. See section 8.3.4.2.

[1531] See Marckx v. Belgium, 1979. For critical remarks, see Meulders-Klein, Marie-Thérèse, Towards a European Civil Code on Family Law? 2003, pp. 105–117 (p. 112 in particular). See also section 8.4 below.

the principle, developed in the Court's jurisprudence, that there must be weighty reasons to justify differential treatment because of a person's sexual orientation. Otherwise the treatment is not justified.[1532]

When the 2010 judgment in Schalk and Kopf was made, it was noted that only 6 out of the 47 Member States had adopted gender-neutral marriage regulations. Thus, the Court held, there was no convergence of standards regarding same-sex marriage in Europe. Because of the diverse partnership schemes, no such standard could be discerned in this respect either. As argued in section 8.3.4.3, given the development in sexual orientation law in Europe, it can be expected to be just a matter of time before the right of same-sex couples to have their relationship formally recognized is established by the Strasbourg Court. Full consensus was not necessary for the Strasbourg Court to establish a right for transsexuals to marry someone of their opposite assigned sex, and full consensus was not necessary in order to establish that a same-sex couple enjoys protection of their "family life" under Art. 8 of the ECHR. Consequently, full consensus will most likely not be found necessary for the Strasbourg Court to find in future cases that protection of one's family life requires legal recognition through access to a formalized union.

Katharina Boele-Woelki advocates that the ECJ and the Strasburg Court should take on an even more active role and use their judicial authority to oblige the national courts to adopt registration schemes – or same-sex marriage regulation – for same-sex couples.[1533] She points out that legal recognition of same-sex couples has in most jurisdictions been initiated through court proceedings, and underlines that in the European Union, a person's civil status, for instance as "registered partner," should be portable.[1534]

On the other hand, it could be argued that protecting the national and cultural diversity in Europe is also a central goal of the EU, against which the goal of achieving equality must be balanced. This was illustrated in the case concerning the right of children with dual citizenships to follow the Spanish tradition regarding surnames, discussed in section 8.2.3.1. In the case, the ECJ found that the protection against discrimination also covered the right to be treated *differently*, for the purpose of safe-guarding diversity.[1535]

Marie-Thérèse Meulders-Klein has criticized the dynamic interpretation by the Strasbourg Court of the ECHR for creating a "case-by-case pattern of development and an unpredictable piecemeal approach depending on

[1532] See section 8.3.2.1.

[1533] Boele-Woelki, Katharina, The Legal Recognition of Same-Sex Relationships Within the European Union, 2007–2008, p. 1970.

[1534] Boele-Woelki, Katharina, The Legal Recognition of Same-Sex Relationships Within the European 2007–2008, p. 1978.

[1535] Case C-148/02, Carlos Garcia Avello v État belge.

unforeseeable majorities of judges".[1536] Meulders-Klein, has advocated that approximation of laws in Europe should take place on the basis of an open democratic dialogue – not by the Court's power of coercion.[1537] From this point of view, the ECJ – and the Strasbourg Court – cannot be expected to "jump ahead" of the legal development in the Member States and "force" moral values upon them, by obliging Member States to adopt registration schemes for same-sex couples. As illustrated in chapter 6, the notion of marriage as a union reserved for a man and a woman can be linked to religious values and cultural traditions. Changing the law does not necessarily mean that fundamental values change. Instead there is a risk that Member States which are forced to adapt to the standards set by the EU become critical toward the EU for intervening in their domestic matters from a "super state" perspective.[1538]

In my opinion, which is in line with Katharina Boele-Woelki's argumentation above, it is problematic if protecting diversity in the Member States is used as an argument in favor of denying same-sex couples basic rights through access to a registration scheme. Same-sex couples need to have access to a registration scheme in order to be safeguarded mutual rights and duties. The EU has prepared for recognition of same-sex unions, although recognition remains on an "if the host-state-so-wishes" level. The Strasbourg Court, however, has taken this one step further by recognizing that same-sex couples enjoy protection of their "family life" under Art. 8. As argued above, the Strasbourg Court can be expected to rule that introducing a registration scheme for same-sex couples is required.

Whereas the main focus of the EU is the internal market, the Strasbourg Court, deals specifically with protecting human rights under the Convention. Against this background the Strasbourg Court can be expected to have a more proactive and dynamic role in respect of the legal recognition of same-sex couples than the ECJ. However, the free movement of persons is limited if a person's civil status, for instance as registered partner, is not portable when moving to another Member State. As illustrated above, human rights have gradually become prioritized at EU level. Since 2009, the EU has a set of legally binding human rights of its own – the Charter of Fundamental Rights of the European Union. Moreover, the EU will accede to the ECHR and be formally

1536 Meulders-Klein, Marie-Thérèse, Towards a European Civil Code on Family Law? 2003. p. 112.

1537 Meulders-Klein, Marie-Thérèse, Towards a European Civil Code on Family Law? 2003. pp. 117 f.

1538 As mentioned in chapter 4, harmonizing family laws of EU Member States through voluntary harmonization projects – such as the work of the CEFL – which may inspire the national legislators, can contribute to creating a common foundation of values in the EU – a European "identity". This "top-down" approach to harmonization is likely to appeal to both "camps" of thought accounted for above. See section 4.4.2.5. See also Antokolskaia, Masha, Harmonisation of Family Law in Europe, 2006, pp. 16–26, for an account of "bottom-up" harmonization.

bound by the "dynamic" jurisprudence of the Strasbourg Court. When the EU accedes to the ECHR, the two different systems will merge completely.[1539]

In this book I claim that the institution of marriage has a special value, as a symbol of commitment between a couple and as a means for a national legislator to officially signal that a relationship is worthy of social recognition.[1540] For same-sex couples, who have a history of being stigmatized in society, this recognition is especially valuable and can contribute to counteracting negative opinions toward homosexuals. Thus granting same-sex couples access to marriage is an important symbolic issue. For the time being the Strasbourg Court is not likely to "force" Member States to recognize that same-sex couples are equal to married couples, by extending Art. 12 to encompass same-sex couples. However, the Strasbourg Court is likely to oblige States to adopt registration schemes for same-sex couples, and although such schemes cannot match marriage on a symbolic level, they are, nevertheless, an important step on the way.

1539 It can be noted that Art. 52(3) of the Charter states that insofar as rights listed in the Charter correspond with the rights laid down in the Convention, meaning and scope of those rights shall be the same as those laid down by the Convention. It is also stated in the preamble to the Charter that the EU may provide more extensive protection. See also Sumner, Ian, The Charter of Fundamental Rights of the European Union and Sexual Orientation, 2004, pp. 883 f.

1540 See for instance section 9.2.2.

PART IV
CONCLUDING ANALYSIS

9. THE ESSENCE OF MARRIAGE

9.1. MARRIAGE: A DIVERSE AND ELASTIC CONCEPT

9.1.1. DIVERSITY: CHARACTERISTIC FEATURE OF MARRIAGE AND PARTNERSHIP REGULATIONS IN EUROPE IN THE TWENTY-FIRST CENTURY

Marriage is a multifaceted concept. The interests and values considered worth protecting through the marriage regulation have differed over time, and from one country to another in Europe and globally. There is not one uniform understanding of the concept of marriage in Europe today. Marriage varies from functioning in practice as a life-long commitment concluded in the presence of God – through a legally binding religious ceremony or through an additional (legally irrelevant) church blessing of a civil marriage – to a legal contract which can be ended unilaterally at any time. For example, in present-day Sweden divorce is regarded as a unilateral right for each spouse, whereas in Malta, where Catholic values have a significant impact on the marriage regulation, the marriage regulation does not permit divorce. Furthermore, in Sweden fault is totally irrelevant for the outcome of divorce proceedings, but in many continental European countries, on the contrary, fault can still be taken into account in divorce proceedings.

Another example of how diverse the concept of marriage is, is that different marriage regulations, signaling different values, can co-exist *within* a jurisdiction today. In some states in the United States, so-called covenant marriage laws have been introduced as an option to the statutory marriage regulation.[1541] These covenant marriage laws limit the grounds for divorce for the purpose of strengthening marriage. Couples can at the time of the marriage choose to conclude a covenant marriage, or they can transform a statutory marriage into a covenant marriage. There is not just one fixed legal definition of marriage, not in Europe and not even necessarily within a jurisdiction.

The European picture of marriage becomes even more complex if the legal recognition of other marriage-like cohabitation models is taken into account. In

---

[1541] The Covenant marriage laws can be found at www.divorcereform.org/cov.html. Accessed 12 October 2010. Counseling is required prior to concluding a covenant marriage and prior to divorce, in order to ensure that the couple understands the terms. See also Baker, Elisabeth H, et al., Covenant Marriage and the Sanctification of Gendered Marital Roles, 2009, pp. 147–178.

many European countries alternative cohabitation models have been legally regulated, and the marriage regulation has often functioned, in this respect, as a source of inspiration. In Sweden the legal situation of unmarried couples was for the first time subject to legal regulation in 1973. In 1987 "marriage-like" division of property rules, although much more limited than the property division rules attached to marriage, were made applicable to unmarried cohabitees of different sex and of the same sex. Since 1994 in Sweden, there is also the institution of registered partnership, reserved for same-sex couples. In 2009, when marriage was extended to encompass couples of the same sex, the Swedish Registered Partnership Act was repealed and only continues to apply to couples who have not transformed their registered partnership into a marriage. The "trend" to use marriage as a source of inspiration when designing new cohabitation models indicates that the marriage regulation appears to have managed to strike a good balance between, on the one hand, safeguarding equality, and, on the other hand, promoting the autonomy of the individuals concerned.

Furthermore, marriage can even provide different legal effects within a jurisdiction depending on if the couple is of the same sex or of different sex. As Macarena Saez put it in her General Report of 2010 for the eighteenth International Congress of the International Academy of Comparative Law: "there are *marriages* and there are *same-sex marriages.*"[1542] For instance, in Portugal, same-sex couples have access to marriage, but without being able to acquire all of the legal effects of marriage, e.g. in respect of legal parenthood.[1543]

Against the decision taken in a country to open the institution of marriage to same-sex couples for the alleged purpose of achieving equal treatment, it could be argued to be counterproductive to attach more limited legal effects to a marriage between a same-sex couple than to a marriage between a different-sex couple. A marriage without full legal effects risks being regarded as a "second class" marriage of lower dignity and symbolic value than a "real" marriage.[1544] This, in turn, might connote *differential treatment* rather than *equal treatment* of same-sex and different-sex couples. In other words, the public recognition of marriage as providing an official stamp of approval – a symbol of the high quality of the relationship – becomes undermined by connotations to inequality and differential treatment.[1545] It follows that there may be good reasons to first introduce a registered partnership act and then replace it with a gender-neutral marriage enactment only when full equality in respect of legal effects can be included also concerning same-sex spouses. This is also largely the legal development that has taken place in Sweden, the Netherlands and Spain.

1542 Saez, Macarena, Same sex marriage, same sex cohabitation, and same sex families around the world: Why "same" is so different? 2010, p. 2. Emphasis added.

1543 Saez, Macarena, Same sex marriage, same sex cohabitation, and same sex families around the world: Why "same" is so different? 2010, p. 44.

1544 See section 6.6.2.2.

1545 This will be further discussed in section 9.2.2.2.

The legal recognition of same-sex couples in special enactments is becoming more of a rule than an exception in Europe, although the form and function of the enactments differ significantly.[1546] Some European jurisdictions have even introduced a gender-neutral marriage concept.[1547] Because of the diversity in legal approaches to same-sex unions, the Strasbourg Court has not yet interpreted the Convention's Art. 12 – the right to marry – to include same-sex couples. However, the Strasbourg Court has found the consensus in Europe regarding same-sex partnerships to be sufficiently strong to include same-sex couples in the family concept (under Art. 8 of the ECHR).[1548] The diversity that exists in respect of legal approaches to same-sex unions in European jurisdictions is likely to decrease gradually, taking into account the "trend" to legally recognize same-sex unions and the recent position taken by the Strasbourg Court when including same-sex unions in the concept of family. However, just like marriage means different things in Europe today, because the substantive content of the marriage regulations differs from one jurisdiction to another, different legal concepts of "registered partnership" are likely to continue to exist, unless harmonization in this field of substantive family law proves successful. Were a harmonization of substantive laws dealing with same-sex unions to take place in Europe, this would most likely improve the rights of the same-sex couples, facilitate free movement in cross border situations and create predictability concerning such couples' civil status and legal rights.

9.1.2. FLEXIBILITY WITHIN THE SWEDISH CONCEPT OF MARRIAGE – HISTORICALLY AND CONTEMPORARILY

In the previous chapters it has been demonstrated that the Swedish marriage regulation has been reformed several times in the past, in order to match new values in a changing society. Against this background, marriage stands out as a flexible and elastic institution. Marriage regulation has even in part been extended to encompass unmarried couples, through the enactment of property division rules applicable upon separation or death, which have been inspired by the marriage regulation. In 1994, a new institution modeled on marriage was introduced to same-sex couples – registered partnership. It follows from the

---

1546 See Boele-Woelki, Katharina, The Legal Recognition of Same-Sex Relationships Within the European Union, 2007–2008, pp. 1956 f., Saez, Macarena, Same sex marriage, same sex cohabitation, and same sex families around the world: Why "same" is so different? 2010, pp. 1–49 and Schalk and Kopf v. Austria, 24 June 2010, Paras. 27–34.

1547 In November 2010, these states are: the Netherlands, Spain, Belgium, Norway, Sweden and Iceland. Also Luxembourg and Slovenia are preparing gender-neutral marriage enactments. See www.fra.europa.eu/fraWebsite/attachments/FRA-LGBT-report-update2010.pdf. (p. 8) Accessed 5 December 2010.

1548 See section 8.3.2.3.

flexible characteristic of marriage that there, in fact, has never been one clear-cut understanding of the concept of marriage in Sweden.

As illustrated in chapter 2, marriage was not even a uniform concept in Sweden in 1734, when the first comprehensive codification of laws was carried out in Sweden, irrespective of the powerful position that the Church of Sweden enjoyed in Swedish society at that time, and irrespective of the church's ambition to establish one uniform Lutheran understanding of marriage. A certain level of flexibility continued to characterize marriage in Sweden considering that the "incomplete marriages", deriving from old Germanic marriage customs, continued to give rise to legal effects under the 1734 Code.[1549] This flexibility was further developed in 1908, when civil marriage became a general option in Sweden, in addition to the religious marriage ceremony. Through the 1908 enactment, the concept of marriage was extended to encompass two ways of concluding a marriage instead of one, namely marriage concluded in the *civil* and in the *religious* form.

However, the deeply rooted symbolism of marriage could not easily be transferred to a secular counterpart. The difference between the religious and the civil marriage ceremonies was not just a formality. A qualitative difference was observed in the Law Commission Report of 1913. More precisely, the Law Commission pointed out that a marriage concluded in the civil form was sometimes perceived as being less valued than a marriage concluded in the religious form.[1550] This perceived difference was irrelevant from a legal point of view, in the sense that the legal effects of a civil and a religious marriage were identical. Nonetheless, according to the Law Commission, it was urgent to strengthen the symbolic value of the civil marriage ceremony. A semantic solution was proposed to come to terms with the alleged difference in value, namely to introduce the predominantly religious term for the marriage ceremony – *vigsel* – also to the civil marriage ceremony, which had previously been called "giftermål".[1551] The new terminology was introduced in the 1915 Act on Conclusion and Dissolution of Marriage, and this Act was incorporated into the Marriage Code of 1920.

In fact, differences on a symbolic level, because of the flexibility of marriage, appear to have attracted the attention of the Swedish legislator at different points in time, and resulted in deliberate political attempts to mitigate or even diminish the substantive and symbolic differences within the concept of marriage, as well as between marriage and registered partnership.[1552] In 2009, extending the same terminology to cover formalized unions between couples of the same sex and

1549 See section 2.5.4.

1550 Law Commission Report of 1913, p. 282.

1551 Law Commission Report of 1913, p. 282. These terms do not translate into English. See section 3.4.3.2.

1552 The political attempts to charge registered partnership with a special symbolic value have been discussed in section 6.5.1.

couples of different sex was a means of creating equality, since it implied granting same-sex couples access to the symbolic dimension of marriage.

The political aim to implement the principle of equality in the marriage regulation has required a flexible understanding of marriage. Through the Marriage Code of 1920 marriage changed, from a legal perspective, from a patriarchal institution into a union between two equals. As discussed in chapter 3, the 1920 Code created formal equality between the spouses, but it did not strive at changing the division of duties within marriage in practice. In society, married men and women continued to divide duties among themselves in a traditional manner, i.e. men provided the financial income and women took care of the children and the home. Nevertheless, giving the principle of equality between men and women statutory support in the Marriage Code laid the foundation for further implementation of the principle of equality in Swedish law and society during the coming decades.

In the past, the "flexibility" with which the legislator has interpreted concepts relating to marriage has sometimes created tension between the secular and religious understandings of marriage, because law and society have tended to change at a faster pace than the church.[1553] A tension between the secular and the religious concept of marriage can be discerned in connection with the 1920 Marriage Code, more precisely in respect of its focus on equality between husband and wife. In the literature on the sociology of religion it has been pointed out that traditional gender roles have been legitimized by the Church of Sweden on the basis of the story of the Creation, according to which men and women were assigned different roles and responsibilities.[1554] Against this background, representatives of the church have periodically opposed law reforms aimed at creating equality between men and women as being contrary to the Bible.[1555] It follows that the interpretation given to the principle of equality was a sensitive issue in certain ecclesiastical circles long before the legal recognition of same-sex relationships as equal to different-sex relationships was considered. The same-sex marriage reform of 2009 was a fundamental challenge of religious values relating to marriage. Therefore, the decision to marry same-sex couples, taken by the Church of Sweden's General Synod in October 2009, was radical and progressive.[1556] Through this decision the Church of Sweden was among the first religious communities in the world to adopt a gender-neutral marriage concept.[1557]

The tension between the religious and the secular understanding of the concept of marriage is a recurring theme in the Swedish legal development concerning marriage. In chapter 6 it has been suggested that it is not always

1553 See Former Archbishop, K.G. Hammar, Svenska kyrkans utredningar 2005:1, 2004, p. 32.
1554 Bäckström et al., Religious Change in Northern Europe, 2004, pp. 142 f.
1555 Bäckström et al., Religious Change in Northern Europe, 2004, p. 142.
1556 Information about the General Synod of 2009 can be found at the website of the Church of Sweden: www.svenskakyrkan.se/default.aspx?id=586596. Accessed 15 October 2010.
1557 See section 6.3.2.4.

possible to distinguish clearly between the "religious" and the "secular" understandings of marriage, because religious connotations to marriage have become embedded in Swedish culture, expressed as basic values also in society.[1558] Below it will be argued that in connection with the same-sex marriage reform of 2009 these religiously founded values remerged, offering an explanation as to why introducing same-sex marriage was controversial in Sweden.[1559]

9.2. THE ESSENCE OF MARRIAGE: CONTRACT, CIVIL STATUS AND SYMBOLISM

9.2.1. MARRIAGE: FROM CIVIL STATUS TO CONTRACT AND BACK AGAIN

From a legal point of view marriage is substantially a contract, in the sense that each party must agree to enter into it. Furthermore, when two persons consent to marrying each other, they also agree to be covered by the special "package" of legal rules attached to marriage, i.e. the legal consequences of marriage. For the marriage contract to be valid, certain forms prescribed by law need to be fulfilled. The consent of the individuals to contracting the marriage needs to be given orally during a civil or a religious ceremony, which, in turn, needs to be concluded by an authorized (state or church) official. The presence of witnesses is also required to safeguard that the marriage is entered into voluntarily.

However, marriage is no ordinary contract, since it also changes the individuals' civil status. The parties are not entirely free to determine the content of the marriage contract. The state has interfered in the couple's autonomy by designing the package of legal rules attached to marriage, and by determining to what extent the spouses are free to alter the content of the marital "contract" through additional agreements, which deviate from the main rules. Historically in Sweden, as illustrated in chapter 2, the marital status was essential for the survival of the individual in society. There was no welfare state with a social security network for the individual to rely on. Instead the family unit based on marriage provided basic services which are now largely being provided by the state. The marital status was also essential to secure the legitimacy of the offspring, as well as for the acquisition of inter-spousal rights. Since the 1970s, the level of autonomy awarded to the couple in respect of modifying the content of the "marriage contract" has increased, but certain aspects of the marital contract have nevertheless remained indispensible, for instance the spouses' obligation to support each other during marriage. Moreover, the types of couples

1558 See Bäckström, et al., Religious Change in Northern Europe, 2004, pp. 87–98. See also section 9.4.

1559 This will be further developed in section 9.2.

granted access to the marital status has been extended since the 1970s, through a reduction of the impediments to marriage to an absolute minimum – even half-siblings are able to marry in Sweden, upon dispensation by a competent authority from the affinity impediment. The significance of the marital status in Sweden can also be seen as having been, to some extent, "weakened" through the divorce regulation, more precisely through turning divorce into a unilateral right for each spouse, possibly giving rise to connotations of marriage as a union with "revolving doors".[1560]

Furthermore, new cohabitation models – cohabitation without marriage and registered partnership – have become legally recognized and socially accepted. More precisely, certain parts of "the marriage contract" have been made available also to unmarried cohabiting couples and registered partners. For instance, unmarried cohabitees and registered partners have been covered by "marriage-like" property division rules. Also, unmarried couples (same-sex couples and different-sex couples) have been granted access to assisted procreation methods, which illustrates that procreation has been legally detached from the marital status. Moreover, all legal distinctions between children born to married and unmarried (or single) parents have been abolished. These reforms can be seen as "weakening" the importance of the marital status, in the sense that marriage is no longer a necessary requisite for exercising legally recognized family life.

In summary, the law reforms carried out in Sweden since the 1970s, aimed to decrease the impact of moral values expressed in the previous regulation governing marriage, can be seen as having resulted in, to some extent, diminishing the significance of the marital status in society, and instead enhancing the "contractual function" of marriage.[1561] However, I would argue that the gender-neutral marriage enactment of 2009 once again brought focus on the importance of the marital status, and as a result increased its value. The symbolic value of granting same-sex couples access to the marital status was the only issue at stake in connection with the 2009 reform – not acquiring the legal effects of marriage, which the Registered Partnership Act already provided. From this point of view, adopting a gender-neutral marriage concept strengthened the institution of marriage.

9.2.2. THE SYMBOLIC DIMENSION OF MARRIAGE

9.2.2.1. The Purpose of Marriage – Religious Connotations

The same-sex marriage reform of 2009 challenged the traditional view of marriage as a union reserved for one man and one woman. Why was this

1560 See section 4.4.1.
1561 See sections 4.2.4.1, 4.2.4.2 and 5.2.3.2.

controversial in twenty-first century Sweden, where the concept of marriage, as illustrated above, has proven quite "elastic" in the past? I have argued that the notion of marriage as a heterosexual union can be traced back to the story of the Creation, which links marriage to procreation. Swedes are, generally speaking, regarded as "secularized" and do not actively participate in church activities,[1562] but the Lutheran faith, nevertheless, forms a part of the Swedish cultural heritage. Values founded in this heritage appear to have come to the surface in connection with the 2009 reform.[1563]

In the wording of the civil marriage ceremony, applicable until 2009, a main purpose of marriage was described as the "upholding of society", i.e. procreation. Referring to procreation as a main purpose of *civil marriage* was an idea quite contrary to the Swedish *legal* conception of marriage, which has clearly distinguished marriage from procreation since the 1970s. In fact, a statute was adopted in 1972, which grants persons who had undergone gender reassignment surgery the right to marry someone of their opposite assigned sex, irrespective of the couple's biological inability to reproduce jointly on their own.[1564] The Strasbourg Court has also established in its jurisprudence that reproduction is not a necessary prerequisite for exercising the right to marry under the European Convention of Human Rights.[1565] Furthermore, cohabitation without marriage has become legally recognized in Sweden and children's birth within or out of marriage has become legally irrelevant. These developments illustrate that from a legal perspective marriage is no longer necessary for the "upholding of society".

The connection between marriage and procreation has a religious foundation. As pointed out in chapter 2, the church and the state used the institution of marriage as a tool to control sexual behavior. Sexual relationships were only allowed for the purpose of procreation within marriage, meaning that same-sex couples who could not reproduce on their own were considered a threat to society. In the registered partnership ceremony, applicable until 2009, procreation was not mentioned. Instead publically and internally manifesting the couple's commitment to each other through a formalized ceremony was underlined as the primary purpose of registered partnership. It is noteworthy that children were not mentioned in the partnership ceremony, not even after all differences in treatment had been abolished as regards registered partners' right to adopt or access to assisted procreation methods in the early 2000s.

1562 It can be noted that in 2008, 73 percent of the Swedes were members of the Church of Sweden (this figure was about 70 percent in 2010), but only two percent of the members stated that they attended religious services on a regular basis. See Jänterä-Jareborg, Maarit, Religion and the Secular State, 2010, p. 669.

1563 See section 6.6.1.

1564 The Gender Identity Act, Lag (1972:119) om fastställande av könstillhörighet. See also section 4.2.1. below.

1565 Christine Goodwin v. The United Kingdom, 2002.

The different purposes of marriage and registered partnership, explicitly reflected in the ceremonies, further strengthen the impression that they were not two symbolically equal institutions, irrespective of the similarity in legal effects. The different purposes, discernable in the civil marriage ceremony by linking marriage to procreation, also suggest that religious values still influenced the essence of marriage in Sweden. It appears as if the historically founded conception of marriage as a cornerstone of society, safeguarding the upholding of society, which was promoted by the church for centuries based on the biblical story of the Creation, has survived in Sweden as a deeply rooted traditional notion. This connotation was found difficult to combine with the gender-neutral marriage concept.

When same-sex marriage was introduced in 2009, the legislator took the opportunity to modernize the civil marriage ceremony by abolishing the references to procreation from its wording. At the same time, the Registered Partnership Act was abolished. In the civil marriage ceremony the spouses' community of life is emphasized as the purpose of marriage, instead of procreation. The Church of Sweden is currently drafting a new marriage liturgy, which will apply to couples of different sex as well as to couples of the same sex. It remains to be seen whether the opening of marriage to couples of the same sex once and for all broke the link between marriage and procreation, retained in the marriage ceremonies, and whether the conception of marriage as a basis for community and love between two adults will be regarded as a main purpose also in the *religious* marriage ceremony.

Since 2009 in Sweden, the marriage concept is gender-neutral. The law does not distinguish between "marriage" and "same-sex marriage."[1566] The Church of Sweden officially shares this understanding and is at present redrafting its marriage liturgy. The advantage of treating same-sex couples and different-sex couples equally in the religious and the civil marriage ceremonies respectively is that it enforces the understanding that "same-sex marriage" is not an institution of its own, with different connotations. As discussed above, connotations to inequality and differential treatment, for instance through different wordings in the marriage ceremonies because of the couple's sex, risk creating the impression that there are two marriages which are not equal in value on a symbolic level.[1567]

9.2.2.2. The Institution of Marriage – Connotations to Values Extending Beyond the Legal Sphere

In this study the form and function of the institution of marriage in Sweden have been analyzed, at different points in time and under divergent societal conditions. It has been claimed that marriage has continued to be regarded as the superior

1566 See section 9.1.2.
1567 See section 9.1.1.

cohabitation model in Swedish society – the paradigm of the good and more secure relationship – because it is not just a legal contract with special legal effects; but because there is also a *symbolic* dimension to marriage, connoting inter alia a life-long relationship founded on love, consideration and mutual obligations.[1568]

It appears as if the traditional fundamental values attached to marriage are more deeply rooted in Swedish society than one might have expected. The symbolic dimension of marriage includes values which extend beyond the legal sphere, deriving from the cultural, social and religious functions of marriage in Swedish society during the last three hundred years studied here, and probably much longer in time. As Eva Ryrstedt points out, values concerning the marital status and the formalities attached to marriage are governed by social norms and perceptions, which are deeply rooted in a country's tradition.[1569]

In Sweden, as illustrated in chapter 2, religious values have been prominent in the marriage regulation because of the past monopoly of the Church of Sweden on celebrating marriages and on setting the general moral standard in society in respect of values attached to sexual relationships and family life. In this study it has been suggested that religious values have continued to be of relevance for the essence of marriage and have contributed to defending its position as the superior cohabitation model.

The tension between religious and secular interpretations of marriage was particularly visible in connection with the 2009 gender-neutral marriage enactment, which highlighted the symbolic dimension of marriage in Sweden. The Swedish Registered Partnership Act had been designed to provide same-sex couples, who could not marry, with a legal institution equivalent to marriage. The legal effects of registered partnership were subsequently broadened to correspond to the legal effects of marriage. Still, the institution of registered partnership could not match the institution of marriage *on a symbolic level*, since by definition it was not a marriage.[1570] In the 2007 Committee Report dealing with same-sex marriage, it was explicitly held, as a reason for reform, that marriage may be deemed to have a higher symbolic value than registered partnership.[1571]

Marriage has a history of being used by the legislator (sometimes together with the church) as a tool to signal approval of – i.e. to legally sanction – a certain category of relationships. Impediments to marriage have been established to exclude certain couples from access to marriage. The same-sex marriage reform is the most recent example of the legislator using the institution of marriage as a

1568 See Committee Report, (SOU 2007:17), p. 32 (English summary) and p. 230, where these qualities were seen as especially closely connected to marriage, more so than to registered partnership.

1569 Ryrstedt, Eva, Bodelning och bostad, 1998, p. 383.

1570 See section 6.6.2.2.

1571 Committee Report, (SOU 2007:17) p. 32.

tool to give public approval of certain relationships, more precisely to signal to society that a relationship between two men or two women is equally valuable as a relationship between a man and a woman. In section 6.6.2 it has been claimed that registered partnership did not suffice as a public signal in this respect, since it did not have the same symbolic connotations as a marriage.

The symbolic dimension of marriage, based on the values and general connotations deriving from a cultural, social and religious heritage, could be a reason why marriage appears to have remained a useful tool to signal official approval of a relationship, and the absence of such connotations could be why the modern construction "registered partnership" fell short in this respect in Sweden. Furthermore, it is worth repeating that this is not the first time that a secular marriage(-like) institution fails to match the symbolic dimension of the institution of marriage. As mentioned above, five years after the 1908 introduction of civil marriage as a general option in Sweden, the 1913 Law Commission observed a symbolic difference between the religious and the secular form of concluding a marriage and attempts were made to mitigate this perceived discrepancy.

The impediments to marriage signal to society which relationships are not found ethically desirable. From this point of view, reversely, granting same-sex couples access to marriage in Sweden was to socially sanction these relationships, and to signal to society that same-sex unions were equally worthy of societal and legal recognition as different-sex couples. What then, more precisely, does this signal mean and why was it controversial in Sweden? According to the American philosopher Sandel, opening up marriage to same-sex couples signals that same-sex couples, from the perspective of the state, are found worthy of serving the purpose of marriage.[1572] The controversy of the topic of same-sex marriage, from this point of view, can be explained with reference to the fact that different understandings of what the purpose of marriage is co-exist in Swedish society, and same-sex marriage does not necessarily fit into a "traditional" prevailing interpretation of what the purpose of marriage is. To persons who adhere to a traditional interpretation of marriage, an increased emphasis on diversity, based on respect for the individuals' own choices, might not be sufficient to alone morally justify introducing same-sex marriage. From a traditional religious perspective, which dominated for centuries in Sweden and influenced the understanding of marriage, the purpose of marriage is procreation based on the story of the Creation in the Bible. In other words, a same-sex couple who cannot reproduce jointly on their own cannot, from this point of view, serve the purpose of marriage and should not be granted access to the institution of marriage.

It has been suggested above that the link between marriage and procreation has remained relevant in Sweden to some extent, in spite of growing secularization, and could be discerned in the *civil* marriage ceremony until

1572 Sandel, Michael J., Justice, What's the Right Thing to Do? 2009, pp. 257 f.

2009.[1573] In chapter 6, I have argued that the symbolic dimension of marriage became particularly visible in contrast to registered partnership, which failed to express the same values or give rise to the same (positive) connotations as marriage.[1574] There was not a massive religiously motivated opposition toward same-sex marriage in Swedish society in general. Nevertheless, it is possible that the idea of marriage as the most prominent cohabitation model – symbolizing a long-term commitment between a man and a woman, a secure base for raising children and sanctioned by the legislator through a package of legal rules – has been reinforced by religiously based values which are a part of our culture. Furthermore, it is possible that these values contributed to the opposition toward opening marriage to same-sex couples in Sweden in 2009 and to the "loudness" and intensity of the voices raised against the reform.

9.3. THE RELEVANCE OF THE RESEARCH OBJECT – THREE PRACTICAL ARGUMENTS REVISITED

9.3.1. THE VALUE OF ANALYZING THE IMPACT OF THE GENDER-NEUTRAL MARRIAGE ENACTMENT ON THE ESSENCE OF MARRIAGE IN SWEDEN

The symbolic Swedish gender-neutral marriage enactment of 2009 was the starting point for this thesis and its search for what characterizes marriage, i.e. the essence of marriage. However, in order to understand what marriage is and what impact the Swedish gender-neutral marriage enactment had on the essence of marriage, it was found adequate to trace the institution of marriage back to the 1734 codification in Sweden and analyze its forms and functions in Swedish society since then.

The overall impression is that marriage is a resilient institution, which remains a relevant cohabitation model in Sweden in the twenty-first century. The institution of marriage has existed under diametrically different societal conditions in Sweden and has "survived" shifting political ideologies. Legislation on marriage has been intentionally used to reform society, but new habits in society have also called for new and more practical legal solutions. The Code of 1734 was based on moral values determined by the Church of Sweden. The Code of 1920, on the contrary, was a major step toward secular values and focused on the principle of equality between husband and wife. Equality was again a key principle in the legal development toward adopting the gender-neutral marriage concept. First the principle of equality focused on the relationship between husband and wife, then on unmarried and married couples and their children

---

1573 See section 9.2.2.1.

1574 See also sections 6.6.1, 6.6.2 (including subsections) and 9.2.2.1.

and, finally, on homosexual and heterosexual individuals and couples. Marriage still creates a tailor-made package of legal rights and duties for *two* persons who have formalized their intimate relationship through a special ceremony. Until 2009 these two persons had to be of different sex.

Challenging the "heterosexual criterion" of marriage was in line with the general equality focus in law and society, but it was contrary to the traditional religious interpretation of the story of the Creation. The analysis of the impact of the same sex marriage reform on the essence of marriage has suggested that religious connotations relating to marriage have continued to be of significance in society, and that these connotations, detectable for instance in the civil marriage ceremony, came to the surface in the opposition to the 2009 reform.

The same-sex marriage reform also illustrated that the institution of marriage has once again been used as a tool to signal official approval of a category of relationships, previously excluded from "the honor and recognition" by the community that marriage entails. This indicates that there still appears to be a need to use the institution of marriage – access to the marital status – as a tool to signal what types of relationships are ethically desirable. In fact this function of marriage, one could say, is an important explanation for why marriage has remained a central legal and societal institution in Sweden. The selection of persons qualifying for marriage is determined through the impediments to marriage. Impediments to marriage no longer prohibit couples from living together outside of marriage, but they nevertheless signal to society what relationships are considered ethically undesirable. Without any impediments to marriage retained in the law, any couple – and any number of persons – could contract a marriage. This has not been found desirable by the legislator.

Cohabitation without marriage and registered partnership are also considered to be legally and socially acceptable cohabitation models in Sweden, but it can be noted that these are both closely modeled on marriage and the couples officially recognized through these enactments are the same as those recognized through the marriage regulation. Irrespective of the aim expressed in the 1970s – to keep moral values in respect of cohabitation models out of the law – the marriage regulation, the Cohabitees Act and the Registered Partnership Act became selective in respect of the types of couples included in the enactments.

The gender-neutral marriage enactment increased the symbolic value of the "civil status side" of marriage. Since the 1970s, the contractual side of marriage – accounted for in section 9.2.1 – has been strengthened through law enactments, which have enhanced marriage as a voluntary contract entered into and exited out of more or less freely.[1575] The renewed focus on marriage as a desirable civil status, from the perspective of same-sex couples, in fact strengthened the institution of marriage, and marriage as an institution was proven to be attractive but in demand of an extension in scope. In short, the introduction of same-sex

[1575] This observation has also been made by Eva Ryrstedt, see Bodelning och bostad, 1998, p. 398.

marriage illustrates that the institution of marriage still serves a purpose in Swedish society, namely as a tool to signal official approval of a certain category of relationships, and thus promote equality (or whatever other political interest found worth protecting through the law at a certain point in time).

9.3.2. THE VALUE OF PROVIDING A FOUNDATION FOR FUTURE CHALLENGES RELATING TO MARRIAGE

What happens next? Was same-sex marriage the end of the line, a final stage of development realized through a long series of equality enactments during the twentieth century? In my opinion, this is most likely not the case. As Masha Antokolskaia points out, the modernization of family law is not likely to have reached an "end point", not least if one takes into account developments in the field of technology, which have opened up for medically assisted procreation techniques, surrogate motherhood etc.[1576] Against this background, it is likely that new challenges for family law will continue to be generated.

In this study I have suggested that marriage is a flexible concept, which has been reconsidered several times in the past and been modified to correspond to prevailing values in society. New legal challenges will most likely arise in the future, for instance, the question of whether or not to allow polygamous marriages.[1577] The conception of marriage as a monogamous union can be linked to Christian values – just like the idea of marriage as a heterosexual union aiming at procreation.[1578]

Polygamy is generally considered to be inconsistent with the principle of equality between men and women, the idea being that women in polygamous marriages – in situations when a man has several wives – are discriminated against from a human rights perspective.[1579] Polygamy will not be discussed in detail here, but it can be briefly mentioned that in Europe polygamy is usually connected to Islam, because it is practiced inter alia in some Muslim societies. As Jänterä-Jareborg points out, it is not only the human rights arguments focusing on equality that have created negative opinions in the West toward polygamous marriages; there would most likely also be opposition on principle grounds toward allowing one woman to marry several men.[1580] However, an individual who is living in a polygamous marriage might need a certain level of legal protection in statutory law, irrespective of an "instinctive" resistance in the

1576 Antokolskaia, Masha, see Harmonisation of Family Law in Europe, 2006, p. 500.

1577 On polygamous marriages, see, for instance, Jänterä-Jareborg, Maarit, Kan polygami vara laglig i Sverige? 2010.

1578 Coester-Waltjen, Dagmar, Coester Michael, International Encyclopedia of Comparative Law, Vol. IV, Persons and Family, Chapter 3, Formation of Marriage, 1997, p. 33.

1579 Jänterä-Jareborg, Maarit, Kan polygami vara laglig i Sverige? 2010, pp. 4 and 9.

1580 Jänterä-Jareborg, Maarit, Kan polygami vara laglig i Sverige? 2010, pp. 13 f.

West toward legally recognizing relationships which extend beyond the deeply rooted idea of the twosome relationship as the desirable form.

This research does not deal with polygamous marriages, but the analysis here of the institution of marriage – illustrating its flexibility and symbolic value – might shed light on and provide a future basis for the study of new legal challenges to the essence of marriage, e.g. in relation to the monogamous characteristic of marriage. In this study it has been claimed that marriage is an important legal institution, which signals official approval of relationships. Against this background, a certain level of moderation and open-mindedness by the Swedish legislator is recommended when encountering foreign cultures with different, but equally strong, religiously and culturally anchored conceptions of marriage. Mosa Sayed has emphasized that the secular state should also take into account cultural and religious customs in a multicultural society.[1581] Anna Singer has also argued along these lines, underlining that in a multicultural society people should be able to live in accordance with their own culture and religion, as long as other people's human rights are not violated.[1582]

However, my study illustrates how deeply rooted the principle of equality is in Swedish law and society. Only reforms which do not compromise the principle of equality between women and men can be expected to gain political and societal support in Sweden.[1583]

9.3.3. THE VALUE OF COMPARING REASONS FOR REFORM IN SWEDEN, SPAIN AND THE NETHERLANDS

The comparative outlooks into the Dutch and Spanish legal developments indicate that the institution of marriage has been used to reform society also outside of Sweden (and Scandinavia), during the last couple of decades, inter alia for the purpose of creating equality between same-sex and different-sex couples. In all three jurisdictions compared – Sweden, Spain and the Netherlands – granting same-sex couples access to marriage has been a way for the state to signal to society that homosexual relationships are worthy of legal recognition. The rights and integrity of the individual within the framework of the human rights discourse in Europe have motivated extending the concept of marriage to same-sex couples. An eagerness to appear progressive in a human rights context is visible, which has contributed to the speedy legal development in Europe during the last decade in respect of legal recognition of same-sex couples.

1581 Sayed, Mosa, Islam och arvsrätt i det mångkulturella Sverige, 2009, p. 375.

1582 Singer, Anna, Familjerätten – en kulturyttring? 2010, p. 272.

1583 Jänterä-Jareborg, Maarit, Kan polygami vara laglig i Sverige? 2010, p. 15. She underlines the necessity of a discussion on polygamy in Sweden and welcomes the tolerance which she finds signifying for Swedish law today, as a contrast to the policies allegedly aimed to strengthen human rights, adopted in Denmark and in many other European states.

The symbolic dimension of marriage is strengthened by its connection to human rights and the focus on equality and non-discrimination. Furthermore, the importance of a person's civil status when EU citizens exercise their right to move freely within the Union has contributed to increasing the relevance of a person's civil status. The human rights discourse is full of symbolism and value-charged concepts such as "equality", "human dignity", "protection of family life" and "democratic society". This has contributed to making the institution of marriage symbolically charged also as a human right. For instance, when the Registered Partnership Act was adopted in Sweden references were made to human rights documents in order to market the Act as "desirable". Still, this was not regarded as sufficient from a human rights perspective. Hans Ytterberg, the former Swedish Ombudsman against Discrimination on Grounds of Sexual Orientation, connected the same-sex marriage issue to the global human rights discussion, namely to the UN Declaration of Human Rights, by referring to registered partnership as "equality in rights without equality in dignity".[1584] According to the UN Declaration, Art. 1 "All human beings are born free and equal in dignity and rights". Along the lines of Ytterberg's reasoning, it can be argued that obtaining equality not only in rights but also in dignity presupposes equal access to marriage for same-sex and different-sex couples.

The international comparisons, and the outlooks into the human rights discourse in the EU and the jurisprudence of the Strasbourg Court, illustrate that equality and non-discrimination are generally considered to form an essential part of a democratic society, and the Strasbourg Court has recently modified the concept of family to include also formalized same-sex unions.

9.4. DOES THE INSTITUTION OF MARRIAGE HAVE A FUTURE?

9.4.1. ABOLISH MARRIAGE? PRO ET CONTRA

In this study it has been claimed that the institution of marriage was strengthened through the same-sex marriage reform. Same-sex marriage placed the symbolic importance of the marital status in the limelight. This was in contrast to the previous development, which can be claimed to have emphasized the contractual side of marriage and toned down its status side. What form and function can the institution of marriage expect to have in the future? Marriage has symbolized long-term commitment, and this may continue to make marriage an appealing cohabitation model, combined with couples' desire to be covered by a full

[1584] Ytterberg, Hans, All Human Beings Are Equal, but Some Are More Equal than Others, 2003, p. 8.

package of legal rules. A slight increase in the number of marriages concluded annually has been observed in Sweden during the last few years.[1585]

As suggested above, a future step might be that the institution of marriage is made available to a wider category of persons – for instance polygamous relationships – although this can also be objected to on numerous grounds which will not be accounted for here. In an increasingly multicultural Swedish society, the religious significance of marriage might become more visible. The decision by the Strasbourg Court to include same-sex couples in the concept of "family life" under Art. 8 of the ECHR is most likely a first step toward granting two men or two women the right to marry under Art. 12.[1586] Such a development can be expected to give rise to discussions on what the essence of marriage is or should be. It follows that the institution of marriage will continue to be of relevance and engage the legislators, the religious communities and the population in general.

I am naturally well-aware of that many may find it tempting to argue now at the dawn of the twenty-first century that time is ripe for the Swedish legislator to once and for all abolish the *legal* institution of marriage, and instead leave it up to the parties themselves to conclude whatever mutual agreements they deem necessary for their relationship. From this point of view, abolishing marriage could be seen as self-evident and a continuation of the Swedish legal development, visible in the marriage regulation since the 1970s, toward trusting the spouses to make rational decisions concerning their relationship and minimizing the public interference in this respect.

I wish to briefly return to the arguments of Sandel. According to his line of reasoning, abolishing marriage would be a way for a state to become truly neutral to moral values concerning cohabitation models. As long as marriage is retained as a state sanctioned union, open to some couples and closed to others, moral judgments are implicitly made concerning desirable and undesirable lifestyles.[1587] Impediments to marriage signal to society which couples are unworthy of legal recognition – i.e. those who are unable to marry each other because of an impediment to marriage. Without impediments to marriage, any couples and any number of persons could marry each other, which would deprive marriage of its symbolic connotations.[1588] This would hardly be a desirable development for reasons further developed below.

An additional argument for abolishing the legal institution of marriage could be claimed to be that it would clarify the distinction between the powers of the state and the religious communities in Sweden in respect of marriage. Such a distinction can be achieved by breaking the traditional "double track system"

1585 Statistics Sweden: www.scb.se/statistik/_publikationer/OV0904_2010A01_BR_04_A01BR1001.pdf. Accessed 5 December 2010. In 2009, however, a slight decrease was noted.

1586 See section 8.3.4.2.

1587 Sandel, Michael J., Justice, What's the Right Thing to Do? 2009, p. 254–257.

1588 See section 9.3.1.

governing conclusion of marriage in Sweden, and instead making civil marriage the only legally valid form of concluding a marriage. It follows that the religious communities would be free to perform religious blessings of civil marriages, but these blessings would be irrelevant from a legal viewpoint. Such a system, which exists for instance in the Netherlands, was considered and dismissed in the Committee Report of 2007, inter alia because of the popularity of the religious marriage ceremony in Swedish society.[1589]

By abolishing the double track system and making civil marriage the only legally valid form – it can be argued that more room would be created for the freedom of religion. In other words, such a reform can be argued to increase the freedom for the religious communities to interpret religious concepts independently in their own pace, without being pressured to follow the rapid legal development and political policies in society. Although there is no *obligation* for the religious communities to marry same-sex couples, the official link between the state and the religious communities through the state delegated authority to marry, risks resulting in adjustments to state policies, by religious communities, in fear of being labeled as regressive or discriminatory. In other words, the willingness to appear progressive and modern can influence not only European states, as discussed in chapter 7, but also the religious communities in relation to the state.

However, as repeatedly stressed above, marriage is not just a legal institution. The institution of marriage is a part of Sweden's cultural heritage. Its traditional and historical function in society has been as a "rite" which unites people and creates a feeling of belonging and identification.[1590] From this point of view, marriage is worth retaining as a unifying legal institution, in addition to retaining the freedom to choose between a religious and a civil marriage ceremony. Moreover, the religious marriage ceremony is popular in Sweden. In fact, more than 40 percent of all marriages concluded annually are celebrated in the Church of Sweden.[1591]

Another motive for retaining the Swedish double track system for concluding a marriage, i.e. through a secular or a religious marriage ceremony, is that in the

---

1589 Committee Report, (SOU 2007:17), pp. 253 f.

1590 Bäckström, et al., Religious Change in Northern Europe, 2004, pp. 87–98. In theological literature, rites such as the marriage ceremony have been defined as: "[…] recurring, culturally transmitted formalised actions which involve a group of people. They have a dramatic, performative character; they are justified by reference to authority and express a symbolic representation of a dimension which in some sense is viewed as supra-individual and timeless i.e. in some sense transcendent." See p. 91.

1591 Jänterä-Jareborg, Maarit, Religion and the Secular State, 2010, p. 669. If the number of marriages concluded by other authorized religious communities are taken into account, this figure increases, but there are no official figures available which distinguish the total number of marriages concluded in the religious form on an annual basis in Sweden. The Church of Sweden has on its own initiative made statistical calculations concerning marriages concluded within the Church of Sweden.

multicultural Swedish society, the religious communities' authority to conclude legally valid marriages can be regarded as an official symbol of inclusion. In this study it has been illustrated that marriage as a tool to signal official approval of relationships that qualify for marriage has proven useful and under demand. In other words, authorizing a variety of religious communities to conclude legally valid marriages is a means to officially signal that religious pluralism is a welcome feature of Swedish society – a cultural enrichment. Furthermore, from a practical viewpoint, the authorization to conclude legally valid marriages can also be a control mechanism to safeguard that certain basic values relating to marriage are respected by the religious communities, for instance the applicable age-limits for conclusion of marriage in the Marriage Code. If the rules dealing with the marriage ceremony or marital impediments in the Marriage Code are not followed, an authorization can be withdrawn.[1592]

9.4.2. THE INSTITUTION OF MARRIAGE – ELASTIC YET TRADITION-BOUND

The overall impression is that the basic elements of the marriage regulation have changed over time in Sweden to match new values in society. It follows that our understanding of marriage has proven to be flexible and elastic as well. It appears that irrespective of the major changes that have taken place in Swedish society over the last three hundred years, marriage has resiliently remained a "cornerstone" of Swedish society, representing an especially eminent form of family life.

A general observation concerning marriage is that the Swedish legislator, since the 1970s, appears to have given up promoting the idea of marriage as a life-long commitment, and has instead introduced legislation based on the principle that each spouse should be free to leave the marriage. However, this understanding of marriage was not adopted by the Church of Sweden. On the contrary, the notion of marriage as a life-long commitment has continued to be reflected and reinforced by the wording of the religious marriage ceremony. In accordance with the religious marriage ceremony, the spouses shall promise to be together until death do them part.[1593] It could be claimed that people in general, irrespective of the changes in the Swedish divorce regulation, have continued to associate marriage with a life-long commitment,[1594] in accordance with its original religious meaning, which for centuries was the dominating

[1592] See Government Bill, (Prop 1992/93:211), p. 14.

[1593] The spouses-to-be are free to, in co-operation with the marriage official, formulate their marriage vows, but the content should reflect their ambition to stay together for life. See www.svenskakyrkan.se/default.aspx?id=647808. Accessed 4 December 2010.

[1594] Also Eva Ryrstedt has noted that marriage rests on the idea of a life-long commitment. See Ryrstedt, Eva, Bodelning och bostad, 1998, p. 383.

conception in Sweden, and is still frequently expressed during the religious marriage service. In other words, people still conclude a marriage with the intent of staying together for a long time – perhaps even for a lifetime. This attitude of the couple has not been fundamentally changed by the liberal divorce rules.

The most significant change relating to marriage in Sweden, noted during the period of time studied here, is the tendency to gradually open up marriage to a broader category of persons, by reducing the impediments to marriage to a minimum and, most recently, by making marriage available to same-sex couples. Furthermore, marriage regulation has been extended to encompass other "marriage-like" relationships. Keeping in mind how elastic and adaptable to change marriage has proven to be in the past, it may appear inconsistent that extending marriage to encompass same-sex couples has been controversial in Sweden in the twenty-first century. Granting same-sex couples the right to access the institution of marriage can be seen as a direct confrontation with the religiously founded conception of marriage as a union for a man and a woman for the purpose of upholding society, i.e. through procreation, as laid down in the story of the Creation in the Bible. Revolutionary, in a sense, is that in Sweden the gender-neutral marriage enactment resulted in a modification, not only of the *secular* understanding of marriage, but also of the Church of Sweden's *religious* understanding of marriage, and the church found it to be in compliance with the message of love in the Bible to solemnize marriages between two persons of the same sex.

In summary, the analysis in the previous chapters has illustrated the significance of marriage in Sweden for centuries, as an elastic institution firmly anchored in Swedish society. Marriage is not just a legal concept that can easily be abolished with reference to the individuals' legal capacity to conclude agreements with each other regulating their relationship. Marriage is a multifaceted and dynamic institution which is an integral part of the Swedish cultural heritage, concluded through a ritual which creates a sense of solidarity in society. The experience with the gender-neutral marriage reform in Sweden strengthens my impression that marriage is still needed as an official symbol of inclusion and tolerance, and as a symbol of commitment and community between the couple. From this point of view, marriage still serves a relevant purpose and should be retained as a legal institution.

REFERENCES

OFFICIAL DOCUMENTS – SWEDEN

Government Bill (Prop 1937 nr. 187), om ändringar i strafflagen.

Government Bill (Prop 1938:146), Kungl. Maj:ts proposition till riksdagen med förslag till lag om upphävande av 18 kap. 13 §2 mom. Strafflagen, m.m.; given Stockholms slott den 25 februari 1938.

Government Bill (Prop 1944 nr 13), utdrag av protokollet över justitiedepartementsärenden, hållet inför Hans Maj:t Konungen i statsrådet å Stockholms slott den 5 november 1943.

Government Bill (Prop 1968:136), Kungl. Maj:ts proposition till riksdagen med förslag till lag om ändring i giftermålsbalken, m.m.; given Stockholms slott den 4 oktober 1968.

Government Bill (Prop 1973:32), Kungl. Maj:ts proposition med förslag till lag om ändring i giftermålsbalken, m.m.; given Stockholms slott den 9 mars 1973.

Government Bill (Prop 1975:76:170), om ändring i Föräldrabalken, m.m.

Government Bill (Prop 1978/79:12), om underhåll till barn och frånskilda, m.m.; beslutad den 5 oktober 1978.

Government Bill (Prop 1986/87:1), om äktenskapsbalk m.m.

Government Bill (Prop 1986/87:124), om de homosexuellas situation i samhället.

Government Bill, (Prop 1992/93:211), om rätt att förrätta vigsel inom andra trossamfund än Svenska kyrkan m.m.

Government Bill (Prop 1997/98:116), Staten och trossamfunden bestämmelser om Svenska kyrkan och andra trossamfund.

Government Bill (Prop 2001/02:123), Partnerskap och adoption.

Government Bill (Prop 2002/03:80), Ny sambolag.

Government Bill (Prop 2004/05:137), Assisterad befruktning och föräldraskap.

Government Bill (Prop 2004/05:170), Ny instans- och processordning i utlännings- och Medborgarskapsärenden.

Government Bill (Prop 2005/06:77), Genomförande av EG-direktiven om unionsmedborgares rörlighet inom EU och om varaktigt bosatta tredjelandsmedborgares ställning.

Government Bill (Prop 2007/08:95), Ett starkare skydd mot diskriminering.

Government Bill (Prop 2008/09:80), Äktenskapsfrågor.

Committee Report (SOU 1935:68), Promemoria angående ändringar i strafflagen beträffande straffsatserna för särskilda brott m.m.

Committee Report (SOU 1936:15), Betänkande angående moderskapspenning och mödrahjälp.

Committee Report (SOU 1936:51), Yttrande angående revision av 18 kap. 13 §strafflagen m.m., avgivet av befolkningskommissionen.
Committee Report (SOU 1936:59), Betänkande i sexualfrågan.
Committee Report (SOU 1938:13), Betänkande angående förvärvsarbetande kvinnors rättsliga ställning vid äktenskaps och barnsbörd, avgivet av befolkningskommissionen.
Committee Report (SOU 1938:57), Slutbetänkande, avgivet av Befolkningskommissionen.
Committee Report (SOU 1941:3), Åtgärder för bekämpande av homosexualitetens samhällsfarliga yttringar.
Committee Report (SOU 1941:32), Strafflagberedningens utlåtande med förslag till lagstiftning angående åtgärder mot homosexualitetens samhällsfarliga yttringar, avgivet den 3 november 1941.
Committee Report (SOU 1947:46), Betänkande angående familjeliv och hemarbete, avgivet av utredningen för hem- och familjefrågor.
Committee Report (SOU 1964:34–35), Äktenskapsrätt, förslag av familjerättskommittén.
Committee Report (SOU 1972:41), Familj och äktenskap I.
Committee Report (SOU 1977:37), Underhåll till barn och frånskilda.
Committee Report (SOU 1981:85), Äktenskapsbalk.
Committee Report, (SOU 1984:63), Homosexuella och samhället.
Committee Report (SOU 1993:98), Partnerskap, Parts A and B, Betänkande av partnerskapskommittén.
Committee Report (SOU 1999:104), Nya samboregler, betänkande av samboendekommittén.
Committee Report (SOU 2001:10), Barn i homosexuella familjer, Parts A and B, Betänkande av Kommittén om barn i homosexuella familjer.
Committee Report (SOU 2007:3) Föräldraskap vid assisterad befruktning.
Committee Report (SOU 2007:17), Äktenskap för par med samma kön, vigselfrågor, Betänkande av äktenskaps och partnerskapsutredningen.
Law Commission Report (1832:1,2,) Förslag till allmän criminallag.
Law Commission Report of 1913, Lagberedningens förslag till revision av giftermålsbalken och vissa delar av ärvdabalken I. Förslag till lag om äktenskaps ingående och upplösning m.m. 1913.
Law Commission Report of 1918, Lagberedningens förslag till revision av giftermålsbalken och vissa delar av ärvdabalken. IV. Förslag till giftermålsbalk m.m. 1918:15.
Law Commission Report (LU 1973:20), Lagutskottets betänkande i anledning av Kungl. Majt:s proposition 1973:32 med förslag till lag om ändring i giftermålsbalken m.m., jämte motioner.
Parliament's Law Commission Report (1991/92:LU32), Registrerat partnerskap m.m.
Parliament's Law Commission Report (1993/94:LU28), Registrerat partnerskap, m.m.
Report of the Committee on Civil Affairs, (Civilutskottet) (2008/09:CU19), Könsneutrala äktenskap och vigselfrågor.
Memorandum of the Ministry of Justice, (Ds 2004:19), Föräldraskap vid assisterad befruktning för homosexuella.
Report by the Committee on Foreign Affairs, (2001/02:UU8) Mänskliga rättigheter m.m. länder, områden, enskilda folkgrupper och vissa FN-frågor.

NJA II, 1910 no 2, Samfälldt lagstiftningsarbete för Sverige, Danmark och Norge.
NJA II 1921, no 1, Den nya giftermålsbalken I.
Government Writ (Regeringens skrivelse), (2005/06:95), April 2010, Uppföljning av den nationella handlingsplanen för de mänskliga rättigheterna.
Protocol of the Second Chamber, 1928.
Guidelines by the head of the Ministry of Justice to the Commission on Family Law, 15 August, 1969, Riksdagsberättelsen 1970, Ju 52.
Directive (Dir 2005:6), Äktenskap och partnerskap.
Motion no 1 1933, Motioner i Andra Kammaren, av herr Lundstedt, om upphävande av 18 kap. 10 §strafflagen m.m.
Motion to Parliament (1973:1793) Av herr Hermansson m.fl. (vpk).
Motion to Parliament (1991/92:L408) Utvärdering av sambolagstiftningarna.
Motion to Parliament (2007/08:C317), Könsneutralt äktenskap.
Motion to Parliament (2008/09:C454). Könsneutral Äktenskapsbalk.

OFFICIAL DOCUMENTS – FOREIGN SOURCES

FINLAND

Government Bill 15 December 2000, (HE 200/2000 vp), Regeringens proposition till Riksdagen med förslag till lag om registrerat partnerskap.
Government Bill (RP 37/2010 rd), Regeringens proposition till Riksdagen med förslag till lag om upplösning av sambors gemensamma hushåll och om ändring av vissa lagar som har samband med den.

NORWAY

Government Bill (Ot.prop.) no. 73 (2007–2008), Om lov om endringer i arveloven mv. (arv og uskifte for samboere).

THE UNITED KINGDOM

Law Commission, Consultation Paper No. 179, Cohabitation: The Financial Consequences of Relationship Breakdown, A Consultation Paper, published 31 May 2006.

GERMANY

The Bundestag's printed papers, Entwurf eines Gesetzes zur Reform des Personenstandsrechts, 15 June 2006, BT-Drucks, 16/1831.

SPAIN

Official Journal of the Spanish government, Boletín Oficial del Estado, BOE 65, 16 March, 2007.

Official Journal of the Spanish government, Boletín Oficial del Estado, BOE, 157, 2 July, 2005.

Catalonia

Government Bill to The Catalan Parliament, Butlletí Oficial del Parlament de Catalunya, 19 January 2009, Number 284.

OFFICIAL DOCUMENTS – EU-LAW

Council Regulation 1612/68 of 15 October 1968 on freedom of movement for workers within the Community [1968/9] OJ Sp Ed (II) 475.

Directive 2004/38/EC on the right of citizens of the Union and their family members to move and reside freely within the territory of the Member States.

COM (2003) 199, Amended proposal for a Directive of the European Parliament and of the Council on the right of citizens of the Union and their family members to move and reside freely within the territory of the Member States.

COM (2004/0401) final, Communication from the Commission to the Council and the European Parliament – Area of Freedom, Security and Justice: Assessment of the Tampere program and future orientations {SEC(2004)680 et SEC(2004)693}.

COM (2005/0184) final, Communication from the Commission to the Council and the European Parliament – The Hague Program: Ten priorities for the next five years The Partnership for European renewal in the field of Freedom, Security and Justice.

COM (2010) final, communication form the Secretary-General of the European Commission to the Secretary-General of the Council of the European Union, 21 October 2010, 15319/10.

Opinion of Advocate General Mischo, delivered on 22 February 2001, Joined Cases C-122/99, P and C-125/99 P, D and Kingdom of Sweden v. Council of the European Union.

OFFICIAL DOCUMENTS – THE CHURCH OF SWEDEN

Sveriges kyrkolag af år 1686: jemte samling af de till 1844 års början utkomna stadganden, hvarigenom densamma blifvit i vissa fall upphäfven, ändrad och tillökt / utgifven och försedd med ett fullständigt alphabetiskt register öfver de ecclesiastiska föreskrifter, som ännu äro till efterlefnad gällande af A.J. Rydén, Jönköping 1844–1845.

Report by the Theological Committee of the Church of Sweden, Svenska kyrkans utredningar (2005:1), Kärlek, samlevnad och äktenskap, Rapport från en offentlig hearing den 6–9 september 2004, Svenska kyrkans teologiska kommitté.
The Worship Commission's Report (2005:2) Cohabitation issues. (Gudstjänstutskottets betänkande (2005:2) Samlevnadsfrågor).
General Instructions, Blessings of Registered Partnerships, Experimental Order, Accepted by the Church Board 6 December 2006. (Kyrkostyrelsen).
Directive from the Church Board, 19 April 2006, Fortsatt arbete med översyn av Den svenska kyrkohandboken.
Report of the Church Board, Kyrkostyrelsens skrivelse 2009:6, Vigsel och äktenskap.

BOOKS AND ARTICLES

Agell, Anders, the Swedish Legislation on Marriage and Cohabitation, a Journey without a Destination, Scandinavian Studies in Law, 1980, pp. 11–48.

Agell, Anders, Individ, familj, stat, om värderingar i familjerättslagstiftningen under 1900-talet, SvJT 1984 pp. 715–739.

Agell, Anders, Samboende utan äktenskap, Rättsläge och rättspolitik, Second Revised Edition, Publica, 1985.

Agell, Anders, Familjebegrepp och lagstiftningsideologi i svensk rätt, De lege, Juridiska fakulteten i Uppsala, årsbok, årgång 3, 1993.

Agell, Anders, Should and Can Family Law Influence Social Behaviour?, The Changing Family, Family Forms & Family Law, Edited by J. Eeklaar / T. Nhlapo, Hart Publishing, 1998, pp. 125–137.

Agell, Anders, Legal Issues of the Late 1990's, Family Forms and Legal Policies, A Comparative View from a Swedish Observer, Scandinavian Studies in Law, 1999, Vol. 38, pp. 197–216.

Agell, Anders, Is There One System of Family Law in the Nordic Countries? European Journal of Law Reform, 2001, pp. 313–330.

Agell, Anders, Äktenskapets giltighet – en civilrättslig och en förvaltningsrättslig fråga, Festskrift till Gösta Wallin, 2002, pp. 21–39.

Agell, Anders, The Legal Status of Same-Sex Couples in Europe – A Critical Analysis, Legal Recognition of Same-Sex Couples in Europe, Edited by Boele-Woelki, K. and Fuchs, A., European Family Law Series No. 1, Intersentia, 2003, pp. 122–134.

Agell, Anders, Nordisk äktenskapsrätt, En jämförande studie av dansk, finsk, isländsk, norsk och svensk rätt med diskussion av reformbehov och harmoniseringsmöjligheter, Nord 2003:2.

Agell, Anders, Äktenskap, samboende, partnerskap, Third Edition, Iustus, 2004.

Agell, Anders, Individual Statement, No 120, 28 January, 2008, Ju2007/3311/L2, circulation for comments regarding Report (SOU 2007:17), Äktenskap för par med samma kön. Vigselfrågor.

Agell, Anders, Brattström, Margareta, Äktenskap, samboende, partnerskap, Fourth Edition, Iustus, 2008.

Almquist, Jan Eric, Den svenska familjerättens historia, Stockholm, 1943.

Ambjörnsson, Fanny, Vad är queer?, Natur och kultur, 2006.

Andersson, Gudrun, Myndig eller omyndig? Kvinnans rättsliga och samhälleliga ställning under stormaktstiden, Kvinnorna och rätten från stormaktstid till rösträttstid, Granström, Andersson, Jansson och Oja, 1996, pp. 9–40.

Andersson, Håkan, "Barthesianska meditationer", Hyldeskrift till Nørgaard, 2003, pp. 71–97.

Andreasson, Martin, Samhällsfara eller samhällsgrupp? Riksdagens syn på homo- och bisexuella, Homo i folkhemmet, Homo- och bisexuella i Sverige 1950–2000, Anamma, 2000.

Andrén, Åke, Sveriges Kyrkohistoria, Reformationstid, Verbum, 1999.

Antokolskaia, Masha, Boele-Woelki, Katharina, Dutch Family Law in the 21st Century: Trend-Setting and Straggling Behind at the Same Time, Dutch Reports for the XVIIth Conference of Comparative Law, Intersentia, 2002, pp. 53–74.

Antokolskaia, Masha, Harmonisation of Family Law in Europe: A Historical Perspective, A Tale of Two Millennia, Intersentia, 2006.

Antokolskaia, Masha, Family Law and National Culture, Arguing against the cultural constraints argument, Debates in Family Law around the Globe at the Dawn of the 21st Century, Edited by Boele-Woelki, Katharina, Intersentia 2009, pp. 37–51.

Atkin, Bill, New Zealand, Reflections on New Zealand's Property Reforms 'Five Years On', The International Survey of Family Law, 2007 Edition, Published on behalf of the International Society of Family Law, General Editor, Bill Atkin, pp. 217–244.

Baker, Elisabeth H, Sanchez, Laura A, Nock, Steven L, Wright, James D, Covenant Marriage and the Sanctification of Gendered Marital Roles, Journal of Family Issues, February 2009 30, First Published on 17 September 2008. pp 147–178.

Bell, Mark, We are Family? Same-Sex Partners and EU Migration Law, Maastricht Journal of European and Comparative Law, Vol. 9, 2002, pp. 335–355.

Bell, Mark, Holding Back the Tide? Cross-Boarder Recognition of Same-Sex Partnerships within the European Union, European Review of Private Law, 5, 2004, pp. 613–632.

Bell, Mark, EU Directive on Free Movement and Same-Sex Families, Guidelines on the Implementation Process, ILGA - Europe, October 2005, pp. 1–20, published at: www.rfsl.se/public/ilga_eudirektivfreedom.pdf.

Björk Eydal, Stefánsson, Kolbeinn, Restrained reform - Securing equality for same-sex couples in Iceland, a presentation given at the conference on same-sex unions in Stockholm, 25–26 September, 2003, Same-Sex Couples, Same-Sex Partnerships and Homosexual Marriages. A Focus on Cross-Country Differentials.

Boele-Woelki, Katharina, Registered Partnership and Same-Sex Marriage in the Netherlands, Legal Recognition of Same-Sex Couples, Edited by Boele-Woelki, Katharina and Fuchs, Angelika, Intersentia, 2003, pp. 41–53.

Boele-Woelki, Katharina, Cherednychenko, Olga and Coenraad, Lieke. Dutch Report concerning the CEFL Questionnaire on Grounds for Divorce and Maintenance Between Former Spouses. www.ceflonline.net/.

Boele-Woelki, Katharina, Schonewille, Fred and Schrama, Wendy, Dutch Report concerning the CEFL Questionnaire on Property Relations Between Spouses. www.ceflonline.net/.

Boele-Woelki, Katharina, Ferrand, Frédérique, Gonzáles Beilfuss, Cristina, Jänterä-Jareborg, Maarit, Lowe, Nigel, Martiny, Dieter, Pintens, Walter (Editors), Principles of European Family Law, Regarding Divorce and Maintenance Between Former Spouses, Intersentia, 2004.

Boele-Woelki, Katharina, Schrama, Wendy and Vonk, Machteld Dutch Report concerning the CEFL Questionnaire on Parental Responsibilities. www.ceflonline.net/.

Boele-Woelki, Katharina, Curry-Sumner, Ian, Marriage in the Netherlands, Report at the request of the Swedish Marriage and Partnership Inquiry Commission, 19th January 2006, 14.00–17.00, Toon Peterszaal, Achter Sint Peter 200, Universiteit Utrecht University.

Boele-Woelki, K, Curry-Sumner, I, Jansen M, Schrama W, Evaluatie 'Wet openstelling huwelijk' en van het geregistreerd partnerschap, University of Utrecht, Molengraaff Institute for Private Law, Report (Ra 13.429) 2006, commissioned by the Dutch

Ministry of Justice. www.wodc.nl/onderzoeksdatabase/evaluatie-wet-geregistreerd-partnerschap.aspx.

Boele-Woelki, Katharina, The Legal Recognition of Same-Sex Relationships Within the European Union, Tulane Law Review, Vol. 82, 2007–2008, pp. 1949–1981.

Bogdan, Michael, Komparativ rättskunskap, Second Edition, Norstedts Juridik AB, 2003.

Bogdan, Michael, Registered Partnerships and EC Law, Legal Recognition of Same-Sex Couples in Europe, Edited by, Boele-Woelki, Katharina, Fuchs, Angelika, Intersentia, 2003, pp. 171–177.

Bogdan, Michael, EG-domstolens och svensk rättspraxis i internationell privat- och processrätt 2006–2008, SvJT 2010, pp. 33–77.

Bonini-Baraldi, Matteo, Variations on the Theme of Status, Contract and Sexuality: An Italian Perspective on the Circulation of Models, Perspectives for the Unification and Harmonisation of Family Law in Europe, Edited by Boele-Woelki, Katharina, Intersentia, 2003, pp. 300–321.

Bradley, David, Family Law and Political Culture, Modern Legal Studies, Scandinavian Laws in Comparative Perspective, Sweet & Maxwell, 1996.

Bradley, David, A Family Law for Europe? Perspectives for the Unification and Harmonisation of Family Law in Europe, Edited by, Boele-Woelki, Katharina, Intersentia, 2003, pp. 65–104.

Brattström, Margareta, Makars pensionsrättigheter, Iustus, 2004.

Brattström, Margareta, The Protection of a Vulnerable Party when a Cohabitee Relationship Ends – An Evaluation of the Swedish Cohabitees Act, The International Survey of Family Law, Edited by Bainham, Andrew, Published on behalf of the International Society of Family Law, 2006, pp. 345–354.

Brattström, Margareta, Singer, Anna, Rätt arv, Fördelning av kvarlåtenskap, Second Edition, Iustus Förlag, 2007.

Briggs, Margaret, The Formalization of Property Sharing Rights for De Facto Couples in New Zealand, Family Finances, Edited by Bea, Verschraegen, Jan Sramek Verlag, 2009, pp. 329–343.

Butruille-Cardew, Charlotte, The 2004 French Divorce Law and International Prospects, The International Survey of Family Law, September 2006, pp. 144–148.

Bäckström, Anders, Edgardh Beckman, Ninna and Pettersson, Per, Religious Change in Northern Europe, The Case of Sweden, Verbum, 2004.

Calvo, Kerman, Sacrifices that Pay: Polity Membership, Political Opportunities and the Recognition of Same-Sex Marriage in Spain, South European Society & Politics, Vol. 12, No. 3, 2007, pp. 295–314.

Cameron, Iain, Kirilova Eriksson, Maja, An Introduction to the European Convention on Human Rights, 2nd Edition, Iustus förlag, 1995.

Cánovas, Pérez Nicolás, Spain: The Heterosexual State Refuses to Disappear, Legal Recognition of Same-Sex Partnerships, A Study of National, European and International Law, Edited by Wintermute, Robert and Andenaes, Mads, Hart Publishing, 2001, pp. 493–504.

Carlberg, Axel, Ekumeniska perspektiv, Homosexuella i kyrkan – en katolsk respons, Kärlek, samlevnad och äktenskap, Rapport från en offentlig hearing den 6–9 september 2004, Svenska kyrkans teologiska kommitté, pp. 203–210.

Carlsson, Lizzie, Jag giver dig min dotter, Trolovning och äktenskap i den svenska kvinnans äldre historia, I, åttonde bandet, A. – B Nordiska bokhandeln, 1965. Skrifter utgivna av Institutet för rättshistorisk forskning grundat av Gustav och Carin Olin.

Carlsson, Lizzie, Jag giver dig min dotter, Trolovning och äktenskap i den svenska kvinnans äldre historia, II, tjugonde bandet, A.-B. Nordiska bokhandeln, 1972. Skrifter utgivna av Institutet för rättshistorisk forskning grundat av Gustav och Carin Olin.

Childs, Marquis, Sweden: The Middle Way on Trial, Yale University Press, 1980.

Coester-Waltjen, Dagmar and Coester, Michael, International Encyclopedia of Comparative Law, Vol IV, Persons and Family, Chapter 3, Formation of Marriage, Martin Nijhoff Publishers, 1997.

Coester-Waltjen, Dagmar, Human Rights and the Harmonization of Family Law in Europe, European Challenges in Contemporary Family Law, Edited by, Boele-Woelki, Katharina, Sverdrup, Tone, Intersentia, 2008, pp. 3–15.

Combalía, Zoila, Roca, María, Religion and the Secular State of Spain, Conference 2010, Washington etc, pp. 629–644. The XVIII International Congress of the International Academy of Comparative Law, Washington, 2010.

Cooper, Davina, Like Counting Stars?: Re-Structuring Equality and the Socio-Legal Space of Same-Sex Marriage, Legal Recognition of Same-Sex Partnerships, A Study of National, European and International Law, Edited by Wintermute, Robert / Andenaes, Mads, Hart Publishing, 2001, pp. 75–96.

Curry-Sumner, Ian, All's well that ends registered? The substantive and private international law aspects of non-marital registered relationships in Europe, Intersentia, 2005. (See also: Sumner, Ian.)

Curry-Sumner, Ian, Private International Law Aspects of Homosexual Couples: the Netherlands Report, Electronic Journal of Comparative Law, Vol. 11.1, 2007, pp. 1–24.

Danelius, Hans, Reflections on some Important Judgments of the European Court of Human Rights Regarding Family Life, Family Life and Human Rights Regarding Family Life, Edited by Lødrup, Peter and Modvar, Eva, Gyldendal Norsk Forlag AS, 2004, pp. 153–162.

Danelius, Hans, Mänskliga rättigheter i europeisk praxis, en kommentar till Europakonventionen om de mänskliga rättigheterna, Third Edition, Norstedts Juridik, 2007.

Danielsen, Svend, Nordisk børnret II – Forældreansvar – en sammenlignende studie af dansk, finsk, islandsk, norsk og svensk ret med drøftelser af harmoniseringsmuligheder og reformbehov, Nord 2003:14.

Davidson, Alexander, Two Models of Welfare: the Origins and Development of the Welfare State in Sweden and New Zealand, 1888–1988, 1989, Publications of the Political Science Association in Uppsala, no 108.

Domínguez, Marta, Castro Martín, Teresa and Mencarini, Letizia, European Latecomers: Cohabitation in Italy and Spain, (First Draft), March 2007, Prepared for the 2007 Annual Meeting of the Population Association of America, New York, Session 71.

Dupuis, Martin D, The Impact of Culture, Society, and History on the Legal Process: An Analysis of the Legal Status of Same-Sex Relationships in the United States and Denmark, International Journal of Law and the Family, Vol. 9, 1995, pp. 86–118.

Ett brev i en folkets livsfråga, Till Svenska kyrkans präster från dess biskopar, Svenska Kyrkan Diakonistyrelses Bokförlag, 1951.

European Family Law in Action, Volume I, Grounds for Divorce, Edited by Boele-Woelki, Katharina, Braat, Bente and Sumner, Ian, Intersentia, 2003.

European Family Law in Action, Volume II, Maintenance Between Former Spouses, Edited by Boele-Woelki, Katharina, Braat, Bente and Sumner, Ian, Intersentia, 2003.

European Family Law in Action, Volume IV, Parental Responsibilities, Edited by Boele-Woelki, Katharina, Braat, Bente and Sumner, Ian, Intersentia, 2005.

European Family Law in Action, Volume IV: Property Relations between Spouses, Edited by, Boele-Woelki, Katharina, Braat, Bente and Curry-Sumner, Ian, Intersentia 2009.

Fagerberg, Holsten (Editor) De homosexuella och kyrkan, Verbum, 1974.

Ferrand, Frédérique, French Report concerning the CEFL Questionnaire on Grounds for Divorce and Maintenance Between Former Spouses, 2002. www.ceflonline.net/.

Ferrand, Frédérique and Braat, Bente, French Report concerning the CEFL Questionnaire on Property Relations between Spouses, 2008. www.ceflonline.net/.

Ferrer Riba, Josep, Same-Sex Marriage, Express Divorce and Related Developments in Spanish Marriage Law, The International Survey of Family Law, September 2006, pp. 139–143.

Friedmann, Wolfgang, Legal Theory, Steven & Sons Limited, 1967.

Garrison, Marsha, Marriage Matters: What's Wrong with the ALI's Domestic Partnership Proposal, Brooklyn Law School Research Papers, No. 103, 2008.

Glendon, Mary Ann, The Transformation of Family Law, State, Law and Family in the United States and Western Europe, The University Chicago Press, 1989.

Glendon, Mary Ann, Comparative Law as Shock Treatment: A Tribute to Jacob W.F. Sundberg, Festskrift till Jacob W.F. Sundberg, Juristförlaget, 1993, pp. 69–84.

Glendon, Mary Ann, Introduction: Family Law in a Time of Turbulence, International Encyclopedia of Comparative Law, Vol. IV, Persons and Family, 2006.

Glendon, Mary Ann, International Encyclopedia of Comparative Law, Vol. IV, Persons and Family, Introduction: Family Law in a time of Turbulence, Martinus Nijhoff Publishers, 2007.

Glendon, Mary Ann, Rheinstein, Max, International Encyclopedia of Comparative Law, Vol. IV, Persons and Family, Interspousal Relations, 2007.

González Beilfuss, Cristina, Spanish National Report, European Family Law in Action, Volume IV: Property Relations between Spouses, 2003. www.ceflonline.net/.

González Beilfuss, Cristina, Parejas de hecho y matrimonios del mismo sexo en la unión Europea, Marcial Pons, 2004.

González Beilfuss, Cristina, Private international law aspects of homosexual couples, Spanish National Report for the XVIIth Congress of the International Academy of Comparative Law, 2006.

Graversen, Jørgen, Family Law as a Reflection of Family Ideology, Scandinavian Studies in Law, 1990, Vol. 34, pp. 69–91.

Greve, Vagn, Hvornår er bigami strafbart? Festskrift till Suzanne Wennberg, Norstedts Juridik 2009, pp. 91–107.

Gunnarsson, Åsa, Familjen – en genusforskningens utmaning, Familjeföreställningar, om familjens betydelse inom juridik, ekonomi och forskning, Edited by Burman, Monica and Gunnarsson, Åsa, Iustus förlag, 2001, pp. 11–22.

Gårdfeldt, Lars, Äkta vill jag också vara, Uppdrag samliv, Om äktenskap och samlevnad, Edited by Lindfelt, Mikael and Gustafsson Lundberg, Johanna, Verbum, 2007, pp. 367–386.

Gähler, Michael, Self-Reported Psychological Well-being among Adult Children of Divorce in Sweden, Acta Sociologica, Vol. 41, No. 3 (1998), pp. 209–225.

Hadenius, Stig, Swedish Politics during the 20th Century, Second Edition, the Swedish Institute, 1988.

Hadenius, Stig, Swedish Politics during the 20th Century, Conflict and Consensus, Fourth Edition, the Swedish Institute, 1997.

Hafström, Gerhard, Den svenska familjerättens historia, 8:e upplagan, Juridiska föreningen i Lund, 1972.

Hammar, K. G. Ärkebiskopens perspektiv, Svenska kyrkans utredningar, 2005:1, Rapport från en offentlig hearing den 6–9 september 2004, Svenska kyrkans teologiska kommitté, pp. 32–41.

Handbok, ther vti är författat, huruledes gudstiensten med christelige ceremonier och kyrckioseder, vti wåra församlingar skall blifwa hållen och förhandlad, förbättrad och förmehrad i Stockholm åhr 1599, öfwersedd åhr 1608, och numera efter nyia kyrckioordningen inrättad åhr 1693.

Handbok för svenska kyrkan: steadfast av konungen år 1917, Svenska kyrkans diakonistyrelses bokförlag, 1918.

Hartley, Trevor C., The Foundations of European Community Law, Sixth Edition, Oxford University Press, 2007.

Helfer, Laurence R., International Decisions: Grant v. Southwest Trains Ltd. (1999). Duke Law Faculty Scholarship. Paper 2026. http://scholarship.law.duke.edu/faculty_scholarship/2026.

Hirdman, Yvonne, Att lägga livet till rätta – studier i svensk folkhemspolitik, Carlssons, 1989.

Hirdman, Yvonne, Social Engineering and the Woman Question: Sweden in the Thirties, Swedish Social Democracy, A Model in Transition, Edited by Clement, Wallace and Mahon, Rianne, Canadian Scholars' Press Inc., 1994, pp. 65–81.

Holdgaard, Marianne, Family Life and Transsexuals, Family Life and Human Rights Regarding Family Life, Edited by Lødrup, Peter and Modvar, Eva, Gyldendal Norsk Forlag AS, 2004, pp. 283–289.

Inger, Göran, Den svenska kyrkolagen 300 år, Riksarkivets rapport nr 7, Kyrkan-lagen-människan, Forskarsymposium kring 1686 års kyrkolag på Hässelby Slott, 2–3 september 1986. pp. 155–176.

Inger, Göran, Svensk rättshistoria, upplaga 4:1, Liber ekonomi, 1997.

Inger, Göran, Kyrkolagstiftningen under 1600-talet, Sveriges kyrkohistoria 4, Enhetskyrkans tid, Montgomery Ingun, Verbum, 2002.

Jaurena i Salas, Francesc, The Law on Stable Unions of Couples in the Catalonia Autonomous Community of Spain, Legal Recognition of Same-Sex Partnerships,

A Study of National, European and International Law, Edited by Wintermute, Robert, Andenæs, Mads, 2001, pp. 505–518.

Jägerskiöld, Stig, Kring tillkomsten av 1734 års lag, Rättshistoriskt bibliotek, trettiosjunde bandet, skrifter utgivna av institutet för rättshistorisk forskning grundat av Gustav och Carin Olin, A.-B Nordiska Bokhandeln, Stockholm, 1984, pp. 7–25.

Jänterä-Jareborg, Maarit, Mot en europeisk (internationell) familjerätt, Om EU-samarbetets utvidgning till familjerätten, JT 2001/02 pp. 48–74.

Jänterä-Jareborg, Maarit, Registered Partnerships in Private International Law: The Scandinavian Approach, Legal Recognition of Same-Sex Couples in Europe, Edited by Boele-Woelki, Katharina and Fuchs, Angelika, Intersentia, 2003, pp. 137–158.

Jänterä-Jareborg, Maarit, Unification of International Family Law in Europe – A Critical Perspective, Perspectives for the Unification and Harmonisation of Family Law in Europe, Edited by Boele-Woelki, Katharina, Intersentia, 2003, pp. 194–214.

Jänterä-Jareborg, Maarit, Sörgjerd, Caroline, The Experiences with Registered Partnership in Scandinavia, FamPra.ch 3/2004, Stämpfli Verlag AG, pp. 577–597.

Jänterä-Jareborg, Maarit, Parenthood for Same-Sex Couples, Liber Memorialis Petar Sarcevic, Universalism, Tradition and the Individual, Sellier. European Law Publishers, 2006, pp. 75–91.

Jänterä-Jareborg, Maarit, Brattström Margareta and Walleng Kajsa, Swedish Report concerning the CEFL Questionnaire on Property Relations Between Spouses, 2008. www.ceflonline.net/.

Jänterä-Jareborg, Maarit, Rechtsregeln für nichteheliches Zusammenleben in Schweden, Beiträge zum europäischen Familienrecht, Band 12, Edited by: Kroppenberg/Schwab/Gottwald/Spickhoff, Gieseking 2009, pp. 207–226.

Jänterä-Jareborg, Maarit, En harmoniserad familjerätt för Europa? Internationellt privaträttsliga och rättsjämförande perspektiv, Tidsskrift for Rettsvitenskap, Vol. 122, 3 2009, pp. 323–353.

Jänterä-Jareborg, Maarit, Family Law in the European Judicial Space – Concerns Regarding Nation-State's Autonomy and Legal Coherence, National Law and Europeanization, Suomalainen Lakimieshydistys 2009, pp. 29–61.

Jänterä-Jareborg, Maarit, Sweden: The Same-Sex Marriage Reform with Special Regard to Concerns of Religion, Zeitschrift für das gesamte Familienrecht, no. 18, 2010, p. 1508.

Jänterä-Jareborg, Maarit, Religion and the Secular State: National Report of Sweden, The XVIII International Congress of the International Academy of Comparative Law, Washington 2010, pp. 669–686.

Jänterä-Jareborg, Maarit, Kan polygami vara laglig i Sverige? Anförande vid Kungliga Svenska Vetenskaps-societeten i Uppsala den 31 augusti 2010.

Kangas, Urpo, Divorce System and Maintenance of Former Spouses in Scandinavian Countries, Juxtapposing Legal Systems and the Principles of European Family Law on Divorce and Maintenance, 2007, pp. 37–54.

Koch, Elisabeth, Das Verbot der kirchlichen Voraustrauung – politische Hintergründe und historische Entwicklung, StaZ Nr. 5/2010, pp. 129–136.

Korpiola, Mia, An Uneasy Harmony: Consummation and Parental Consent in Secular and Canon Law in Medieval Scandinavia, Nordic Perspectives on Medieval Canon Law, Edited by Korpiola Mia, Publications of Matthias Calonius Society II, 1999.

Korpiola, Mia, Between betrothal and bedding: marriage formation in Sweden 1200–1600, Brill, 2009.

Kälvemark, Ann-Sofie, More Children of Better Quality? Aspects of Swedish Population Policy in the 1930s, Studia Historica Upsaliensia, Historiska Institutionen vid Uppsala Universitet genom Sven A. Nilsson, Sten Carlsson and Carl Göran Andrae 1980.

Lahey, Kathleen A, Alderson, Kevin, Same-Sex Marriage, The Personal and the Political, Insomniac Press, 2004.

Lando, Ole, The Worries of a Comparatist, Julebog 2000, Jurist- og økonomforbundets forlag, 2000, pp. 21–32.

Legrand, Pierre, European Legal Systems are not Converging, International and Comparative Law Quarterly, 1996, pp. 52–81.

Lind, Göran, Common Law Marriage – Ett rättsinstitut för samboende – Ursprung – gällande rätt – framtid, Electronic Publishing Centre, 2006.

Lødrup, Peter, The Reharmonisation of Nordic Family Law, European Challenges in Contemporary Family Law, Edited by, Boele-Woelki, Katharina, Sverdrup, Tone, Intersentia, 2003, pp. 17–26.

Lødrup, Peter, Agell, Anders and Singer, Anna, Nordisk børneret I – farskap og morskap samt underhåll til barn – en sammenlignende studie af dansk, finsk islandsk, norsk og svensk ret med drøftelser af harmoniseringsmuligheder og reformbehov, Nord 2003:4.

Lødrup, Peter, Nordisk Arverett, En sammenlignende studie av dansk, finsk, islandsk, norsk og svensk rett med drøftelser av harmoniseringsmuligheter og reformbehov, Nord 2003:3.

Malmström, Åke, Rättssociologiska forskningsuppgifter inom äktenskapsrätten, Tidskrift utgiven av Juridiska Föreningen i Finland, 1957, nittiotredje årgången, pp. 231–242.

Martín-Casals, Miquel, Ribot, Jordi, Solé, Josep, Spanish Report concerning the CEFL Questionnaire on Grounds for Divorce and Maintenance Between Former Spouses. www.ceflonline.net/.

Martín-Casals, Miquel, Same-Sex Partnerships in the Legislation of Spanish Autonomous Communities, Legal Recognition of Same-Sex Couples in Europe, Intersentia, 2003.

Martín-Casals, Miquel, Family Law of Spanish Autonomies: Following a Similar Pattern? Convergence and divergence of family law in Europe, Edited by Antokolskaia, Masha, Intersentia, 2007, pp. 63–75.

Martínez de Aguirre Aldaz, Carlos and De Pablo Contreras, Pedro, Four years of Same-Sex Marriage in Spanish Law: A Discussion Ranging from Constitutionality to the obstinacy of biology, pp. 1–15, article presented at The XVIII International Congress of the International Academy of Comparative Law, Washington 2010.

Martiny, Dieter, German Report concerning the CEFL Questionnaire on Grounds for Divorce and Maintenance Between Former Spouses. www.ceflonline.net/.

Maxwell, Nancy G, Opening Civil Marriage To Same-Gender Couples: A Netherlands-United States Comparison, Arizona Journal of International and Comparative Law, Vol. 18, 2001, pp. 141–207.

McCrudden, Christopher, The New Concept of Equality, Tier, 2–3 June 2003, ERA Congress Center, pp. 1–24.
Melby, Kari, Pylkkänen, Anu, Rosenbeck, Bente, Carlsson Wetterberg, Christina, Inte ett ord om kärlek, Äktenskap och politik i norden, ca 1850–1930, Makadam förlag, 2006.
Meulders-Klein, Marie-Thérèse, Towards a European Civil Code on Family Law? Ends and Means in Perspectives for the Unification and Harmonisation of Family Law in Europe, Edited by Katharina Boele-Woelki, Intersentia, 2003, pp. 105–117.
Modéer, Kjell Å, Secularization, Liberalization and Modernization: Family Law in Scandinavian Welfare States in the 1960s-1970s, Japanese Family Law in Comparative Perspective, Regents of the University of California, 2009, pp. 205–220.
Myrdal, Alva and Myrdal, Gunnar, Kris i befolkningsfrågan, Albert Bonniers Förlag, 1935.
Myrdal, Alva, Folk och familj, Kooperativa förbundets bokförlag, 1944.
Nielsen, Linda, Family Rights and the Registered Partnership in Denmark, International Journal of Law and the Family, Vol. 4, 1990, pp. 297–307.
Nilsson, Gert (Editor) En fråga om kärlek, Homosexuella i kyrkan, En bok från samtalsgruppen Kyrkan och de homosexuella, Verbum, 1988.
Nilsson, Mattias, Lundberg, Jenny, Europarätten – en introduktion till EG-rätten och Europakonventionen, Second Edition, Jure förlag AB, 2006.
Normann, Carl-E, Enhetskyrka och upplysningsidéer, Studier i svensk religionspolitik vid 1700-talets mitt, CWK Gleerup, 1963.
Nygren, Rolf, Kyrkorätt, Äktenskap och sekularisering – I and II, Svensk pastoraltidskrift – kyrkligt forum, trettioförsta årgången, 1989, pp. 25–54.
Olivecrona, Om makars giftorätt i bo, Fourth Edition, 1878.
Payne, Stanley G, The Franco Regime, 1936–1975, The University of Wisconsin Press, 1987.
Persson, Per Erik, Att tolka Gud idag, Debattlinjer i aktuell teologi, Liber 1971.
Petersson, Stig-Åke, En svensk homorörelse växer fram, RFSL 1950–2000, Homo i Folkhemmet.
Pichardo Galán, José Ignacio, Same-Sex Couples in Spain. Historical, Contextual and Symbolic Factors, Same-Sex Couples, Same-Sex Partnerships and Homosexual Marriages: A Focus on Cross-National Differentials, Documents de Travail, no. 124, Edited by Digoix, Marie and Festy, Patrick, Ined, 2004, pp. 159–173.
Pichardo Galán, José Ignacio, Same-Sex Marriage in Spain: Overcoming Moral Panic, written contribution to the 5th IASSCS International Conference: "Sexual Rights and Moral Panics" at San Francisco State University, 21–24 June, 2005, pp. 1–8.
Pichardo Galán, José Ignacio, Beyond Marriage: LGTB Families in Spain, draft English version of the article "Espagne. Le marriage homosexuel au pays de la famille", Conference on LGBT families in Europe, 4–6 March, 2008, Slovenia.
Pintens, Walter, Europeanisation of Family Law, Perspectives for the Unification and Harmonisation of Family Law in Europe, Edited by, Boele-Woelki, Katharina, Intersentia, 2003, pp. 3–33.
Platero, Raquel, Love and the State: Gay Marriage in Spain, Fem. Leg. Stud, No 15, 2007, pp. 329–340.

Platero Méndez, Raquel, Intersecting Gender and Sexual Orientation: An Analysis of Sexuality and Citizenship in Gender Equality Policies in Spain, Critical Review of International Social and Political Philosophy, Vol. 10, No 4, December 2007, p. 587.

Platero, Raquel, Outstanding Challenges in a Post-Equality Era: The Same-Sex Marriage and gender identity Laws in Spain, International Journal of Iberian Studies, Vol. 21, No. 1, 2008, pp. 41–49.

Popenoe, David, Disturbing the Nest, Family Change and Decline in Modern Societies, Aldine de Gruyter, 1988.

Principles of European Family Law Regarding Divorce and Maintenance Between Former Spouses, Commission on European Family Law, Edited by, Boele-Woelki, Katharina, Ferrand Frédérique, Gonzáles Beilfus, Cristina, Jänterä-Jareborg, Maarit, Lowe, Nigel, Dieter, Martiny, Pintens, Walter, Intersentia, 2004.

Rheinstein, Max, Marriage Stability, Divorce, and the Law, the University of Chicago Press, 1972.

Rheinstein, Max, König, René, International Encyclopedia of Comparative Law, Vol. IV, Persons and Family, Chapter 1, Introduction, 2006, pp. 1–19.

Roca, Encarna, Same-Sex Partnerships in Spain: Family, Marriage or Contract? European Journal of Law Reform, Vol. 3, No. 3, 2001, pp. 365–382.

Rydström, Jens, Sinners and Citizens, Bestiality and Homosexuality in Sweden 1880–1950, Department of History, Stockholm, 2001.

Rydström, Jens, Tvåsamhetens brunn: Registrerat partnerskap i Norden, Queersverige, Edited by Kulick, Don, Natur och Kultur, 2005, pp. 308–335.

Ryrstedt, Eva, Bodelning och bostad, ekonomisk självständighet eller gemenskap, juristförlaget i Lund, 1998.

Ryrstedt, Eva, Delning mellan sambor i Sverige, Normativa perspektiv, Festskrift till Anna Christensen, Juristförlaget i Lund, 2000, pp. 373–402.

Ryrstedt, Eva, Legal Status of Cohabitants in Sweden, Die Rechtsstellung nichtehelicher Lebensgemeinschaften, the Legal Status of Cohabitants, Edited by Jens, M. Scherpe and Nadjma Yassari, Max-Planch-Institut, Mohr Siebeck, 2004, pp. 415–454.

Saez, Macarena, Same sex marriage, same sex cohabitation, and same sex families around the world: Why "same" is so different? General Report for the XVIII International Congress of the International Academy of Comparative Law, Washington 2010, pp. 1–49. (Cited with permission from the author.)

Sandel, Michael J., Justice, What's the Right Thing to Do?, Library of Congress Cataloging-in-Publication Data, 2009.

Savolainen, Matti, The Finnish and Swedish Partnership Acts – Similarities and Divergences, Legal Recognition of Same-Sex Couples, Edited by Boele-Woelki, Katharina and Fuchs, Angelika, Intersentia, 2003, pp. 24–40.

Sayed, Mosa, Islam och arvsrätt i det mångkulturella Sverige, En internationellt privaträttslig och jämförande studie, Iustus, 2009.

Schmidt, Folke, The Prospective Law of Marriage, Scandinavian Studies in Law, 1971, p. 191–218.

Schmidt, Folke, Äktenskapsrätt, Fifth Edition, P. A Norstedt & söners förlag, 1974.

Schrama, Wendy, Registered Partnership in the Netherlands, International Journal of Law, Policy and the Family, 13, 1999, p. 315–327.

Schwenzer, Ingeborg, Methodological Aspects of Harmonization of Family Law, Perspectives for the Unification and Harmonization of Family Law in Europe, Edited by Boele-Woelki, Katharina, Intersentia, 2003, pp. 143–158.

Schwenzer, Ingeborg, in Collaboration with Dimsey, Mariel, Model Family Code From a Global Perspective, Intersentia, 2006.

Silverstolpe, Fredrik, Praxis och teori 1726–1864, Sympatiens hemlighetsfulla makt: Stockholms homosexuella 1860–1960, Edited by Göran Söderström, Stockholmia förlag, 1999.

Singer, Anna, Familjerätten – en kulturyttring? Familj Religion Rätt, En antologi om kulturella spänningar i familjen – med Sverige och Turkiet som exempel. Edited by Singer, Anna, Jänterä-Jareborg, Maarit and Schlytter, Astrid, Iustus, 2010, pp. 243–272.

Stalford, Helen, Concepts of Family under EU Law – Lessons from the ECHR, International Journal of Law, Policy and the Family, No. 16, 2002, pp. 410–434.

Strandbakken, Asbjørn, Lov om registrert partnerskap, Jussens Venner, 1993, pp. 300–351.

Strömholm, Stig, Användning av utländskt material i juridiska monografier, Några anteckningar och förslag, SvJT 1971, pp. 251–263.

Sundberg, Jacob, Familjerätt i omvandling, institutet för rättsvetenskaplig forskning [LV], P. A Norstedt & söners förlag, 1969.

Sundberg, Jacob, Marriage or No Marriage in Swedish Law, International and Comparative Law Quarterly, Vol. 20, 1971, pp. 223–238.

Sundby, Olof, Luthersk äktenskapsuppfattning: en studie i den äktenskapliga debatten i Sverige efter 1900, Svenska kyrkans diakonistyrelses bokförlag, 1959.

Sumner, Ian, Going Dutch? A Comparative Analysis and Assessment of the Gradual Recognition of Homosexuality with respect to the Netherlands and England, Maastricht Journal of European and Comparative Law, 2002, Vol. 9, No 1, pp. 29–56. (See also: Curry-Sumner, Ian.)

Sumner, Ian, Warendorf, Hans, Family Law Legislation of the Netherlands, A Translation Including Book 1 of the Dutch Civil Code, Procedural and Transitional Provisions and Private International Law Legislation, Intersentia, 2003.

Sumner, Ian, The Charter of Fundamental Rights of the European Union and Sexual Orientation, Family Life and Human Rights Regarding Family Life, Edited by Lødrup, Peter and Modvar, Eva, Gyldendal Norsk Forlag AS, 2004, pp. 869–887.

Sumner, Ian, Dissolution of Registered Partnerships: Excursion in Conversion!, International Family Law, 2004, pp. 213–237.

Svenska kyrkohandboken, kap 1–11, jämte tvenne register, A. Ahlström förlag, 1882.

Sverdrup, Tone, An Ill-Fitting Garment: Why the Logic of Private Law Falls Short between Cohabitants, Family Finances, Edited by Bea, Verschraegen, Jan Sramek Verlag, 2009, pp. 355–368.

Söderström, Göran, En aktiviströrelse växer fram, Sympatiens hemlighetsfulla makt: Stockholms homosexuella 1860–1960, Edited by Göran Söderström, Stockholmia förlag, 1999.

Terrett, Steve A Bridge too Far? Non-discrimination and Homosexuality in European Community Law, European Public Law, Issue 4:4, 1998, pp. 487–506.

Thue, Helge, Gift uten samtykke, Tidsskrift for familierett, arverett og barnevernrettslige spørsmål (FAB), No 2 2009, pp. 68–69.

Tobío, Constanza, Marriage, Cohabitation and the Residential Independence of Young People in Spain, International Journal of Law, Policy and the Family, 15, 2001, pp. 68–87.

Toner, Helen, Partnership Rights, Free Movement and EU Law, Modern Studies in European Law, Hart Publishing, 2003.

Tottie, Lars, The Elimination of Fault in Swedish Divorce Law, Marriage and Cohabitation in Contemporary Society, Butterworths, 1980, pp. 131–137.

Tridimas, Takis, The General Principles of EU Law, Second Edition, Oxford University Press, 2006.

Tripp, C.A., Homosexualitet, Bokförlaget Prisma, i sambarbete med RFSL, 1981.

Verschraegen, Bea, The Right to Private Life and Family Life, the Right to Marry and to Found a Family, and the Prohibition of Discrimination, Legal Recognition of Same-Sex Couples in Europe, Edited by, Boele-Woelki, Katharina, Fuchs, Angelika, Intersentia, 2003, pp. 194–211.

Vonk, Machteld, One, Two or Three Parents? Lesbian Co-Mothers and a Known Donor with Family Life Under Dutch Law, International Journal of Law, Policy and the Family, no 18, 2004, pp. 103–117.

Vonk, Machteld, The role of formalised and non-formalised intentions in legal parent-child relationships in Dutch law, Utrecht Law Review, Volume 4, Issue 2, June 2008, pp. 117–134.

Waaldijk, Kees, "Civil Developments: Patters of Reform in the Legal Position of Same-Sex Partners in Europe, Canadian Journal of Family Law, Vol. 17, No. 1, 2000, pp. 62–88.

Waaldijk, Kees, "Small Change: How the Road to Same-Sex Marriage Got Paved in the Netherlands", Legal Recognition of Same-Sex Partnerships, A Study of National, European and International Law, Edited by Wintermute, Robert, Andenæs, Mads, 2001, pp. 437–464.

Westermarck, Edvard, The History of Human Marriage, Firth Edition, vol I-III, Macmillian and Co., Limited, 1925.

Westring, Hjalmar, Den nya giftermålsbalken jämte dithörande författningar med förklaringar, Second Edition by Ekeberg Birger and Stenbeck Einar, P.A. Norstedt & söners förlag, 1933.

Winroth, Alfred, Äktenskaps ingående/af A. Winroth, Gleerup, 1892.

Wintermute, Robert, Strasbourg to the Rescue? Same-Sex Partners and Parents Under the European Convention, Legal Recognition of Same-Sex Partnerships, A Study of National, European and International Law, Edited by Wintermute, Robert, Andenæs, Mads, Hart Publishing, 2004, pp. 713–730.

Wintermute, Robert, Written Comments of Fidh, ICJ, AIRE Centre & Ilga-Europe, concerning the Case of Shalk and Kopf v. Austria, Submitted on 26 June 2007, pp 1–16.

Ytterberg, Hans, All Human Beings Are Equal, but Some are More Equal than Others – Equality in Dignity without Equality in Rights?, Legal Recognition of Same-Sex Couples in Europe, Edited by Boele-Woelki, Katharina and Fuchs, Angelika, European Family Law Series No. 1, Antwerp/Oxford/New York, 2003, pp. 1–9.

Zweigert, Konrad, Kötz, Hein, An Introduction to Comparative Law, Third Edition, Clarendon Press, 1998.

Ängarne-Lindberg, Teresia, Grown-Up Children of Divorce - Experiences and Health, Linköping University Medical Dissertations No. 1173 2010.

Örücü, Esin, The Principles of European Family Law put to the Test: Diversity in Harmony or Harmony in Diversity? Juxtapposing Legal Systems and the Principles of European Family Law on Divorce and Maintenance, 2007, pp. 233–254.

Österberg, Eva, Historiska perspektiv, Kyrkan, äktenskapet och konstruktionen av det "normala": samlevnadsformer i historiskt perspektiv, Kärlek, samlevnad och äktenskap, Rapport från en offentlig hearing den 6–9 september 2004, Svenska kyrkans teologiska kommitté, pp. 43–51.

Östermalm, Torsten, Föreställningar/vanföreställningar, Allmänhetens attityder till homosexualitet, Swedish National Institute of Public Health, Compiled by Carpelan, Lars.

JURISPRUDENCE

SWEDEN

Decision by the Supreme Court, NJA 1950 p. 513.
Decision by the Supreme Court, NJA 1955 p. 63.
Decision by the Supreme Court, NJA 1968 p. 126.
Decision by the Supreme Court, NJA 1972 p. 612.
Decision by the Supreme Court, NJA 1985 p. 172.
Decision by the Supreme Administrative Court, RÅ 1993 ref 102.
Decision by the Supreme Court, NJA 1994 p. 61.
Decision by the Supreme Court, NJA 2005 p. 805.
Decision by the Court of Appeal, RH 1994:29.
Decision by the Court of Appeal, RH 1997:98.
Decision by the Court of Appeal, RH 1998:5.
Decision by the Court of Appeals, 10 October, 1967.

THE NETHERLANDS

The Dutch Supreme Court: Hoge Raad, 19 October 1990 (1992).

THE EUROPEAN COURT OF JUSTICE (EU)

Van Gend en Loos v. Nederlandse Administratie der Belastingen, C-26/62 [1963] ECR 1.
Milac, C-8/78 [1978] ECR 1721.
Netherlands v. Reed, C-59/85 [1986] ECR 1283, Para. 15.
P v. S and Cornwall County Council, C-13/91 [1996] ECR I-2143.
Grant v. South West Trains Ltd, C-249/96 [1998] ECR I-621.
D and Kingdom of Sweden v. Council, C-122/99 P & C-125/99, C-120/78 P [2001] 1.
Carlos Garcia Avello v État belge, Case C-148/02.
Tadao Maruko v. Versorgungsanstalt der deutschen Bühnen, C-267/06.
Grunkin-Paul v Standesamt Niebüll, Case C-353/06.

THE EUROPEAN COURT OF HUMAN RIGHTS

Marckx v. Belgium (application No. 6833/74), 13 June 1979.
X and Y v. United Kingdom (application no. 9369/81), 3 May 1983.
Johnston and Others v Ireland, (application no. 9697/82), 18 December 1986.
Norris V. Ireland, (application no. 10581/83), 26 October 1988.
Eriksson and Goldschmidt v. Sweden, (application no. 14573/89), 22 June 1989.
Modinos v. Cyprus, (application no. 15070/89), 22 April 1993.
A.D.T. v. United Kingdom, (application no. 35765/97), 31 July 2000.

Christine Goodwin v. The United Kingdom, (application no. 28957/95), 11 July 2002.
L and V v. Austria, 9 January 2003 (applications nos. 39392/98 and 39829/98), 9 January 2003.
Karner v. Austria (application no. 40016/98), 24 July 2003
Wena and Anita Parry v. United Kingdom (application no. 42971/05), (declared inadmissible on 28 Nov. 2006.)
R. and F. v. the United Kingdom (application no. 35748/05), 28 November 2006.
Dudgeon v. United Kingdom, (application no. 7525/76), 4 October 2007.
E.B. v. France, January 22 2008 (application no. 43546/02), 22 January 2008.
Burden v. The United Kingdom, (application no. 13378/05), 29 April 2008.
Korelc v. Slovenia, (application no. 28456/03), 12 May 2009.
Schalk and Kopf v. Austria, (application no. 30141/04), 24 June 2010.
P.B. and J.S. v. Austria, (application no. 18984/02), 22 July 2010, 22 July 2010.

OTHER SOURCES

Report by the National Board of Health and Welfare, Transsexuella och övriga personer med könsidentitetsstörningar, rättsliga villkor för fastställelse av könstillhörighet samt vård och stöd, June 2010.
Available at: www.socialstyrelsen.se/Lists/Artikelkatalog/Attachments/18087/2010-6-31.pdf.
Circulation for comments regarding Report (SOU 2007:17), Äktenskap för par med samma kön. Vigselfrågor. Yttrande från trossamfundet Romersk-Katolska kyrkan över äktenskaps- och partnerskapsutredningens betänkande (SOU 2007:17), dnr Ju2007/3311/L2, pp. 1–10.
Cecilia Malmström, Presentation at the Conference "Youth Perspectives on Security, Peace and Democracy, Gothenburg, 25 May 2007. Available at: http://regeringen.se/sb/d/8603/a82935.
Information concerning Dutch law provided by Katharina Boele-Woelki to the author, 19 November 2010.
Information concerning Spanish law, provided by Professor Cristina González Beilfuss to the author, 10 November 2010.
Lecture given by docent Michael Gähler, Swedish Institute for Social Research, Stockholm University, at the Uppsala Faculty of Law, 24 April 2008, 6 pm – 8 pm.
Information provided by Marie Alm at the Swedish Intercountry Adoptions Authority to the author, 25 November 2010.

WEBSITES

NEWSPAPERS AND NEWS

http://www.sydsvenskan.se/sverige/article546491/Fa-samfund-ar-villiga-att-viga-samkonade-par.html
www.dn.se/DNet/jsp/polopoly.jsp?d=147&a=495316.

www.svd.se/opinion/brannpunkt/artikel_471557.svd.
www.nytimes.com/2005/06/30/international/europe/30cnd-spain.html.
www.elmundo.es/elmundo/2004/09/30/sociedad/1096545670.html.
www.cbsnews.com/stories/2005/04/21/world/main689929.shtml?source=search_story.
www.cbc.ca/world/story/2009/05/26/f-same-sex-timeline.html.

STATISTICS

www.scb.se/statistik/_publikationer/OV0904_2010A01_BR_04_A01BR1001.pdf.
www.cbs.nl.
www.cbs.nl/en-GB/menu/themas/bevolking/publicaties/artikelen/archief/2010/2010-3044-wm.htm?Languageswitch=on.
www.cbs.nl/.
www.cbs.nl/en-GB/menu/themas/bevolking/publicaties/artikelen/archief/2010/2010-3044-wm.htm?Languageswitch=on.
www.cis.es/cis/opencm/ES/2_barometros/depositados.jsp.
www.ine.es.

THE CHURCH OF SWEDEN

www.svenskakyrkan.se.
www.svenskakyrkan.se/default.aspx?id=586596
www.svenskakyrkan.se/default.aspx?id=647808.
www.svenskakyrkan.se/default.aspx?di=252610
www.svenskakyrkan.se/default.aspx?di=310232&ptid=0.
www.svenskakyrkan.se/gudstjanstbanken/service_book/20Vigsel.htm.

MISCELLANEOUS WEBSITES

www.riksdagen.se/templates/R_PageExtended____6309.aspx.
http://web.eduskunta.fi/Resource.phx/riksdagen/index.htx.
www.timesonline.co.uk/tol/news/world/article384255.ece.
www.nrk.no/nyheter/1.6673894
www.rawstory.com/rs/2010/0704/spain-church-samesex-marriages/
www.ne.se/lang/feminism?i_whole_article=true
http://runeberg.org/nfbe/0213.html
www.law.leiden.edu/general/img/Translation%20of%20Dutch%20laws%20against%20sexual%20orientation%20discrimination_tcm19-55182.pdf
http://ec.europa.eu/civiljustice/divorce/divorce_spa_en.htm
www.homo.se/o.o.i.s/2711
www.socialstyrelsen.se
www.ceflonline.net/

www.ilga-europe.org/home/issues/families/recognition_of_relationships/legislation_and_case_law/marriage_and_partnership_rights_for_same_sex_partners_country_by_country
www.ne.se
https://svt.se/svt/jsp/Crosslink.jsp?d=62242&a=1201620&lid=senasteNytt_793033&lpos=rubrik_1201620
www.norden.org/start/start.asp.
www.norden.org/da/nordisk-raad/om-nordisk-raad/nordisk-raads-historie/1953–1971.
http://english.justitie.nl/currenttopics/pressreleases/archives-2008/new-acts-as-from-1-january-2009.aspx
www.cis.es/cis/opencm/ES/2_barometros/depositados.jsp.
www.ilga-europe.org/home/issues/beyond_europe/united_nations/consultative_status_in_the_economic_and_social_council_ecosoc_of_the_united_nations/more_lgbt_groups_gain_consultative_status_with_un
http://electionresources.org/es/congress.php?election=1996&community=09
http://electionresources.org/es/congress.php?election=1996
http://electionresources.org/es/congress.php?election=2004
http://en.wikipedia.org/wiki/Municipal_elections_in_Madrid
www.vatican.va/archive/ENG1104/__P45.HTM.
www.fides.org/eng/news/2005/0505/02_4784.html
www.buddybuddy.com/zapat-01.html
www.echr.coe.int/NR/rdonlyres/D5CC24A7-DC13–4318-B457–5C9014916D7A/0/EnglishAnglais.pdf
www.divorcereform.org/cov.html
http://missionskyrkan.se/Svenska-Missionskyrkan/Missionskyrkan/Enstaka/En-kyrka-med-sjalvstandiga-forsamlingar---brev-till-forsamlingar-och-pastorer/
www.bibelsajten.nu/fragelada/117-homosexualitet-/11445-homosexualitet-i-bibeln
www.dagenmagazinet.no/Nyheter/Innenriks/tabid/248/Default.aspx?articleView=true&ModuleId=69289
www.internetconsultatie.nl/ouderschapduomoeder
www.typicallyspanish.com/news/publish/article_6619.shtml
www.partidofamiliayvida.es/sitio/index.php
http://news.bbc.co.uk/2/hi/europe/3695748.stm.
www.fra.europa.eu/fraWebsite/attachments/FRA-LGBT-report-update2010.pdf
www.religlaw.org/template.php?id=173

European Family Law Series

1. *Legal Recognition of Same-Sex Couples in Europe*, K. Boele-Woelki and A. Fuchs (eds.)
2. *European Family Law in Action Volume I: Grounds for divorce*, K. Boele-Woelki, B. Braat and I. Sumner (eds.)
3. *European Family Law in Action Volume II : Maintenance Between Former Spouses*, K. Boele-Woelki, B. Braat and I. Sumner (eds.)
4. *Perspectives for the Unification and Harmonisation of Family Law in Europe*, K. Boele-Woelki (ed.)
5. *Family Law Legislation of the Netherlands*, I. Sumner and H. Warendorf
6. *Indépendance et interdépendance patrimoniales des époux dans le régime matrimonial légal des droits néerlandais, français et suisse*, B. Braat
7. *Principles of European Family Law Regarding Divorce and Maintenance Between Former Spouses*, K. Boele-Woelki, F. Ferrand, C. González Beilfuss, M. Jänterä-Jareborg, N. Lowe, D. Martiny and W. Pintens
8. *Inheritance Law Legislation of the Netherlands*, I. Sumner and H. Warendorf
9. *European Family Law in Action Volume III : Parental Responsibilities*, K. Boele-Woelki, B. Braat and I. Curry Sumner (eds.)
10. *Common Core and Better Law in European Family Law*, K. Boele-Woelki (ed.)
11. *All's well that ends registered?*, I. Curry-Sumner
12. *Model Family Code – From a global perspective*, I. Schwenzer and M. Dimsey
13. *Harmonisation of Family Law in Europe. A Historical Perspective*, M. Antokolskaia
14. *Brussels II bis: Its Impact and Application in the Member States*, K. Boele-Woelki and C. González Beilfuss (eds.)
15. *Tensions between Legal, Biological and Social Conceptions of Parentage*, I. Schwenzer (ed.)
16. *Principles of European Family Law Regarding Parental Responsibilities*, K. Boele-Woelki, F. Ferrand, C. González Beilfuss, M. Jänterä-Jareborg, N. Lowe, D. Martiny and W. Pintens (eds.)
17. *Juxtaposing Legal Systems and the Principles of European Family Law on Divorce and Maintenance*, E. Örücü and J. Mair (eds.)
18. *Convergence and Divergence of Family Law in Europe*, M. Antokolskaia (ed.)
19. *European Challenges in Contemporary Family Law*, K. Boele-Woelki and K. Sverdrup (eds.)
20. *Children and their parents*, M. Vonk

21. *La capacité de l'enfant dans les droits français, anglais et écossais*, L. Francoz-Terminal
22. *Joint Parental Authority*, C.G. Jeppesen de Boer
23. *Debates in Family Law around the Globe at the Dawn of the 21st Century*, K. Boele-Woelki (ed.)
24. *European Family Law in Action Volume IV: Property Relations between Spouses*, K. Boele-Woelki, B. Braat and I. Curry-Sumner (eds.)
25. *Foundational Facts, Relative Truths. A Comparative Law Study on Children's Right to Know Their Genetic Origins*, J. Blauwhoff
26. *Imperative Inheritance Law in a Late-Modern Society. Five Perspectives*, Christoph Castelein, René Foqué and Alain Verbeke (eds.)
27. *Juxtaposing Legal Systems and the Principles of European Family Law on Parental Responsibilities*, Esin Örücü and Jane Mair (eds.)
28. *La justice des mineurs en Europe*, Yann Favier and Frédérique Ferrand (eds.)
29. *The Future of Family Property in Europe*, Katharina Boele-Woelki, Jo Miles and Jens M. Scherpe (eds.)
30. *The Place of Religion in Family Law: A Comparative Search*, Jane Mair and Esin Örücü (eds.)
31. *Reconstructing Marriage. The Legal Status of Relationships in a Changing Society*, Caroline Sörgjerd (ed.)

www.ingramcontent.com/pod-product-compliance
Ingram Content Group UK Ltd.
Pitfield, Milton Keynes, MK11 3LW, UK
UKHW051925100926
8556IPUK00022B/1384